Music Therapy Assessment

of related interest

Music Therapy with Families
Therapeutic Approaches and Theoretical Perspectives
Edited by Stine Lindahl Jacobsen and Grace Thompson
ISBN 978 1 84905 630 4
eISBN 978 1 78450 105 1

Advanced Methods of Music Therapy Practice
Analytical Music Therapy, The Bonny Method of Guided Imagery and
Music, Nordoff-Robbins Music Therapy, and Vocal Psychotherapy
Nicki S. Cohen
ISBN 978 1 84905 776 9
eISBN 978 1 78450 008 5

Collaboration and Assistance in Music Therapy Practice
Roles, Relationships, Challenges
Edited by John Strange, Helen Odell-Miller and Eleanor Richards
ISBN 978 1 84905 702 8
eISBN 978 1 78450 223 2

Music Therapy Assessment

Theory, Research, and Application

Edited by Stine Lindahl Jacobsen,
Eric G. Waldon, and Gustavo Gattino
Foreword by Barbara L. Wheeler

Jessica Kingsley *Publishers*
London and Philadelphia

Chapter 9 contains extracts from the work of Tony Wigram that are reproduced
by permission from Jessica Kingsley Publishers and Jenny Wigram.

First published in 2019
by Jessica Kingsley Publishers
73 Collier Street
London N1 9BE, UK
and
400 Market Street, Suite 400
Philadelphia, PA 19106, USA

www.jkp.com

Library of Congress Cataloging in Publication Data
A CIP catalog record for this book is available from the Library of Congress

British Library Cataloguing in Publication Data
A CIP catalogue record for this book is available from the British Library

ISBN 978 1 78592 295 4
eISBN 978 1 78450 602 5

Printed and bound in the United States

To our clients: Stine, Eric, and Gustavo

To Benjamin, Silje, and Kristian: Stine

To my husband, Piero: Eric

To my wife, Salomé: Gustavo

Contents

Foreword

Barbara L. Wheeler

Assessment is essential to music therapy treatment, but music therapists' understanding of assessment and methods of assessing have not always kept up with their clinical needs. While many clinical techniques have advanced over the years, it has taken longer for the assessment process to progress. This is changing, and this book can play an important role in helping to move music therapy assessment forward. In addition to presenting a variety of perspectives, the book includes important psychometric information that can inform music therapy assessment.

In the first chapter, the editors state, "The purpose of this text is to assist the reader in making effective assessment decisions which involve: reviewing pertinent records, documents, and clinical artifacts; employing effective interviewing skills and methods; carrying out appropriate observational strategies; and selecting, administering, and interpreting findings from clinically relevant tests and measures." This book will assist music therapists with all of these.

The grounding in psychometric concepts that the book provides can be valuable as music therapists continue to develop assessment tools for various needs and clientele. In Chapter 2, "Assessment in Music Therapy: Psychometric and Theoretical Considerations," the editors discuss the relationship of theory to the processes of collecting, interpreting, and applying assessment information and also provide an overview of psychometric concepts as they relate to clinical assessment in music therapy. Developing assessment tools with acceptable psychometric properties is crucial as music therapists move forward in this area, and the integration of these concepts with the material in the book will be invaluable in this process. The data-based decision-making model that is introduced helps put different aspects of the assessment process into a context, with reviewing, interviewing, observing, and testing serving certain functions across all phases of the treatment process (from referral through termination). The emphasis on assessment tools (and specifically these tests and scales that yield scores) in the book draws attention to this area of clinical practice—that is, the development of standardized tools (in which the tools/items have been developed in a systematic way, the tool is administered in a standardized way, and the results are interpreted/used in a standardized way).

The discussion of "Music Therapy Assessment Without Tools: From the Clinician's Perspective," found in Chapter 3, gives an overview of 29 non-test tools that are available for music therapy assessment. The authors of this chapter say that they aim "to focus on non-test tools in music therapy, including a literature review, types of observation, and conduct a guide on how to do assessment without a pre-developed tool. The guide aims to help clinicians by suggesting what to be aware of before, during, and after collecting, analyzing, interpreting, and disseminating assessment data." This makes it clear that music therapists have numerous tools for assessment in addition to the relatively formal and developed tools that are the primary focus of the book.

Following this chapter and a brief introductory chapter on what follows, the presentation of a number of music therapy assessment instruments will be helpful to music therapists who wish to use and adapt them. Most of these summaries are written by those who developed the tools, and having them together in one extensive collection is a first and should be useful to music therapists. This part of the book includes 16 assessment tools. They come from the US, South America, and northern Europe, with authorship from the following countries: US (6), Germany (4), Denmark (3), the UK (2), Argentina (1), Faroe Islands (1), and Finland (1) (two are attributed to more than one country, thus the total is higher than 16). Not all of the tools are population-specific, but, generally, the populations covered include autism and autism spectrum disorder; communication disorders; children, adolescents, and adults with psychiatric disorders; acquired brain injury; older adults, including those with dementia; children and parents with no specific diagnoses; and people with a variety of diagnoses.

The assessment tools are varied, although almost all include some type of psychometric evidence, primarily calculating and reporting information on reliability and validity. The advances in psychometric development are both necessary and impressive, as evidenced in overviews of assessment tools over the past 20 or so years. Referring to assessment tools in music therapy, Gfeller and Davis said, in 2008, "The drawback for some of these tests is that reliability and validity have not yet been fully established. In such cases, caution must be used when interpreting the results" (p. 437). Two extensive surveys of music therapy assessment tools, both published in 2000 (Gregory 2000; Wilson and Smith 2000), did not include psychometric information, although Wilson and Smith did refer to weaknesses in the assessment tools due to the lack of information on reliability and validity. This in itself seems significant in that, at that time, psychometric properties were not a focus of these inquiries. In 2005, Meadows and his colleagues said, "A second issue concerns the reliability and validity of music therapy assessments. This issue has not been adequately addressed in music therapy assessment, even though it has been raised previously (Bruscia, 1988)" (p. 45).

Movement towards recognizing the importance of psychometric properties of assessment tools does seem to have occurred in the second decade of this century. Most reviews of assessment tools now refer to the psychometric properties of the tools. In 2013, Wheeler referred to reliability, validity, and other aspects of assessments that she reviewed, while Lipe (2015) summarized 20 assessment tools on a chart. She evaluated 13 of these as including no psychometric information, while six did report it (an additional tool stated that it had this information but did not include the numbers describing it). Waldon and his colleagues (Waldon 2014; Waldon, Monje, and Powell 2014) looked at the psychometric properties of 25 music therapy assessment tools that were published from 1981 to 2014. They found that 17 included information on both reliability and validity, three on reliability only, one on validity only, and four had none.

It is not possible to compare all of these overviews of music therapy assessment tools directly, as they used different criteria for inclusion and focused on different areas. This overview, though, does suggest that increasing emphasis is being placed on the psychometric properties of music therapy assessment tools—an important step in this area. And it brings us to this book, which makes an important contribution to music therapy assessment, including the psychometric properties of the assessment tools that are included.

This book will help music therapists move towards more effective assessment. This movement will in turn move the discipline of music therapy in a positive direction, both in the assessment of clients and in credibility with other disciplines.

References

Gfeller, K. E. and Davis, W. B. (2008) 'The Music Therapy Treatment Process.' In W. B. Davies, K. E. Gfeller, and M. H. Thaut (eds) *An Introduction to Music Therapy: Theory and Practice.* Silver Spring, MD: American Music Therapy Association.

Gregory, D. (2000) 'Test instruments used by *Journal of Music Therapy* authors from 1984–1997.' *Journal of Music Therapy, 37,* 2, 79–94.

Lipe, A. W. (2015) 'Music Therapy Assessment.' In B. L. Wheeler (ed.) *Music Therapy Handbook.* New York, NY: Guilford Press.

Meadows, A., Wheeler, B. L., Shultis, C. L., and Polen, D. W. (2005) 'Client Assessment.' In B. L. Wheeler, C. L. Shultis, and D. W. Polen (eds) *Clinical Training Guide for the Student Music Therapist.* Gilsum, NH: Barcelona Publishers.

Waldon, E. G. (2014) '*Research Committee Presents: Designing Tests and Measures in Music Therapy.*' Paper presented at the American Music Therapy Association Conference, Louisville, KY.

Waldon, E. G., Monje, J., and Powell, A. (2014) *Music Therapy Tests and Measures: A Review of AMTA Journals (1981–2014)*. Poster session presented at the American Music Therapy Association Conference, Louisville, KY.

Wheeler, B. L. (2013) 'Music Therapy Assessment.' In R. F. Cruz and B. Feder (eds) *Feders' The Art and Science of Evaluation in the Arts Therapies*. Springfield, IL: Charles C. Thomas.

Wilson, B. L. and Smith, D. S. (2000) 'Music therapy assessment in school settings: A preliminary investigation.' *Journal of Music Therapy, 37,* 95–117.

Acknowledgements

Many people were involved in the creation of this book and we (the editors) are very grateful for each individual contribution. It has been a long and exciting journey, and even now towards the end of the process, it seems we are already thinking about a second edition. The need for this book is quite clear and we are happy to finally share it through the aid of Jessica Kingsley Publishers.

A special thank you to our colleagues from the International Music Therapy Assessment Consortium (IMTAC), who offered their support through initial ideas, writing, reviewing, and ongoing encouragement. These colleagues are Daniel Thomas, Esa Ala-Ruona, John Carpente, Sanne Storm, Thomas Wosch, and Wendy Magee.

Thank you to the chapter authors for sharing personal and professional descriptions of their assessment tools as well as offering attention, participating in the peer review process, and being available throughout the book's development. Your motivation and compassion for assessment and your genuine respect for clients and colleagues shines through your writing and inspires us all. In particular, we extend a special thank you to Grace Thompson, Tali Gottfried, and Tereza Alcântara-Silva for their additional care and guidance in reviewing certain chapters.

A special thank you to Barbara Wheeler for providing a reflective and historic perspective on assessment in music therapy. We greatly appreciate how you prepared the reader for a dive into general theory and an exploration of various assessment tools by providing professional context.

Thank you to our students and colleagues at Aalborg University and the University of the Pacific for allowing us to "get smarter" about how we teach and do research about music therapy assessment. We also thank our institutions for agreeing to join the IMTAC and supporting all of our scholarly endeavors.

Thank you to clients for giving meaning to our work and for having taught us how our role as music therapists involves collaboration and striving for meaningful and positive change. Thank you to music therapists from all over the world for giving us inspiration and ideas for different themes addressed in the introductory chapters.

Stine would like to give warm thanks to her family—the true meaning of life lies here with Benjamin, Silje, and Kristian. Endless gratitude to Tony Wigram, her mentor, friend, and fellow assessment companion.

In addition to his husband, family, and friends, Eric would like to recognize the influence of his mentors in both music therapy and psychology: Brian L. Wilson, David Wolfe, Linda Webster, Rachelle Hackett, and Tracy Gayeski. Eric recognizes the presence of your wise counsel in his work (and occasionally his students hear that same wisdom in his words).

Gustavo would like to thank God for the opportunity to work on this project. Thank you to Tony Wigram, a primary source of inspiration in music therapy and the area of assessment in music therapy. Your writings and support were close by during the process of writing and editing. Thanks to his incredible wife Salomé, for giving emotional support and love during the development of this project. Thanks to his parents Paulo and Nilce and his brother Rafael, who taught him to be someone loving, responsible, and having a desire to enjoy life. A special thanks to all his kids: Isabela, Gabriela, Inês, Beatriz, and David.

CHAPTER 1

Assessment in Music Therapy

Introductory Considerations

Eric G. Waldon and Gustavo Gattino

Introduction

The practice of music therapy involves art and science. Music is the creative and flexible vehicle through which discovery, growth, and change occur. Theory and science provide the systematic structure used to explain and predict how music functions therapeutically. And while theory and science play roles in the evaluation of the efficacy and effectiveness of music-based interventions, they have another job to fulfill: clinical assessment. Therapists employ science-based approaches when collecting information about clients, while theory guides clinicians in designing assessments as well as understanding and interpreting what has been collected (Greenberg, Lichtenberger, and Kaufman 2013). A challenge for some involves applying science and theory to assess client strengths and needs, monitor therapeutic progress, and evaluate treatment effectiveness. The purpose of this text is to assist the reader in making effective assessment decisions which involve: reviewing pertinent records, documents, and clinical artifacts; employing effective interviewing skills and methods; carrying out appropriate observational strategies; and selecting, administering, and interpreting findings from clinically relevant tests and measures.

This chapter introduces and orients the reader to the theory, science, and processes involved in music therapy assessment. Following a brief history of the early forms of music and healing and a look at music therapy assessment across the world, a number of issues related to music therapy assessment are discussed. After defining selected assessment terms and looking at evidence-based assessment, attention is turned to presenting a data-based decision-making model for assessment and a brief summary of the state of assessment and assessment tools in the music therapy profession.

History of the early forms of music and healing

That music has been used in the healing arts since antiquity has been established elsewhere. In early societies, the cause of disease was connected to supernatural forces and music was seen as a way to appease and entreat the forces responsible for causing illness (DuBois 2009). In ancient Egypt, musicians continued to enjoy equal status with priests and healers as music was viewed as a force exerting special influence over mental and physical health (Davis, Gfeller, and Thaut 2008). And although science and rational medicine replaced supernatural explanations for illness and disability, the Greeks continued to view music as an integral part of society, with some notable figures who continued to extol music's healing virtues. For example, Aristotle suggested that music be used for catharsis and as a means of relaxation (Catharsis 2013), while Plato "described music as medicine for the soul" (Gfeller 2005, p. 61). And while Davis and Hadley (2015) caution against considering these early forms of music and healing as a form of music therapy, Grocke (2014) states that the profession recognized today as music therapy was established soon after World War II and is clearly different from those earlier musical healing arts.

Music therapy assessment across the world

Music therapy assessment in Asia and Australia

In Asia, few publications on assessment in music therapy have been produced in English; for this reason, it is not possible to estimate the impact of this topic in this region. One exception is a study by Jeong (2013) from South Korea concerning the psychometric exploration of the Music-Based Attention Assessment: Revised (MAA-R). This test was created to identify types of attention impairments and recommend appropriate clinical interventions to aid in attention rehabilitation. The aggregate findings suggest that the MAA-R provides a valid and reliable measure with regard to differentiating types of auditory attention deficits. It is important to highlight that this validation was carried out using a sample from the United States.

In Australia, Langan (2009) cited the lack of a uniform assessment process and the challenging accountability climate resulting from a "combination of evidence-based practice in health, statistically driven results in education, and economically motivated decision-making" (p. 79) as reasons to develop a music therapy assessment tool for use in special education. Based on nationwide educational standards and results from a survey distributed to 40 practicing music therapists, Langan designed the Music Therapy Special Education Assessment Tool to be accessible to therapists and educators as a means of determining appropriateness of a referral and tracking outcomes. Lem (2015), another music therapist from Australia, developed an evaluation tool for music therapists working with those who have dementia. The Scale of Musical Engagement in Dementia, administered individually by a trained music therapist, is based on the assumption that level of musical engagement is a stronger predictor of self-reported quality of life in older adults than cognitive ability or behavior.

Music therapy assessment in Europe

In Europe, the term "music therapy assessment" has been widely used to describe activities including clinical assessment, clinical evaluation, and measurement. Within recent decades, more attention has been given to developing assessment tools and procedures, much of it inspired by the work of Tony Wigram who focused on assessing the psychiatric and developmental needs of children (Wigram 2000, 2007). In an extensive comparison of 20 assessment and microanalysis methods, Wosch and Wigram (2007) found many similarities, including: a consistently high level of precision regarding how the assessment and analysis methods are described; a focus on the interpretation of musical parameters and how they relate to extra-musical clinical purposes; the use of music improvisational techniques to assess client interaction and communication; and research-based assessment models involving rigorous analysis methods. They point out, however, that none of these reviewed methods had been systematically tested or standardized, which requires financial resources and collaboration between clinicians and researchers.

According to Jacobsen, Wigram, and Rasmussen (2019) there appear to be two general philosophical schools regarding assessment in Europe: those who promote a predominantly humanities-oriented music therapy direction and those who advocate for a predominantly natural science-oriented approach consistent with the disciplines of medicine, psychology, and other allied professions (e.g. occupational, physical, and speech therapy). There has been some reluctance to adopt fixed procedures that standardized tools require, but the question in Europe is no longer whether it is possible and/or desirable to develop standardized assessment methods in music therapy, but how these methods can be developed and how they should be used (Jacobsen *et al.* 2019). Music therapy assessment, like much of the field, has evolved from a purely clinically based discipline to a more research-based discipline—the focus now is on providing detailed descriptions of assessment methods and evidence of reliability and validity. Still, the variety of analytical methods used and clinical populations served by these tools is large. Diagnostic assessment tends to involve research-based construction, and in the last five years there have been few attempts to develop tools that include standardized procedures and norms.

Music therapy assessment in North America

During the 1950s and 60s in the United States and Canada, music therapy was viewed predominantly as a form of diversion or recreation within the larger context of healthcare. And while Braswell (1959) and others recommended that music therapy interventions be employed in the service of accomplishing therapeutic goals, early practice studies of music therapists suggested this was not the case. Michel (1965) found that among 336 professionally practicing music therapists only 36 percent responded to questions about evaluating treatment progress, which suggested little interest among respondents with regard to assessment of outcomes. This seeming disinterest continued as evidenced in later surveys by Braswell, Maranto, and Decuir (1979a, 1979b), who found no mention of clinical assessment. The 1980s, however, would see increased interest in clinical assessment, including the development of music therapy-specific measures to assess psychiatric clients (Braswell *et al.* 1983, 1986), those with developmental disabilities (Boxhill 1985), cognitive skills (Rider 1981), and motor functioning (Sutton 1984). In addition to the establishment of assessment standards by the National Association for Music Therapy in 1982 (Lipe 2015) and calls for the profession to make assessment a priority (Clark and Ficken 1988), findings from practice surveys by Lathom (1982) and Taylor (1987) reflected the need to evaluate therapy recipients and base therapeutic aims on assessment findings. The 1990s saw growth in the area of assessment tool development for use in psychiatric (Cassity and Cassity 1994) and older adult (Lipe 1995; York 1994) clinical areas and this culminated in 2000 with special issues of *Music Therapy Perspectives* and the *Journal of Music Therapy* devoted solely to issues of assessment. More recently, Waldon (2014b) indicated that the number of measures examined in the American Music Therapy Association literature from 2004 to 2014 (18 in total) was more than twice that reported during the previous decade (8).

Music therapy assessment in South America

The research and development of music therapy assessment in Latin America has seen recent growth (Merrill 2016). In the last ten years, studies on different types of music therapy assessment, the development of music therapy measurement tools, the translation and validation of scales, and the consideration of cultural issues in music therapy assessment have been carried out across different countries (Ferrari 2013; Gattino *et al.* 2016). For example, the following tools were translated, culturally adapted, and validated for use in Brazil: the Category System of Music Therapy KAMUTHE (KAtegoriensystem MUsikTHERapie) (Gattino *et al.* 2017); the Individual Music-Centered Assessment Profile for Neurodevelopmental Disorders (IMCAP-ND) (Carpente 2016); the Intramusical Relationship Scale (IRS) (Ferrari 2013); the Individual Music Therapy Assessment Profile (IMTAP) (Mauat, Gattino, and Riesgo 2017); the Improvisation Assessment Profiles (IAPs) (Gattino *et al.* 2016); and the Music in Everyday Life (MEL) (Gottfried *et al.* 2016). Additionally, André, Gomes, and Loureiro (2016) from the Minas Gerais Federal University (UFMG) in Brazil are currently validating two scales from the Nordoff-Robbins Evaluation Scales (Scale I: Child-Therapist(s) Relationship in Coactive Musical Experience and Scale II: Musical Communicativeness). Karina Ferrari (2013), an Argentinian music therapist, published *Music Therapy: Aspects of Systematization and Assessment of the Clinical Practice*, which includes the Intramusical Relationship Scale (IRS), a tool that analyzes intramusical issues of a client using nine levels. Finally, the Colombian music therapist Juanita Eslava-Meija (2017) is developing a music therapy assessment on neuropsychological development for children as part of her doctoral studies in music therapy at the Aalborg University (Denmark).

Issues related to music therapy assessment

The role or purpose of music therapy assessment within clinical settings has also attracted a considerable amount of attention. Some concerns include: the extent to which music therapy assessment should overlap (or duplicate) the efforts of other professional members of the treatment team (Lipe 2015); whether a music therapy-specific assessment is necessary; or whether music should be used as part of the assessment process (Wilson 2005). On the issue of whether music should be incorporated into assessment, Wigram (1999) suggests that therapist reluctance to acknowledge the unique contributions of music in assessment may originate from a desire for acceptance from disciplines perceived to be "more scientific." In response, Lathom (1980), Bruscia (1988), and Pavlicevic (1995) all highlight the unique contributions music makes to the assessment process, including: (a) the observation of client responses under music versus non-music conditions; (b) the unique expressive pathway afforded through music which is not available to other disciplines; and (c) the client-therapist interactions through music which are distinct from other forms of therapy.

Focusing on the available literature, Isenberg-Grzeda (1988) gleaned four factors that influence the ways in which music therapists conduct assessments across various populations. Those factors include: music (which includes the musical abilities of the therapist and the extent to which music is perceived as a therapeutic force); theoretical framework (which comes as a result of training or personal philosophy grounded in the therapist's life experience or culture); client population (which refers to the level of ability or specific diagnoses of the person being assessed); and institution (which relates to the particular requirements of the facility or persons requesting the assessment).

Wilson and Smith (2000) conducted a survey of articles published in the *Journal of Music Therapy* using named assessments from 1980 to 1997. Results from their investigation showed that no standardized assessments were used; replication of assessment procedures or use of repeated tests occurred only twice with two different assessment instruments; and the majority of assessment instruments used were researcher-designed. In most cases, Wilson and Smith found that the assessment instruments were not published, were unavailable, not referenced, or not included with the study. More recently, Waldon,

Monje, and Powell (2014) and Waldon (2014a) conducted hand and electronic searches of English-language music therapy articles featuring tests and measures published between 1980 and 2014 from ten peer-reviewed journals. Although they indicated that the number of published measures has shown an increase in recent years, many instruments continue to be difficult to obtain, not all tools described possessed the necessary evidence of technical adequacy (e.g. reliability and validity), and few instruments had undergone repeated study. This suggests the need for more work.

Assessment and evaluation terminology

According to Hunsley and Mash (2014), assessment permeates nearly every aspect of 21st-century life: in hospitals, patients are weighed, tested, and evaluated; in education, students are assessed from the time they begin school to when they graduate; and in the workplace, employees are evaluated based on their performance. Generally speaking, *assessment* is an information-gathering process whereby a clinician builds a body of knowledge about a client or group of therapy recipients. This idea is reflected by Urbina (2004), who explains that psychological assessment is "a flexible, not standardized, *process* aimed at reaching a defensible determination concerning one or more psychological issues or questions, through the collection, evaluation, and analysis of data" (p. 24). With regard to music therapy assessment, Hanser (1999) explains how "*Assessment* is a systematic approach to determining strengths and needs" (p. 76). Furthermore, the assessment *process* is one that occurs continuously—from referral to treatment discharge/termination (Waldon 2013). Describing a data-based decision-making approach to music therapy, Waldon asserts that "The work of all music therapists involves the collection, synthesis, and analysis of data to meet clinical aims of consumers. Differences exist, however, in how music therapists conceptualize data and the ways in which data are used to make treatment decisions" (p. 46). For example, some may conceptualize data as consisting only of numbers and, subsequently, place little emphasis on quantitative expressions of client behavior. Others may place a premium on test scores and weigh the importance of other factors in making treatment decisions.

Frequently the terms *assessment* and *evaluation* are used interchangeably, but in practice they have different meanings. Generally speaking, evaluation is a process that occurs at the end of a defined period of time (e.g. following preliminary data collection or treatment) for the purpose of making a decision or judgement (Frey 2015). This is consistent with Wheeler (2013), who indicates that music therapy evaluation refers to processes that occur after the initiation of services to determine whether treatment has been successful. Wheeler contrasts this with the term *assessment*, which occurs before treatment and "documents the initial contact with the client, the client's caregiver and significant other" (pp. 344–345). The term *evaluation*, therefore, refers to a specific case of assessment, one in which a decision is being made (e.g. determining appropriateness of a client referred for treatment, or conferring a diagnosis). Regarding referral appropriateness, music therapists are responsible for collecting and reviewing clinical information to establish whether a client and their presenting problem is most suitably addressed using music-based interventions (see Hanser 1999 for a suggested list of referral criteria). And while not typically in the practice of conferring diagnoses (a task left to other clinicians), music therapists do generate pertinent data through assessment which can be used in concert with other professionals to assist in the diagnostic or evaluative process.

Measurement is another concept that is related to, but distinct from, assessment. Measurement refers to any quantitative expression of a characteristic or trait usually obtained through some form of apparatus. In psychology and other allied professions, this may be through a test (defined below) or, as frequently encountered in medicine, another device (e.g. stethoscope, medical equipment) or procedure (e.g. laboratory tests). In clinical practice, measurements may be used as *part of* an assessment but they alone do not comprise an assessment in its entirety. An assessment (a broader term) may consist of measures (e.g. test scores) in addition to observations, client history (obtained through interviews), and a review of pertinent records.

A *test* (or a measure) is a specific procedure or set of tasks used to assess one or more clearly definable, clinically relevant abilities or traits which yields a *score*. The score is a meaningful quantification of the assessed characteristic that provides a way to: (a) describe present levels of functioning or performance; (b) establish baseline levels of functioning or performance for later comparison; and (c) identify client strengths and needs (Sattler 2001). It is important to note that while tests and measures are involved in assessment, assessment itself does *not* imply that a test (standardized or otherwise) has been used. Instead, tests are seen as constituting one piece of the assessment process wherein multiple methods are used to gather information about therapy recipients.

The term *standardized* is often misunderstood and has often been met with opposition from those who do not appreciate the meaning of the label. In practice, standardization refers primarily to two characteristics of tests and measures: *uniformity* and *normative comparison*. According to Urbina (2004), uniformity refers to the consistency with which a test's items are developed and administered, and client responses are scored and interpreted. While much of this (e.g. item development and statistical structure of the measure) takes place during the design of the assessment tool, ensuring that tests are administered and responses interpreted using uniform standards by trained clinicians is an issue of therapist skill and ethical assessment practices. Most frequently, however, standardization is associated with the establishment of norms used to estimate a person's performance by comparing it to the performance of others for whom the measure is intended (Colman 2009). More precisely, this meaning of standardization is called *norm-referenced interpretation* and not all standardized tests involve this approach for understanding scores or interpreting an examinee's performance.

Evidence-based assessment in music therapy

Evidence-based assessment (EBA) is the systematic use of theory and research-supported methods to answer specific assessment-related questions within a clinical context (Hunsley and Mash 2014). EBA is further supported by Sattler and Hoge (2006), who suggest that good assessment practices are based on an understanding of theory, development, pathology, and ethics. Theory is important because it underpins a clinician's understanding of personality, the development and remediation of problems, and how music therapists select appropriate assessment methods (e.g. interviews, observations, and tests). Additionally, theory provides a framework for analyzing assessment findings to better understand a client's strengths, needs, and responses to interventions. Therapist knowledge about development informs the selection of assessment methods, assists in building rapport during the assessment process, and impacts the ways in which assessment findings are communicated to clients and other professionals. Knowing about specific pathology or having a conceptual idea about the problems and challenges clients bring to music therapy helps generate referral questions, aids in the selection of assessment methods, and assists the therapist in analyzing and synthesizing assessment information (e.g. constructing a case formulation). Regarding ethics, a therapist (or trainee) should know about, and follow, guidelines that pertain to: training in assessment (i.e. having adequate education, knowledge, and expertise); awareness of bias and its impact on the assessment process; laws and regulations which may govern assessment practices; the valid and appropriate interpretation of assessment findings; the protection of assessment procedures or test items; and storage of clinical assessment data.

A data-based approach to assessment

There are various ways to go about conceptualizing assessment in music therapy. The American Music Therapy Association (AMTA) Standards of Clinical Practice (2015) include: referral and acceptance, assessment, treatment planning, implementation, documentation, and termination of services. As the second Standard, assessment is conceptualized as a comprehensive, multi-method approach which gauges a client's functioning across multiple domains; estimates a client's strengths and needs; explores a client's culture; and ascertains a client's musical ability, musical preferences, and responses to music.

Jacobsen *et al.* (2019) expand the timing and purpose of assessment beyond that which occurs at the beginning of treatment using the following five terms: (a) diagnostic assessment (to obtain evidence to support a diagnostic hypothesis); (b) general assessment (to identify the general needs of the client from a holistic perspective and recommend relevant intervention); (c) assessment of music therapy intervention (to obtain evidence supporting the value of music therapy as an intervention); (d) assessment prior to treatment (to determine in the first two to three sessions a therapeutic intervention relevant to the client); and (e) assessment of effectiveness of treatment (to evaluate the effectiveness of music therapy near the conclusion of treatment). Similarly, Bruscia (1998) delineates assessment functions using five categories: diagnosis, description, interpretation, prescription, and evaluation. Furthermore, Wilson (2005) also identified four traditional methods of assessment shared by all music therapists: interviewing, observing, testing, and reviewing existing materials.

Connecting these perspectives of assessment described above, Waldon (2013) postulates that music therapy assessment could be expanded to comprise any information collection and analysis process used to build a body of knowledge about therapy recipient(s). This conceptualization of assessment is prevalent in the field of clinical psychology, specifically with the definition of the four pillars of assessment postulated by Sattler (2001). The pillars are: standardized tests, interviews, observations, and informal assessment procedures. When one considers these fundamental pillars, assessment occurs during all phases of the music therapy process, because it is possible to apply observations, tests, interviews, and informal assessment methods during referral, initial assessment, planning treatment, implementation, and termination. Moreover, data collection, analysis, and decision making occur at all treatment stages and, when data suggests it, a return to an earlier treatment stage is made. A data-based decision-making model by Waldon (2013) illustrates this understanding (Figure 1.1).

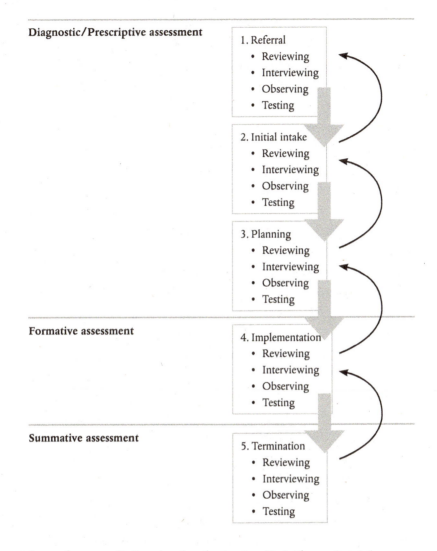

Stages of treatment (1–5) are based on the American Music Therapy Association Standards of Clinical Practice and represent the general progression of treatment from referral through termination (downward, shaded arrows). At each stage, four data-based methods for collecting clinically relevant information are suggested: reviewing, interviewing, observing, and testing. Upward, curving arrows indicate that data collected at a later treatment stage may serve as an impetus to review, re-conceptualize, or recollect data at an earlier stage. Dashed lines suggest points at which the functions of assessment (i.e. diagnostic/prescriptive, formative, and summative) change.

Figure 1.1: A data-based decision-making model in music therapy

According to Sattler (2001), standardized tests can describe the client's present functioning in reference to peer group, identify strengths and weaknesses, and provide a baseline for follow-up testing. Further, the use of tests and measures can be conceptualized into three broad purposes or functions across the treatment process. When used *diagnostically and prescriptively*, testing occurs at the beginning of treatment for the purpose of planning treatment or assisting with conferring a diagnosis. Test data is used to assess client characteristics, estimate functional abilities, formulate therapeutic aims (i.e. goals and objectives), and establish a pre-treatment level of functioning. During therapy implementation, tests and measures used *formatively* can be used to monitor client progress and responsiveness to interventions. Therapists use this data when documenting performance toward goals and objectives, justifying the establishment of new therapeutic aims, or revising existing treatment plans. When measures are used *summatively*, therapists evaluate client responses following a course of treatment with the purpose of summarizing treatment effectiveness, which may be used to justify terminating treatment or recommending a client for additional services (Waldon 2014a). Applied more broadly, one sees that all data-based assessment procedures (reviewing, interviewing, observing, and testing) can fall under one of these purposes (diagnostic/prescriptive, formative, and summative) depending on the point at which these assessment activities occur (Figure 1.1).

The four assessment methods (or processes) proposed by Waldon (2013) and others form the acronym RIOT: reviewing records, documents, or other artifacts; interviewing; observing; and testing/ measuring. There is no predetermined order for these assessment methods (i.e. reviewing does not precede interviewing, observing, and testing) as these methods vary by clinical setting wherein some may occur simultaneously (e.g. a music therapist working in an acute care medical setting conducts observations simultaneously with interviewing methods) and others not at all (e.g. where the use of a standardized music therapy-specific measure is not available). Each is described with more detail on the following pages.

Reviewing

The review of documents or pertinent records is an assessment method common to music therapists working across many clinical settings. In many cases, therapists can obtain much of the information they need by accessing a client's school files or medical records. In an age of electronic record keeping, this task is made simpler as much of the desired information is contained in one place as opposed to across various locations. But reviewing can also constitute the inspection of work samples or other clinically relevant artifacts. This is sometimes referred to as *permanent product recording* (Van Houten and Hall 2001), and therapists may find value in examining writing samples, art work, or other tangible products that result from client behavior as they may reveal pertinent information regarding a client's functioning across multiple clinical domains.

Interviewing

Direct, interpersonal methods to obtain information from clients and others are essential at all stages of the treatment. Interviews may be structured, semi-structured, or free flowing (Sattler 2001) and involve therapist-informant interaction to obtain clinically relevant information within a client's familiar environment (involving family members or caregivers), therapeutic environment (involving therapists, nurses, or other professionals), or everyday life environment (peers from work, school, church, or social institutions). While there are some published interview protocols available (e.g. Structured Clinical Interview for the DSM (SCID)), music therapists typically create their own questionaries or adapt the interviews in line with their approach or theoretical framing in music therapy (Ferrari 2013).

Observing

Observations consist of systematic (e.g. frequency or duration recording) or informal methods which involve data collection using the senses (e.g. through seeing or listening) (Sattler 2001). Descriptive observations are generally less structured and can serve as an excellent preliminary means of capturing information about a therapy recipient, their environment, and the quality of activities, interactions, or tasks that are relevant to the assessment process. A common observational practice in music therapy involves examining video and audio recordings of therapy sessions (Gfeller 2016) to analyze clinically significant events, understand client responses, reflect on client or music therapist manifestations, and plan subsequent sessions (Oldfield 2006).

In many cases, these observations may lead to structured, or systematic, observation methods which focus on the quantity (e.g. frequency, intensity, or duration), sequencing, or location of clinically relevant responses, interactions, or behaviors. There are two important uses of systematic observations in music therapy: the applied behavior analysis and the microanalysis approaches. The applied behavior analysis approach concerns defining behaviors, their antecedents, and consequent events which may serve to increase, decrease, or maintain the behavior. Furthermore, emphasis is placed on the function (or purpose) of the behavior so that interventions can be designed to support a client in developing more environmentally adaptive responses. Music therapy microanalysis (Wosch and Wigram 2007) involves video, audio, and text analysis of a portion of (or an entire) music therapy session to understand the therapeutic processes involved during clinically significant points during the implementation phase of therapy.

Observational approaches may also assist therapists in testing hypotheses about clients as well as identifying particular strengths and needs. In this manner, a music therapist can apply a conjunct of musical tasks or musical activities to access and observe functioning across different domains (i.e. communication, motor, and cognitive). For example, Wigram and Gold (2006) postulate that music therapy assessment (using musical improvisation) allows a more flexible approach to exploring the creative potential of a child (in cognitive terms) when compared to standardized methods for assessing intellectual or cognitive abilities.

Testing

As with reviewing records, interviewing, and observing, testing can also be used to build a body of knowledge about a client or group for the purposes of assessment. According to Frey (2015), "A test is *an organized set of procedures, questions, or tasks, which produces interpretable quantitative results meant to reflect an individual's level of some characteristic*" (p. 3, italics in original). Given this definition, tests may take any number of forms, including rating scales, checklists, and inventories, all of which can be administered by the clinician, while others are self-administered by clients. While the use of tests in music therapy clinical practice is not common (Waldon 2014b), music therapists have a number of music-based assessment tools from which to choose (see Lipe 2015), some of which will be described later in this text.

Updated information on tests and measures in music therapy

This section presents an overview of tests and measures in music therapy that are published in peer-review journals in the period between 1981 and 2016, based on work conducted by Waldon (2014a) and Waldon *et al.* (2014). Waldon and colleagues searched for tests and measures published from 1981 to 2014 in the following peer-reviewed journals: *Arts and Psychotherapy, Australian Journal of Music Therapy, British Journal of Music Therapy, Canadian Journal of Music Therapy, Journal of Music Therapy, Journal of the Association of Music and Imagery, Music and Medicine, Music Therapy Perspectives, Nordic Journal of Music Therapy,* and *Psychology of Music.* References to measures reviewed in other peer-reviewed journals potentially meeting inclusion criteria were also surveyed.

In identifying tests and measures for inclusion, the following selection criteria were applied:

- The primary purpose of the article is the development, technical exploration, or clinical application of a specific test.

- The test must incorporate musical stimuli into the assessment process.

- The test must yield a measure (i.e. quantifiable score) representing an identifiable construct, domain, or clinical phenomenon.

- The test must be intended for use in a clinical (as opposed to research) setting.

- The article must be published in English.

After cataloging the articles, the authors abstracted the following information: test title, author(s), and year; population served; journal source and publication year; additional studies investigating the test; purpose(s) of the test; construct(s) measured; and type of psychometric evidence reported. Of the 25 tests and measures meeting inclusion criteria, Waldon (2014a) and Waldon *et al.* (2014) found that: (a) seven measures lacked evidence of either reliability or validity, while three lacked both; and (b) the majority of measures were designed for formative and diagnostic/prescriptive purposes, while four were designed for summative purposes.

A more current analysis conducted for the purposes of this chapter found six new tests/measures published in music therapy peer-reviewed journals, only one of which did not include evidence of reliability. Moreover, three tests/measures found in this recent review were updated with new publications: Music Attentiveness Screening Assessment, Revised (MASA-R; Waldon *et al.* 2016); Music Therapy Assessment Tool for Awareness in Disorders of Consciousness (MATADOC; Magee *et al.* 2016); and Assessment of Parenting Competencies (APC; Jacobsen and Killén 2014). Compared to previous analyses by Wilson and Smith (2000) and Sabatella (2004), issues of psychometric quality are receiving increased attention, but the number of assessment instruments in the prominent music therapy journals continues to be small. It is also important to consider that this review did not include ongoing studies, publications from other journals (i.e. non-music therapy journals), and measures published in non-English journals.

Final considerations

Assessment in music therapy is necessary for quality treatment and provides a unique opportunity to use music to evaluate client functioning using the creative and flexible medium of music. As a standard for clinical practice, assessment consists of multiple procedures (i.e. reviewing, interviewing, observing, and testing) working in concert to address important clinical questions about therapy recipients. As discussed in this chapter, the number of standardized tests and measures in music therapy is small and the array of tools does not cover all fields of clinical practice. Additionally, the number of studies investigating the psychometric and technical proprieties of measures is limited, and in some cases the tools are not published in peer-reviewed journals, as is the case of some publications from Latin America. In this sense, increased attention should be focused on developing new tests and thoroughly exploring the psychometric properties of new and existing measures and their uses with different populations.

References

American Music Therapy Association (2015) *Standards of Clinical Practice*. Retrieved 03/01/2017 at www.musictherapy.org/about/standards.

André, A. M., Gomes, C. M. A., and Loureiro, C. M. V. (2016) '*Translation and Validation of the Nordoff-Robbins Scale I: Child-Therapist(s) Relationship in Coactive Musical Experience and Nordoff-Robbins Scale II: Musical Communicativeness.*' Paper presented at the 17th ANPPOM Congress, Belo Horizonte, Brazil.

Boxhill, E. H. (1985) *Music Therapy for the Developmentally Disabled*. Rockville, MD: Aspen Systems.

Braswell, C. (1959) 'The Goal-Directed Hospital Music Program.' In E. H. Schneider (ed.) *Music Therapy 1959*. Lawrence, KS: National Association for Music Therapy.

Braswell, C., Brooks, D., Decuir, A., Humphrey, T., Jacobs, K., and Sutton, K. (1983) 'Development and implementation of a music/activity therapy intake assessment for psychiatric patients. Part I: Initial standardization procedures in data from university students.' *Journal of Music Therapy, 20*, 88–100.

Braswell, C., Brooks, D., Decuir, A., Humphrey, T., Jacobs, K., and Sutton, K. (1986) 'Development and implementation of a music/activity therapy intake assessment for psychiatric patients. Part II: Standardization procedures in data from psychiatric patients.' *Journal of Music Therapy, 23,* 126–141.

Braswell, C., Maranto, C. D., and Decuir, A. (1979a) 'A survey of clinical practice in music therapy. Part II: The institutions in which music therapists work and personal data.' *Journal of Music Therapy, 16,* 2–16.

Braswell, C., Maranto, C. D., and Decuir, A. (1979b) 'A survey of clinical practice in music therapy. Part II: Clinical practice, educational, and clinical training.' *Journal of Music Therapy, 16,* 50–69.

Bruscia, K. (1988) 'Standards for clinical assessment in the arts therapies.' *Arts in Psychotherapy, 15,* 5–10.

Bruscia, K. (1998) *Defining Music Therapy* (2nd edition). Gilsum, NH: Barcelona.

Carpente, J. (2016) *Versão Brasileira da escala Individual Music-Centered Assessment Profile for Neurodevelopmental Disorders (IMCAP-ND): Manual de Aplicação.* New York, NY: Regina Publishers.

Cassity, M. D. and Cassity, J. E. (1994) *Multimodal Psychiatric Music Therapy for Adults, Adolescents, and Children: A Clinical Manual* (2nd edition). St. Louis, MO: MMB Music.

Catharsis (2013) *New World Encyclopedia.* Retrieved 11/10/2016 at www.newworldencyclopedia.org/entry/Catharsis.

Clark, M. E. and Ficken, C. T. (1988) 'Music therapy in the new healthcare environment.' *Music Therapy Perspectives, 5,* 23–28.

Colman, A. M. (2009) 'Standardized test.' In *Oxford Dictionary of Psychology* (3rd edition). Oxford: Oxford University Press.

Davis, W. and Hadley, S. (2015) 'A History of Music Therapy.' In B. L. Wheeler (ed.) *Music Therapy Handbook.* New York, NY: Guilford Press.

Davis, W. B., Gfeller, K. E., and Thaut, M. H. (2008) *An Introduction to Music Therapy: Theory and Process* (3rd edition). Silver Spring, MD: American Music Therapy Association.

DuBois, T. A. (2009) *An Introduction to Shamanism.* Cambridge: Cambridge University Press.

Eslava-Meija, J. (2017) 'The Attention Profile in MT Assessment for Children: Development and Pilot Study of Validity and Reliability.' Unpublished PhD thesis, Aalborg University.

Ferrari, K. (2013) *Musicoterapia: Aspectos de la Sistematización y Evaluación de la Práctica Clínica.* Buenos Aires, Argentina: Ediciones MTD.

Frey, B. B. (2015) *100 Questions (and Answers) about Tests and Measures.* Thousand Oaks, CA: Sage.

Gattino, G., Ferrari, G., Azevedo, G., de Souza, F., Pizzol, F. C. D., and Santana, D. d. C. (2016) 'Translation, transcultural adaptation and validity evidences of the improvisational assessment profiles scale (IAPs) for use in Brazil: Section 1.' *Brazilian Journal of Music Therapy, 20,* 1, 92–116.

Gattino, G. S., da Silva, A. M., Figueiredo, F. G., and Schüler-Faccini, L. (2017) 'KAMUTHE video microanalysis system for use in Brazil: Translation, cross-cultural adaptation and evidence of validity and reliability.' *Health Psychology Report, 5*, 1, 1–13.

Gfeller, K. E. (2005) 'Music as a Therapeutic Agent: Historical and Sociological Perspectives.' In R. F. Unkefer and M. H. Thaut (eds) *Music Therapy in the Treatment of Adults with Mental Disorders: Theoretical Bases and Clinical Interventions.* Gilsum, NH: Barcelona.

Gfeller, K. E. (2016) 'Music as Communication and Training for Children with Cochlear Implants.' In N. M. Young and K. Iler Kirk (eds) *Pediatric Cochlear Implantation.* New York, NY: Springer.

Gottfried, T., Thompson, G., Carpente, J., and Gattino, G. (2016) 'Music in everyday life by parents with their children with autism' [Supplement]. *Nordic Journal of Music Therapy, 25,* 89–90, doi: 10.1080/08098131.2016.1180085.

Greenberg, D., Lichtenberger, E. O., and Kaufman, A. S. (2013) 'The Role of Theory in Psychological Assessment.' In D. H. Saklofske, C. R. Reynolds, and V. Schwean (eds) *The Oxford Handbook of Child Psychological Assessment.* Oxford: Oxford University Press.

Grocke, D. E. (2014) 'Music Therapy.' In W. F. Thompson (ed.) *Music in the Behavioral Sciences: An Encyclopedia, Vol II.* Thousand Oaks, CA: Sage.

Hanser, S. E. (1999) *The New Music Therapist's Handbook* (2nd edition). Boston, MA: Berklee Press.

Hunsley, J. and Mash, E. J. (2014) 'Evidence-Based Assessment.' In D. H. Barlow (ed.) *Oxford Handbook of Clinical Psychology* (4th edition rev.). Oxford: Oxford University Press.

Isenberg-Grzeda, C. (1998) 'Music therapy assessment: A reflection of professional identity.' *Journal of Music Therapy, 25,* 156–169.

Jacobsen, S. L. and Killén, K. (2014) 'Clinical application of music therapy assessment within the field of child protection.' *Nordic Journal of Music Therapy, 24,* 148–166, doi: 10.1080/08098131.2014.908943.

Jacobsen, S. L., Wigram, T., and Rasmussen, A. M. (2019) 'Assessment and Clinical Evaluation in Music Therapy.' In L. O. Bonde, I. N. Pedersen, and S. L. Jacobsen (eds) *Comprehensive Guide to Music Therapy* (2nd edition). London: Jessica Kingsley Publishers.

Jeong, E. (2013) 'Psychometric validation of a music-based attention assessment: Revised for patients with traumatic brain injury.' *Journal of Music Therapy, 50,* 66–92.

Langan, D. (2009) 'A music therapy assessment tool for special education: Incorporating educational outcomes.' *Australian Journal of Music Therapy, 20,* 78–98.

Lathom, W. (1980) *Role of Music Therapy in the Education of Handicapped Children and Youth.* Lawrence, KS: National Association for Music Therapy.

Lathom, W. (1982) 'Survey of functions of a music therapist.' *Journal of Music Therapy, 19,* 2–27.

Lem, A. (2015) 'The evaluation of musical engagement in dementia: Implications for self-reported quality of life.' *Australian Journal of Music Therapy, 26,* 30–52.

Lipe, A. (1995) 'The use of music performance tasks in the assessment of cognitive functioning among older adults with dementia.' *Journal of Music Therapy, 32,* 137–151.

Lipe, A. W. (2015) 'Music Therapy Assessment.' In B. L. Wheeler (ed.) *Music Therapy Handbook.* New York, NY: Guilford Press.

Magee, W. L., Siegert, R. J., Taylor, S. M., Daveson, B. A., and Lenton-Smith, G. (2016) 'Music Therapy Assessment Tool for Awareness in Disorders of Consciousness (MATADOC): Reliability and validity of a measure to assess awareness in patients with disorders of consciousness.' *Journal of Music Therapy, 53,* 1–26, doi: 10.1093/jmt/thv017.

Mauat, A., Gattino, G., and Riesgo, R. (2017) 'Validity evidence of the Individualized Music Therapy Assessment Profile (IMTAP) for ASD Children.' Unpublished doctoral dissertation, Universidade Federal do Rio Grande do Sul, Brazil.

Merrill, T. R. (2016) 'Music Therapy Research: A Historical Portrait.' In B. L. Wheeler and K. M. Murphy (eds) *Music Therapy Research* (3rd edition). Dallas, TX: Barcelona.

Michel, D. E. (1965) 'Professional profile: The NAMT member and his clinical practices in music therapy.' *Journal of Music Therapy, 2,* 124–129.

Oldfield, A. (2006) *Interactive Music Therapy in Child and Family Psychiatry: Clinical Practice, Research, and Teaching.* London: Jessica Kingsley Publishers.

Pavlicevic, M. (1995) 'Interpersonal Processes in Clinical Improvisation: Toward a Subjectively Objective Systematic Function.' In T. Wigram, B. Saperston, and R. West (eds) *The Art and Science of Music Therapy: A Handbook.* London: Routledge.

Rider, M. (1981) 'The assessment of cognitive functioning level through musical perception.' *Journal of Music Therapy, 18,* 110–119.

Sabatella, P. E. (2004) 'Assessment and clinical evaluation in music therapy: An overview from literature and clinical practice.' *Music Therapy Today, 5,* 1, 1–32. Retrieved 27/11/2016 at http://musictherapyworld.net.

Sattler, J. M. (2001) *Assessment of Children: Cognitive Applications* (4th edition). La Mesa, CA: Jerome M. Sattler, Publisher Inc.

Sattler, J. M. and Hoge, R. D. (2006) *Assessment of Children: Behavioral, Social, and Clinical Foundations* (5th edition). La Mesa, CA: Jerome M. Sattler, Publisher Inc.

Sutton, K. (1984) 'The development and implementation of a music therapy physiological measures test.' *Journal of Music Therapy, 21,* 160–169.

Taylor, D. (1987) 'A survey of professional music therapists concerning entry-level competencies.' *Journal of Music Therapy, 24,* 114–145.

Urbina, S. (2004) *Essentials of Psychological Testing.* Hoboken, NJ: Wiley.

Van Houten, R. and Hall, R. V. (2001) *The Measurement of Behavior: Behavior Modification* (3rd edition). Austin, TX: Pro-Ed.

Waldon, E. G. (2013) 'Data-based decision making in music therapy.' *Imagine: Early Childhood Music Therapy, 4,* 46–50.

Waldon, E. G. (2014a) *Tests and Measures in Music Therapy: A Systematic Review (1994–2014).* Poster session presented at the World Congress of Music Therapy, Krems, Austria.

Waldon, E. G. (2014b) *Research Committee Presents: Designing Tests and Measures in Music Therapy.* Paper presented at the American Music Therapy Association Conference, Louisville, KY.

Waldon, E. G., Lesser, A., Weeden, L., and Messick, E. (2016) 'The Music Attentiveness Screening Assessment-Revised (MASA-R): A study of technical adequacy.' *Journal of Music Therapy, 53,* 75–92.

Waldon, E. G., Monje, J., and Powell, A. (2014) *Music Therapy Tests and Measures: A Review of AMTA Journals (1981–2014).* Poster session presented at the American Music Therapy Association Conference, Louisville, KY.

Wheeler, B. L. (2013) 'Music Therapy Assessment.' In R. F. Cruz and B. Feder (eds) *Feder's The Art and Science of Evaluation in the Arts Therapies* (2nd edition). Springfield, IL: Charles C. Thomas.

Wigram, T. (1999) 'Assessment methods in music therapy: A humanistic or natural science framework?' *Nordic Journal of Music Therapy, 8,* 7–25.

Wigram, T. (2000) *Assessment and Evaluation in the Arts Therapies: Art Therapy, Music Therapy and Dramatherapy.* Radlett: Harper House Publications.

Wigram, T. (2007) 'Event-Based Analysis of Improvisation using the Improvisational Assessment Profiles (IAPs).' In T. Wosch and T. Wigram (eds) *Microanalysis in Music Therapy – Methods, Techniques and Applications for Clinicians, Researchers, Educators and Students.* London: Jessica Kingsley Publishers.

Wigram, T. and Gold, C. (2006) 'Music therapy in the assessment and treatment of autistic spectrum disorder: Clinical application and research evidence.' *Child: Care, Health, and Development, 32,* 535–542, doi: 10.1111/j.1365-2214.2006.00615.x.

Wilson, B. L. (2005) 'Assessment of Adult Psychiatric Clients.' In R. F. Unkefer and M. H. Thaut (eds) *Music Therapy in the Treatment of Adults with Mental Disorders: Theoretical Bases and Clinical Interventions.* Gilsum, NH: Barcelona.

Wilson, B. L. and Smith, D. S. (2000) 'Music therapy assessment in school settings: A preliminary investigation.' *Journal of Music Therapy, 37,* 95–117.

Wosch, T. and Wigram, T. (eds) (2007) *Microanalysis in Music Therapy – Methods, Techniques and Applications for Clinicians, Researchers, Educators and Students.* London: Jessica Kingsley Publishers.

York, E. (1994) 'The development of a quantitative music skills test for patients with Alzheimer's disease.' *Journal of Music Therapy, 31,* 280–296.

CHAPTER 2

Assessment in Music Therapy

Psychometric and Theoretical Considerations

Eric G. Waldon, Stine Lindahl Jacobsen,
and Gustavo Gattino

Introduction

Both the underlying philosophy (theory) and technical adequacy (psychometrics) of assessment are important with regard to building a body of clinical knowledge. Many argue that music therapy offers unique avenues for change and a distinctive way of clinically understanding our clients (Wigram and Wosch 2007), and this calls for evidence-based assessment approaches that meet the rigor of modern test theory, thereby strengthening the integrity of the profession. Without profession-specific and standardized assessment tools, the field of music therapy is less robust and less equipped to meet the demands of a respected healthcare profession. Clinical and research relevance should guide the development of assessment tools and procedures that have a purpose and add meaningfully clinical work. Additionally (and where appropriate) assessment procedures should be based on solid theory and possess relevant psychometric properties. The purposes of this chapter are to: (a) discuss how theory underlies the processes of collecting, interpreting, and applying assessment information; and (b) provide an overview of psychometric concepts as they relate to clinical assessment in music therapy.

Please know that a full discussion of theory and psychometrics is beyond the scope of the current text and we have cited notable authors and volumes throughout the chapter that will provide a deeper understanding of these topics.

Assessment theory

Test theory and assessment theory have had a long history and encompass many fields such as psychology, education, social science, and medicine. While there is some disagreement about best practice or methods of gauging psychometric (or statistical) adequacy, there are accepted guidelines and standards to which the music therapy field should adhere in the use and construction of assessment in both research and clinical practice.

History of testing

The most typical use of psychological testing occurs when one needs to make decisions about people. In the early part of the 20th century, psychological testing was developed as a result of the rise of urban, industrial, and democratic societies because of the need to make decisions about people in building these modern societies (Urbina 2014). The origin of psychometrics can be traced back to Galton, a polymath inspired by evolutionary theory who in 1884 measured differences between people from different backgrounds. Although he was not successful in detecting these differences or correlations between academic level and class, this work established some of the fundamentals of test theory, some of which survive to this day (Rust and Golombok 2014). Prior to this time, the oldest known form of psychological testing related to occupational management and competitive examinations dating to approximately 200BC when the ancient Chinese imperial court selected individuals for government positions (Urbina 2014).

Within the field of education, tests were being used in the 13th century, as the first universities had to ensure that students were acquiring adequate knowledge and skills. With a desire to differentiate between normal and abnormal functioning, the late 19th century saw the rise of the first clinical psychology tests, which focused on cognitive functioning. While these early clinical tests were based on the subjective and unstructured collection of information, Wundt (the first self-proclaimed psychologist) introduced a more scientific approach to studying psychology in 1879 (Urbina 2014). Soon afterwards, this more systematic approach was put to use in developing intelligence tests in 1904, when the Minister of Public Instruction in Paris appointed a committee to find a way to differentiate normal children from those with mental retardation. A member of that committee, Alfred Binet, is considered by many to be the father of IQ (intelligence quotient) testing, and his measures were used for almost 60 years. Today, the use of IQ testing is a controversial topic as the historic use of these measures is often criticized for being discriminating and judgemental (Rust and Golombok 2014). To meet these types of challenges and to provide acceptable use standards, the International Test Commission (ITC) was formed in 1978 with the aim of establishing guidelines on the use of tests and evaluating the technical characteristics of test instruments (Urbina 2014).

Types of foci

Psychological tests do not measure physical objects but rather intervening constructs or hypothetical entities, which require a fundamental understanding of concepts (Rust and Golombok 2014). There are two main psychometric schools or foci involved: functional focus and trait focus. Functional testing is completely determined by its use and has no other meaning than this application. The focus is to discriminate between people who perform well and people who perform poorly, and the presence of underlying traits is considered irrelevant. Trait approaches are less concerned with performance and focus more on underlying sets of characteristics that may explain intellect or personality. Early trait testing endeavored to assign and connect specific skills with specific occupational tasks (Urbina 2014), and as a result, scores are interpreted along continua. For example, personality is considered a matter of degree where strengths and weaknesses of the individual are profiled by providing separate scores on various factors (Rust and Golombok 2014; Urbina 2014).

Assessment criteria

One should consider many aspects before considering developing or constructing clinical tools in music therapy. In 1987, Bruscia described criteria for clinical and effective assessment and they are still relevant today.

First, one should consider the *purpose* (Bruscia 1987; Urbina 2014). Inspired by Bruscia, Wigram described the different purposes of music therapy assessment, which include diagnostic, general assessment, music therapy relevance and effect, or long-term assessment (Jacobsen, Wigram, and Rasmussen 2019). Other purposes worth mentioning are predictive (Urbina 2014). Diagnostic assessment should involve objectivity and ethical caution, as estimating skills, deficits, competences, traits, and so on relevant to certain clinical challenges can have long-lasting consequences. While music therapists are not usually authorized to confer diagnoses, they can aid the diagnostic process by capturing information that other disciplines find difficult to obtain (Wigram—see Chapter 9). Frequently music therapists develop customized assessment processes to gather information about clients' strengths and needs and the appropriateness of music therapy during the early stages of treatment as there are very few tools available (see Chapter 3). A focus on documentation of effect also calls for objectivity and the consideration of ethical standards as there may be a conflict of interest when music therapists evaluate the effect of music therapy. Without objectivity (e.g. psychometric considerations) one risks subjectively evaluating the outcome of therapy or the potential benefit to the client (e.g. appropriateness or eligibility for services) for the therapist's personal gain (Jacobsen 2017).

Besides a clear purpose and relevant function, an assessment tool should offer *unique information* (Bruscia 1987). Developing a tool that already exists or that collects data that is already collected with other tools may be unnecessary and may waste time and effort in something that will not add to clinical knowledge. However, uniqueness might involve collecting data in a more nuanced way to obtain a clearer picture of the individual in question. The focus on uniqueness also links back to the aspect of integrity and acknowledgement of music therapy as an independent healthcare profession. If the aim is to decrease depression symptoms, one needs a tool that assesses how individuals act, feel, and change within music therapy as opposed to a tool built to assess functioning in psychotherapy or other clinical settings. Without profession-specific information, we fail to collect information about how music uniquely affects individuals with depression. One example from music therapy assessment is the Voice Assessment Profile (VOIAS), the results from which might indicate signs of improvement or worsening of depression before other measures (e.g. psychiatric questionnaires or interviews) reveal the state and prognosis of the client (Storm—see Chapter 16).

Additionally, one needs to *professionally administer* the assessment with fidelity (i.e. the way in which it is intended) and employ expertise, which may involve the appropriate selection of instruments, scoring, interpretation, and the cautious use of findings to draw conclusions. As such, test user qualifications are of major concern and all assessment tools should have clear guidelines on who may be qualified to administer them and the training that is required (Bruscia 1987; Urbina 2014).

Collecting data during assessment also needs to be *effective* (Bruscia 1987). Effectiveness is important for the researcher, the clinician, and the individual in question for many reasons, including time, costs, value, relevance, and accuracy. The client certainly has an interest in effective methods as an expedient, in-depth, and accurate assessment might lead to a swifter, meaningful recovery. The cost-benefit perspective is relevant in terms of clinical application for both clinicians and potential commissioners as the assessment method has to be clinically manageable and worth the effort compared to other options. Matching purpose or referral with relevant data is also an important part of the puzzle when you strive for effective assessment methods. Wigram identified different types of unique music therapy data including musical data, musical behavioral data, behavioral data, and comparative data (Jacobsen *et al.* 2019). *Musical data* includes specific musical events or individual characteristic expressions, while *musical behavioral data* consists of behaviors evidenced during music without musical descriptions (e.g. how one plays an instrument or moves when playing). *Behavioral data* includes characteristic behaviors observed in the music therapy setting, whereas *comparative data* is assessment information that is obtained outside music therapy (e.g. reports from staff or other clinicians).

According to Bruscia, a final criterion for effective clinical assessment involves adhering to *ethical standards* (Bruscia 1987). For example, clients need to consent to participate in the assessment as well as agree on whether (and what type of) media may be used to record the assessment (e.g. audio or video recording). Additionally, one might argue that an assessment yielding neither valid nor reliable information should not be used for any purpose. Furthermore, if results are portrayed as objective but are truly subjective, characterizing it otherwise may not be ethical. Finally, if the tool does not uniquely contribute to knowledge, one might also question the clinical relevance of the tool and its uses (Bruscia 1987).

Construction process

All tests that involve psychometrics as a way of gauging their technical adequacy are composed of individual items, and the utility of a test depends on the sufficiency of its items (Rust and Golombok 2014). In constructing an assessment tool, one needs to consider items carefully. They can be *knowledge-based* or *person-based*. Knowledge-based items focus on aspects including ability, aptitude, and achievement, and assess maximum performance, whereas person-based test items focus on personality traits, clinical symptoms, mood, interest, and so on, and assess typical performance. Knowledge-based tests are necessarily hierarchical and cumulative, whereas person-based ones are not. Therefore, scoring of knowledge-based items tends to be unidimensional, while person-based items may represent multiple factors (Rust and Golombok 2014). Items can also be *objective* or *open-ended*, which relates to whether there is a correct answer. Right and wrong answers used predominantly in educational settings make statistical analysis straightforward but also more reductionist, while open-ended items call for more subjective interpretation (like projective techniques such as those used in the Rorschach test) (Rust and Golombok 2014).

A consideration between norm-referenced and criterion-based item interpretation is also important when constructing measures. Until 1970, items had a tendency to be selected in way that test scores would have a normal distribution if administered to a large sample (Rust and Golombok 2014). The individual result or score was thus always understood in relation to the average. Occasionally, however, comparisons against the norm are irrelevant and comparing performance to external criteria is more appropriate. When items are constructed with particular reference to performance on some objectively defined criterion, it is considered criterion-referenced. These types of items are less common in psychological testing because criterion-referenced interpretation tends to be skill-specific (i.e. asking whether an examinee can perform a specific task) and provides limited generalizable information about the specific examinee (i.e. client). As such, criterion-referenced testing is used most frequently in educational or trade fields (pass/fail tests) (Rust and Golombok 2014). Following item construction, one decides how or whether to sum the items' values into scores or factors. The importance of each should be reviewed as one might have results from factor analysis that argue for more weight on some items over others (Rust and Golombok 2014).

Types of bias

In assessment theory, bias is a term often used, and any assessor or assessment developer should consider different types of biases. *Response bias* concerns whether individual responses are systematically biased in a way that makes their scores a poor reflection of their true psychological traits or states. Response biases can be conscious or unconscious and there are several types to consider (Furr 2011). *Acquiescence bias* refers to when individuals always say "yes" or "no" to specific items on a questionnaire, and *extremity bias* refers to differences in participants' willingness to use extreme response options. *Social desirability response bias* is the tendency to respond in a manner that seems socially appealing, regardless of an individual's true characteristics. All types of bias can lead to inaccurate conclusions, and test developers should guard against response biases by providing assurances of anonymity, minimizing respondent fatigue, and striving for brief and comfortable measurement periods (Furr 2011; Rust and Golombok 2014).

Response biases systematically obscure outcomes or differences among respondents, while *test bias* or *intrinsic test bias* systematically obscures the true differences among groups of respondents (Rust and Golombok 2014). If we understand questions or tasks differently, those differences might have important theoretical, personal, and (potentially) societal implications. *Construct bias* is a type of statistical skewedness and concerns whether people from different groups respond differently to items that are not due to group differences (which can be referred to as *extrinsic test bias*) (Rust and Golombok 2014). For instance, if females and males respond differently to an item measuring aggression, the item may be gender-biased (Furr 2011). Factor analysis can aid the detection and management of construct biases (see description below). Finally, *predictive bias* is another form of test bias and concerns the degree to which a scale equally predicts an outcome for two groups (Furr 2011). For example, suppose a test developer designed a tool for determining whether someone (based on their musical skill and interpersonal warmth) was suitable for a career in music therapy. Predictive bias may be present if the test did not consistently forecast professional success for vocalists versus instrumentalists.

Psychometric concepts

Psychometrics is the field of science concerned with the construction, administration, and interpretation of tests designed to measure psychological variables such as intelligence, aptitude, and personality traits (Lall and Sharma 2009). The study of assessment in music therapy uses concepts and processes from this field to describe, organize, and analyze various characteristics of standardized tests, observations, interviews, and other informal assessment procedures. What follows are descriptions of key psychometric concepts that are of concern when designing and evaluating the overall use of clinical tools.

Validity

According to the *Standards for Educational and Psychological Testing* (American Educational Research Association (AERA), American Psychological Association (APA), and National Council on Measurement in Education (NCME): Joint Committee on Standards for Educational and Psychological Testing 2014), *validity* (and its various dimensions) is a matter of *accuracy* that represents the extent to which a testing procedure assesses what it claims to measure. Historically, most of the attention was paid to the types of validity a particular test possessed, a conceptual understanding, which is similar to how types of reliability are considered (see below). For example, factor analyses would be used to explore or confirm the underlying structure of how a test measures a characteristic in an effort to establish construct validity. Likewise, with regard to criterion validity, an investigator may conduct a study to examine whether performance on a test predicts performance on another measure or external standard. However, validation is a process (rather than a product), and for this reason the validity of an instrument falls along a continuum; therefore, it is not correct to state whether or not a tool is valid. In this contemporary perspective, there is only one type of validity: construct validity.

CONSTRUCT VALIDITY

A *construct* is understood as any phenomenon created by the human mind that is not directly observable. Constructs are abstractions that refer to concepts or ideas used to describe features, processes, conditions, or traits which can only be inferred based on overt client responses. Therefore, constructs are the traits, characteristics, or conditions that assessment tools are designed to assess (AERA *et al.* 2014). Furthermore, the goal of all validation procedures and evidence is in the service of establishing construct validity, i.e. the extent to which an assessment process or tool measures a given characteristic (or construct). Given the emphasis placed on construct validity by AERA *et al.* (2014), the expression "types of validity" has been abandoned and replaced with sources of "evidence of validity."

EVIDENCE BASED ON CONTENT

Traditionally referred to as "content validity," evidence related to the subject matter being assessed or the items being used in a test or measure refers to evidence based on a test's content. Content refers to an assessment tool's items, the procedures used to obtain information, and the extent to which the items sufficiently cover the subject matter being addressed. Content can be derived from a list of standards, body of research, theory, or a set of competencies or skills established by a professional organization.

As an initial step in developing an assessment tool, a panel of "content experts" may review the set of proposed test items and evaluate the extent to which the subject matter (or construct) is being sufficiently addressed. As an example, Adler (2001) recruited a team of researchers and clinicians from various fields to evaluate the content of the Musical Assessment of Gerontologic Needs and Treatment (MAGNET). In her manual, Adler describes a multi-stage review and revision process, which resulted in an initial pool of 1825 items being reduced to 152 items. Baxter *et al.* (2007) employed a similar procedure that involved a panel of music therapists, speech-language pathologists, special educators, and researchers who helped design the Individual Music Therapy Assessment Profile. Regarding content-related evidence, it is important for the consumer to review the purpose for the assessment tool and examine the procedures used (e.g. review of items by an expert panel) to determine whether or not the domain being assessed is sufficiently addressed.

Another term, *face validity*, is often confused with content; instead, face validity refers to how a test or assessment tool's items appear to cover the content under consideration and is based on the perspective of the examinee (as opposed to a panel of content experts). Face validity is a concern when the appearance of a test's items and procedures are important to the motivation of the examinee, which can affect the extent to which they respond in a desired (or predicted) manner. For example, if a music-based procedure is said to assess musical preference, then one (the examinee) would expect the items (e.g. questions about the relative liking or disliking of genres, songs, or artists) or procedures (e.g. rating preference after listening to a musical example) to be present. An example includes Gold *et al.*'s (2013) Interest in Music Scale (IiM), which involves a self-report questionnaire that includes items on the extent to which examinees engage with various music activities.

However, it may be important to obscure the purpose of a test. In these situations, it may be unimportant (or counter-productive) to reveal the intent of a testing procedure's purpose; therefore, concealing the purpose of an assessment tool's items is important. An example of this is how the Assessment of Parent-Child Interaction (APCI) includes the voice of the parent in the report having presented the initial APCI results to them (Jacobsen—see Chapter 14). In this way, the experience and thoughts of the parent are part of the analysis of the parent-child interaction without them fully knowing how this will be further interpreted. They know what the focus of the assessment is, but they don't know how their experience and reflections might further inform the results and the final report.

EVIDENCE BASED ON INTERNAL STRUCTURE

When a measure's construct validity is based on the nature of how, and extent to which, items within the tool relate to each other, then the authors should provide evidence based on the internal structure. Typically involving factor analytic techniques, one of the objectives of examining a measure's internal structure is to see whether one, two, or more constructs are being estimated (or assessed) and the extent to which those constructs are related to each other. When a measure provides multiple scores assessing different dimensions of functioning, evidence of structural characteristics is necessary before any interpretation of the scores, or use of the findings, is possible. Bergmann and colleagues (2015) provided this type of structural evidence in their study and development of the Music-based Scale for Autism Diagnostics (MUSAD; Bergmann—see Chapter 7), a music-based measure used to help with the differential diagnosis of adults with autism spectrum disorder (ASD) with suspected intellectual disabilities. According to the authors, the MUSAD evidenced three latent factors (social interaction; stereotyped, restricted, or repetitive behavior; and motor coordination) which correspond with widely accepted clinical and diagnostic guidelines (*International Statistical Classification of Diseases and Related Health Problems, 10th Revision* and the *Diagnostic and Statistical Manual of Mental Disorders, Version 5*) relevant to ASD.

EVIDENCE BASED ON SIMILAR MEASURES

Another common method of evaluating construct validity is to examine the degree to which scores on an assessment tool relate to other variables or test scores, which are theoretically related. One may argue that developing a measure of an important clinical construct is not necessary if such a tool already exists; however, new theories, methods, and procedures for understanding clinically relevant constructs are being discovered that result in better assessment processes. As discussed in the previous chapter, because music occasions unique responses not otherwise elicited under other (non-music) conditions (Bruscia 1998; Lathom 1980;

Pavlicevic 1995), assessment methods that incorporate music may yield additional information to the overall clinical picture. Therefore, it would seem important to determine whether music-based assessment tools estimate, at least in part, the constructs and characteristics they claim to measure by using conceptually related (non-music-based) tests.

To achieve this there are two typically accepted methods of obtaining validity evidence based on relationships with conceptually similar or dissimilar measures: obtaining convergent and/or discriminant evidence. *Convergent validity evidence* is "based on the assumption that different measures of the same hypothetical construct ought to correlate highly with one another" (Coleman 2009, p. 171) if they measure the same construct. Waldon and his team (Waldon and Broadhurst 2014; Waldon *et al.* 2016) used a convergent evidence approach by comparing scores from two auditory attention neuropsychological subtests to establish the extent to which MASA (and its revision, MASA-R) sampled the construct of auditory attention. Similarly, Bergmann *et al.* (2015) used three scales (the Autism Diagnostic Observation Schedule, the Pervasive Developmental Disorder in Mental Retardation Scale, and the Social Communication Questionnaire) to determine whether MUSAD measured similar constructs. *Discriminant validity evidence* assumes that measures which assess different constructs do not correlate significantly with one another. Returning to the MUSAD, Bergmann and his team used the Modified Overt Aggression Scale and the Aberrant Behavior Checklist to generate discriminant evidence because high scores on these measures do not relate strongly with diagnostic indicators of ASD.

EVIDENCE BASED ON EXTERNAL CRITERIA

When considering evidence based on external criteria (previously referred to as criterion or criterion-related validity), one is concerned with how an assessment tool's outcomes (e.g. scores or findings) relate to an accepted independent standard. There are two general approaches to examining criterion-related evidence: establishing the presence of predictive evidence and/or concurrent evidence. Establishing *predictive evidence* involves determining how well an assessment tool predicts *future* performance on another measure or against an established standard. In the field of music therapy, Waldon and Wolfe (2006) investigated whether results from the Computer-based Music Perception Assessment for Children (CMPAC) would assist music therapists in making a decision as to whether to refer a child for music therapy during invasive medical procedures. Using a sample of music therapists working in pediatric medical settings, they asked the panel to determine whether the data obtained through CMPAC would be useful in making a future referral decision (an external standard). The *concurrent validity approach* is similar to that of predictive validity except the objective is to determine how well an assessment tool estimates *current* (as opposed to future) performance on an external standard. Working with a sample of pediatric patients, Magee, Ghetti, and Moyer (2015) conducted a pilot study to determine whether ratings from MATADOC (Magee—see Chapter 20) could comparably assess disorders of consciousness to the same extent as a set of external measures of the same construct.

EVIDENCE BASED ON CONSEQUENCES

The final source of validity evidence described here is that which is based on *consequences*. Evidence of this type is less statistical in nature and is largely related to the social consequences that result from the use of assessment tools like standardized tests. As Frey (2015) explains, "validity is the extent to which the *scores* from a test reflect the intended construct. Under that widely accepted understanding of the term, the unintended social consequences of test use, while important to consider, do not affect the validity of the test" (p. 21). This means that while a sufficient standard for validity evidence may have been met, consumers must still consider whether the assessment finding is being used in the spirit of beneficence. This means that decisions about which assessment tools and procedures should be used and how that assessment data should be used rests on the shoulders of clinicians, institutional administrators, and policy-making bodies. While appearing less relevant to the types of assessment procedures used in music therapy, an understanding of the consequences that result (directly or indirectly) from assessment (and test scores specifically) is important because music therapists will encounter clients who have experienced consequences (e.g. diagnostic decisions, residential placement determinations, and disability qualification verdicts) resulting from test scores and other forms of assessment.

Reliability

Reliability, in a general sense, is understood as the consistency of scores across replications of a testing procedure, regardless of how this consistency is estimated or reported (AERA et al. 2014). Therefore, reliability explains whether an assessment procedure gives the same results each time it is used under the same conditions. From the perspective of classical test theory, reliability is conceived as the extent to which scores from an assessment procedure are free from measurement error—that is, the more consistency is present from one occasion to the next, the less random error is present. Therefore, reliability is a matter of *precision*: greater precision (or fineness of measure) means less measurable variability between test administrations, and can be illustrated (in the simplest sense) as a ratio:

$$\text{Reliability} = \frac{\text{What one intends to measure}}{\text{What is measured}}$$

Therefore, the higher the reliability index (e.g. expressed using a correlation coefficient and interpreted as a percentage), the higher the consistency and the less error is present (see Waldon 2016 for additional information). As with validity, there are a number of procedures used to estimate reliability, some of which are discussed here.

INTERNAL CONSISTENCY

Internal consistency (sometimes referred to as internal reliability) denotes the consistency to which multiple items within a test or measure assumed to measure the same characteristic or trait relate to each other. The need for this type of reliability comes from the notion that an examinee will respond with a certain degree of inconsistency across items or procedures during an assessment process. For example, a client's music improvisation performance may vary across an assessment as a function of fatigue, motivation, time, or other factors. While some of these are intended to be measured by the assessment tool, others are not (e.g. fatigue), which would contribute to the inconsistency of the measure. Two examples of internal consistency analyses can be found in the Assessment of Parent-Child Interaction (APCI) and the Attention Profile in MT assessment for children (APMT) (Jacobsen—see Chapter 14; Eslava-Meija 2017). One would expect the consistency between parent-child interaction scores such as Nonverbal Communication and Mutual Attunement to be evident like the consistency between different types of attention skills in children. On a measure gauging perceived engagement with music, a person's responses will vary as a function of factors (i.e. measurement error) that are not intended to be assessed by the test's authors or the therapist administering it (see Gold *et al.* 2013). Internal consistency procedures estimate true score (versus unintended error) variability of a measure or assessment procedure using a number of procedures, including Chronbach's alpha, split-half reliability, and the Kuder Richardson 20 formula (for assessment items scored dichotomously). For more details on these methods, the reader is referred to Urbina (2014).

TEST-RETEST RELIABILITY

At times, it is important to know whether a measure taken on one occasion will remain viable (or stable) after a period of time has passed. In this regard, test-retest reliability indicates the extent to which a test or measure administered on two separate occasions consistently yields the same score. This would be especially important in assessment situations where a therapist is gauging a trait that is not expected to vary significantly (e.g. personality or motor ability) in the absence of intervention or other training. For example, Waldon and Broadhurst (2014) and Waldon et al. (2016) developed MASA (and MASA-R) to assess the degree to which a child can attend to specific musical cues—information that can be used to design music-based interventions during invasive medical procedures. Confidence in the stability of the assessment finding is important with regard to designing interventions because a score obtained on one occasion (e.g. at admission) may be used across a child's hospitalization. Another example of established test-retest reliability in music therapy assessment is Music in Dementia Assessment Scales (MIDAS) where the client reaction in music therapy in relation to aspects such as enjoyment, involvement, and initiation correlates positively in different sessions (McDermott—see Chapter 19). Usually estimated by calculating correlations from scores between the two testing occasions, test-retest reliability provides an estimate of how applicable a measure taken at one point will be at another.

INTER-RATER RELIABILITY

Whenever an assessment process involves a judgement in scoring during the course of its administration there is a chance that the observer (or "rater") may be inconsistent in executing the assessment's procedures or scoring rules. This would result in measurement error and may be a sign of: unclear administration directions, poorly defined operational definitions, or inadequate training of the assessment administrators. Estimates of inter-rater reliability (sometimes referred to as inter-observer, inter-scorer, or inter-scorer agreement) provide a gauge of consistency between different observers of the same examinees or clients. A common approach to calculating inter-rater reliability when the number or frequency of observances (e.g. behavior or event counts) is relevant is to calculate *percentage agreement* expressed by the following:

$$\frac{\text{Number of observations (agreements)} \times 100}{\text{Total number of observations}}$$
$$\text{(i.e. agreements + disagreements)}$$

Additional approaches to calculate agreement on observed frequencies, both of which account for "chance agreement" between observers, can be calculated using Cohen's kappa (for two observers) or Fleiss's kappa (when more than two observers are involved). Carpente and Gattino (2018) explored weighted kappa (ordinal data) in establishing inter-rater reliability for the IMCAP-ND (Carpente—see Chapter 5). Other assessment and measurement situations, particularly those involving continuous levels of measurement (e.g. ratings of clinical phenomena), require the computation of correlations which may include intraclass correlation, Pearson's r, or Spearman's Rho (Waldon 2016). Magee *et al.* (2016) and Waldon *et al.* (2016) both used interclass correlation to estimate inter-observer agreement for the MATADOC and MASA-R, respectively.

ALTERNATE (PARALLEL) FORMS RELIABILITY

There may be an occasion when a clinician wants to assess a client at the beginning of treatment (e.g. during initial assessment) and then again at a point following intervention. While the clinician may elect to use the same measure twice, there may be an advantage to administering two forms of the same measure to ensure that performance on the second measure was not unduly influenced by the first. For situations like this, where two versions of the same test or measure are available, one would want evidence of equivalence (Waldon 2016). Alternate (or parallel) forms reliability estimates two measures that have similar content (i.e. coverage of the domain of interest) and procedures (i.e. identical tasks) yet consist of different items.

RELATIONSHIP BETWEEN RELIABILITY AND VALIDITY

It is important to note that, while different psychometric concepts, validity and reliability are related in important ways. Validity refers to the accuracy of an assessment process and represents the magnitude to which a measure represents the construct it was designed to measure. Reliability refers to precision and is a gauge of how consistently an approach (e.g. a score yielded from an assessment tool) assesses the intended construct and its freedom from error. This means that a test score may yield a consistent (reliable) measure of a phenomenon but it does not mean that the score accurately represents the construct you intend (validity). Furthermore, if a measure does not evidence acceptable reliability (i.e. one that is relatively free from error), that same score could not be considered valid. In short, reliability is a requirement for validity but, alone, is insufficient for validity (Waldon 2016).

In closing the discussion that specifically relates to reliability, it is important to note that certain types of reliability are more important than others depending on the nature of the test, measure, or assessment situation. In other words, it may not be important for all measures to evidence stability (test-retest reliability) because the construct being measured is expected to vary greatly within a period of time. Similarly, if an apparatus (e.g. an electronic or computerized mechanism) as opposed to an examiner is used to obtain a measure, then the error of human administration is largely absent and, therefore, the need to establish inter-rater reliability is unnecessary. What is important to keep in mind is that one understands how different types of reliability evidence are important given the features of the test or measure being considered. For example, MUSAD (Bergmann *et al.* 2015) involves an administrator's judgement of behavioral manifestations in the assessment of those with suspected autism spectrum disorder and intellectual disabilities. This requires a degree of administrator consistency, and the authors calculated the inter-rater agreement using interclass correlation. In contrast, the IiM (Gold *et al.* 2013) is a self-administered questionnaire that does not involve an administrator's judgement with regard to administration and scoring—therefore inter-rater agreement is an unnecessary consideration. As with validity, it is not simply the relative presence or absence of reliability that is important; instead, the suitable type of reliability evidence (in sufficient degrees) is important.

Other psychometric concepts

CROSS-CULTURAL ADAPTATION

The process of *cross-cultural adaptation* is related to test instrument translation but concerns the application of an assessment tool in a different culture from the original instrument (Wild *et al.* 2005). Cross-cultural adaptation applies when items need to be modified to maintain equivalent meaning for people from a specific culture in the target language (*semantic equivalence*) and to ensure that methods of survey administration are appropriate for the target culture (*operational equivalence*) (Byrne 2016).

TRANSLATION

Test instrument *translation* involves converting an assessment instrument (including its administration instructions and test items) from the original language to the target idiom (Wild *et al.* 2005). Ridder, McDermott, and Orrell (2015) explained in detail how this process works in music therapy and highlighted that few assessment tools use international standard procedures in carrying out translations in the field. Internationally, there is a consensus to which assessment tools should adhere regarding forward-backward translation, an example of which appears in Wild *et al.* (2005), who suggest using ten steps: (1) preparation; (2) forward translation; (3) reconciliation; (4) back-translation; (5) back-translation review; (6) harmonization; (7) cognitive debriefing (analysis from a small sample of the target population and/or from a committee of judges); (8) review of cognitive debriefing results and finalization; (9) proofreading; and (10) final report.

TREATMENT VALIDITY

While psychometric concepts are generally applied to understanding and exploring the technical adequacy of tests (i.e. assessment tools that produce a score), when they are considered more broadly one must weigh the extent to which the assessment processes being used contribute meaningfully to treatment. Referred to as treatment validity, Gresham and Witt (1997) explain that the concept involves three important, and interrelated, considerations. The first is *utility*, or the degree to which evidence exists that supports the assessment tool's use in clinical work. Such evidence may include how well an assessment result informs clinical recommendations or affects the design of treatment programs. There has been considerable attention in the school psychology and psychotherapy literature (Aljunied and Frederickson 2015) about the extent to which testing contributes in a meaningful way to treatment beyond disability qualification or conferring a diagnosis. Critics in those fields frequently question whether intelligence or personality tests yield information that informs how interventions are designed or executed. While there is little written about the extent to which data yielded from music therapy assessment informs treatment decisions, Bruscia's (1987) ethical considerations regarding assessment would seem relevant (see discussion above).

The second treatment validity consideration is *cost benefit* and refers to whether the expense of conducting a particular assessment procedure is justified given the impact on treatment. The concern relates to whether time and money spent is balanced with the benefits to the client. Largely, music therapists do not collect assessment data or subject clients to unnecessary assessment procedures. Music therapists, however, can be mindful to avoid unnecessary duplication of assessment by thoroughly reviewing other sources of data and limiting the use of methods that require client involvement (e.g. interviewing or testing) which are not otherwise required.

Finally, Gresham and Witt discuss *incremental validity* as the third treatment validity consideration. In this instance, one is concerned with whether a specific assessment process or procedure contributes meaningfully to assessment information beyond that which is already provided by conventional means. While incremental validity can be calculated statistically, from a conceptual perspective a therapist would want to determine whether the evidence yielded from an assessment procedure contributes to an understanding of the client and their level of functioning. Within the music therapy field, ongoing study of MATADOC (Magee *et al.* 2016; O'Kelly and Magee 2013) has shown that it evidences more sensitivity for functioning in the auditory and visual domains for those with disorders of consciousness versus comparator instruments. This suggests that MATADOC may provide diagnostic evidence beyond that which other non-music-based methods can provide. More research like this which highlights the unique contribution that music provides during the assessment process will benefit clients and serve to advance the field.

Conclusion

It is easy to argue that an understanding of assessment theory and psychometrics is important. What may be less obvious is that assessment involves more than collecting data using archival records, observations, interviews, and tests. One does not simply review a set of records to collect information; educated music therapists know what information to look for to answer the referral question. Interviews involve more than asking a series of disparate questions; skilled music therapists conduct interviews as if they were conversations that lend themselves to both a depth and breadth of clinical information. When conducted by experienced music therapists, observations can yield important information that cannot be captured through other means. Regarding the use of assessment tools, trained music therapists know that test scores capture a fraction of the clinical picture and alone (i.e. in the absence of other sources of information or a disregard of context) are insufficient to draw conclusions. We would expect all readers to seek out appropriate training to supplement the information included in this chapter (and throughout this book) because only assessment-informed music therapists can use these skills and their clinical acumen to draw relevant inferences about client functioning.

References

Adler, R. (2001) *Musical Assessment of Gerontologic Needs and Treatment: The MAGNET Survey*. Saint Louis, MO: MMB Music, Inc.

Aljunied, M. and Frederickson, N. L. (2015) 'Assessing cognitive abilities in children with autism: Practitioner evaluation of treatment validity.' *International Journal of Developmental Disorders, 61*, 231–241, doi: 10.1179/2047387714Y.0000000057.

American Educational Research Association (AERA), American Psychological Association (APA), and National Council on Measurement in Education (NCME): Joint Committee on Standards for Educational and Psychological Testing (2014) *Standards for Educational and Psychological Testing.* Washington, DC: AERA.

Baxter, H. T., Berghofer, J. A., MacEwan, J. N., Peters, J., and Roberts, P. (2007) *The Individualized Music Therapy Assessment Profile.* London: Jessica Kingsley Publishers.

Bergmann, T., Sappok, T., Diefenbacher, A., Dames, S., Heinrich, M., Ziegler, M., and Dziovek, I. (2015) 'Music-based Autism Diagnostics (MUSAD): A newly developed diagnostic measure for adults with intellectual developmental disabilities suspected of autism.' *Research in Developmental Disabilities, 43–44,* 123–135, doi: 10.1016/j. ridd.2015.05.011.

Bruscia, K. E. (1987) *Improvisational Models of Music Therapy.* Springfield, IL: Charles C. Thomas.

Bruscia, K. E. (1998) *Defining Music Therapy* (2nd edition). Gilsum, NH: Barcelona.

Byrne, B. M. (2016) 'Testing Instrument Equivalence Across Cultural Groups: Basic Concepts, Testing Strategies, and Common Complexities.' In N. Zane, G. Bernal, and F. T. L. Leong (eds) *Evidence-Based Psychological Practice with Ethnic Minorities: Culturally Informed Research and Clinical Strategies.* Washington, DC: American Psychological Association.

Carpente, J. A. and Gattino, G. S. (2018) 'Inter-rater reliability on the Individual Music-Centered Assessment Profile for Neurodevelopmental Disorders (IMCAP-ND) for autism spectrum disorder.' *Nordic Journal of Music Therapy.* Advance online publication. doi: 10.1080/08098131.2018.1456480.

Coleman, A. M. (2009) *Oxford Dictionary of Psychology* (3rd edition). New York, NY: Oxford University Press.

Eslava-Meija, J. (2017) 'The Attention Profile in MT Assessment for Children: Development and Pilot Study of Validity and Reliability.' Unpublished PhD thesis, Aalborg University.

Frey, B. B. (2015) *100 Questions (and Answers) about Tests and Measures.* Thousand Oaks, CA: Sage.

Furr, M. (2011) *Scale Construction and Psychometrics for Social and Personality Psychology.* London: Sage.

Gold, C., Rolvsjord, R., Mössler, K., and Stige, B. (2013) 'Reliability and validity of a scale to measure interest in music among clients in mental health care.' *Psychology of Music, 41,* 665–682, doi: 10.1177/0305735612441739.

Gresham, F. M. and Witt, J. C. (1997) 'Utility of intelligence tests for treatment planning, classification, and placement decisions.' *School Psychology Quarterly, 12,* 249–267.

Jacobsen, S. L. (2017) 'Ethics and Transparency.' In D. Thomas and V. Abad (eds) *The Economics of Therapy.* London: Jessica Kingsley Publishers.

Jacobsen, S. L., Wigram, T., and Rasmussen, A. M. (2019) 'Assessment and Clinical Evaluation in Music Therapy.' In L. O. Bonde, I. N. Pedersen, and S. L. Jacobsen (eds) *Comprehensive Guide to Music Therapy* (2nd edition). London: Jessica Kingsley Publishers.

Lall, M. and Sharma, S. (2009) *Personal Growth and Training and Development.* New Delhi, India: Excel Books.

Lathom, W. (1980) *Role of Music Therapy in the Education of Handicapped Children and Youth*. Lawrence, KS: National Association for Music Therapy.

Magee, W. L., Ghetti, C. M., and Moyer, A. (2015) 'Feasibility of the Music Therapy Assessment Tool for Disorders of Consciousness (MATADOC) for use with pediatric populations.' *Frontiers in Psychology, 6*, 1–12, doi: 10.3389/fpsyg.2015.00698.

Magee, W. L., Siegert, R. J., Taylor, S. M., Daveson, B. A., and Lenton-Smith, G. (2016) 'Music Therapy Assessment Tool for Awareness in Disorders of Consciousness (MATADOC): Reliability and validity of a measure to assess awareness in patients with disorders of consciousness.' *Journal of Music Therapy, 53*, 1–26, doi: 10.1093/jmt/thv017.

O'Kelly, J. and Magee, W. L. (2013) 'The complementary role of music therapy in the detection of awareness in disorders of consciousness: An audit of concurrent SMART and MATADOC assessments.' *Neuropsychological Rehabilitation, 23*, 287–298, doi: 10.1080/09602011.2012.753395.

Pavlicevic, M. (1995) 'Interpersonal Processes in Clinical Improvisation: Toward a Subjectively Objective Systematic Function.' In T. Wigram, B. Saperston, and R. West (eds) *The Art and Science of Music Therapy: A Handbook*. London: Routledge.

Ridder, H. M., McDermott, O., and Orrell, M. (2015) 'Translation and adaptation procedures for music therapy outcome instruments.' *Nordic Journal of Music Therapy, 26*, 1–17, doi: 10.1080/08098131.2015.1091377.

Rust, J. and Golombok, S. (2014) *Modern Psychometrics: The Science of Psychological Assessment*. New York, NY: Routledge.

Urbina, S. (2014) *Essentials of Psychological Testing* (2nd edition). Somerset, NJ: Wiley.

Waldon, E. G. (2016) 'Measurement Issues in Objectivist Research.' In B. L. Wheeler and K. M. Murphy (eds) *Music Therapy Research* (3rd edition). Dallas, TX: Barcelona.

Waldon, E. G. and Broadhurst, E. H. (2014) 'Construct validity and reliability of the Music Attentiveness Screening Assessment (MASA).' *Journal of Music Therapy, 51*, 154–170, doi: 10.1093/jmt/thu008.

Waldon, E. G. and Wolfe, D. E. (2006) 'Predictive validity of the Computer-based Music Perception Assessment for Children (CMPAC).' *Journal of Music Therapy, 43*, 356–371.

Waldon, E. G., Lesser, A., Weeden, L., and Messick, E. (2016) 'The Music Attentiveness Screening Assessment-Revised (MASA-R): A study of technical adequacy.' *Journal of Music Therapy, 53*, 75–92, doi: 10.1093/jmt/thv021.

Wigram, T. and Wosch, T. (2007) 'Microanalysis in Music Therapy: A Comparison of Different Models and Methods and their Application in Clinical Practice, Research and Teaching Music Therapy.' In T. Wosch and T. Wigram (eds) *Microanalysis in Music Therapy – Methods, Techniques and Applications for Clinicians, Researchers, Educators and Students*. London: Jessica Kingsley Publishers.

Wild, D., Grove, A., Martin, M., Eremenco, S., McElroy, S., Verjee-Lorenz, A., and Erikson, P. (2005) 'Principles of good practice for the translation and cultural adaptation process for patient-reported outcomes (PRO) measures: Report of the SPOR Task Force for Translation and Cultural Adaptation.' *Value in Health, 8*, 94–104, doi: 10.1111/j.1524-4733.2005.04054.x.

CHAPTER 3

Music Therapy Assessment Without Tools

From the Clinician's Perspective

Gustavo Gattino, Stine Lindahl Jacobsen, and Sanne Storm

Introduction

The therapeutic process is complex in music therapy and requires a holistic perspective to be understood, particularly regarding the inherent subjective dynamics (Hiller 2016). Even though most of the chapters presented in this book are focused on tests, the music therapist can also use interviews, reviews of documents, and observations to assess the different stages of the clinical process in music therapy. Some clinicians systematize these non-test assessments, transforming them into tools, while other clinicians implement and apply assessment according to the circumstances. Some music therapists confuse the use of the term "assessment" with the concept of "test" (Gattino 2017). In some cases, clinicians claim that they do not use assessment in music therapy because they do not want to quantify what happens in clinical practice with a client. A more precise formulation would be that there is no interest in testing. Perhaps this confusion is the reason why there are few publications focusing only on non-test tools and assessment without a pre-developed tool in music therapy.

In order to discuss the implementation of non-test assessment, this chapter aims to focus on non-test tools in music therapy, including a literature review, types of observation, and a guide on how to conduct assessment without a pre-developed tool. The guide aims to help clinicians by suggesting what to be aware of before, during, and after collecting, analyzing, interpreting, and disseminating assessment data.

Literature review of non-test tools in music therapy

In order to provide an overview of the publications on clinical assessment without a tool, we performed an integrative literature review. The integrative review is a methodology that provides the synthesis of knowledge and incorporates the applicability of results from essential studies into practice (de Souza, da Silva, and de Carvalho 2010). The review defined one main research question: how are the non-test assessment tools characterized considering author, assessment methods, types of assessment processes (reviewing, interviewing, and observing), clinical population, theoretical framework, and level of systematization?

Search strategy

The first author of this chapter conducted a systematic search of the literature using the following databases: Cumulative Index to Nursing and Allied Health Literature (CINAHL), Embase, PubMed, the Digital Access to Research Theses (DART)-Europe E-theses Portal, Open Access Theses and Dissertations, ProQuest Dissertations and Theses Database Web of Science, and Primo (Aalborg University library search database).

The keywords used were "music therapy" and "assessment." The search covered articles that had been written in English and published in peer-reviewed journals, theses, and dissertations between 1968 and November 2017. The beginning date was chosen to encompass the advent of formal studies in music therapy, including the earliest use of assessment procedures (Gaston 1968). The end date represents when the author initiated the final version of the review.

Study eligibility

The inclusion criteria for this review were organized in conditions:

1. The subject "assessment in music therapy" is the main topic within the publication.

2. The non-test tool needs to present some level of systematization.

3. The selected non-test tool needs to be classified in one or more of the following types of assessment: observing, reviewing, and interviewing.

4. Publications are in English.

The search excluded studies if only an abstract was published or in cases of duplication. Furthermore, publications where the assessment method was not sufficiently clear were excluded.

Data abstraction

The results that followed the requirements established in the search strategy were organized according to the following classifications: publication citation, publication type (article, dissertation, thesis, or book chapter), assessment method (purpose and data type), type of assessment (interview, observation, and documents review), client group, theoretical frames, and levels of systematization (slightly systematic, systematic, or highly systematic). The types of assessments were based on the rationale description proposed by Waldon and Gattino in the first chapter of this book. In relation to theoretical orientation, we prioritized the clinical theoretical perspective, although we did consider the theories or authors that grounded the method of analysis (phenomenology, hermeneutics, etc.). Moreover, the criteria to assess the level of systematization were defined in the number of systematic procedures described in the publication. From none to three systematic procedures, the study was classified as slightly systematic. If the study had four or five procedures, it was considered systematic, and for more than six procedures, it was considered highly systematic.

Results from the literature review

A total of 29 studies met the criteria described above and were further analyzed. The classifications for each study (publication type, assessment method, type of assessment, client group, theoretical frames, and level of systematization) are described in Table 3.1. The classification of the client population followed the terms used in the original publication.

PUBLICATION AUTHORS

The author with most publications in this area is Kenneth Bruscia with five (17%) publications (1987a, 1987b, 1987c, 1987d, 2002), followed by Joanne Loewy (1994, 2000) with two publications (7%).

TYPE OF PUBLICATIONS

Book chapters were the most frequent publication, with 19 publications (65%). In addition, eight articles (28%), one dissertation (3%), and one master's thesis (3%) were registered.

ASSESSMENT PURPOSE AND DATA-FOCUS

Regarding the diverse number of methods, general assessment was the most frequent method with 11 publications (38%); six reported musical analysis (21%), four applied video analysis (14%), and three used text analysis (10%); and there were two studies on intake procedures (7%), one study on diagnostic assessment (3%), one publication on voice analysis (3%), and one study on psychoacoustic analysis (3%).

TYPE OF ASSESSMENTS

Taking into account the classifications of assessment established by Waldon and Gattino in the first chapter of this book, there were 17 observations (59%), six reviews (21%), four methods combining observation and review (14%), one method combining observation and interview (3%), and one interview (3%).

CLINICAL POPULATIONS

Most of the assessment methods did not define the clinical population, reported in 14 publications (48%). Furthermore, we found three studies for people with autism spectrum disorder (10%), two studies on dementia (7%), two on emotionally disturbed people (7%), one on communication difficulties (3%), one on multiple disabilities (3%), one on psychotic patients (3%), one on brain injury (3%), one on people with anorexia nervosa (3%), one on people with developmental disorders (3%), and one on psychotic clients (3%).

THEORETICAL FRAMEWORK

There was a balance between the number of publications that described the clinical theoretical framework and studies that focused on the theories regarding the method of analysis. Four studies reported a behavioral perspective (14%), five did not define the theoretical frame (17%), four described a phenomenological background (14%), three were centered in psychodynamic theories (10%), and there were two on hermeneutics (7%), two on developmental psychology (7%), two on the Bonny Method and Guided Imagery and Music (BMGIM) (7%), one on psychoacoustics (3%), one about improvisational music therapy (3%), one on four levels of experience and analysis from Even Ruud *et al.* (1999) (3%), one that connected analytic, cognitive, and humanistic models of psychotherapy (3%), one with gestalt and existential orientation (3%), and one on a qualitative method for describing and interpreting musical works developed by Langenberg, Frommer, and Tress (3%).

LEVEL OF SYSTEMATIZATION

Twelve publications presented a slight level of systematization (41%), followed by 9 systematic publications (36%) and eight highly systematic publications (27%).

TABLE 3.1: OVERVIEW OF LITERATURE REVIEW

Citation	Publication category	Assessment purpose and data-focus	Type	Client group	Theoretical frames	Levels of systematization
Thaut (2014)	Book chapter	Transformational design model (general assessment purpose)	Observing	Undefined	Neurologic music therapy	Slightly systematic
Melhuish (2013)	Article	General assessment	Observing	People with dementia	Behavioral	Slightly systematic
Martin *et al.* (2012)	Book chapter	Eligibility procedures based on a formulation of an individual education plan (IEP) and goals assessment according to the SCERTS (Social Communication, Emotional Regulation and Transactional) approach	Observing	Children with autism spectrum disorder (ASD)	Behavioral	Systematic
Wang (2010)	Thesis	Music analysis of clinical improvisations	Observing and reviewing	Adolescents with communication difficulties	Hermeneutics	Systematic
Lucht and Gatzsche (2009)	Article	Emotional assessment using an interactive system (audio signals are encoded within different physical, psychoacoustic, or musical parameters)	Reviewing	Typical adults	Psychoacoustic	Slightly systematic
Holck (2007)	Book chapter	An ethnographic descriptive approach to video microanalysis	Observing	Children with ASD	Phenomenology	Systematic
Plahl (2007)	Book chapter	Video microanalysis of pre-verbal communication in music therapy	Observing	Children with multiple disabilities	Developmental psychology	Highly systematic
Ridder (2007)	Book chapter	Microanalysis on selected video clips with focus on communicative response in music therapy	Observing and reviewing	Undefined	Undefined	Highly systematic

cont.

Citation	Publication category	Assessment purpose and data-focus	Type	Client group	Theoretical frames	Levels of systematization
Scholtz et al. (2007)	Book chapter	Video Microanalysis of Interaction in Music Therapy (MIMT)	Observing	Children with developmental disorders	Developmental psychology	Highly systematic
Baker (2007)	Book chapter	Voice analysis software to analyze the sung and spoken voice	Observing and reviewing	Young males who had sustained traumatic brain injury	Undefined	Highly systematic
De Backer (2007)	Book chapter	Analysis of notated music examples selected from improvisations of psychotic patients	Reviewing	Psychotic patients	Phenomenology	Highly systematic
Sutton (2007)	Book chapter	The use of micro-musical analysis and conversation. Analysis of improvisation: "The Invisible Handshake" —free musical improvisation as conversation	Observing	Undefined	Undefined	Systematic
Trondalen (2007)	Book chapter	A phenomenologically inspired approach to microanalyses of improvisation in music therapy	Observing	Undefined	Phenomenology	Highly systematic
Bonde (2007)	Book chapter	Researching the music in therapy	Reviewing	Undefined	Four main properties or encompassing four levels of experience and analysis from Even Ruud	Systematic

Grocke (2007)	Book chapter	Structural Model of Music Analysis (SAMA)	Observing and reviewing	Undefined	Bonny Method of Guided Imagery and Music (BMGIM)	Systematic
McFerran and Grocke (2007)	Book chapter	Phenomenological text microanalysis	Reviewing	Undefined	Phenomenology	Systematic
Ortlieb, Sembdner, and Frommer (2007)	Book chapter	Text Analysis Method for Micro Processes (TAMP) of single music therapy sessions	Reviewing	Undefined	A qualitative method for describing and interpreting musical works used in treatment developed by Langenberg, Frommer, and Tress	Systematic
McFerran et al. (2006)	Article	Retrospective lyrical analysis of songs	Reviewing	Adolescents with anorexia nervosa	Undefined	Systematic
Bruscia (2002)	Book chapter	General description of the main proposals of assessment in the BMGIM—diagnostic, prescriptive, interpretive, or evaluative	Observing	Undefined	BMGIM	Slightly systematic
Munk-Madsen (2001)	Article	Qualitative observation/description of both the client and the music therapy process	Observing	People with dementia	Undefined	Slightly systematic
Wigram (2000)	Article	A method of music therapy assessment for the diagnosis of autism and communication disorders in children	Observing	Children with ASD	Improvisational music therapy	Slightly systematic

cont.

Citation	Publication category	Assessment purpose and data-focus	Type	Client group	Theoretical frames	Levels of systematization
Loewy (2000)	Article	Music psychotherapy assessment	Observing	Undefined	Analytic, cognitive, and humanistic models of psychotherapy	Slightly systematic
Loewy (1994)	Dissertation	A hermeneutic panel analysis	Observing	Emotionally disturbed children	Hermeneutics	Slightly systematic
Bruscia (1987a)	Book chapter	General assessment in Free Improvisation Therapy (Alvin model)	Observing	Undefined	Psychodynamic theories	Slightly systematic
Bruscia (1987b)	Book chapter	General assessment in Analytical Music Therapy (Priestley model)	Interviewing and observing	Undefined	Psychodynamic theories	Slightly systematic
Bruscia (1987c)	Book chapter	General assessment in Experimental Therapy (Riordon-Bruscia model)	Observing	Undefined	Gestalt and existential orientation	Slightly systematic
Bruscia (1987d)	Book chapter	General assessment in Paraverbal Therapy (Helmlich model)	Observing	Undefined	Psychodynamic theories	Slightly systematic
Wells (1988)	Article	Individual music therapy assessment procedure	Observing based in specific music activities	Emotionally disturbed young adolescents	Behavioral	Highly systematic
Braswell et al. (1983)	Article	Music/activity therapy intake assessment	Interviewing	Psychiatric patients	Behavioral	Highly systematic

Reflections on the literature review results

The data of this review point to an almost equal number of non-test tools (29) in comparison with the number of tests with evidence of reliability and validity described in the first chapter of the book (25). In fact, the number of non-test assessment tools is slightly higher in comparison with assessment tests. In this sense, there is not a representative predominance that allows affirming either focus being a central tendency in music therapy assessment.

Regarding the period of publication, it is possible to claim that between 2000 and 2010 there was a higher number of reports on non-test assessment. It is interesting because this period is slightly earlier than the time when the test publications increased, which began in 2010. In other words, the results of this review confirm the current trend of a fundamental concern about the creation and evidence of reliability and validity for testing today in music therapy. Since many of the review publications come from the book *Microanalysis in Music Therapy* (Wosch and Wigram 2007), this can explain why the majority of publications are between 2000 and 2010. The method of microanalysis (analysis of small fragments of audio, video, or text) was in fact the most predominant within the presented data (12 reports). As was the case with the book on microanalysis, the book *Improvisational Models of Music Therapy* (Bruscia 1987) also had a representative number of chapters on the use of assessment and evaluations in improvisational music therapy, with four publications.

In addition to the results of the books cited above, considering the chapter on assessment and evaluation in the BMGIM method (Bruscia 2002) and the chapter on assessment in the book *Early Childhood Music Therapy and Autism Spectrum Disorders: Developing Potential in Young Children and their Families* (Martin et al. 2012), the total number of book chapters is 18, more than half of the publications. It should be noted that the book chapters reported during the review process were only accessible due to the high degree of efficiency of the search tools used. This means that a clinician may have difficulties finding such information since access to databases is often restricted to researchers, teachers, and students.

The results in this review point to a low number of interviews. This might be due to clinicians preferring to create their models based on the particularities of their own clinical practice and reality (Ferrari 2013). Regarding the quality of the evaluation methods, two factors can be highlighted: empirical basis and level of detail, and examples of application. Most of the non-test assessment tools created were based on the experience from clinical practice, and there are no clear descriptions on the use of these methods in research or applications used by other professionals. Furthermore, some models do not show much detail on how to use the methods, and there are only a small number of case studies that illustrate the application of the models.

Focusing on the trends of the models, it is possible to highlight three points: diversity between objectivist and interpretative models, the variety of theoretical approaches, and high level of complexity of some methods. Among the methods presented, there is a precise balance between the number of objectivist and interpretative evaluations, since many behavioral models are focused on obtaining objective data, while others require a subjective analysis that mainly involves the use of specific forms of interpretation. The methods show a considerable variability of theoretical orientations that allow the clinicians to find a model that suits their way of theoretically understanding the clinical practice. Finally, we highlight the high level of complexity of some microanalysis tools that require a lot of time and specific tools to be applied. In this way, it is possible to imagine that these tools may have a more excellent application in the field of research. In conclusion, this review found that the area of non-test assessment tools is still in development and needs more publications, as well as investigations that can access the quality of these methods.

Observing without pre-developed tools

As the literature review shows, music therapists mostly apply observational methods in their assessments. The following sections aim to further inspire clinicians on ways to choose, understand, and structure their observations by describing selected areas of focus, including tactile and body observations, behavior observation, and interaction/communication observations. We selected the three foci based on our experience and knowledge and completely acknowledge that other foci including intrapersonal perspectives, symbolism, emotions, and so on are equally relevant and important. Often the clinical population and their needs and challenges determine the focus and process of observing in assessment. A good example of this is the doctoral study of Ala-Ruona (2005, 2007) who focused on different practical approaches in initial music therapy assessment within the context of psychiatric music therapy, including looking at methods and theoretical frameworks used. Based on interviews of experienced clinicians and grounded theory analyses, Ala-Ruona's study describes a useful non-structured assessment process including theoretical frameworks and a model to understand the therapist's process of gaining understanding of new clients within the context of psychiatry (Ala-Ruona 2005, 2007). Each assessment process is unique and context dependent. The following is meant as inspiration to guide the process of observation.

Behavior observation

According to the Oxford Dictionary, behavior is defined as the way in which one acts or conducts oneself, especially towards others (Oxford Dictionary 2017). Considering this definition, behavior observation is an important part of the assessment process in music therapy. The therapists observe behaviors that are affecting or need to be considered in the therapeutic process, independent of the theoretical orientation. When the client is avoiding interaction or is presenting aggressive behaviors in the treatment implementation, the therapist needs to observe the target behaviors to plan future interventions to explore these behaviors (increasing their presence) or to decrease or eliminate these actions. In a different perspective, the music therapist can observe how much time the client spends playing different musical instruments during an initial assessment session, including only instruments in which the client showed interest in subsequent sessions.

WHAT TO OBSERVE

Basically, there are three types of behavior observations: descriptive observation, number of rummaging occurrences (frequency), and time duration (normally in minutes or seconds) (Plahl 2007).

- Descriptive observation: The therapist describes all the details on actions performed by the client, avoiding any type of interpretation. This description will include a characterization about the target behaviors, with a meticulous report of the whole situation, focusing on when, how, and the consequences of these behaviors (Hanley, Iwata, and McCord 2003).

- Number of occurrences (frequency): The therapist counts how many times one event happens. These events could be observed in an audio or video excerpt and should be evident in the observation. Figure 3.1 includes a hypothetical example from an observation of the number of vocalizations from a client with ASD over ten sessions.

- Duration: In some situations, behavior frequency is not the most relevant factor in the analysis because the therapist wants to verify how much time the client engages in the target behavior in each occurrence. Measuring duration is essential when the therapist compares how much the client is doing one behavior when the therapist is doing the same behavior. Figure 3.2 shows a hypothetical example comparing the time duration of "playing a musical instrument" (between client and therapist) within a music therapy session in a fragment of ten seconds.

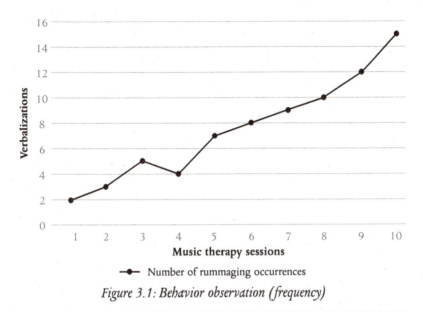

Figure 3.1: Behavior observation (frequency)

SECONDS	1	2	3	4	5	6	7	8	9	10	11
Therapist playing	░	░	░	░	░	░	░	░	░	░	░
Client playing	▓								▓	▓	▓

Figure 3.2: Time observation (duration)

Tactile and body observation

Mind and body are highly integrated in most types of actions, and we find that awareness of this knowledge can be used constructively and embraced in clinical approaches within music therapy (Storm 2013). The somatosensory system is receptive to both physical and psychological phenomena because both somatic and psychic operations are, at one level, neurological processes (Damasio 1999; Hart 2008) and include somatic senses like touch, body position and movement, and vocal sounding.

Observations of the body in action and tactility go hand in hand with the aim of the psychotherapy offered and the choice of instrument. However, in cases where the body and the human voice are the primary instruments, the clients are the instruments and therefore additionally activated through the sensation of breathing, and body and vocal exercises. No matter what the means of instrumentation are, the somatosensory system will be activated by different stimuli connected to a tactile sensation provided by the instrument.

A consciousness towards how and what to observe about the body in action and the tactility can support the music therapist's choices of approaches in clinical practice as well as analytical conclusions of the therapeutic processes. With attention towards body action and tactility, there appears an opportunity for consciously blending bottom-up (sensory stimulations) and top-down (cognitive approaches and verbal dialogue) interventions (Storm 2013).

VITALITY FORMS

Kinesthesia is related to the use of muscles and body parts, as well as the sensation of position and movement of the body. Every touch, movement, or action is connected to a certain level of intensity and pleasantness versus unpleasantness (Storm 2013). The sensation of pleasantness is connected with an affective touch and provides information about the dysregulation in numerous clinical conditions such as autism, eating disorders, depression, and chronic pain (Case *et al.* 2016). A client's sensation of pleasantness or unpleasantness is something which may be observed in the way the feet move on and are in contact with the floor, how the hands move and are in contact with the body, or the hands hold on to or are in contact with instruments (Storm 2013).

According to Stern (2010a), the form in which the energy, strength, and power takes in a movement is defined as "dynamic forms of vitality," and can best be described and explained in kinesthetic terms as surging, relaxing, gliding, tense, accelerating, weak, fluttering, and so on.

Damasio (1999) links the vitality affects to his definition of background feelings. Background feelings are not always conscious to our mind, and in these situations, there is a tendency to focus on other mental matters or contents. Background feelings are more internally directed and may be observable to others in myriad ways like body posture, the speed and design of our movements, the tone of our voice, and the prosody in our speech as we communicate thoughts that may have little to do with the background emotion. According to Damasio (1999), background feelings include fatigue, energy, excitement, wellness, sickness, tension, relaxation, surging, dragging, stability, instability, balance, imbalance, harmony, and discord (Storm 2013).

Therefore, it is very important to train a special kind of attention and awareness, or more specifically, train the listening perspective and attitude in a broad sense towards the vitality forms in the applied music therapeutic interventions in the clinical setting. The dynamics of the vitality forms will reveal the amount of excitement or engagement, distance to the narrative stance from the "here and now," or deadness sensation or the amount of defensive blockage in the passage from mind to speech, and much more (Stern 2010a). Dynamic forms of vitality therefore provide a possibility of accessing non-conscious experience, memories, and dissociative experiences (Storm 2013).

When body movement and the human voice are applied as a primary instrument, one would therefore consider that the use of body and voice work blends theory and technique from cognitive and dynamic theory with focus on somatic awareness and movement and vocal interventions (Storm 2013). Within this approach, the clients are taught to observe or rather "listen" to themselves and explore the relationship between their physical sensations, postures, movements, and voice, and how these affect their emotional and psychological state as well as influence the words and content they describe in therapy.

WHAT TO OBSERVE

The client's psychological state clearly affects the body posture, breathing pattern, freedom of movement, heart rate, and so on, and there seems to be a tendency to stabilize oneself through tension and rigidity rather than through a flexible, integrated body with solid support through the legs (Storm 2013). This understanding is supported by Lowen (1972, 1975) and Ogden, Minton, and Pain (2006).

The body scan: A body scan conducted while the client is in a standing position may provide information about the level of natural gravity the body has present or missing. A body scan may focus on: (1) the client's feet and how these have contact with the floor; (2) whether the knees are locked or unlocked; (3) the posture or position of the chest and pelvis; (4) whether the shoulders are lifted or held in a stiff position or relaxed; (5) how the client places their arms in relation to the body; (6) whether the client unconsciously clenches their fists, spreads their fingers, or finds the hands are relaxed; and (7) the neck and head. As an example, one may examine whether tension, the figurative lack of force or effectiveness in the feet and legs, and the presence of locked knees create an illusion of security and diminish the experience of feeling grounded. It is all about observing natural and economical use of muscle activity (Storm 2013).

Locking the knees creates a tremendous pull on the whole torso, making free or flexible vocal output and expression almost impossible (F. M. Alexander in Heirich 2005), while simultaneously inhibiting the body from having an energetic flow (Lowen 1975). Therefore, generally speaking, somatic resources that involve awareness and movement of the core of the body (centering, grounding, breathing, vocal exercises, and alignment) may provide a sense of internal physical and psychological stability and teach the client how to recognize the feeling of being centered and grounded, and in that way support an autoregulation and the experience of being present (Storm 2013).

Body movement: Kinesthetics is the study of body motion, and of the perception (both conscious and unconscious) of one's body motions. The perception of continuous movement (kinesthesia) is largely unconscious. A conscious proprioception is achieved through increased awareness. Kinesthetics involves the teaching and personal development of such awareness. In order to structure what to observe, inspiration can be drawn from Laban Movement Analysis (LMA), which itself draws from multiple fields including anatomy, kinesiology, and psychology.

Body: The body category describes structural and physical characteristics of the human body while moving. This category relates to describing which body parts are moving, which parts are connected, which parts are influenced by others, and general statements about body organization. For instance, the head is still but the rest of the body is moving vividly.

Interaction and communication observation

A client's ability or interest to interact and communicate both non-verbally and verbally is quite relevant in music therapy, as the aim or focus is often related to social and communicative aspects across age groups and clinical areas. Attachment is essential to social and interaction skills and behavior in any individual. Attachment, however, is difficult and complex to observe as it requires profound understanding of the concept and extensive interpretation, which might call for a more test-oriented approach that allows for more objectivity.

ATTUNEMENT

The ability to engage in attuned interaction is important if the focus in assessment or treatment is related to interpersonal and communication skills. In his theory of how the self develops in infants, Stern (2000) described affect attunement as a key feature in basic communication and interaction skills. Stern described how caregivers imitate their infant and vary the repetition of the imitation in order to keep the infant interested and attentive. The repetition over a specific theme is particularly appealing to the infant, because it tends to organize the world by looking for invariants. It organizes both the known and the unknown parts of theme, and this is ideal for the infant to learn how to identify interpersonal invariants. The infant learns about complex behavior and recognizes which parts to regard more than others. Thus, infants are taught to identify the invariant features in interpersonal behavior (Stern 2000). Affect attunement occurs when the parent acknowledges an infant's feeling and that emotions are shared non-verbally. These complex intersubjective exchanges of emotions consist of three steps:

1. The parent reads the infant's emotional state (correctly) based on their non-verbal communication.

2. The parent imitates and varies the response of the infant.

3. The infant reads the corresponding response as something related to itself.

Stern also called this a musical process, and many music therapists have incorporated this into music therapy theory as an understanding of and a part of clinical practice. For example, Holck (2008) referred to the concept of communicative musicality as a human capacity, while Stern (2010) characterized Wigram's (2004) matching in music therapy as affect attunement and described it as "the base of so much of the relationship and the transmission and communication between therapist and child" (Stern 2010, p. 94). He then further linked it with parent-infant interaction and the different types of affect attunement, and described it as a vital technique in emotional communication: "Music is fabulous at [affect attunement]" (p. 98). Stern believed this type of intersubjective contact to be the single most necessary aspect of any successful therapy, because it is a type of contact that two people can expand on (Stern 2010).

NON-VERBAL COMMUNICATION

Furthermore, interpersonal interaction relies predominantly on non-verbal channels of communication. The verbal language is an insufficient medium for expressing quality, intensity, nuance of emotion, and affect in different social situations (Mandal and Ambady 2004). In music therapy, it seems highly relevant to observe non-verbal communication skills and interaction when assessing one or more clients. Interplay with turns is a particularly important part of human interaction both verbally and non-verbally, and here we can learn a lot from conversation analysis. The theory of conversation analysis describes turn-organization in detail, but as Holck (2004) pointed out, this is not yet a common perspective within music therapy assessment. Holck used conversation analysis to describe and understand the concept of turn-interplay in music therapy with children with communication disorders. Holck explained how conversation analysis has developed a series of concepts useful in describing and observing interplay in music therapy (Holck 2004).

Conversation analysis originates in sociology and concerns the underlying social organization of interactional rules, procedures, and conventions. It is a methodological approach to the study of verbal interaction and includes analysis of ordinary conversation and other forms of talk-in-action such as debates and interviews. It examines language as social action, but also includes the prosody and non-verbal gestures that accompany the spoken words, including the organization of turns (Goodman and Heritage 1990; Schegloff 2007; Wooffitt 2005). Although the content of the conversation is considered a contextualizing factor, the main focus in turn-organization is the sequence, form, and structure of exchanging turns (Goodman and Heritage 1990).

Knapp and Hall (2009) argued that the ability to send and receive non-verbal messages is an important part of communication capacity. They described this capacity and the understanding of social communication to be dependent on proper feedback from carers or parents in early and later childhood. This seems to have many similarities with Stern's theories of affect attunement and the concept of communicative musicality (Malloch and Trevarthen 2009). "Nonverbal skills are gained by imitating and modelling ourselves after others and by adapting our responses to the coaching feedback and advice of others" (Knapp and Hall 2009, p. 64). Knapp and Hall further suggested that without some sort of common understanding of non-verbal communication, two people cannot effectively interact.

CUES

Part of non-verbal negotiation in conversations involves implicit cues indicating passing of turns and who is to speak when. The non-verbal cues can consist of facial expression, body language, and prosody. More specifically, Knapp and Hall (2009) distinguished between the cues of listeners and speakers, where turn-yielding and turn-maintaining behaviors are speakers' cues, and turn-requesting and turn-denying behaviors are listeners' cues. While Knapp and Hall used the term turn-yielding, it is more commonly known in music therapy literature as turn-giving. The following concepts of turn-giving and turn-maintaining are applied to the current study in the flexible design and microanalysis and are thus described in detail. In common conversation, turn-giving is when the speaker gives up his turn. This can include many different types of signals at the end of the speaker's utterance such as:

- kinetic markers that rise or fall with the speaker's pitch level

- decreased loudness

- a slowed-down tempo

- termination of gestures accompanying the speech

- gazing at the listener

- an extended unfilled pause.

Cues that are more explicit can consist of touching the listener, holding the eyebrow in expectation, or saying something like "Well?" The speaker uses these if the listener does not perceive the signals as turn-giving.

Turn-maintaining is when the speaker does not want to pass the turn, which can result in one or more of the following behaviors:

- increasing voice volume as turn-requesting cues are perceived from the listener

- continuing accompanying movement, creating a gestural equivalent to the filled pause

- increasing the frequency and duration of silent pauses decreases

- lightly touching the other person and using a patting motion (as if saying, "Hold on just a little bit longer").

Turn-requesting is when the listener wants to talk and exhibits one or more of the following behaviors:

- an upraised index finger (raised hand)

- an audible inspiration of breath

- a straightening and tightening of posture

- rapid head nods

- when interrupting, the listener (becoming speaker) speaks louder than the partner, begins gesturing, and looks away to indicate the turn-shift.

Turn-denying is when the listener has received a turn-giving signal but does not want to speak. Here behavior may consist of:

- maintaining a relaxed listening pose

- maintaining silence

- gazing intently at something else

- smiling, nodding, or briefly restating the speaker's last word to indicate that the speaker should continue

- shaking the head.

FAILS AND REPAIRS

Exchange of turns is a jointly negotiated and complicated process, and it can easily fail. According to Knapp and Hall, sometimes two non-verbal signals can contradict one another, turns can overlap each other, or cues can be missed. Sacks, Schegloff, and Jefferson (1974) explained different repair mechanisms in turn-organization such as repairing interruption and repairing a failure of turn-transfer. Building on this, Holck (2004) stated that, in evaluating the mutuality of interactions, how and if a repair of these not so uncommon mistakes occurs is important (p. 46).

A non-verbal focus in conversation analysis provides knowledge about what kind of social behavior one can expect from non-verbal interplay between therapist and client or between clients. However, as a method, conversation analysis can be time consuming and often requires a micro-level analysis. In her study on interaction themes, Holck (2007) developed a method where some of the concepts and microanalysis from conversation analysis were applied to the transcriptions of the music therapy improvisations.

WHAT TO OBSERVE

Based on these theories and using a relevant data collection method such as video recording, you can assess interaction or social skills by observing whether the client is able to imitate or synchronize with others in the music, with the body, and/or outside the music. The ability to share emotions with others is essential to human communication, but it is not easy to observe as one cannot know how the client feels unless a self-report is given (and this may not reflect reality). However, we can assess how we feel ourselves in interacting with the client by describing the behavior that led us to the sensations as addressed in the above section on body and tactile foci. Furthermore, you can assess the level of autonomy in the client's interaction with others by observing the balance between following and leading tendencies (Bruscia 1987; Jacobsen—see Chapter 14; Wigram and Jacobsen—see Chapter 9). You can gain knowledge of the non-verbal skills by observing if the client is able to wait for their turn, or if the client has a tendency to interrupt. Observing the clarity of non-verbal signals both gesturally and musically may be helpful in determining whether the client can self-monitor (or repair) communication failures or their misunderstanding of others.

A guide to assessment without a pre-developed tool

In this section, we intend to summarize and present a guide on how to organize an assessment without a pre-developed tool. The seven steps are as follows:

1. Consider the previous information about the client.

2. Determine the purpose and goal for your assessment (diagnostic perspective, initial assessment, relevance of music therapy, general assessment, etc.).

3. Determine the types of assessment procedures to be used: reviewing, interviewing (structured or unstructured), observing (structured or unstructured).

4. Determine the focus and data source (traits and skills: communicative, social, musical, motor, emotional, cognitive, sensorial, etc.; data source: behavior, body, interaction, etc.).

5. Determine the nature of your outcome (quantitative or qualitative).

6. Consider the context of the assessment process (theoretical framework, the clinical population, the institutional context, etc.).

7. Customize and choose activities to fit steps 2–6 (active, receptive, structured/free, songwriting, group/individual).

1 Consider the previous information about the client

The therapist should consider previous relevant information regarding the client to ensure ethical standards, quality, and relevance in the assessment process. There might be a client journal with information and the therapist might have access to this. When reading a client journal, it is also important to keep an open mind as circumstances and the state of the client might have changed. To adjust expectations and be clear on the purpose and content of the assessment process, it is relevant to arrange a meeting with the client and/or relatives prior to the actual assessment sessions. At this meeting and when relevant, the therapist can gently enquire about important information concerning early traumas, psychiatric conditions, or medical issues the client or relatives would like to share. It is also necessary to ask permission to use video or audio recording prior to the actual assessment sessions.

2 Determine the purpose and goal for your assessment

Based on the referral and prior information about the client, the therapist has to be aware of and define the purpose of the assessment. The classification of Jacobsen, Wigram, and Rasmussen (2019) might be useful and includes diagnostic impressions, initial assessment, and relevance of music therapy as a treatment, and pre-treatment assessment and evaluation. Although there might be a predominant referral reason, assessment often involves several of the aims and purposes. Sometimes the main purpose might shift during the assessment process due to information gathered during the assessment.

3 Determine the types of assessment procedures

According to definitions from Chapter 1, the primary assessment methods (processes) include reviewing, interviewing, observing, and testing. Assuming that the option of testing is not possible, the therapist has to define the assessment type and consider existing options or new methods of assessment. This choice is intimately connected with the referral and the assessment purpose. No single assessment method is better than the other except choosing the approach(es) that best fit the reason for the referral. One may find it helpful to review the data-based decision-making model presented in Chapter 1 and in Waldon (2013).

4 Determine the focus and data source

At this stage, the music therapist determines the skills and traits they will assess. Baxter *et al.* (2007) describe seven domains that may be helpful: communicative, social, musical, motor, emotional, cognitive, and sensorial. In addition, it is important to establish the main data source according to the selected focus. As described earlier, possible observational data sources might involve a behavioral focus, body focus, and interaction/interpersonal focus (although there are many more options such as an intrapersonal focus, verbal focus, or emotional focus), with the optimal focus being that which is the best fit considering steps 1–3.

5 Determine the nature of your outcome

Closely linked with step 4, the therapist has to determine how to report the data collected. If the therapist is considering frequency of behavior, it is necessary to think in quantitative outcomes and numbers. If the data involves thick descriptions, then the therapist may be considering more of a qualitative focus. Choices made in steps 4 and 5 are often connected to the theoretical framework and therapeutic approach adopted by the therapist.

6 Consider the context of the assessment process

As described in the first chapter, different elements influence the assessment process. The main factors include theoretical framework, clinical population, and institutional context. If the therapist has a psychodynamic theoretical overview, it may be harder for them to manage assessment methods based on behavioral observations. Therefore, before designing an intervention, the therapist needs to be aware of the strengths and weaknesses of the clinical population in order to meet individual client needs in the musical and non-musical activities. Therapists may also need to adjust their assessment approaches (or philosophy) depending on the institution's overarching philosophy of care. For example, a therapist who uses a cognitive behavioral or applied behavioral analytic approach may need to modify the assessment methods used or the types of information obtained while working in a healthcare facility that has adopted a humanistic or family-centered care philosophy.

7 Customize and choose activities

After the therapist has considered steps 1–6, it is necessary to customize and define activities. What type of assessment activities will be needed to collect relevant data? The therapist needs to consider client characteristics and try to facilitate personalized activities. Some clients call for more active or live-music experiences, while others may require verbal activities (like interviews), or receptive and less invasive musical experiences, as they might have difficulties in expressing their ideas musically. Moreover, the therapist needs to consider client discomfort or adverse reactions to music or musical instruments.

Conclusion

It is not always possible for music therapists to use discipline-specific assessment tools because the resources are not available or because a tool that matches the clinical need does not exist. However, before treatment begins, assessment is necessary to ensure quality and adherence to ethical standards. Taking cues from the literature reviewed and the observational methods described here, there are many ways to structure a customized assessment plan. Furthermore, these plans can vary in terms of structure and flexibility as well as how they are placed within a positivist and a constructivist paradigm.

References

Ala-Ruona, E. (2005) 'Non-structured initial assessment of psychiatric client in music therapy.' *Music Therapy Today*, vol. VI, 1/2005. University of Witten-Herdecke. Retrieved 27/07/2018 at https://www.wfmt.info/music-therapy-today/.

Ala-Ruona, E. (2007) 'Initial Assessment as a Clinical Procedure in Music Therapy of Clients with Mental Health Problems – Strategies, Methods and Tools.' Unpublished PhD thesis. Jyväskylä, Finland: University of Jyväskylä.

Baker, F. (2007) 'Using Voice Analysis Software to Analyse the Sung and Spoken Voice.' In T. Wosch and T. Wigram (eds) *Microanalysis in Music Therapy – Methods, Techniques and Applications for Clinicians, Researchers, Educators and Students.* London: Jessica Kingsley Publishers.

Baxter, H. T., Berghofer, J. A., MacEwan, J. N., Peters, J., and Roberts, P. (2007) *The Individualized Music Therapy Assessment Profile: IMTAP.* London: Jessica Kingsley Publishers.

Bonde, L. O. (2007) 'Steps in Researching the Music in Therapy.' In T. Wosch and T. Wigram (eds) *Microanalysis in Music Therapy – Methods, Techniques and Applications for Clinicians, Researchers, Educators and Students.* London: Jessica Kingsley Publishers.

Braswell, C., Brooks, D. M., Decuir, A., Humphrey, T., Jacobs, K. W., and Sutton, K. (1983) 'Development and implementation of a music/activity therapy intake assessment for psychiatric patients. Part I: Initial standardization procedures on data from university students.' *Journal of Music Therapy, 20,* 2, 88–100.

Bruscia, K. E. (1987) *Improvisational Models of Music Therapy.* Springfield, IL: Charles C. Thomas.

Bruscia, K. E. (1987a) 'Free Improvisation Therapy: Assessment and Evaluation.' In K. Bruscia (ed.) *Improvisational Models of Music Therapy.* Springfield, IL: Charles C. Thomas.

Bruscia, K. E. (1987b) 'Analytical Assessment: Assessment and Evaluation.' In K. Bruscia (ed.) *Improvisational Models of Music Therapy.* Springfield, IL: Charles C. Thomas.

Bruscia, K. E. (1987c) 'Experimental Improvisation Therapy: Assessment and Evaluation.' In K. Bruscia (ed.) *Improvisational Models of Music Therapy.* Springfield, IL: Charles C. Thomas.

Bruscia, K. E. (1987d) 'Paraverbal Therapy: Assessment and Evaluation.' In K. Bruscia (ed.) *Improvisational Models of Music Therapy.* Springfield, IL: Charles C. Thomas.

Bruscia, K. E. (2002) *Guided Imagery and Music: The Bonny Method and Beyond.* Gilsum, NH: Barcelona Publishers.

Case, L. K., Laubacher, C. M., Olausson, H., Wang, B., Spagnolo, P. A., and Bushnell, M. C. (2016) 'Encoding of touch intensity but not pleasantness in human primary somatosensory cortex.' *The Journal of Neuroscience, 36,* 21, 5850–5860.

Damasio, A. (1999) *The Feeling of What Happens: Body and Emotion in the Making of Consciousness.* New York, NY: Harcourt Books.

De Backer, J. (2007) 'Analysis of Notated Music Examples Selected from Improvisations of Psychotic Patients.' In T. Wosch and T. Wigram (eds) *Microanalysis in Music Therapy – Methods, Techniques and Applications for Clinicians, Researchers, Educators and Students.* London: Jessica Kingsley Publishers.

de Souza, M. T., da Silva, M. D., and de Carvalho, R. (2010) 'Revisão integrativa: O que é e como fazer.' *Einstein, 8,* 1, 102–106.

Ferrari, K. (2013) *Musicoterapia: Aspectos de la sistematización y la evaluación de la práctica clínica.* Buenos Aires: MTD.

Gaston, E. T. (1968) *Music in Therapy.* New York, NY: Macmillan.

Gattino, G. (2017) *Musicoterapia y autismo: Consideraciones sobre la enseñanza basada en la evidencia* [*Music Therapy and Autism: Considerations about Evidence-Based Teaching*]. Paper presented at III Ibero-American Congress of Research in Music Therapy, Valencia Catholic University Saint Vincent Martyr, Valencia, Spain.

Goodman, G. and Heritage, J. (1990) 'Conversation analysis.' *Annual Review of Anthropology, 19,* 283–307.

Grocke, D. (2007) 'A Structural Model of Music Analysis.' In T. Wosch and T. Wigram (eds) *Microanalysis: Methods, Techniques and Applications in Music Therapy for Clinicians, Researchers, Educators and Students.* London: Jessica Kingsley Publishers.

Hanley, G. P., Iwata, B. A., and McCord, B. E. (2003) 'Functional analysis of problem behavior: A review.' *Journal of Applied Behavior Analysis, 36,* 2, 147–185.

Hart, S. (2008) *Brain, Attachment, Personality: An Introduction to Neuroaffective Development.* London: Karnac Books.

Heirich, J. R. (2005) *Voice and the Alexander Technique: Active Explorations for Speaking and Singing.* Berkeley, CA: Mornum Time Press.

Hiller, J. (2016) 'Epistemological Foundations of Objectivist and Interpretivist Research.' In B. Wheeler and K. Murphy (eds) *Music Therapy Research.* Gilsum, NH: Barcelona Publishers.

Holck, U. (2004) 'Turn-taking in music therapy with children with communication disorders.' *British Journal of Music Therapy, 18,* 2, 45–53.

Holck, U. (2007) 'An Ethnographic Descriptive Approach to Video Microanalysis.' In T. Wosch and T. Wigram (eds) *Microanalysis in Music Therapy – Methods, Techniques and Applications for Clinicians, Researchers, Educators and Students.* London: Jessica Kingsley Publishers.

Holck, U. (2008) 'Kommunikativ musikalitet. Kognition & pædagogik.' *Tidsskrift om Gode Læring, 18,* 70–79.

Jacobsen, S. L., Wigram, T., and Rasmussen, A. M. (2019) 'Assessment and Clinical Evaluation in Music Therapy.' In L. O. Bonde, I. N. Pedersen, and S. L. Jacobsen (eds) *Comprehensive Guide to Music Therapy* (2nd edition). London: Jessica Kingsley Publishers.

Knapp, M. and Hall, J. (2009) *Nonverbal Communication in Human Interaction: International Edition.* Boston, MA: Wadsworth Cengage Learning.

Loewy, J. (2000) 'Music psychotherapy assessment.' *Music Therapy Perspectives, 18,* 1, 47–58.

Loewy, J. V. (1994) *A Hermeneutic Panel Study of Music Therapy Assessment with an Emotionally Disturbed Boy.* UMI Dissertation Services //9502432. Ann Arbor, MI: Bell & Howell.

Lowen, A. (1972) *Depression and the Body: The Biological Basis of Faith and Reality.* New York, NY: Penguin Compass.

Lowen, A. (1975) *Bioenergetics.* New York, NY: Penguin Compass.

Lucht, M. and Gatzsche, G. (2009) 'Assessment of Emotions in Music Therapy.' Proceedings of the Audio Mostly Conference. Glasgow, Scotland: Glasgow Caledonian University.

Malloch, S. and Trevarthen, C. (2009) *Communicative Musicality.* Oxford: Oxford University Press.

Mandal, M. K. and Ambady, N. (2004) 'Laterality of facial expressions of emotion: Universal and culture-specific influences.' *Behavioural Neurology, 15* (1–2), 23–34.

Martin, L., Snell, A., Wakworth, D., and Humpal, M. (2012) 'Assessment and Goals: Determining Eligibility, Gathering Information, and Gathering Treatment Goals for Music Therapy Services.' In P. Kern and M. Humpal (eds) *Early Childhood Music Therapy and Autism Spectrum Disorders: Developing Potential in Young Children and their Families.* London: Jessica Kingsley Publishers.

McFerran, K. and Grocke, D. (2007) 'Understanding Music Therapy Experiences through Interviewing: A Phenomenological Microanalysis.' In T. Wosch and T. Wigram (eds) *Microanalysis in Music Therapy – Methods, Techniques and Applications for Clinicians, Researchers, Educators and Students*. London: Jessica Kingsley Publishers.

McFerran, K., Baker, F., Patton, G. C., and Sawyer, S. M. (2006) 'A retrospective lyrical analysis of songs written by adolescents with anorexia nervosa.' *European Eating Disorders Review, 14,* 6, 397–403.

Melhuish, R. (2013) 'Group music therapy on a dementia assessment ward: An approach to evaluation.' *British Journal of Music Therapy, 27,* 1, 16–31.

Munk-Madsen, N. M. (2001) 'Assessment in music therapy with clients suffering from dementia.' *Nordic Journal of Music Therapy, 10,* 2, 205–208.

Ogden, P., Minton, K., and Pain, C. (2006) *Trauma and the Body: A Sensorimotor Approach to Psychotherapy*. London: W. W. Norton & Company.

Ortlieb, K., Sembdner, M., and Frommer, J. (2007) 'Text Analysis Method for Micro Processes (TAMP) of Single Music Therapy Sessions.' In T. Wosch and T. Wigram (eds) *Microanalysis in Music Therapy – Methods, Techniques and Applications for Clinicians, Researchers, Educators and Students*. London: Jessica Kingsley Publishers.

Oxford Dictionary (2017) *Oxford English Dictionary*. Retrieved 27/11/2017 at https://en.oxforddictionaries.com.

Plahl, C. (2007) 'Microanalysis of Preverbal Communication in Music Therapy.' In T. Wosch and T. Wigram (eds) *Microanalysis: Methods, Techniques and Applications in Music Therapy for Clinicians, Researchers, Educators and Students*. London: Jessica Kingsley Publishers.

Ridder, H. M. O. (2007) 'Microanalysis on Selected Video Clips with Focus on Communicative Response in Music Therapy.' In T. Wosch and T. Wigram (eds) *Microanalysis in Music Therapy – Methods, Techniques and Applications for Clinicians, Researchers, Educators and Students*. London: Jessica Kingsley Publishers.

Ruud, E., Holck, U., Schepelern, T., Bonde, L. O., *et al.* (1999) 'Book symposium on Even Ruud's book "Music Therapy: Improvisation, Communication, and Culture".' *Nordisk Tidsskrift for Musikkterapi, 8,* 1, 76–88.

Sacks, H., Schegloff, E. A., and Jefferson, G. (1974) 'A simplest systematics for the organization of turn-taking for conversation.' *Language, 50,* 696–735.

Schegloff, E. A. (2007) *Sequence Organization in Interaction: A Primer in Conversation Analysis*. New York, NY: Cambridge University Press.

Scholtz, J. (2007) 'Video Microanalysis of Interaction in Music Therapy (MIMT).' In T. Wosch and T. Wigram (eds) *Microanalysis in Music Therapy – Methods, Techniques and Applications for Clinicians, Researchers, Educators and Students*. London: Jessica Kingsley Publishers.

Stern, D. (2000) *The Interpersonal World of the Infant*. New York, NY: Basic Books.

Stern, D. (2010) *Forms of Vitality*. Oxford: Oxford University Press.

Storm, S. (2013) 'Research into the Development of Voice Assessment in Music Therapy.' Unpublished PhD thesis. Aalborg, Denmark: Aalborg University.

Sutton, J. (2007) 'The Use of Micro-Musical Analysis and Conversation Analysis of Improvisation: "The Invisible Handshake" – Free Musical Improvisation as Conversation.' In T. Wosch and T. Wigram (eds) *Microanalysis in Music Therapy – Methods, Techniques and Applications for Clinicians, Researchers, Educators and Students.* London: Jessica Kingsley Publishers.

Thaut, M. H. (2014) 'Assessment and the Transformational Design Model (TDM).' In M. Thaut and V. Hoemberg (eds) *Handbook of Neurologic Music Therapy.* London: Oxford University Press.

Trondalen, G. (2007) 'A Phenomenologically Inspired Approach to Microanalyses of Improvisation in Music Therapy.' In T. Wosch and T. Wigram (eds) *Microanalysis in Music Therapy – Methods, Techniques and Applications for Clinicians, Researchers, Educators and Students.* London: Jessica Kingsley Publishers.

Waldon, E. G. (2013) 'Data-based decision making in music therapy.' *Imagine: Early Childhood Music Therapy, 4,* 46–50.

Wang, A. P. A. (2010) 'Music Analysis of Clinical Improvisations with an Adolescent who has Communication Difficulties.' Unpublished master's thesis. Wellington, New Zealand: New Zealand School of Music.

Wells, N. F. (1988) 'An individual music therapy assessment procedure for emotionally disturbed young adolescents.' *The Arts in Psychotherapy, 15,* 1, 47–54.

Wigram, T. (2000) 'A method of music therapy assessment for the diagnosis of autism and communication disorders in children.' *Music Therapy Perspectives, 18,* 1, 13–22.

Wigram, T. (2004) *Improvisation.* London: Jessica Kingsley Publishers.

Wooffitt, R. (2005) *Conversation Analysis and Discourse Analysis: A Comparative and Critical Introduction.* London: Sage Publications.

Wosch, T. and Wigram, T. (2007) *Microanalysis in Music Therapy – Methods, Techniques and Applications for Clinicians, Researchers, Educators and Students.* London: Jessica Kingsley Publishers.

CHAPTER 4

Introduction to Assessment Chapters

Eric G. Waldon and Stine Lindahl Jacobsen

What is plainly evident in the preceding chapters is that the practice and technology (e.g. the tools and methods) of music therapy assessment have not developed along the same trajectory as clinical music therapy practice. In fact, music therapy assessment has only recently been at the forefront among researchers, professional organizations, and clinicians (Waldon and Gattino—see Chapter 1). And while assessment as a professional competency is evaluated among those being trained for work as music therapists, there exists a lack of assessment tools (or a compendium of tools) available to clinicians, students, researchers, and commissioners. Furthermore, it has traditionally been difficult for stakeholders to obtain these instruments because they have not been published, they are no longer in print, or it is unclear where or how the assessment tool is available. This text (and particularly the forthcoming chapters) intends to fill those needs.

The editors compiled a list of known assessment tool developers and invited each to contribute a chapter summarizing their work:

Dear Author

As members of the International Music Therapy Assessment Consortium (IMTAC), we are developing a new text on assessment and we would like you to write a chapter about your measure/ assessment tool. In the chapter you will be given the opportunity to describe your measure/assessment tool, its development, and (if appropriate) how to administer the measure/assessment tool in a clinical setting. You will be asked to follow a template and we will provide you with a draft chapter to use as a guide.

In particular, each author was asked to:

- provide some context (e.g. setting and motivation) for their assessment tool

- explain the theoretical foundations underpinning their tool

- describe the development of the assessment tool

- describe the administration and data collection procedures

- describe how data is analyzed and interpreted

- report on the research, psychometric properties (when applicable), or evidence supporting the assessment tool's use in a clinical setting

- describe how results are documented and disseminated

- describe training requirements

- discuss the challenges and future plans for the assessment tool.

In different manners and orders, the authors answered these requests. In some cases, the authors provide a general overview of their assessment tool with background on its development and its clinical utility. In one case, the author has agreed to have the measure published so that readers can put the tool into practice. In all cases, the authors offer a reflective and thoughtful review of their assessment tools and include information for the reader on how to obtain them.

Naturally, not all music therapy assessment tools are presented in this book. Many tools could have been included and more authors were invited to contribute. This compendium of music therapy assessment tools is still only a selection of tools. The International Music Therapy Assessment Consortium offers access to short descriptions of the tools presented in this book and more tools through the catalogue on the website www.imtac.aau.dk.

CHAPTER 5

The Individual Music-Centered Assessment Profile for Neurodevelopmental Disorders

John Carpente

Setting and motivation

In 2005, I was invited to implement a music therapy program for a school in New York City that incorporates the Developmental Individual-differences Relationship-based (DIR) Floortime model—a developmental framework for assessment and intervention for neurodevelopmental and related disorders that utilizes affect-based interactions and experiences to promote development (Greenspan and Weider 2006). At the time, the school was supervised by Dr. Stanley Greenspan, co-creator of the DIR Floortime model, and provided educational and clinical services for school-aged children from preschool to high school age diagnosed with a range of neurodevelopmental disorders. The majority of the classes, however, were made up of children and teenagers with autism spectrum disorder (ASD).

Although the theoretical tenets of the DIR model closely aligned with my own world view and theoretical orientation as a music therapist (music-centered, existential, relationship-based), integrating the two interventions into practice proved to be very challenging in terms of assessment and treatment. The DIR model focuses on the client's social-emotional capacities such as the ability to co-regulate, engage in reciprocal communication and shared problem solving, use symbols and abstract thinking, and create and bridge ideas with others (Greenspan and Wieder 2006). Music-centered music therapy (MCMT) emphasizes the client's musical capacities in the areas of musical responsivity, mutuality, expressivity, and creative freedom (Aigen 2005; Ansdell 2016; Nordoff and Robbins 2007). The DIR practitioner considers individual differences (i.e. sensory processing, visual spatial ability, motor-planning, etc.) that may impede the client's ability to engage in play, whereas the music-centered music therapist may explore the various musical strategies, such as altering elements and musical styles as a means to foster engagement, and generally will not consider the client's individual differences.

Finally, although both Floortime and MCMT share similar values in that they are relationship based, client centered, and stress the importance of spontaneous interactions and creativity, the areas in which the interventions are carried out vary considerably in terms of the targeted responses and outcomes (Carpente 2013). Moreover, extra- or non-musical responses such as a smile, motion, or gesture, or a hug, which are highly regarded in the DIR Floortime assessment, are generally not emphasized areas of MCMT assessment and treatment.

During the process of implementing a music therapy program at this DIR-based school, I began exploring various assessment ideas that would maintain the integrity of my work as a music therapist, while also incorporating and carrying out the principles and values of the DIR Floortime model. At the same time, I was developing my dissertation research, which involved exploring the effectiveness of MCMT within a DIR-based program. While developing my research I drafted a music-centered assessment instrument that would generate music-centered goals within the context of relational play experiences. In addition, it would consider the client's needs for extra-musical supportive interventions geared towards supporting their individual differences. The assessment tool was later developed into the Individual Music-Centered Assessment Profile for Neuro-developmental Disorders (IMCAP-ND) (Carpente 2013).

The IMCAP-ND's constructs were consistent with the DIR Floortime assessment instrument, the Functional Emotional Assessment Scale (FEAS)—a standardized criterion-referenced instrument designed to measure social-emotional functioning in children with constitutional- and maturation-based challenges. The FEAS provides a systematic assessment of the child's ability to organize play interactions with objects and persons, to self-regulate mood and organize attention, to form an attachment with the caregiver, to engage in reciprocal emotional interactions, and to represent feelings and ideas through play interactions (Greenspan, DeGangi, and Weider 2001). In addition, two Nordoff and Robbins assessment scales inspired the IMCAP-ND: (1) Tempo-Dynamic Schema (TDS) and (2) Thirteen Categories of Response (TCR) (Nordoff and Robbins 2007). The TDS associates emotional states with musical expressivity as manifest through tempo and dynamic range, while the TCR was designed to describe drum response to the therapist's music and how the child reacts to different musical idioms and elements (Bruscia 1987; Nordoff and Robbins 2007). Furthermore, the IMCAP-ND incorporates a variation of Bruscia's taxonomic classification of 64 clinical techniques (Bruscia 1987) as a means of protocolizing musical-clinical techniques in order to target specific musical responses.

The development of the IMCAP-ND included a five-year process in which it was implemented at the Rebecca Center for Music Therapy at Molloy College where a team of therapists were trained to use the instrument in their daily practice. During this process, the IMCAP-ND was shaped by continuously reviewing video recorded sessions alongside discussions with the practicing music therapists as well as parents whose children were being treated at the Center.

Theoretical background

Human beings are affectively connected in everything that they do in relation to others. For infants and toddlers, affective relationships have always been a context for developing and integrating motor skills, cognition, social-emotional capacities, speech and language skills, and so on (Greenspan and Greenspan 1985; Rogers and Pennington 1991; Stern 2009; Trevarthen 2011). During interpersonal communications, individuals perceive and respond to each other's micro-level communicative responses and behaviors as they engage in a mutual affective message (Feldman 2007a). This may include facial expressions, tone and prosody of voice, eye-gaze, arousal level, or body awareness, and the ability to follow modulation in such behaviors, which are all essential for the participation in any emotional exchange (Feldman 2007a; Greenspan and Greenspan 1985).

According to Stern (2009), infants are sensitized to the temporal components of emotional communication as young as 2–3 months via the caregiver's ongoing coordination or synchrony with the infant's micro-level behaviors. Thus, parent-infant synchrony, early in life, provides essential affective interactions during a critical period for brain growth that can help shape future development (Feldman 2007b). Moreover, if the infant is provided with a wide range of affective experiences, they become sensitized to the temporal relations between isolated behaviors of self and others while integrating and assimilating this into lived experiences (Fogel 1993). This theoretical structure suggests that the foundational skills for healthy development are a result of a wide range of early-life physical, sensory, and pre-verbal affective back-and-forth interactions in which the child is able to connect affect and sensory-motor to emerging symbols through a wide range of experiences (Greenspan 2001; Greenspan and Shanker 2004; Mahler 1963; Mahler, Pine, and Bergman 2000).

Individuals diagnosed with ASD are impacted in the areas of social communication that involve the ability to express and comprehend non-verbal and verbal communication, maintain peer relationships, and engage in long chains of back-and-forth dialogue (American Psychiatric Association 2013). Therefore, children at risk for ASD may not experience the essential affective interactions early in life that are needed to develop foundational capacities required for healthy development. Greenspan's Affect Diathesis Hypothesis theorizes that children at risk for ASD present with a unique type of processing challenge that inhibits the process of connecting affect to motor-planning, sequencing, and emerging symbolic formation (Greenspan 2001). Therefore, these children present with constrictions in their ability to engage in long chains of reciprocal affective interactions. (Greenspan 2001; Greenspan and Shanker 2009). This suggests that the assessment process when working with individuals with ASD should focus on examining the individual's capacities for relational and communicative interactions. How can music therapy assess clients' abilities in the area of verbal and non-verbal social communication, including the foundational skills required for social communication (i.e. self-regulation, joint attention and engagement, shared-problem solving, etc.)?

Musical play can offer many opportunities for assessing verbal and non-verbal communications which are not only core features of ASD but are also embedded in co-active music making (Aigen 2005; Pavlicevic 2002; Wigram and Gold 2006). Moreover, when clients engage in relational musical play, they are linking the physical, emotional, cognitive, and expressive resources that are embodied in all domain areas of health (Abrams 2011; Aigen 1995; Alvin 1965).

Music making with another person represents a living embod-iment of relational affect and can provide opportunities for assessing strengths as well as challenges that impede health across several domains. Thus, a shift in a client's way of relating and communicating in musical play also indicates a shift in that client's way of relating in life (Abrams 2011).

Child-led improvisational music therapy is viewed as a meaning-ful framework, similar to early mother-infant interactions, that can provide a range of affective experiences used to foster the ability to affectively attune, relate, and communicate in two-way back-and-forth dialoguing (Holck 2004; Kim, Wigram, and Gold 2009). The process of tuning into the child's musical and non-musical expression has been an integral feature of improvisational music therapy (IMT) work with children with ASD (Alvin and Warwick 1991; Geretsegger *et al.* 2015) and has been shown to be an effective intervention to foster joint attention (Kim, Wigram, and Gold 2008), affective reciprocity (Kim *et al.* 2009), non-verbal communication (Gattino *et al.* 2011), social-emotional skills (Carpente 2016), and parent-child social communication (Oldfield and Bunce 2001; Thompson, McFerran, and Gold 2013).

Procedure and population

The IMCAP-ND is a musical play-based evaluation instrument made up of three quantitative criterion-referenced rating scales designed to examine how clients perceive, interpret, and make music with the therapist while participating in individual music therapy. Administering the IMCAP-ND requires the therapist to improvise music experiences based on the client's interests, music, and affect while providing specific musical cues that target musical responses relevant to ASD (e.g. musical attention involving sharing, shifting, and maintaining attention; adaption to musical play dealing with joining and adjusting to music experiences, etc.). The IMCAP-ND examines social-emotional abilities, cognition, and perception skills, as well as overall responsiveness pertaining to musical preferences, perceptual efficiency, and self-regulation. Furthermore, it identifies the type of support provided—that is, verbal, visual, and physical—in order for the client to demonstrate a musical-social capacity.

Music-based protocols and procedures

Administering the IMCAP-ND involves following a set of protocols and procedures that guide the music therapist in how to target each musical response outlined in the rating scales. In other words, the music therapist is required to provide specific musical opportunities and conditions for the client in order to assess their capacity to demonstrate the ability to express specific musical responses. Administering instructions include: music protocols, clinical techniques, musical procedures, and outcome observations (Carpente and Kelliher 2017).

The IMCAP-ND's musical protocols provide the therapist with a method of how to structure the music in order to target particular responses. It does not provide the music therapist with guidance on what type of music, style, song, mode, or scale to be used during the assessment but suggests how to format the music in terms of form—A-B-A. Determining the style of music, scale, or mode to be used is based on the therapist's judgement during the creative musical process that occurs between the therapist and the client. The clinical techniques provide an operation and/or interaction to elicit or target a specific response from the client. These techniques derive from Bruscia's taxonomic classifications of improvisational music therapy techniques (Bruscia 1987) and guide the therapist as to how to play and deliver a musical offering as per the desired musical target. The IMCAP-ND's musical procedures consist of an organized sequence of operations and interactions that the therapist uses to foster a musical experience while targeting a specific musical response.

Outcome observations

Finally, the IMCAP-ND defines outcomes and observations in order for the therapist to determine the client's ability in each assessed area. This data consists of observable and audible musical responses expressed by the client within a particular targeted area. Outcomes provide the therapist with criteria of what to "look" or "hear" for following specific musical offerings. Depending on the area of assessment, client responses may be expressed while engaged with either the therapist, music, play, or therapist-music:

- Therapist: the client responds to the therapist in an interpersonal manner but does not necessarily respond to specific musical elements or play.

- Music: the client's receptive response to musical elements uses specific musical elements to match and engage the therapist's music. Here, the client is engaging in the therapist's music as cued and not offering original musical ideas (parallel/ interactive play).

- Play: the client is actively involved in musical play, via instrument, and/or movement, and/or voice, in which the client times their own participation in response to the therapist. Here, the client follows what the therapist is doing as a play partner, but does not necessarily respond to specific musical elements (parallel play).

- Therapist-music: the client initiates and contributes original musical ideas with the intent to engage the therapist's music (interactive play).

The IMCAP-ND is made up of three quantitative scales that evaluate the client's ability to engage in co-active musical play:

- Scale I: Musical Emotional Assessment Rating Scale (MEARS)

- Scale II: Musical Cognitive/Perception Scale (MCPS)

- Scale III: Musical Responsiveness Scale (MRS)

Data collection and interpretation

Sources of data for the IMCAP-ND are historical records, client-therapist musical interactions, and clinical observations. The first step of the assessment process is to collect historical data and caregiver reports of current functioning. This may include reports from the client's other therapists and educators. The purpose of examining the reports is to note any factors that may inform the improvisation assessment.

When administering the IMCAP-ND, the therapist's main focus is on engaging the client in a wide variety of musical interactions. Sessions may involve the client playing instruments, singing, and moving. As the client participates in these musical activities, the therapist has an opportunity to assess the client's musical perception and ability to engage in play. This is followed by the therapist providing experiences to engage the client in increasingly more challenging musical tasks until the client's musical resources and strengths can be clearly defined.

Clinical observations are the third source of data, and these observations may be made during or after the session by either the therapist conducting the session or by a trained observer. The therapist may choose to observe the client through the course of one or two 45-minute sessions depending on the completion of the entire IMCAP-ND. It is recommended that sessions be video recorded. If, however, video-recording of sessions is not an option, it is then required that the therapist score and take notes immediately following the session.

During each session, the therapist improvises music based on the client's responses, reactions, and behaviors. Thus, observations are focused on how the client perceives, interprets, and creates music with the therapist. All aspects of the client's responses and reactions in musical play must be observed. These include musical components, facial expressions, movements, postures, reactivity (i.e. hyper, hypo), visual spatial capacities, motor-planning and sequencing abilities, and sensory sensitivities (e.g. tactile vestibular proprioception).

Scoring

Each of the three scales that make up the IMCAP-ND are interconnected in that each examines different aspects of the client's capacities to musically interact with the therapist. Therefore, in essence, each scale is attempting to dissect a musical interaction based on three interrelated categories—musical emotional, cognition/perception, and preference, efficiency, and self-regulation—in order to provide an overall profile of the client's ability to relate to and communicate in musical play.

It is recommended that when scoring the IMCAP-ND, therapists first rate each item in Scale I: MEARS. While scoring the MEARS, therapists should also consider the related areas in Scales II and III. For example, when scoring the ability to shift musical attention on Scale I, the therapist simultaneously is examining this capacity in relation to the client's cognitive and perceptual abilities (Scale II) as well as their overall responsiveness (Scale III: MRS). This helps the therapist determine the musical conditions needed in order for the client to exhibit the ability to shift musical attention. After scoring Scale I, the therapist will then formally score Scale II (MCPS), followed by Scale III (MRS).

Scale I: Musical Emotional Assessment Rating Scale (MEARS)

Scale I: Musical Emotional Assessment Rating Scale (MEARS) assesses the client's social-emotional capacities in musical play. It rates clients in 24 areas organized into five, hierarchically structured levels of functional social-emotional capacities:

- attention

- affect

- adaption to musical play

- engagement

- interrelatedness.

The MEARS assumes a developmental sequential structure, based on Greenspan's developmental sequential theory (2001), in which each musical-social capacity builds on the previous. Each area is broken down into subcategories that identify its critical features. For example, musical attention is composed of four subcategories assessing how the client attends to musical-play: (1) focuses, (2) maintains, (3) shares, and (4) shifts. Each of these subcategories is rated on the frequency of response and support provided in order for the client to demonstrate capacity in a specific targeted area. Frequency is scored according to a six-point scale which ranges from zero (does not exhibit response) to five (consistently exhibits response). Each of the subcategories is also rated for the support the therapist provides in order for the client to express a targeted musical response. The support scale is also based on a six-point scale from zero (not applicable due to child's functional incapacity); one, maximum (full physical, i.e. hand over hand); two, moderate (partial physical); three, mild (visual); four, minimal (verbal); and five, no support (independently exhibits response).

TABLE 5.1: SCALE I: MUSICAL EMOTIONAL ASSESSMENT RATING SCALE

I MUSICAL ATTENTION		
	Frequency	Support
Focuses		
Maintains		
Shares		
Shifts		
TOTALS/AVG.		
II MUSICAL AFFECT		
	Frequency	Support
Facial		
Prosody		
Body		
Motion		
TOTALS/AVG.		

Scale II: Musical Cognitive/Perception Scale (MCPS)

Scale II: Musical Cognitive/Perception Scale (MCPS) evaluates the client's ability to react, focus, recall, follow, and initiate five musical elements:

- rhythm

- melody

- dynamic

- phrase

- timbre.

Scoring is based on frequency of response using the same frequency rating scale as the MEARS. The MCPS was developed as a means to understand the cognitive processes that support musical behaviors involved in relational music making such as awareness, comprehension, memory, attention, and performance. Furthermore, it was created as a means to understanding the client's musical sensitivity in musical play, including receptiveness to relational rather than absolute properties of rhythm, melody, dynamics, phrasing, and timbre. Rating the MCPS involves using the same frequency scale as the MEARS. Support is not rated with the MCPS.

TABLE 5.2: SCALE II: MUSICAL COGNITIVE/PERCEPTION SCALE

	Rhythm	Melody	Dynamic	Phrase	Timbre
Reacts					
Focuses					
Recalls					
Follows					
Initiates					

Scale III: Musical Responsiveness Scale (MRS)

Scale III: Musical Responsiveness Scale (MRS) is designed to examine the overall responses and tendencies of the client at various ranges of tempo, dynamics, pitch, and attack in musical play based on three areas:

- preferences—the extent to which the client responds with positive affect

- perceptual efficiency—the relative success the client has when performing perceptual tasks

- self-regulation—the extent to which the client maintains attention and availability for interaction in musical play.

The MRS was developed to identify client preferences, motivations, and efficiency as well as their ability to self-regulate in musical play. Scoring the MRS is based on the same frequency scale as the MEARS and MCPS. Support is not scored with the MRS.

TABLE 5.3: SCALE III: MUSICAL RESPONSIVENESS SCALE

	Tempo range			Dynamic range			Pitch range			Attack		
	Slow	Med	Fast	Soft	Med	Loud	Low	Mid	High	PS	SL	PL
Preference												
Efficiency												
Self-regulation												

Interpretation and report

Scale I: MEARS generates a total of 48 raw scores. These scores consist of 24 frequency and 24 support scores that are based on five main musical-emotional areas: attention, affect, adaption to play, engagement, and interrelatedness.

Each of these five areas generate an overall mean score that is gauged by using the frequency rating scale. While mean scores for each area provide an overall portrait of the client's strengths and challenges in musical play, the raw scores are considered when determining specific goals.

Goals are developmentally prioritized. For example, if a client displays difficulty in the areas of musical attention (i.e. how the client attends to musical play), adapting to musical play (e.g. how the client adjusts to tempo and/or dynamics changes), and initiating musical ideas, musical attention may take priority. Capacities for musical attention, such as the ability to focus, share, and shift attention in play, can be considered a prerequisite for musical interaction and therefore may be considered foundational to more sophisticated forms of musical play such as adaption and initiating.

Scale II: MCPS generates five raw scores in five areas: reacts, focuses, recalls, follows, and initiates. Scale III: MRS provides 12 raw scores in each of the three areas that deal with musical responsiveness: preference, efficiency, and self-regulation. Scales I, II, and III work together to generate a musical profile narrative for each client. The MEARS determines the client's musical-social-emotional abilities in terms of how they interactively engage in musical play with the therapist. Scales II and III work together to help the therapist determine the musical conditions needed for the client to engage in those musical-social-play experiences. Hence, Scales II (MCPS) and III (MRS) provide outcomes that act as descriptors which indicate the client's musical tendencies, interests, preferences, and preferred media, i.e. instruments, vocals, and/or movement, while engaged in co-active musical play.

This data helps to inform and guide the therapist's musical choices in order to maximize musical interactions. For example, a client may exhibit the ability to sustain sharing music attention as scored in Scale I. Scale II, however, determined that, during moments of shared attention, the client has a propensity towards music experiences driven by tempo and dynamics. Finally, Scale III informed the therapist that the client's preferences (extent to which the client responds with positive affect), perceptual efficiency (the relative success the client has when performing perceptual tasks), and self-regulatory capacities (extent to which the client maintains emotional availability for interaction) include music that is allegro (tempo) and forte. Thus, this informs the therapist that, although the client displays the ability to share musical attention in play, they require music that is allegro and forte. Furthermore, this data will assist the therapist in developing a goal for this client that may focus on the client playing in music that contains a wider range of tempo and dynamic.

Training

In order to ensure proper use of the IMCAP-ND, music therapists with professional credentials, interested in employing this assessment, are required to attend a three-day certificate training course. The training encompasses both didactic and experiential learning and includes how to administer the musical and non-musical protocols, rate the items in each of the three scales, interpret results, create clinical goals, and write reports. There are plans to create a level II course for music therapists who have already completed level I. Level II will provide clinicians with real-life practical experience within their own clinical practice of administering and completing IMCAP-ND assessments while being supervised. The level II course will include one-to-one individualized supervision and involve video review of sessions. This course may be completed in person or via video conferencing.

Research and psychometrics

The IMCAP-ND has been tested for inter-rater reliability in order to empirically determine the degree to which two music therapists were consistent in their judgements of music therapy videos of 30 children with ASD. Inter-rater reliability was tested using "weighted kappa" (Landis and Koch 1977). Results for the MEARS indicated that 98 percent of the 48 weighted kappa coefficients for the frequency and support ratings can be characterized as "almost perfect" using current interpretive standards for evaluating inter-rater reliability coefficients. In addition, all of the weighted kappas (100%) for the subscales of this music therapy observational instrument as well as the subscales of the MCPS and MRS can be categorized as "almost perfect," that is, the highest level of inter-rater reliability (Carpente and Gattino 2018).

Future plans

Currently the IMCAP-ND is being tested for predictive, concurrent, and convergent validity with children with ASD. The study involves correlating the IMCAP-ND with standardized and validated diagnostic and assessment instruments that are used to evaluate children with ASD. Correlations will include comparing Scale I: MEARS with the Autistic Diagnostic Observational Schedule (ADOS), Autism Diagnostic Interview-Revised (ADI-R), and Pervasive Developmental Disorder Behavior Inventory (PDDBI); Scale II: MCPS with Intelligent Quotient (IQ) scores, the Social Responsive Scale (SRS), and PDDBI; and Scale III: MRS with ADOS, SRS, and PDDBI. An additional future project will be to develop automation software that will generate assessment reports based on the IMCAP-ND scoring.

Discussion and summary

The IMCAP-ND is a play-based assessment instrument in which the music therapist provides various improvised musical contexts to assess musical-emotional capacities related to core features of ASD.

The IMCAP-ND takes into account and rates supportive interventions required for a client to express a particular musical response. Furthermore, it considers clients' musical differences, preferences, tendencies, and range of responses during play as a means of informing clinical-musical processes. Finally, it provides the therapist with a musical understanding of the client within the context of relational musical play.

Among some of the IMCAP-ND's limitations are the absence of validity testing and other reliability methods, such as test-retest. In addition, for therapists with minimal IMCAP-ND experience, rating and examining subjective interactive dynamics with an objective lens may pose some scoring challenges and inconsistencies. Moreover, the relevence of the IMCAP-ND depends greatly on the therapist's approach and level of clinical improvisation skill. Thus, clinicians that work within a behaviorally based context, and/or generally provide pre-composed and/or activity-based experiences, may encounter difficulties employing the IMCAP-ND protocols and rating system.

The uniqueness of the IMCAP-ND is that it provides therapists with a way to assess clients in the manner most aligned with the very modality through which the work takes place: the music (Abrams 2013). Hence, the IMCAP-ND does not relegate music to a separate "domain"—rather, it is understood as the experience and act of developmental, relational, and communicative functioning that is the core basis for the client's challenges related to intentionality, spontaneity, affective attunement, and interactive relating (Abrams 2013). Therefore, rather than viewing clients through the lens of conventional health domains (i.e. motor, cognition, etc.) independently from music, the IMCAP-ND seeks to assess and consider music and all of its social, dynamic, and aesthetic dimensions as the only domain area. Hence, just as a physical therapist assesses a client's motor capacities and a speech therapist focuses on evaluating speech skills, the music therapist implementing the IMCAP-ND attends to the client's musical capacities such as musical intent, communication, problem solving, and expressivity in musical play.

References

Abrams, B. (2011) 'Understanding music as a temporal-aesthetic way of being: Implications for a general theory of music therapy.' *The Arts in Psychotherapy, 38,* 2, 114–119.

Abrams, B. (2013) 'Foreword.' In J. A. Carpente, *Individual Music-Centered Assessment Profile for Neurodevelopmental Disorders (IMCAP-ND): Clinical Manual.* Baldwin, NY: Regina Publishers.

Aigen, K. (1995) 'Cognitive and affective processes in music therapy with individuals with developmental delays: A preliminary model for contemporary Nordoff-Robbins practice.' *Music Therapy, 13,* 1, 13–46.

Aigen, K. (2005) *Music-Centered Music Therapy.* Gilsum, NH: Barcelona Publishers.

Alvin, J. (1965) *Music for the Handicapped Child.* London: Oxford University Press.

Alvin, J. and Warwick, A. (1991) *Music Therapy for the Autistic Child* (2nd edition). London: Oxford University Press.

American Psychiatric Association (2013) *Diagnostic and Statistical Manual of Mental Disorders* (5th edition). Arlington, VA: American Psychiatric Publishing.

Ansdell, G. (2016) *How Music Helps in Music Therapy and Everyday Life.* New York, NY: Routledge Publishing.

Bruscia, K. E. (1987) *Improvisational Models of Music Therapy.* Springfield, IL: Charles C. Thomas.

Carpente, J. A. (2013) *Individual Music-Centered Assessment Profile for Neurodevelopmental Disorders (IMCAP-ND): A Clinical Manual.* Baldwin, NY: Regina.

Carpente, J. A. (2016) 'Investigating the effectiveness of a developmental, individual difference, relationship-based (DIR) improvisational music therapy program on social communication for children with autism spectrum disorder.' *Music Therapy Perspectives, 35,* 2, 160–174.

Carpente, J. A. and Gattino, G. (2018) 'Inter-rater reliability on the Individual Music-Centered Assessment Profile for Neurodevelopmental Disorders (IMCAP-ND) for autism spectrum disorder.' *Nordic Journal of Music Therapy, 27,* 297–311.

Carpente, J. A. and Kelliher, M. (2017) 'IMCAP-ND Musical Protocols & Procedures.' Unpublished manuscript.

Feldman, R. (2007a) 'On the origins of background emotions: From affect synchrony to symbolic expression.' *Emotion, 7,* 3, 601–611.

Feldman, R. (2007b) 'Parent-infant synchrony and the construction of shared timing: Physiological precursors, developmental outcomes, and risk conditions.' *Journal of Child Psychology and Psychiatry, 48,* 329–354.

Fogel, A. (1993) *Developing Through Relationships.* Chicago, IL: University of Chicago Press.

Gattino, G. S., Riesgo, R. D. S., Longo, D., Leite, J. C. L., and Faccini, L. S. (2011) 'Effects of relational music therapy on communication of children with autism: A randomized controlled study.' *Nordic Journal of Music Therapy, 20,* 2, 142–154.

Geretsegger, M., Holck, U., Carpente, J. A., Elefant, C., Kim, J., and Gold, C. (2015) 'Common characteristics of improvisational approaches in music therapy for children with autism spectrum disorder: Developing treatment guidelines.' *Journal of Music Therapy, 52,* 2, 258–281.

Greenspan, S. I. (2001) 'The affect-diathesis hypothesis: The role of emotions in the core deficit in autism and in the development of intelligence and social skills.' *Journal of Developmental and Learning Disorders, 5,* 1–47.

Greenspan, S. I. and Greenspan, N. T. (1985) *First Feelings.* New York, NY: Viking Press.

Greenspan, S. I. and Shanker, S. (2004) *The First Idea: How Symbols, Language, and Intelligence Evolved from our Primate Ancestors to Modern Humans.* New York, NY: Da Capo Press.

Greenspan, S. I. and Weider, S. (2006) *Infant and Early Childhood Mental Health: A Comprehensive Developmental Approach to Assessment and Intervention.* New York, NY: American Psychiatric Association.

Greenspan, S. I., DeGangi, G., and Weider, S. (2001) *The Functional Emotional Assessment Scale (FEAS) for Infancy and Early Childhood: Clinical and Research Applications.* New York, NY: Interdisciplinary Council on Developmental and Learning Disorders.

Holck, U. (2004) 'Turn-taking in music therapy with children with communication disorders.' *British Journal of Music Therapy, 18,* 45–53.

Kim, J., Wigram, T., and Gold, C. (2008) 'The effects of improvisational music therapy on joint attention behaviors in autistic children: A randomized controlled study.' *Journal of Autism and Developmental Disorders, 38,* 9, 1758.

Kim, J., Wigram, T., and Gold, C. (2009) 'Emotional, motivational and interpersonal responsiveness of children with autism in improvisational music therapy.' *Autism, 13,* 4, 389–409.

Landis, J. R. and Koch, G. G. (1977) 'The measurement of observer agreement for categorical data.' *Biometrics, 33,* 159–174.

Mahler, M. S. (1963) 'Thoughts about development and individuation.' *The Psychoanalytic Study of the Child, 18,* 1, 307–324.

Mahler, M. S., Pine, F., and Bergman, A. (2000) *The Psychological Birth of the Human Infant: Symbiosis and Individuation.* New York, NY: Basic Books.

Nordoff, P. and Robbins, C. (2007) *Creative Music Therapy: A Guide to Fostering Clinical Musicianship* (2nd ed. revised and expanded). Gilsum, NH: Barcelona Publishers.

Oldfield, A. and Bunce, L. (2001) '"Mummy can play too…" Short-term music therapy with mothers and young children.' *British Journal of Music Therapy, 15,* 1, 27–36.

Pavlicevic, M. (2002) 'Dynamic interplay in clinical improvisation.' *Voices: A World Forum for Music Therapy, 2.* Retrieved 13/12/2017 at https://voices.no/index.php/voices/article/view/88/70.

Rogers, S. J. and Pennington, B. F. (1991) 'A theoretical approach to the deficits in infantile autism.' *Development and Psychopathology, 3,* 2, 137–162.

Stern, D. N. (2009) *The First Relationship: Infant and Mother.* Boston, MA: Harvard University Press.

Thompson, G. A., McFerran, K. S., and Gold, C. (2013) 'Family-centred music therapy to promote social engagement in young children with severe autism spectrum disorder: A randomized controlled study.' *Child: Care, Health and Development, 40,* 6, 840–852.

Trevarthen, C. (2011) 'What is it like to be a person who knows nothing? Defining the active intersubjective mind of a newborn human being.' *Infant and Child Development, 20,* 1, 119–135.

Wigram, T. and Gold, C. (2006) 'Music therapy in the assessment and treatment of autistic spectrum disorder: Clinical application and research evidence.' *Child: Care, Health and Development, 32,* 5, 535–542.

CHAPTER 6

The Music Therapy Expression and Communication Scale

Dorothee von Moreau

Setting and motivation

For many years, I worked as a music therapist in a psychiatric university clinic for children and adolescents. The children or adolescents were referred to the clinic with specific symptoms, such as aggression, depression, enuresis, and psychosis, but when we got to know them better we noticed that most of them had further problems. Some were not aware of their sensations or feelings; others were not able to cope with emotions; some felt lonely and had never learned how to make friends; others rejected any contact or did not know how to initiate or maintain contact; and some seemed disconnected from their inner world or did not know how to express their feelings. There were so many other phenomena behind the symptoms. Beside the symptoms, we also detected individual strengths of the clients: creativity, emotional intensity, esprit, empathy, power, and richness of imagination.

As clinicians, we need to focus not only on the main symptoms but also to be concerned with the hidden problems and resources behind the symptoms, in order to plan and provide effective treatment. Within a psychodynamic framework, we could regard the symptom as a symbolization of an inner state or conflict; a systemic framework would regard symptoms as the weak point of a whole system, for example a family or a school class. Sometimes we find that symptoms are the summit of a range of deficits or the peak of a long development. Regardless of the theoretical approach, we always try to cover the main problems of our clients in an individual, specific and inclusive, client-centered way.

Because of the emotional and interactive potential of music, the role of music therapists within a multidisciplinary context or team is to focus on mental sensations, feelings and emotions, and the client's ability to arrange contact and communication. Our contribution to an effective treatment is to help the client to connect and express, to deal with emotions and conflicts, to understand and to feel understood, or to develop further emotional or social skills. Sometimes these goals are central to therapy, sometimes they are adjunctive to symptom-oriented therapy that aims mainly to relieve the person's main symptoms.

I was fortunate that my work as a music therapist focusing on these broader needs was acknowledged by my colleagues and the head physician. Nonetheless, I was inspired to evaluate my therapy outcomes in order to present the results more objectively and transparently. However, in the early 1990s there were no research-based assessment instruments for music therapy available in this field. With the support of colleagues and the university, I built expert panels and conducted pilot studies and further investigations for developing a music therapy assessment tool focusing on my main clinical goals of emotional expression and communication. My objective was to develop an assessment tool that could be used in clinical and research contexts to evaluate clients' initial and final psychological states and to give objective evidence of therapy outcomes.

Theoretical background

In constructing an assessment tool for music therapy, my intention was to create a tool that was independent of therapeutic schools.

Therefore, the theoretical background of this tool is purely phenomenological. The phenomenological approach was developed by E. Husserl (1859–1938) and is based on the work of E. Kant. This philosophical method also influenced Heidegger, Foucault, Merleau-Ponty, Buber, and Habermas. From the very beginning it was also closely connected to developments in psychology, psychopathology (Karl Jaspers), and particularly Gestalt therapy (Laura Perls).

The theory of phenomenology emphasizes the "phenomenological reduction" (Husserl 1952), which intends to focus on pure experience (phenomenon) without evaluations, concepts, hypotheses, ideas, predictions, or comparisons. Following Husserl, phenomenological reduction leads to pure knowledge and cognizance. When transferred to a psychological or clinical setting, the phenomenological approach helps us to distinguish the main problems of a client by describing their sensations and experiences or observing their behavior.

There are several music therapy approaches that follow this theoretical background, such as the morphological music therapy approach developed by Tüpker, Weymann, Grootaers, and Weber (Tüpker 2001), based on the theories of Salber (1986). These clinicians describe dynamic mental processes of the client by analyzing their musical play in terms of musical patterns, form, dynamics, and construction. They verified that it is possible to reconstruct a client's inner state, and their symptoms, diagnosis, or problem, by carefully describing the phenomenon of their (musical) expression and behavior in a structured, qualitative way. Our everyday clinical experience as music therapists also suggests that there are specific diagnosis-related patterns of musical expression and communication, and we use this knowledge for a subjective diagnostic rating. Similarly, in the field of psychology, and in particular when working with very young or very old persons without reflecting or verbal skills, therapists emphasize observation in their assessments and evaluation to gain detailed clinical information about the mental state, psychodynamics, and psychopathology of the client.

The challenge in constructing a rating scale for these observation purposes lies in defining observation categories with representative, significant, meaningful, unidimensional, and unambiguous items. The items should describe the category in an accurate, objective, and comprehensive way and they should cover the entire phenomena of the relevant behavior (Döring and Bortz 2015; Fisseni 2004). Therefore, I surveyed music therapy experts and reviewed existing assessment tools in music therapy and related fields in order to find categories and items that describe music therapy phenomena. Based on the results of my survey and my direct clinical experience, I developed the Music Therapy Expression and Communication Scale (MAKS = German: Musiktherapeutische Ausdrucks- und Kommunikations-Skala).

Population

The MAKS assessment tool was developed for children and adolescents who suffer from different psychiatric disorders. The scales were evaluated in two studies: first within a population of healthy and psychiatric adolescents (male and female, aged 17) (Moreau 1996, 2003), and second within a population of healthy and psychiatric ill boys, aged 7–12 (Moreau 2009). The evaluation studies showed that MAKS differentiates between diagnostic groups, is highly sensitive to change, and is independent of age (Moreau 2010). The items correlate to the client's psychopathological state and some aspects of personality.

MAKS can be applied for clinical and research purposes: the assessment at the beginning of a therapy process may detect strengths and deficits of a client's non-verbal expressive and communicative behavior. Providing this relevant information, MAKS supports the clinical assessment process. This information may also be useful for treatment planning: therapy goals such as supporting the client's strength, creativity, flexibility, vitality, independency, or contact behavior may be detected by MAKS.

A final assessment at the end of therapy is recommended in order to evaluate the therapy outcome: comparing the first assessment at the beginning and the final assessment at the end of therapy helps to detect in what aspects and to what extent the client's behavior has changed through the therapy process. This provides a rather objective evaluation of the therapy outcome. If necessary, a MAKS assessment can also be useful in the middle of a long therapy process as an interim evaluation.

The Music Therapy Expression and Communication Scale (MAKS)

The Music Therapy Expression and Communication Scale (MAKS) is an assessment tool consisting of two subscales: one for describing the client's musical expression during a solo improvisation (solo-play), and one for describing the client's musical communication during a client-therapist improvisation (duo-play).

Each subscale has different items grouped into foci of observation (see Figure 6.1), and each item is divided into seven levels (Likert-type scales). Each item is also precisely operationalized, and each level accurately described in order to support objective rating. Table 6.1 shows the entire expression scale consisting of 15 items. The communication scale has a similar structure of 14 items, and is in the process of being translated.

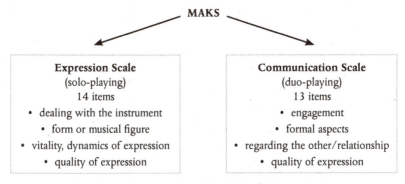

Figure 6.1: MAKS and its foci of observation

TABLE 6.1: MAKS: EXPRESSION SCALE (SOLO CONDITION)

1 INTERACTION WITH THE INSTRUMENT

Instrument choice	Does not voluntarily choose instrument	Chimes, small tonal or noise instruments	String instruments (lyre, psalter, kantele)	Mallet instruments (xylophone, metallophone)	Drums, slit drums	Gongs, large slit drums, drum kit	Piano, cello, wind instruments
Playing space (size of the area of the instrument used when playing)	Playing space not used or not used as originally intended	Smallest possible playing space	Small playing space (3%)	Half of the playing space (50%)	Large playing space (70%)	Entire playing space (100%)	Expansion of playing space (100% plus further sound generation)
Initiative (frequency with which the player realizes or develops their own impulses or ideas)	No initiative (only plays on request or with assistance)	Very limited initiative (plays exclusively familiar music)	Limited initiative (1–2 ideas)	Medium initiative (2–3 ideas)	High initiative (3–4 ideas)	Very high initiative (more than 4 ideas)	Excessive initiative (unable to limit themselves)

2 FORM/STRUCTURE

	Disconnected individual notes	Notes seem barely connected (also: scale or monotonous beat)	Short motifs discernible (2–3 connected notes)	Medium-length motifs (4–6 connected notes)	Musical phrase (8–16 connected notes)	Development and continuation of phrases	Overdevelopment of phrases (mannered)
Connectedness (combination of individual notes into complex forms)							
Structure (inner order of the playing, e.g. the subdivision through pauses, accents, repetition)	No discernible structure (chaotic, scattered, vague)	Very little structure (the structural elements are chaotic and disordered)	Little structure, freely changing structural elements	Medium structure (relatively ordered, clear)	Highly structured (constant, stable)	Very highly structured (tightly fixed, inflexible)	Excessively structured (formulaic, lifeless)
Variation (flexibility, changeability of the composition, e.g. playing technique, form, or rhythm)	No discernible variation	Very limited variation	Limited variation in 1–2 characteristics	Medium variation in 1–2 characteristics	High variation in 1–2 characteristics	Very high variation in More than 2 characteristics	Excessive high variation in More than 2 characteristics

3 LIVELINESS/DYNAMICS OF EXPRESSION

Tension (amount of energy transformed to the instrument in relation to the instrument's expression potential)	Instrument's potential not used	Far below the instrument's potential	At the lower end of the instrument's potential	Medium level of the instrument's potential used	At the upper potential of the instrument	Surpassing the potential of the instrument	Instrument breaks
Audibility (volume)	Extremely quiet (*hardly audible*)	Very quiet (*very weak*)	Quiet (*weak*)	Medium	Loud (*clear*)	Very loud (*powerful, strong*)	Extremely loud (*forceful, unpleasant*)
Liveliness (perceived tempo)	Extremely low (*listless, becomes slower and slower*)	Very low (*appears very slow, sluggish, cautious*)	Low (*feels slow, solemn*)	Medium (*walking pace*)	Accelerated (*lively, buoyant*)	Very accelerated (*fast, agitated*)	Excessive (*overexcited, overexerting themselves*)
Flow (degree of inhibition/lack of inhibition)	Very inhibited (*faltering*)	Inhibited (*very cautious, very controlled*)	Rather inhibited (*cautious, controlled*)	Medium (*continuous, relaxed, neither inhibited nor uninhibited*)	Rather uninhibited (*rather urgent*)	Uninhibited (*very urgent*)	Very uninhibited (*complete lack of restraint*)
Dynamics (variation in tempo and volume)	No dynamics (*monotonous, uniform*)	Very weak dynamics	Weak dynamics	Medium dynamics	Strong dynamics	Very strong dynamics	Excessive dynamics (*forced, erratic*)

4 QUALITY OF EXPRESSION

Sound quality (degreee of forcefulness/softness used when producing sound)	Very soft *(cautious)*	Soft *(delicate)*	Rather soft *(gentle, sonorous)*	Medium	Rather forceful *(thudding, not sonorous)*	Forceful *(hard, rough)*	Very forceful *(harsh, severe)*
Quality of expression (intensity of the expression of emotion)	No intensity *(completely devoid of expression)*	Very low intensity *(no expression, expressionless)*	Low intensity *(slightly expressive)*	Medium intensity *(expressive)*	High intensity *(very expressive)*	Very high intensity *(overflowing with expression)*	Excessive intensity *(decompensated)*
Clarity of emotion (perceptibility and clarity of the emotional experience)	No discernible expression	Very vague, indistinct expression	Vague, but some degree of discernible expression	Clear, distinct expression	Overlapping expression	Fragmented, ambivalent expression	Disjointed, disordered expression
Experience (degree of player's involvement in/response to their own playing)	No discernible response *(seems detached, cut-off)*	Very weak response *(seems absent, indifferent)*	Weak response *(seems little affected)*	Medium response *(seems involved, interested)*	Strong response *(seems very involved, excited)*	Very strong response *(deeply moved, agitated)*	Overly strong response *(subsumed by/lost in the music)*

Procedure and protocol

The protocol for the assessment session consists of at least one client solo and one client-therapist improvisation (duo-play) in a single music therapy setting. Each assessment session takes about 20 minutes. The client should be familiar with the instruments, the setting, and the therapist. Therefore, it is common to complete the first assessment at the end of the first or at the beginning of the second therapy session, when the client feels fairly secure, free, and confident in improvising. The assessment session should not be loaded with specific feelings or conflicts. The final assessment at the end of the therapy should not happen during the very last session.

Clinical protocol

For the solo improvisation (solo-play), the client is invited to choose an instrument. They are instructed to play for a while, following their own interests, ideas, and creativity. The instructions are the same as those for a free improvisation. The therapist sits facing the client, listening carefully to the improvisation, with an accepting and appreciating attitude towards the client's expression, without forcing contact.

For the client-therapist improvisation (duo-play), the therapist invites the client to choose one instrument for themselves and one for the therapist; or the therapist may invite the client to play together on one joint instrument. The instrument in this case should have enough space for both players (e.g. piano or table drum). The instructions are the same as those for a turn-taking style of improvisation, with one player starting, the other player answering, and then following the process of the improvisation and ending up playing together. The therapist follows the lead of the client, carefully answering the client's requirements and level of contact, and, if necessary, supports an animated dialogue by exaggerating techniques like intensifying or provocation (see Bruscia 1987).

After the assessment session, the therapist rates the client's musical behavior using the MAKS rating scale and focusing on the predominant behavior of the client. A video or audio record may support an accurate rating process, but is not usual or obligatory for clinical purposes.

Research protocol

For research purposes, the assessment protocol (solo and duo) is the same as for the clinical context, but we recommend a different setting, documentation, and rating process. For research, it is obligatory that the assessment session be video recorded. The setting must be standardized for consistent visual and auditory quality and to minimize disruptive side effects (placement of the instrument and the players, placement of camera and microphone, no zooming, no fading in or out). We would even suggest standardizing the instruments (drums, mallets, or piano, even for solo improvisations). Pilot studies showed that the sound of string or small instruments is often difficult to hear on the video recording and therefore rating will be difficult, imprecise, and not reliable.

The therapist should then choose about 30 seconds of solo and about 40 seconds of duo improvisations, either from the video itself or from a transcript. The scene chosen should be representative of the client's behavior at this stage of therapy. That means the client's typical behavior should be represented in the short scene. The therapist should choose a scene that could stand on its own, so as not to interrupt a musical line or a dialogue sequence, in order not to confuse the raters. Pilot studies showed that a scene of 30–40 seconds provides complex-enough information for the rating.

Following research standards, the rating is executed not by the therapist but by trained, independent, and "blind" observers. For the rating, the scene is shown three times: twice before and once again during the rating process. The auditory and visual quality of the video needs to be excellent and free from distractions. The raters are instructed to rate the client's predominant behavior.

Data analysis and results

The rating by the therapist (clinical condition) or an independent observer (research condition) gives two profiles of the client's behavior: one profile of their expressive behavior in a solo improvisation (expression scale profile), and one profile of their social behavior in a client-therapist improvisation (communication scale profile).

The second evaluation study (Moreau 2009) tested the interval level of the scale. This is essential for further data analysis in a research context. For data analysis and interpretation, we have two relevant levels for consideration: item and category.

Data analysis on an item level

The structure of MAKS is based on a working hypothesis that normal musical behavior is rated in the middle range (3–5) of a seven-point Likert scale, and pathological behavior on the edges (1–2 or 6–7). Therefore, descriptive data analysis in the first step considers the balanced and extreme items in order to detect resources and deficits of a client's non-verbal behavior in terms of musical expression and communication skills.

In a second step, we may look at items which are relevant for the client's diagnosis; for example, for clients with schizophrenic disorders, it would be reasonable to consider the results of the items Connectedness and Structure (expression scale) and Logic Structure (communication scale). Clinical experience shows that patients with schizophrenic disorders show specific musical patterns when improvising (De Backer 2008; Kunkel 2009).

Data analysis on a category level

Statistical factor analysis of MAKS produced seven categories across the two scales. This means that items within one category describe similar aspects of the category and that we can calculate sums and averages across the items of one category for further statistical analysis. Table 6.2 shows the categories with their loading items.

TABLE 6.2: CATEGORIES OF MAKS AND THEIR LOADING ITEMS

MAKS

Expression scale				Communication scale		
Flexibility	Form	Power	Vitality	Emotionality	Independence	Contact
• Playing surface	• Connectedness	• Tension	• Flow	• Quality of expression	• Autonomy	• Involvement
• Initiative	• Structure	• Audibility	• Liveliness	• Clarity of emotions	• Dominance	• Contact behavior
• Variation		• Sound quality		• Experience	• Affective quality	• Dynamic quality
• Dynamics					• Turn-taking	• Playing quality
						• Intro/ extraversion

For individual analysis within the clinical context, we look at whether the items within a category show similar profiles. Deviant item profiles within a category point out inconsistency within that category. This is always interesting for clinical reasoning and interpretation.

Data analysis across categories

For clinical reasoning, it is also interesting to compare the results of some single items in the client-solos and client-therapist improvisations, as some items of the expression and communication scales are closely related (see box below). In clinical experience, we see some clients performing very well in a solo-play, but highly dysfunctional in duo-plays with the therapist. By contrast, some clients perform better in duo and are more dysfunctional in a solo condition.

Expression scale (solo-playing)	vs	Communication scale (duo-playing)
Choice of instrument (solo)	vs	Choice of instrument (duo)
Playing space	vs	Social space
Variation	vs	Behavior variation
Flow	vs	Flow quality
Dynamics	vs	Dynamic quality
Connectedness	vs	Logical structure

Interpretation and report

MAKS evaluates seven categories that are closely related to core aspects of mental health or psychopathology. Some items and categories also correlate with dimensions of temperament and personality (Moreau 2009; Moreau 2010). Thus, the MAKS assessment tool allows us to make the following specific statements about these categories.

Solo categories (expression scale)

Musical flexibility evaluates the range of melody or instrumental space the client uses, how many musical ideas they initiate, and to what extent they change dynamics, musical patterns, instrumental space, musical form, or rhythm. Clinical experience shows that clients with pain, depression, and compulsive or anxiety disorders play with reduced flexibility; by contrast, clients with attention deficit, hyperactivity, impulsive disorders, or mania often play with increased flexibility (Kashdan and Rottenberg 2010). Balanced flexibility in musical expression suggests an improved mental state (Matten 2014).

Musical power evaluates the energy the client releases through playing the instrument, whether they take into account the potential of the instrument and are able to develop their musical expression in relation to the instrument's potential, and how clearly or weakly this is expressed. In a clinical context, we find that clients with depression, pain disorders, or anxious personality disorders typically play with low musical power. Their musical power increases when they recover. By contrast, clients with mania, hyperactivity, or impulsive disorders often show great musical power. Balanced musical power suggests an improved emotional state for these clients.

Musical vitality evaluates the tempo and flow of musical expression. It indicates the degree of or lack of inhibition in the client's improvisation. Again, from clinical experience we know clients whose vitality appears sluggish or cautious—or by contrast agitated or excessive—while the musical flow may be uniform and controlled or uninhibited or urgent. Discrepant rating of the two items in this category is an indication of ambiguity in the client's inner state, with strong vitality and strong inhibition at the same time. Thus, the scores in this category are indicators of emotional self-regulation. A balanced score is an indication of a balanced and well-regulated emotional state.

Musical emotionality evaluates how intensively the client expresses their emotional experience and how clear, vague, or fragmented this experience may be perceived by the therapist/observer. It also describes the client's response to and involvement in their own playing. Thus, this category refers to the client's ability to detect and musically express emotions, and to be connected to their emotions. It also draws attention to ambivalent or conflicted emotions. From clinical experience, we are familiar with the whole range of clients with indistinct, disjointed, or chaotically disordered musical expression. Increased and balanced musical emotionality indicates adaptive emotionality as a sign of a healthy mental state or a positive therapy outcome (Greenberg and Watson 2006).

Musical structure evaluates the inner and logical order of the client's playing and their ability to build complex musical structures in terms of musical motives, melodies, or phrases. From clinical experience, we know that this ability is substantially lower in clients with psychosis (De Backer 2008; Kunkel 2009) and fragmented in clients with impulsive disorders. We observe increased musical structure when clients improve their psychological state.

Duo categories (communication scale)

Musical independence evaluates how autonomously the client brings in their own ideas and initiatives in a client-therapist improvisation, how elaborately they answer to another's statement, whether they dominate or subordinate, and their tendency to act in a gentle and empathic versus a powerful and intense (rough, heavy) way in a duo-play. In clinical experience, we see little independence in clients with depression, anxiety disorders, or psychosis, and clients show more independence when recovering from these psychiatric disorders. However, we observe excessive independence in clients with disorders such as narcissistic personality disorder, mania, social disorder, or impulsive disorder.

Musical contact describes the interest and involvement of a client in a client-therapist improvisation, their tendency towards intro- or extraversion, and to what extent the dialogue is fluent, agile, and inspired versus blocked, rigid, and numb. In clinical experience, we see less or poorer contact in many disorders such as autism, depression, anxiety, psychosis, and also some personality or social disorders. The ability to initiate, maintain, and modulate contact is evidence of well-being and good mental health (Mössler *et al.* 2012).

Interpretations across categories and conditions

Comparing the results of some single items in the client solos and client-therapist improvisations (duo), we gain specific information about the client's independence, need for support, or distress in contact situations. If clients perform better in solo than in duo conditions, we could reason that they feel more independent and secure without contact, and might feel distressed by contact with the therapist. Alternatively, clients show that they benefit from or need support when they perform better in a duo-play condition. If both conditions bring the same results, we assume that the client's performance is independent of contact and more related to their mental state itself.

Training

A MAKS training program for qualified music therapists has been prepared. The training will include two periods of training for each scale, each period consisting of two full days. The first period introduces the background and the scale, provides an overview of the items and how they work, and offers training samples. The participants then use the scales for their clinical practice. For the second training period, the participants bring their video-recorded clinical examples and discuss the MAKS scoring with the trainer and the group. The training ends with a certification test at the end of this period. Research using the MAKS should be completed no later than six months post-certification.

Research and psychometrics

The MAKS scales were validated in two different studies. The first study included a sample of ten adolescents with a broad range of diagnoses. Fifty-two untrained raters completed the scales twice (Moreau 1996, 2003). The second study included a large sample of 62 boys, 24 healthy and 38 with a psychiatric disorder (n = 62, age range 5.8 to 13.2 years, average 8.7). Three trained raters rated three times: at the beginning, in the middle, and at the end of a music workshop or therapy process (Moreau 2009, 2010).

The first investigations (Moreau 1996, 2003) showed that MAKS scores allow significant differentiation between clients with various psychiatric disorders (p < .001) and gave an initial impression of the scale's inner structure (independence of items, stable factor structure for the two rating times as an aspect of construct validity). The second investigations (Moreau 2009; Moreau 2010) showed that the results are independent of age (p = .198, tested by analysis of variance (ANOVA)) and therefore free of developmental influences.

The study also tested MAKS' significant sensitivity of change (p=.023 for the expression scale and p = .001 for the communication scale, tested by multivariate analysis of variance (MANOVA)). Some items and categories also correlate with core aspects of psychopathology (Strengths and Difficulties Questionnaire (SDQ), Goodman 2001), and dimensions of temperament and personality (Junior Temperament and Character Inventory (JTCI), Cloninger 1994). Cluster analysis detected specific group profiles across the tested population—these groups differed significantly in clinical state (p = .017, tested by ANOVA) and self-directedness (p = .035, tested by ANOVA). After eliminating five weak items that need further adaptation, the scale showed a reliability of α > .70 (Cronbach's alpha) and an objectivity of r > .7 (Pearson's inter-rater correlation) for at least one condition (the training or the rating condition).

Future plans

Within the last decade, weak items were revised but need to be re-evaluated within a clinical group. Prototypical scenarios for a training manual were video recorded and validated with students. Currently, the expression scale is being translated and validated for an English version (Winkler 2017); a translation of the communication scale is planned. A study involving adult psychiatric patients and a healthy control group may contribute to diagnosis-specific MAKS profiles.

Discussion

MAKS was developed with the support of music therapy experts as a specific music therapy assessment tool for psychiatric children and adolescents. As MAKS is independent of age, we expect that the scales may be used also in psychiatric populations (adults). As psychopathological dimensions show a high variety and ambiguity in children and adolescents, we expect even clearer results (e.g. differences in groups and correlation to psychopathology) for adult psychiatric patients. Plum *et al.* (2002) and Isermann (2001) used MAKS to show the effectiveness of music therapy with psychiatric adults. Matten (2014) tested the hypothesis that music therapy may increase flexibility in (adult) pain patients. However, to date there has been no MAKS evaluation with adult patients, nor do we know typical MAKS profiles of healthy and normal populations. A standardization study is needed.

The accurate description of each interval of the items allows a detailed reflection of a client's musical behavior. Validation testing shows that MAKS provides an objective, reliable, and valid measure for clinical and research application; we also hope the same will prove true for the items that were revised. As validation supported the interval level of the scale, strong statistical methods are permissible for future data analysis.

The two scales of MAKS focus on expressive and communicative musical behavior and detect typical nuances of mental conspicuousness or ambiguity. MAKS is mainly focused on observable behavior and cannot describe a client's inner state or emotional experience. Its factor structure allows statements about a client's musical flexibility, power, vitality, emotionality, structure, independence, and contact behavior, in addition to self-confidence, need for support/contact, or distress in client-therapist improvisations. All of these phenomena are of clinical relevance, either for assessment or treatment planning. Although these phenomena are not the most relevant characteristics for a clinical diagnosis, they are often correlated with clinical symptoms or disorders. Regional and international expert panels determined that these phenomena are those that are most commonly addressed in music therapy treatment: they are relevant for statements about treatment outcomes.

MAKS focuses exclusively on the client, not on the therapist and their behavior. This approach requires a controlled therapeutic attitude and behavior during assessment: the client needs support to perform to their potential, but the influence of the therapist should be kept to a minimum. All certified and experienced music therapists will be able to perform and reflect these specific requirements, if they follow the protocol.

Acknowledgements

I would like to thank Prof. David Aldridge, Prof. Fritz Pouska, Prof. Heiner Ellgring, and Prof. Andreas Warnke for the chance and support to follow my ideas. I thank Dr. Kirstin Goth for the statistical support. Warm thanks to my students for their ideas and further investigations, especially Jan Cohrs, Kai Matten, and Janik Winkler. Alice Spendley, Erin Goldfinch, Silvie Zeller, and Prof. Douglas Keith put in enormous efforts for the English translation. Without the interest and support of music therapy experts, students, clients, and colleagues, MAKS would have never succeeded.

References

Bruscia, K. E. (1987) *Improvisational Methods in Music Therapy*. Springfield, IL: Charles C. Thomas Publishers.

Cloninger, C. R., Pryzbeck, T. R., Svrakic, D. M., and Wetzel, R. D. (1994) *The Junior Temperament and Character Inventory (JTCI): A Guide to its Development and Use*. St. Louis, MO: Washington University Center for Psychobiology and Personality.

De Backer, J. (2008) 'Music and psychosis.' *Nordic Journal of Music Therapy, 17*, 2, 89–104.

Döring, N. and Bortz, J. (2015) *Forschungsmethoden und Evaluation in den Sozial- und Humanwissenschaften*. Heidelberg: Springer.

Fisseni, H. J. (2004) *Lehrbuch der psychologischen Diagnostik*. Göttingen: Hogrefe.

Goodman, R. (2001) 'Psychometric properties of the strengths and difficulties questionnaire.' *Journal of the American Academy of Child and Adolescent Psychiatry, 40*, 11, 1337–1345.

Greenberg, L. S. and Watson, J. C. (2006) *Emotion-Focused Therapy for Depression*. New York, NY: American Psychological Association.

Husserl, E. (1952) *Ideen III: Die Phänomenologie und die Fundamente der Wissenschaften*. Tübingen: Max Niemeyer Verlag.

Isermann, H. (2001) 'Einzelfalluntersuchung einer Gruppenmusiktherapie mit schizophrenen Patienten.' Unpublished thesis in music therapy, University Enschede.

Kashdan, T. B. and Rottenberg, J. (2010) 'Psychological flexibility as a fundamental aspect of health.' *Clinical Psychology Review, 30*, 7, 865–878.

Kunkel, S. (2009) 'Möglichkeiten und Formen emotionaler Differenzierung im musiktherapeutischen Erstkontakt mit schizophrenen Patienten.' In Deutsche Musiktherapeutische Gesellschaft (ed.) *Musiktherapie und Emotionale Differenzierung*. Jahrbuch Musiktherapie Bd. 5. Wiesbaden: Reichert.

Matten, K. M. (2014) 'Darstellung einer Flexibilisierung des erstarrten Bezugskorrelats durch 4 Items der Musiktherapeutischen Ausdrucks- und Kommunikationsskala.' Unpublished bachelor thesis, SRH University, Heidelberg.

Moreau, D. v. (1996) 'Entwicklung und Evaluation eines Beschreibungssystems (MAKS) zum Ausdrucks- und Kommunikationsverhalten in der Musiktherapie.' Unpublished diploma thesis, Universität Würzburg.

Moreau, D. v. (2003) 'MAKS—a scale for measurement of expressive and musical behaviour.' *Music Therapy Today, 4*, 4. Retrieved 13/11/2017 at www.wfmt.info/Musictherapyworld.

Moreau, D. v. (2009) 'Evaluation der Musiktherapeutischen Ausdrucks- und Kommunikationsskala (MAKS).' Unpublished PhD thesis, Universität Witten-Herdecke.

Moreau, D. v. (2010) 'Psychometric results of the music therapy scale (MAKS) for measuring expression and communication.' *Music and Medicine, 2*, 1, 41–47.

Mössler, K., Assmus, J., Heldal, T. O., Fuchs, K., and Gold, C. (2012) 'Music therapy techniques as predictors of change in mental health care.' *The Arts in Psychotherapy, 39*, 333–341.

Plum, F. J., Lodemann, E., Bender, S., Finkbeiner, T., and Gastpar, M. (2002) 'Gruppenmusiktherapie mit schizophrenen Patienten. Entwicklung des Kontaktverhaltens, des improvisatorischen Spielausdrucks und der Psychopathologie.' *Nervenheilkunde, 10*, 522–528.

Salber, W. (1986) *Morphologie des Seelischen Geschehens*. Bonn: Bouvier.

Tüpker, R. (2001) 'Morphologisch orientierte Musiktherapie.' In H. H. Decker-Voigt (ed.) *Schulen der Musiktherapie*. München: E. Reinhardt.

Winkler, J. (2017) 'Übersetzung der Musiktherapeutischen Ausdrucks- und Kommunikationsskala (MAKS) ins Englische.' Unpublished master's thesis, SRH Hochschule, Heidelberg.

CHAPTER 7

The Music-Based Scale for Autism Diagnostics

Thomas Bergmann

Setting and motivation

For more than ten years, I have been working at a specialized treatment center for people with intellectual disability and co-morbid psychiatric disorder, including severe, challenging behaviors. The Assessment of the Quality of Relationship (AQR; Schumacher and Calvet 2007) became a helpful tool for intervention planning to support a therapeutic approach based on early infant research and attachment theory. Music therapy as a non-verbal, interactive method is indicated for clients with severe communication deficits and problems with emotion regulation in an individual setting. I was increasingly attracted to working with individuals with pervasive developmental disorders, who were often isolated from the social world. Short moments of contact felt like a window that opened briefly; tuning into a different way of thinking and perceiving felt like walking on another planet. Both enriched my experience, touched my heart, and created curiosity, thus motivating research in the area of autism.

Together with a specialist in neurology and psychiatry and a psychological psychotherapist, I formed a clinical research group aiming to improve diagnostics and treatment in adults with intellectual developmental disorders. First, we reviewed literature and implemented a weekly diagnostic consensus conference allowing for a multi-professional procedure in autism diagnostics. In parallel, we investigated the applicability of diagnostic measures for children and youth (Sappok *et al.* 2013) and developed specific scales for assessing adults with intellectual disability (Sappok *et al.* 2014). We changed the treatment and support for those diagnosed with autism, for example reducing psychotropic medication, consulting the client and their relatives, implementing an autism-friendly environment, and developing specific educational concepts, like the Autism Competence Group (Bergmann, Herberger, Birkner, and Sappok 2016).

Video documentation for diagnostic purposes was implemented as a resource for discussion in the consensus conference. I had already developed a semi-structured music therapy approach for people with autism to provide a routine, meeting clients' need for sameness and structure (Bergmann *et al.* 2009), and had systematically started video documentation. These videos became an essential part of the diagnostic workup and helped in decision making, especially in clients with limited speech. Motivated by this experience, I began considering the operationalization of diagnostically relevant behaviors. This was the starting point in developing the Music-based Scale for Autism Diagnostics (MUSAD), which went along with my PhD and growing research activity in this field.

Theoretical background

Autism spectrum disorder (ASD) is an umbrella term to describe a continuum of neurodevelopmental conditions, including autism. All conditions within the spectrum are characterized by qualitative impairments in social interaction and communication along with stereotyped and repetitive patterns of behavior and the early onset of symptoms. The *DSM-5* (American Psychiatric Association 2013) includes sensory peculiarities as ASD core features. Motor clumsiness is often observed in higher functioning individuals with ASD (Gillberg and Gillberg 1989) and is discussed as an ASD cardinal feature throughout the entire spectrum (Fournier *et al.* 2010). ASD is a life-long disorder with a varied severity of symptoms across the lifespan (Howlin *et al.* 2004). Clinical characteristics caused by ASD, such as deficits in social reciprocity or restricted patterns of interests, influence the relationship to the self, to other people, and to objects, and thus include all areas of life (Williams 2008).

Intellectual disability (ID) is a generalized neurodevelopmental disorder characterized by significantly impaired intellectual and adaptive functioning. It is defined by an $IQ < 70$ in addition to deficits in two or more adaptive behaviors that affect everyday living (American Psychiatric Association 2013). About 1 percent of the general population are affected (Maulik *et al.* 2011). ASD and ID frequently co-occur, with an increasing prevalence of ASD being linked to the increasing severity of cognitive impairment (Bryson *et al.* 2008). Challenging behaviors and self-injury are very often observed in this group (McCarthy *et al.* 2010) and may lead to hospitalization and long-term treatment with anti-psychotic medication (Tsakanikos *et al.* 2007). Clarifying a suspicion of ASD in individuals with ID is essential to ensure appropriate treatment and improve mental health and quality of life (Howlin 2000).

Given the lack of biological markers specific for ASD, diagnosis is based on the client's medical history and behavioral assessment. ASD diagnostics are especially challenging in adults with ID and speech impairments due to limited self-report and the overlap of ASD- and ID-related markers in the areas of adaptive functioning, speech, social interaction, and stereotyped behaviors. Differential diagnostics may be further complicated because of an ASD-like picture of schizophrenia, hospitalization, emotional development disorders, and sensory impairments. Furthermore, all these conditions are potential co-morbidities. Unfortunately, there is a lack of appropriate diagnostic instruments for this clinical group.

For diagnostic clarification, the gold standard from children and youth diagnostics is potentially useful. Here, the Autism Diagnostic Interview-Revised (ADI-R; Lord, Rutter, and Le Couteur 1994) provides important information about early childhood development, but is feasible only in one third of cases (Sappok *et al.* 2013). The Autism Diagnostic Observation Schedule (ADOS; Lord *et al.* 2012) was originally developed for assessing children in a play-based framework. The protocol consists of a series of structured and semi-structured tasks that involve social interaction between the examiner and the client. The examiner observes and identifies segments of the client's behavior and assigns these to predetermined observational categories associated with ASD symptomatology.

Although the ADOS is applicable in adults with ID, the child-like design and materials seem inappropriate for assessing adults (Berument *et al.* 2005; Sappok *et al.* 2013). Musical interaction as a non-verbal and age-independent form of play helps to overcome these limitations. There is a wide use of music in the therapy and education of children and youth with ASD (Srinivasan and Bhat 2013), supporting the ASD-friendliness of a music-based framework. Based on these potentials and challenges, the MUSAD has been developed as an alternative and complement to the ADOS in assessing adults with ID.

Procedure

By introducing musical situations that demand social interaction in various forms, as well as non-social activities, such as playing and handling instruments, the MUSAD seeks to identify an ASD-defining symptomatology. Comparable to the different tasks and prompts of the ADOS, situations linked to instruments and activities generate certain client behaviors that can be assessed systematically with respect to ASD symptomatology.

Implementation procedure

The bird's-eye view of the semi-structured diagnostic setting, as shown in Figure 7.1, involves all 12 instruments/objects with corresponding activities wherein the arrangement of the instruments corresponds to the chronological order of the investigation.

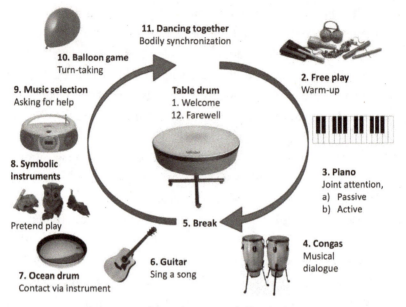

Figure 7.1: The semi-structured diagnostic setting

The required set of instruments corresponds to the music therapy standard equipment supplemented by a big, colored balloon and a selection of CDs with dance music of different styles. The table marks the beginning and end of the investigation (1, welcome—12, farewell). By working clockwise through the instruments and tasks, with a short break in the middle, the setting structures the time and provides a predictable ending. This is in line with the principles of structuring and visualization to further improve the feasibility of the measure (Mesibov, Shea, and Schopler 2004). The participation of an observing caregiver (parent/tutor) is desirable, but not obligatory.

To enhance feasibility, a sequence of increasing demands on interactional skills and physical contact was used. After the welcome, a preparatory talk, and the introduction of the camera at the table (1), the investigation starts with a "warm-up" (2), allowing the client to explore the room and instruments without a reciprocal contact request. The intersubjective challenge increases with the request for joint attention at the piano (3) in conjunction with physical proximity in sitting together at the piano in parallel alignment. The first invitation for a dialogue occurs at the conga situation (4), which demands social reciprocity in a physical face-to-face situation. After a break (5), the sing-a-song task with guitar (6) raises the challenge of sharing joy in social-emotional togetherness by smiling directly at the client. The ocean drum (7) is the first offering of physical contact via an instrument. Role play with symbolic instruments (8) requires the capacity for social imagination, and this is followed by selection of music (9), with the necessity to ask for help to make the CD run. The balloon game (10) assesses back and forth interaction followed by dancing together (11). This activity represents a maximum requirement by coordinating whole body movements and direct bodily contact by joining hands, before the investigation ends with a debriefing at the table (12).

Coding procedure

A two-step coding procedure was adopted from the ADOS to support the examiner in changing roles and perspectives from being an active partner in the musical-interactive diagnostic setting to being an external rater assessing the client's behavior. The conga situation below illustrates the entire diagnostic workup.

IMPLEMENTATION

The examiner (music therapist) initiates joint play with a common pulse, followed by slight tempo changes and re-stabilization of a basic beat. The next task is to hit the drum with alternating right and left hand. Next are simple motifs and breaks to initiate interplay; if the client does not react, or stops, they are supported verbally and gesturally. Finally, a crescendo with release of the suspense in a final blow invites the client to share affectivity.

DESCRIPTION

To change perspective, the examiner is first asked to describe the client's behaviors in free-text along predetermined observation priorities. For example:

Drums

Joint drumming allows for the observation of motor skills and musical reciprocity:

1. *Motor coordination* (right-left, gaze-hand) as well as the speed and the fluidity of rhythmic movements.

2. *Imitative ability* and *metric adaptation* during tempo changes by the investigator.

3. Reaction to the offer of a musical dialogue—degree and quality of musical *reciprocity* and *variability* in the use of motifs and breaks.

4. *Emotional reaction* (signs of joy and social reassurance) to the build-up of musical tension through the drum roll and the offload of the last bang.

SCORING

Task-specific items like "rhythmic synchronization of tempo changes" or overall items like "joy in playing together" are scored on a four-point Likert scale to operationalize ASD-related behaviors. For example:

Rhythmic synchronization of tempo changes

Drumming

3 There is no common rhythmic pulse.

2 There is a common rhythmic pulse. However, the client does not react to changes in tempo that are initiated by the investigator.

1 Metric adaptation is delayed or the musical play stops when the tempo changes.

0 Spontaneous synchronization to changes in tempo is present.

Items and scale construction

The process of item development was based on the *ICD-10* and *DSM-5* diagnostic guidelines, further ASD symptoms, as discussed in the literature, existing ASD scales and assessments, and our own clinical experience of how autistic features manifest in a music therapy setting. Scale construction resulted in an original draft with 88 MUSAD items—musical and non-musical behavioral issues operationalizing an ASD symptomatology. In further scale development, the MUSAD has been streamlined to select the most valuable items for diagnostic classification, and so enhance economy and user-friendliness. Thus, the current version comprises 46 items grouped into the following domains: (1) social communication and interaction, (2) stereotyped patterns of interests and behaviors including sensory issues, and (3) motor coordination (Bergmann *et al.* 2018).

Data analysis and interpretation

The MUSAD scoring results in values from 0 to 3 indicating increasing severity of ASD symptomatology. Of the 46 items, the 20 most valuable items were selected for a diagnostic algorithm. These 20 items are added up to provide a simple sum score. A well-balanced cut score is warranted to allow for a valid categorical decision, that is, the correct identification of ASD (sensitivity) as well as of non-ASD (specificity). Using a cut-off point of 26 resulted in a sensitivity/specificity of about 80 percent. In addition, the total score is indicative for the overall ASD severity. Next to the algorithm, the remaining 26 items are suitable to provide additional diagnostic information and may be valuable to be considered in diagnostic discussions. Regardless of quantitative results, the qualitative aspect of assessing the client in a structured setting related to ASD characteristics allows for an expert judgement.

International guidelines recommend a comprehensive, team-based workup undertaken by trained and competent professionals and using a wide range of resources for diagnostically relevant information (National Institute for Health and Clinical Excellence 2012). According to these recommendations, the MUSAD widens the range of professions and resources in diagnosing ASD. However, as with other scales and measures, the MUSAD alone is not sufficient to make a final diagnostic decision.

Training

The implementation and evaluation of a structured diagnostic tool requires comprehensive training. Basic knowledge about ASD is crucial. Furthermore, the implementation of the procedure needs standardization to ensure use of the MUSAD is identical across different clients and examiners to make scores comparable. Scoring needs calibration, and interpretation needs regular discussions. While psychologists often have sophisticated knowledge in applying diagnostic instruments, they may need musical training, whereas music therapists need instruction in taking a diagnostic perspective. The professional self-conception of a music therapist is based on establishing a therapeutic relationship and focusing on the client's strengths. However, using music-based interaction for diagnostic proposes means it is necessary to focus on specific symptoms in a short period of time—this may clash with this self-conception. Finally, changing the therapist's own role from active participation to a more distant view assessing the client's behaviors is challenging.

Consequently, there are many interesting things to be learned and practiced. A three-day introductory course followed by a one-day certification test has been conceptualized to implement the MUSAD. A detailed manual contains comprehensive information and instructions, and additional video tutorials are planned. A regular re-certification is envisaged, ensuring correct calibration of the scorings and allowing for discussions about the interpretation of results.

Research and psychometrics

Investigation of the psychometric properties of the MUSAD has been performed using the criteria for test quality, oriented towards the evaluation of established diagnostic tools and measures in the field. Two studies were applied. First, we piloted the new instrument (Bergmann, Sappok, Diefenbacher, Dames *et al.* 2015; Bergmann, Sappok, Diefenbacher, and Dziobek 2015). In a second sample, we validated the revised test draft (Bergmann *et al.* 2018).

Sample characteristics and study aims

Study 1 (1/2010–12/2011) was based on 80 adults with ID. Implementation and interpretation of the MUSAD failed in four cases due to a high level of irritability and sensory impairment. ASD was diagnosed in 50 participants (66%). The remaining 26 participants did not show ASD, but were diagnosed with schizophrenia, mood disorders, obsessive-compulsive behaviors, attention deficit hyperactivity disorder, and/or challenging behaviors. Study aims were to investigate:

- feasibility

- plausibility of the MUSAD concept and user-friendliness of scorings

- factorial validity

- construct reliability

- convergent and discriminant validity

- inter-rater agreement

- test-retest reliability.

Study 2 (1/2012–4/2016) was based on a sample of 129 adults. ASD was diagnosed in 78 cases (60%), compared to a non-ASD group of 51. Differential diagnoses were comparable to Study 1;

the ASD and non-ASD group did not differ significantly regarding gender, IQ, and age. Study aims were:

- item selection

- replication of the confirmatory factor analysis (Study 1)

- improvement of inter-rater reliability

- calculation of diagnostic validity.

Participants were consecutively included in the diagnostic procedure. Inclusion criteria were age > 18 years and the presence of an ID (*ICD-10*: F70–73), resulting in an ad-hoc sample reflecting clinical reality.

Procedure

MUSAD investigations were carried out by the test developer, who was also part of the multi-professional diagnostic workup. All sessions were videotaped, allowing for third-party behavioral observation. The ASD diagnosis decision was made by a multidisciplinary team consensus conference, consisting of at least one psychiatrist, a clinical psychologist, a special needs caregiver, therapists, and a member of the nursing staff who was experienced in the fields of ID and ASD. This multidisciplinary diagnostic workup was evaluated internally (Bergmann, Diefenbacher, Heinrich, and Sappok 2016) and is in accordance with current guidelines (National Institute for Health and Clinical Excellence 2012).

Results

Feasibility was 95 percent with a total failure rate of 4/80 (two incomplete due to rejection, two excluded due to sensory impairment). A subsample of 40 individuals was investigated with the MUSAD and the play-based ADOS. Again, feasibility of the MUSAD was 95 percent, and higher compared to 85 percent applying the ADOS.

Plausibility of the MUSAD concept and the user-friendliness of scorings have been supported by the fact that 12 independent raters completed the scoring of one case based on the written explanations according to the coding booklet without previous training. The absolute agreement among raters was acceptable (Intraclass Correlation Coefficient 2, 1=.67), and a questionnaire survey gained positive expert feedback on items, scorings, and procedure.

Factorial validity asks for the structural model of the MUSAD—which domains (factors) are necessary to describe the inter-correlation between the different items properly. The confirmatory factor analysis (CFA) was performed and revealed an adequate fit of a slightly modified three-factorial model (factor 1: social communication and interaction; factor 2: stereotyped, restricted, and repetitive behaviors, plus sensory issues; factor 3: motor coordination). Fit indices provide clues about the robustness of the scale structure. Fit indices of the CFA for all 37 items assessed in Study 1 were comparative fit index (CFI) = .97 and root mean square error of approximation (RMSEA) = .06, 90 percent confidence interval (CI) (.05, .07), indicating a good model fit. After including the deferred items in Study 2, the replication of the CFA based on 44 items resulted in slightly poorer values, but still supported the MUSAD factorial structure, which is in line with the *DSM-5*.

The construct reliability of each subscale, measured with McDonald's omega (McDonald 1999), was > .90 ($\Omega 1$ = .98; $\Omega 2$ = .94; and $\Omega 3$ = .92). This value can be interpreted as excellent in terms of internal consistency according to Cronbach's alpha (Cronbach 1951). Calculating Cronbach's alpha in Study 2, the average value for the total score increased to .95.

Convergent and discriminant validity indicate construct validity, i.e. the degree to which the MUSAD measures what it claims, or purports, to be measuring. This was done by comparing the MUSAD score with the scores of ASD and non-ASD measures applied in the same sample. The MUSAD total score was significantly correlated with the sum scores of the PDD-MRS (Kraijer and Bildt 2005), $r(37)$ = .55, p < .001, one-sided, an ASD interview measuring the same construct. As expected, analyses of divergent validity revealed a non-significant and negligible relationship between the MUSAD and the Modified Overt Aggression Scale (MOAS; Oliver *et al.* 2007), $r(56) = .15$, $p = .252$, a screener for aggressive behaviors not highly associated with core ASD symptomatology.

Inter-rater reliability refers to the degree of agreement among raters. This was measured by the Intraclass Correlation Coefficient (ICC; Shrout and Fleiss 1979). The agreement among two blinded raters was based on a stratified random sampling of 12 in Study 1. The ICC (2, 1) was .71, 95 percent CI (.59, .82), based on the final version including 37 items. The ICC (2, 1) across three raters (two blinded raters and the test developer) was .67, 95 percent CI (.62, .72). A value of .7 was seen as appropriate for a newly developed measure; however, when finalizing the MUSAD in Study 2, the improvement of inter-rater reliability was intended. Here, agreement among four independent raters based on n=25 cases and 24 selected items for the diagnostic algorithm resulted in an average ICC (1, 1) of .75 and ranged from .60 to .90. Agreement based on sum scores was excellent (ICC = .93).

Test-retest reliability was calculated by the correlation among four tests and retests in Study 1. Values ranged from .45 to .80 and resulted in an average ICC (3, 1) of .69. The high variation was caused by a statistical outlier, a person with severe impairment hard to assess. Including three retests from Study 2, the average ICC was .73, indicating good agreement.

Item selection was performed to identify the most valuable items for the calculation of a diagnostic algorithm. Balanced characteristics defined by thresholds, i.e. low rate of missing data ($\leq 5\%$), discriminant power (Gamma $> .5$, $r > .3$), and high inter-rater reliability (ICC $> .7$), were used for selection. Additionally, a wide range of item difficulties and content-related aspects were taken into account. This process resulted in 24 items overall: 13 items assessing social communication and interaction, 8 items assessing restricted and repetitive behaviors, and 3 items referring to motor coordination. There was a wide range of difficulties from self-injurious behavior (.04) to reaction to symbolic sounds (.74), but most items were of moderate difficulty.

Criterion validity is the extent to which a measure is related to an outcome. In this case, the external criterion was the diagnostic decision of a multidisciplinary consensus conference, based on biographical anamnesis, everyday observations, and established ASD measures. This was calculated using a Receiver Operating Characteristic (ROC) analysis indicating to what extent the MUSAD is able to recognize ASD (sensitivity) versus non-ASD (specificity) given a cut-off point for group separation. Applying a cut-off score of 29, sensitivity was 78 percent and specificity 76 percent. The area under the curve (AUC) was .80.

Taken together, the MUSAD was shown to be appropriate for assessing ASD in adults with limited speech: its plausibility was supported by expert judgement; objectivity (inter-rater reliability) was good to excellent, and reliability (test-retest, construct) was good to excellent as well; and the validity of the MUSAD construct was supported. A diagnostic algorithm based on 24 selected items correctly identified ASD and non-ASD in about 80 percent of cases, seen as appropriate against the background of a naturalistic study design reflecting clinical reality.

Future plans

A research version of the MUSAD coding booklet exists in German, and has already been translated into English and French. We are currently revising the instructions for implementation to make them more precise, comprehensive, self-explanatory, and straightforward. We hope that, at the time of publication of this essential assessment book, the MUSAD manual will be available in German. A current small-sized study includes potential users—music therapists, psychologists with musical experience, and psychologists with only basic musical skills—and aims to evaluate the width of implementability of the MUSAD and the objectivity of its application.

In applying the MUSAD in different areas of culture and speech, a new verification of its psychometric properties is required.

Colleagues working with children and youth highlighted the desire to implement the MUSAD for those with ID and limited speech. For use alongside the ADOS, a MUSAD short version as a simple ad-hoc screening measure seems reasonable. This version should be applicable during a regular music therapy session, should be also implementable by non-music therapists, and should require less training. Currently, a growing international network of music therapists and psychologists follows the notions of:

- implementing the MUSAD procedure with children and identifying appropriate musical-interactional situations

- selecting the most significant items and most valuable situations

- evaluating its psychometric properties.

Discussion

In summary, the MUSAD is a structured approach that uses the unique non-verbal and interactive quality of musical play in detecting ASD-specific behaviors in adults with limited speech. The instrument is well accepted among the group investigated, and its psychometric properties have been widely assessed, providing evidence for its diagnostic quality and its use within a multidisciplinary diagnostic workup. Here, music therapists in the field of people with ID are supported by the possibility of contributing substantially to ASD diagnostics by using an instrument comparable to established measures in the field. This expands the professional profile and may also contribute to anchoring music therapy more firmly within an institutional setting. The MUSAD fills a gap in diagnostic observational instruments assessing adults with ID. Perspectively, a short version for children and youth on a lower level of functioning may contribute to diagnostic clarification.

The above-mentioned AQR and the Individual Music-Centered Assessment Profile for Neurodevelopmental Disorders (IMCAP-ND;

Carpente 2013) are both assessments for intervention planning and therapy evaluation based on developmental theories requiring sensitivity to change in measuring a therapy process. Here, the MUSAD differs fundamentally in:

- assessing a state

- being free of theory but oriented to diagnostic manuals

- being structured in implementation

- focusing on a disorder.

Correct diagnostic classification is needed to ensure that appropriate treatment and support are identified and that this may result in radical changes, for example from medical treatment to non-medical strategies like education, shaping the environment, or even music therapy. The World Health Organization's International Classification of Functioning, Disability and Health (ICF; World Health Organization 2001) marked a paradigm shift in how health and disability are understood and measured. A comprehensive set of multiple dimensions of human functioning, synthesizing biological, psychological, social, and environmental aspects, allows for a more individualized picture of the client. Contemporary research in ASD aims to develop ICF core sets for children and youth with a broad range of items describing also strengths and potentials corresponding with a more dimensional view of autism as a spectrum (Schipper et al. 2015). Perceptively, this gives more detailed clues for support, treatment, and therapy planning, and may also influence further development of music therapy assessments in the field of ASD.

Acknowledgements

I wish to thank Stiftung Irene in Hamburg for financial support. Special thanks to Manuel Heinrich for a comprehensive review of this chapter.

References

American Psychiatric Association (2013) *Diagnostic and Statistical Manual of Mental Disorders: DSM-5.* Washington, DC: American Psychiatric Association.

Bergmann, T., Diefenbacher, A., Heinrich, M., and Sappok, T. (2016) 'Perspektivenverschränkung: Multiprofessionelle Autismusdiagnostik bei erwachsenen Menschen mit Intelligenzminderung und Autismusverdacht' [Entangled perspectives: A multiprofessional approach in diagnosing autism in adults with intellectual disability]. *Zeitschrift für Psychiatrie, Psychologie und Psychotherapie, 64,* 257–267.

Bergmann, T., Heinrich, M., Ziegler, M., Dziobek, I., Diefenbacher, A., and Sappok, T. (2018, forthcoming) 'Musical interaction helps in diagnosing autism in adults with intellectual disability: Validation of the MUSAD.'

Bergmann, T., Herberger, K., Birkner, J., and Sappok, T. (2016) 'A musical-bodily-based group training supporting adults with autism and intellectual disability.' *Nordic Journal of Music Therapy, 25,* 1, 119, doi.org/10.1080/08098131.2016.1180140.

Bergmann, T., Sappok, T., Diefenbacher, A., Dames, S., *et al.* (2015) 'Music-based autism diagnostics (MUSAD): A newly developed diagnostic measure for adults with intellectual developmental disabilities suspected of autism.' *Research in Developmental Disabilities, 43–44,* 123–135, doi.org/10.1016/j.ridd.2015.05.011.

Bergmann, T., Sappok, T., Diefenbacher, A., and Dziobek, I. (2015) 'Music in diagnostics: Using musical interactional settings for diagnosing autism in adults with intellectual developmental disabilities.' *Nordic Journal of Music Therapy, 25,* 4, 319–351, doi.org/10.1080/08098131.2015.1039567.

Bergmann, T., Sappok, T., Schumacher, K., and Diefenbacher, A. (2009) 'Musiktherapeutischer Ansatz in der Behandlung von Erwachsenen mit Autismus und geistiger Behinderung' [Music-therapeutic approach in the treatment of adults with autism and intellectual disability]. In F. Schneider and M. Groezinger (eds) *Psychische Erkrankungen in der Lebensspanne: Abstractband zum DGPPN Kongress 2009.* Berlin: DGPPN.

Berument, S. K., Starr, E., Pickles, A., Tomlins, M., Papanikolauou, K., Lord, C., and Rutter, M. (2005) 'Pre-Linguistic Autism Diagnostic Observation Schedule adapted for older individuals with severe to profound mental retardation: A pilot study.' *Journal of Autism and Developmental Disorders, 35,* 6, 821–829, doi.org/10.1007/s10803-005-0027-4.

Bryson, S. E., Bradley, E. A., Thompson, A., and Wainwright, A. (2008) 'Prevalence of autism among adolescents with intellectual disabilities.' *Canadian Journal of Psychiatry, 53,* 7, 449–459.

Carpente, J. A. (2013) *IMCAP-ND: The Individual Music-Centered Assessment Profile for Neurodevelopmental Disorders: A Clinical Manual.* North Baldwin, NY: Regina Publishers.

Cronbach, L. J. (1951) 'Coefficient alpha and the internal structure of tests.' *Psychometrika, 16,* 3, 297–334, doi.org/10.1007/BF02310555.

Fournier, K. A., Hass, C. J., Naik, S. K., Lodha, N., and Cauraugh, J. H. (2010) 'Motor coordination in autism spectrum disorders: A synthesis and meta-analysis.' *Journal of Autism and Developmental Disorders, 40,* 10, 1227–1240, doi.org/10.1007/s10803-010-0981-3.

Gillberg, I. C. and Gillberg, C. (1989) 'Asperger syndrome? Some epidemiological considerations: A research note.' *Journal of Child Psychology and Psychiatry, 30,* 4, 631–638, doi.org/10.1111/j.1469-7610.1989.tb00275.x.

Howlin, P. (2000) 'Autism and intellectual disability: Diagnostic and treatment issues.' *Journal of the Royal Society of Medicine, 93,* 7, 351–355.

Howlin, P., Goode, S., Hutton, J., and Rutter, M. (2004) 'Adult outcome for children with autism.' *Journal of Child Psychology and Psychiatry, 45,* 2, 212–229, doi.org/10.1111/j.1469-7610.2004.00215.x.

Kraijer, D. W. and Bildt, A. de (2005) 'The PDD-MRS: An instrument for identification of autism spectrum disorders in persons with mental retardation.' *Journal of Autism and Developmental Disorders, 35,* 4, 499–513.

Lord, C., Rutter, M., DiLavore, P. C., Risi, S., Gotham, K., and Bishop, S. L. (2012) *Autism Diagnostic Observation Schedule* (2nd edition). Los Angeles, CA: Western Psychological Services.

Lord, C., Rutter, M., and Le Couteur, A. (1994) 'Autism Diagnostic Interview-Revised: A revised version of a diagnostic interview for caregivers of individuals with possible pervasive developmental disorders.' *Journal of Autism and Developmental Disorders, 24,* 5, 659–685.

Maulik, P. K., Mascarenhas, M. N., Mathers, C. D., Dua, T., and Saxena, S. (2011) 'Prevalence of intellectual disability: A meta-analysis of population-based studies.' *Research in Developmental Disabilities, 32,* 2, 419–436, doi.org/10.1016/j.ridd.2010.12.018.

McCarthy, J., Hemmings, C., Kravariti, E., Dworzynski, K., Holt, G., Bouras, N., and Tsakanikos, E. (2010) 'Challenging behavior and co-morbid psychopathology in adults with intellectual disability and autism spectrum disorders.' *Research in Developmental Disabilities, 31,* 2, 362–366, doi.org/10.1016/j.ridd.2009.10.009.

McDonald, R. P. (1999) *Test Theory: A Unified Treatment.* Mahwah, NJ: L. Erlbaum Associates.

Mesibov, G. B., Shea, V., and Schopler, E. (2004) *The TEACCH Approach to Autism Spectrum Disorders.* New York, NY: Springer.

National Institute for Health and Clinical Excellence (2012) *Autism Spectrum Disorder in Adults: Diagnosis and Management.* Retrieved 27/01/2018 from www.nice.org.uk/guidance/cg142/chapter/1-guidance.

Oliver, P. C., Crawford, M. J., Rao, B., Reece, B., and Tyrer, P. (2007) 'Modified Overt Aggression Scale (MOAS) for people with intellectual disability and aggressive challenging behaviour: A reliability study.' *Journal of Applied Research in Intellectual Disabilities, 20,* 4, 368–372, doi.org/10.1111/j.1468-3148.2006.00346.x.

Sappok, T., Diefenbacher, A., Budczies, J., Schade, C., *et al.* (2013) 'Diagnosing autism in a clinical sample of adults with intellectual disabilities: How useful are the ADOS and the ADI-R?' *Research in Developmental Disabilities, 34,* 5, 1642–1655, doi.org/10.1016/j.ridd.2013.01.028.

Sappok, T., Gaul, I., Bergmann, T., Dziobek, I., *et al.* (2014) 'The Diagnostic Behavioral Assessment for Autism Spectrum Disorder—Revised: A screening instrument for adults with intellectual disability suspected of autism spectrum disorders.' *Research in Autism Spectrum Disorders, 8,* 4, 362–375, doi.org/10.1016/j.rasd.2013.12.016.

Schipper, E. de., Lundequist, A., Coghill, D., Vries, P. J., *et al.* (2015) 'Ability and disability in autism spectrum disorder: A systematic literature review employing the International Classification of Functioning, Disability and Health—Children and Youth Version.' *Official Journal of the International Society for Autism Research, 8,* 6, 782–794, doi.org/10.1002/aur.1485.

Schumacher, K. and Calvet, C. (2007) 'The "AQR-Instrument" – An Observation Instrument to Assess the Quality of Relationship.' In T. Wosch and T. Wigram (eds) *Microanalysis in Music Therapy – Methods, Techniques and Applications for Clinicians, Researchers, Educators and Students.* London: Jessica Kingsley Publishers.

Shrout, P. E. and Fleiss, J. L. (1979) 'Intraclass correlations: Uses in assessing rater reliability.' *Psychological Bulletin, 86,* 2, 420–428.

Srinivasan, S. M. and Bhat, A. N. (2013) 'A review of "music and movement" therapies for children with autism: Embodied interventions for multisystem development.' *Frontiers in Integrative Neuroscience, 7,* 22, doi.org/10.3389/fnint.2013.00022.

Tsakanikos, E., Costello, H., Holt, G., Sturmey, P., and Bouras, N. (2007) 'Behaviour management problems as predictors of psychotropic medication and use of psychiatric services in adults with autism.' *Journal of Autism and Developmental Disorders, 37,* 6, 1080–1085.

Williams, J. H. (2008) 'Self–other relations in social development and autism: Multiple roles for mirror neurons and other brain bases.' *Autism Research, 1,* 2, 73–90, doi.org/10.1002/aur.15.

World Health Organization (2001) *ICF: The International Classification of Functioning, Disability and Health.* Geneva: World Health Organization.

CHAPTER 8

The Individual Music Therapy Assessment Profile

Penny Roberts

Setting and motivation

The process of writing and publishing the IMTAP (Individual Music Therapy Assessment Profile) took four years and innumerable weekend and after-work meetings, all done without funding from any source. The longest portion of that time was spent determining the skills that were appropriate for each level and ensuring the IMTAP could be applied to a wide variety of ages, followed by settling on a scoring system. The IMTAP came about as a practical solution to a number of workplace challenges, including differences in training, philosophical approach, and communication. When I joined the team in 2002, Ron Borczon and Judy Nelson (JN) were both teaching music therapy at California State University, Northridge. Ron had an extensive background in his work with a number of populations and had settled into working with adults in trauma at the clinic, teaching classes, and serving as the Director of the Music Therapy Wellness Clinic (MTWC). Judy was considering returning to school to pursue a degree in speech and language pathology and taught several music therapy courses.

The other members of the clinical team at the MTWC were Holly Tuesday Baxter, MT-BC (HTB), Kasi Ann Peters, MT-BC (KAP),

Julie Berghofer, RMT (JAB), and Lesa MacEwan, MT-BC (LME). HTB
utilized technology and included song-writing, self-expression, and
performance goals in groups with at-risk youth from impacted areas of
Los Angeles. JAB was the most experienced clinician and a seasoned
Nordoff-Robbins therapist with training from Clive Robbins himself.
LME had a master's degree in special education and worked as a
special education teacher in the Los Angeles Unified School District
in grades kindergarten to 12. In her work with children with autism,
KAP used the Floortime™ method both at the MTWC and another
clinic. I came from a background in piano pedagogy and a master's
degree in music therapy at Florida State University, with its emphasis
on behavioral techniques and quantitative-driven data collection. We
were a unique mix of talents, abilities, and strong opinions.

The clinic had recently become much more solidified in its
position in the community, both literally and figuratively. We had
recently acquired a clinic space with two treatment rooms, each with
piano, guitar, two-way mirrors, and audio wiring to allow for parent
and student observation. This was a huge change from the original
clinic, which was located in an off-hours classroom and had only a
piano and chair! This dedicated space epitomized Ron's efforts to
make the MTWC a presence in the community, and also suggested
it was time to adopt a coherent assessment and documentation tool
that would accommodate and support all the styles of music therapy
we practiced.

Like many other music therapists, the therapists at the MTWC
were using a self-created assessment appropriate for our clients and
setting (Wigram, Bonde, and Pedersen 2002). Prior to the IMTAP,
our assessment was narrative-based and had specific blanks for
gross motor, fine motor, vocalizations, and overall client strengths
and weaknesses, and a section for client goals, objectives, and the
dates met. The assessment was supplemented by reports from other
therapists (occupational, speech, etc.), the local Regional Center
(which provided funding for music therapy clients at that time),
individual education plans (IEPs), and any other information or

reports we may access. In Ron Borczon we were fortunate to have leadership that acknowledged each of our strengths and different approaches to music therapy and encouraged this individuality. However, in staff meetings we grappled to communicate with each other to explain which techniques we were using and why, how we had assessed which skill, and how this related to the overall picture of each client.

The IMTAP team began to meet regularly in 2003, although at that time working only to create an assessment solely for clinic use. However, as we realized the scope of this project, we began to consider the state of music therapy assessments in general, recognized the need in the community, and considered publication. Through the many discussions about goals, objectives, data collection, and techniques, as the IMTAP meetings progressed, our goal remained the same—to produce a thorough music therapy assessment—but we soon discovered we all used different jargon and had different assessment priorities. Unsurprisingly, JAB's focus gravitated toward the music the child produced, KAP's inclined toward how the client used instruments, JN was captivated with the child's emerging language, HTB was concerned about looming adolescent skills, LME wanted to make sure music therapy treatment goals translated to IEP goals, and I was concerned with observable pre- and post-data. To complicate matters, we sometimes used different terminology to describe the same thing, and we weren't sure if this was a strength or a weakness of our team.

Further, what seemed at first like mere differences in jargon also revealed differences in approach that were not always easy to resolve. This was most memorably demonstrated as we struggled to come to an agreement on the word "appropriate." Although inherently understood, this word is problematic for several reasons: What is appropriate? Who determines that? What are the metrics involved? Is a child with autism striving to be socially appropriate, or to be socially comfortable? What is the purpose of social appropriateness? To which cultural norm are we appealing? We discussed this as a group over several IMTAP meetings, resolved it, circled back, and tackled it again. It was frustrating, time consuming, and ultimately enlightening. After the "appropriate" dust settled, we realized we also had to define each and every skill (374!)—after all, what exactly is a simple/intermediate/advanced rhythmic pattern? Our disparities may be most easily understood in the framework of validity, and we asked each other and ourselves several questions regarding validity: Did/could/should the IMTAP relate to current IEP and other therapeutic goals? Did the IMTAP domains accurately translate to real-world skills, and abilities? And, if we all approached music therapy from different theoretical frameworks, how could we be sure we were all assessing the same thing? These discussions were often frustrating; however, it is a representation of the true nature of the music therapy community at our clinic that, although we believed and worked in different ways, we all had the topmost benefit of the client, the music therapy community, and our clinic at the center of our practice.

Perhaps most uniquely, the IMTAP included an assessment specifically for musical ability. As late as 2004, a survey of music therapists working with children with special needs found only 35 percent assessed for musical responses and/or abilities (Chase 2004). In particular, we believed it was important to the overall picture of a child's abilities to include their innate musical talent: for example, in our experience, a child may be developmentally delayed in language and fine motor skills, but may show an intrinsic sense of rhythm via drumming and display a talent for musical form and structure by unprompted harmonization (Heaton 2009; Wigram 2000). It is unlikely these strengths would have been discovered by any other therapy! Further, the acknowledgement of cross-domain and related skills (those that are present in two or more domains) may reveal areas of deficit in one area and an area of strength in another. For example, a child with a low oral motor score may display a high score in vocalizing, suggesting a natural area of work and progression. We felt—and feel—strongly that music therapy is unique in its ability to recognize, assess, elicit, and develop these talents and abilities, and we believe that the inclusion of a client's musical tastes, abilities, and accomplishments is paramount in every music therapy document or report. For this reason, although the therapist may include or remove any of the other nine domains, the "Musicality" domain in the IMTAP is always indicated as appropriate for assessment. JAB took the lead in creating a sensitive and thoughtful menu of activities, interpretations, and suggestions that are accessible to both new and experienced therapists, and these are included for therapist reference.

We assessed our own clients using the IMTAP-beta, and then performed blinded (to the domain being scored) inter-rated reliability tests with our clinic clients. The team discussed scores that were significantly different, altered and edited the document, and then tested and scored another session. We continued this process until we reached a within-clinic therapist reliability greater than 75 percent. After the team settled on the final product, we chose several therapists (including music, speech, occupational, and physical therapists) and sent them the entire package for beta testing. These generous professionals returned the IMTAP-beta with feedback and suggestions, and we were able to implement necessary changes immediately. Ultimately, the IMTAP accommodated all of our primary concerns and preferences and allowed for individuality of the client, culture, and community.

Theoretical background

In particular, music therapy is both blessed and cursed with a lack of standardization (Bieleninik, Ghetti, and Gold 2016; Hohmann *et al.* 2017). That is, music is fraught with numerous fluid variables (pitch, rhythm, inflection, etc.), and music therapists often respond to clients by adapting these elements (Jackson 2010; Spiro and Himberg 2016). In fact, it is the ability to adapt in every moment, allowing music therapists to communicate their attention and dedication to their clients, that fosters a unique connection. However, this unique personalization—on the part of the client, the therapist, and the client-therapist relationship and, therefore, resulting lack of standardization in the methodology—has also been one major criticism of music therapy research (Raglio *et al.* 2008). Unfortunately, "well intentioned, and often rigorous work, is spoiled by a lack of research methodology" (Aldridge 1994, p. 204; Silverman 2007). That is, without reproducibility of research, we cannot be sure the results are reliable; however, in a dynamic therapeutic relationship such as music therapy, the conditions are—and we would argue should be—invariably different.

In the Nordoff-Robbins approach, "therapists' interventions occurred in the music, the clients' developmental process was ascertained through musical responses" (New York University 2017). In this way, each client's music is personal, poetic, and a meaningful communication that is un-measurable in value. Like the Nordoff-Robbins approach, Floortime™ seeks to use the responses of the client as a starting point for reciprocal interaction and "takes into account an individual's intrinsic level of interest and then expands on that initial level of motivation to incorporate mutual interest of others" (Hess 2013, p. 269). Behavioral music therapy also shapes behavior, but uses musical cue, somatic and temporal structure, reward, and attention focus (Wheeler *et al.* 2012). This method can be more focused on the reaction to intervention—that is, tracking and recording desired responses—rather than their interpretation.

The IMTAP's current form and function were informed by several impactful realizations. First, we wanted to create an assessment that focused on what the clients could do, rather than on what they were unable to do. This was a major shift in our thinking, and caused us to rewrite anything that had been written with a view towards deficits in a more client-positive manner. We remained in this mode of thought and approach to the project until completion.

Second, domain goals were shaped in terms of developmental milestones; that is, we determined that Level 1 skills were those present at 0–18 months, Level 2 skills present at 36 months, and so on. This form was influenced by the work of several resources, including the Centers for Disease Control and Protection (2018) and interviews with our colleagues at physical, occupation, speech, and music therapy centers.

The IMTAP tool

Psychometrics

The validity of the IMTAP was one of our primary concerns. We felt that a useful music therapy assessment required concurrent validity (relationship to current IEP and other therapeutic goals), face validity (agreement that it measures what it aims to measure), and predictive validity (accurate predictions of future behavior).

The IMTAP utilizes an ordinal measurement scale. It has an absolute zero and can be ordered; however, the difference between values is not exactly the same between ranks—that is, the difference between "rarely" and "inconsistent" is not the same as between "inconsistent" and "consistent" in one skill, and likely not the same between two skills. There are ten skill domains (gross motor, fine motor, sensory, receptive communication, auditory perception, expressive communication, cognitive skills, emotional skills, social skills, and musicality) and 306 scoreable items.

The IMTAP was different at the time in two ways. First, it came with a CD-ROM that placed quantitative measurement at the clinician's fingertips. The software then generated a report immediately that could be printed out to include in a client file and referenced later for IEP or team meetings, to view and track progress, discuss development with parents, and so on. Further, it allowed for a client's unique profile to be developed within a framework of general functional goals. However, we also recognized that not all music therapists would have access to or be comfortable with computerized assessment, and so we chose to ensure that the paper system would be accessible and easy to manually score.

Population

Second, although our clinic served mostly children with special needs at the time of the IMTAP's creation, including skills for those aged 5 years and above ensures that adolescents and adults can be assessed with this tool. Unlike other assessments that are for specific age groups (e.g. a geriatric assessment), the IMTAP is applicable to a variety of ages and abilities. The intake and session planning are conducted by the therapist, allowing for cultural considerations as well, making the IMTAP a flexible resource. In particular, the IMTAP was, to our knowledge, the first to clarify the progression through intake and assessment by providing parents, guardians, and therapists with an interview format specifically designed to narrow the domains to be assessed and, therefore, tailor the assessment sessions.

Procedure

The IMTAP procedure is as follows:

1. Complete intake.

2. Plan and prepare session.

3. Conduct assessment sessions.

4. Compute final score, evaluation of cross-domain skills, and summary.

5. Create goals and objectives.

6. Create domain and subdomain profile graphs.

Interpretation

The IMTAP includes several forms that assist with ensuring the assessment procedure can be consistent from client to client and therapist to therapist, increasing methodological stability. An intake form is included that collects relevant information in each of the ten domains, then refers the therapist to the domains indicated;

for example, if the intake questions indicate deficits in emotional processing, the emotional processing box is checked on the intake summary. There are several suggestions for musical activities appropriate for assessment sessions, and the IMTAP guides the therapist through completing assessment. Importantly, the activities included are suggestions; the completing music therapist is ultimately the creator of the assessment sessions! In each unit of the profile package there are music therapist signature and date lines, creating a logical, progressive, signed, and dated document.

For those collecting quantitative data, behavior is observed and the percentage of time a client displays this behavior during that observation period is recorded in an interval recording technique: never (0%), rarely (<50%), inconsistently (50–79%), or consistently (80–100%) (NRIC). In this way, the recording is both an interval and a frequency recording: we are recording the number of times (converted to a percentage range with NRIC schema) a behavior occurred during a predetermined amount of time. The number of NRIC scores is then tallied to give an overall indicator of functionality in each domain. Relating to our desire to view the client in a positive light, the resulting score is not necessarily a composite of scores across a normality scale; rather, it is an indication of which skills the client was able to perform successfully. For example, a very young child would not be expected to perform level IV skills—their absence is not a failure; rather, the therapist can choose to omit them from the assessment or not include them in the final output. Therefore, the resulting document is a profile of each client's performance, and all subsequent assessments are compared to the original rather than a pre-existing composite gold standard of appropriate accomplishments at a certain age.

The therapist either then manually calculates, or the IMTAP software creates, a profile of client responses, and a graph is generated that is the total sum of client abilities and needs in all assessed domains.

Analysis and results

The total result of this assessment is a document that can be invaluable in a number of settings such as IEPs and the parental progress meeting, and referenced on change of therapist. Most importantly, when an assessment is filmed, the therapist is recording objective NRIC responses—there is no in-the-moment discernment required, leaving no room for interpretation or disagreement. This disproves the oft-cited concern that music therapy's results are subjective, and provides quantitative data to support findings.

Training

An additional advantage of the IMTAP is its accessibility as a professional tool. That is, it contains extensive yet thoroughly explained and detailed instructions on how to use the IMTAP. It does not require specialized training, nor do the authors require an annual certification or licensure renewal; the IMTAP was designed with intent that, after using it for the first time, the music therapist would be easily able to use it from then onward.

Research

Since its publication in 2007, the IMTAP has been used for numerous studies, articles, theses, and dissertations (Berger 2009; de Araujo *et al.* 2018; Mariath *et al.* 2017; Moereira *et al.* 2016; Salokivi 2012; Twyford and Watters 2016) and has been translated or mentioned in publications in Korean (Yong 2014), Portuguese (da Silva *et al.* 2013), and Finnish (Letule 2016). In addition to music therapy schools in the United States, students and researchers in Israel, Finland, Taiwan, Latvia, and Brazil have contacted the IMTAP team to request permission (and it was granted!) to use it for school-related work. We look forward to its continued use.

Future plans and discussion

The IMTAP software—the CD accompanying each book—is due for an upgrade. HTB dabbled in *FileMaker* programming prior to the IMTAP, and the project was a huge undertaking. However, because she has continued her professional development in areas other than computer programming, the software has not been updated. Further, because technology has changed such that students seem to rarely use CD-ROMs, we anticipate an online replacement. We are also interested in expanding the format to include populations other than children and young adults, and continue to communicate with one another on this possibility.

Screening for developmental milestones has also continued to evolve, with the pediatrics community changing its guidelines and suggestions for assessment (Brooke 2006; Hicks *et al.* 2010; Limbos and Joyce 2011). For example, the American Academy of Pediatrics (2016) continues to release statements that include updated developmental screening materials; a revised release of the IMTAP will certainly include the latest developmental recommendations and data from the medical and therapeutic communities.

Additionally, the music therapy community has benefited from several excellent assessments published since our original 2007 publication. Currently, there are three assessments for children available—the IMTAP (Baxter *et al.* 2007), the Music Therapy Social Skills Assessment and Documentation (MTSSA; Dennis *et al.* 2014), and the Individual Music-Centered Assessment Profile for Neurodevelopmental Disorders (IMCAP-ND; Carpente 2013)— and none available for purchase on the American Music Therapy Association website. The MTSSA focuses on social skills in a group context, while the IMTAP is applicable to both group and individual and includes social skills among the domains. Like the IMTAP, the MTSSA has suggestions for session planning and includes a CD-ROM with forms, and its scoring is designed to collect the highest number of times a behavior was observed in a timeframe. The IMCAP-ND is scored in three domains: Musical Emotional (emotional response to music, including attention, engagement, and playing), Musical Cognitive/Perception (including initiation, recall, and follow musical elements), and Musical Responsiveness (incorporating a client's preferences and self-regulation in response to music). This tool and the IMTAP have many features in common, including a criterion-based frequency of response scoring system and the populations for which they were designed and are appropriate.

Last, when deciding to publish, we were faced with another difficult research issue. While we had struggled with these concepts in our own team, we recognized that we did not have the resources to fully study the IMTAP's reliability and validity. Although the beta testing indicated it was both valid and reliable, we did not have the time, funding, or resources to conduct a larger study prior to dissemination. We chose instead to place the IMTAP immediately into the hands of our greatest resource: our fellow music therapists. We hope the IMTAP will continue to be used for dissertations, theses, and studies that will inform future editions, and look forward to learning more about how it can best serve the music therapy community.

In a recent email to me, HTB said that our goal was to produce a "usable, functional multi-domain assessment that gave clear indications for goals, provided a quantitative means to assess client progress, and allowed therapists of all levels (from entry to master therapist) to use it." In summary, the IMTAP was a response to:

- a diverse team of music therapists who respected the approaches of one another and sought to foster teamwork

- a diverse client population

- understandable and correct reactions to music therapy that asked for more quantification

- the desire to acknowledge and protect the uniqueness of the music therapy intervention

- the challenge to meld the quantitative and qualitative assessment styles to create a fuller picture of our clients

- the need to create a profile that could be understood by and collaborated on with therapists from other disciplines.

We have attempted to balance the quantification with an acknowledgement of client uniqueness by shaping it as a profile of many different domains rather than a measurement of developmental norms. We further recognize the distinct intervention of music therapy by including a musicality domain that is rich in opportunities for clients to show musical ability and preferences. We are eager to see the field grow and change and we welcome new assessments and continue to be honored to be among them.

References

Aldridge, A. (1994) 'An overview of music therapy research.' *Complementary Therapies in Medicine, 2,* 204–216.

American Academy of Pediatrics (2016) 'Recommendations for pediatric and preventive healthcare.' *Pediatrics, 137,* 1, doi: 10.1542/peds2015-3908.

Baxter, H. T., Berghofer, J. A., MacEwan, L., Nelson, J., Peters, K. A., and Roberts, P. (2007) *The Individualized Music Therapy Assessment Profile.* London: Jessica Kingsley Publishers.

Berger, D. (2009) 'On developing music therapy goals and objectives.' *Voices: A World Forum for Music Therapy, 9,* 1, doi: 10.15845/voices.v9i1.362.

Bieleninik, L., Ghetti, C., and Gold, C. (2016) 'Music therapy for preterm infants and their parents: A meta-analysis.' *Pediatrics, 138,* 3, doi: 10.1542/peds.2016-0971.

Brooke, S. (2006) *Creative Arts Therapies Manual: A Guide to the History, Theoretical Approaches, Assessment, and Work with Special Populations of Art, Play, Dance, Music, Drama, and Poetry Therapies.* Springfield, IL: Charles C. Thomas.

Carpente, J. (2013) *The Individual Music-Centered Assessment Profile for Neurodevelopmental Disorders (IMCAP-ND): A Clinical Manual.* North Baldwin, NY: Regina Publishers.

Centers for Disease Control and Protection (2018) *Developmental Milestones.* Retrieved 27/01/2018 from www.cdc.gov/ncbddd/actearly/milestones/index.html.

Chase, K. M. (2004) 'Music therapy assessment for children with developmental disabilities: A survey study.' *Journal of Music Therapy, 41,* 28–54, doi: 10.1093/jmt/41.1.28.

da Silva, A. M., Gattino, G. S., de Araujo, G. A., Mariath, L. M., Riesgo, R. S., and Schuler-Faccini, L. (2013) 'Translation to Brazilian Portuguese language and validation of the Individualized Music Therapy Assessment Profile (IMTAP) scale for use in Brazil.' *Revista Brasileira de Musicoterapia, 14,* 67–80.

de Araujo, G., Leite, J., Gattino, G. S., Heck, C., *et al.* (2018, forthcoming) 'Music therapy intervention effects in the non-declarative memory of children with Williams syndrome.' *Arts in Psychotherapy.*

Dennis, A., Ho, P., West, R., Peyton, K., *et al.* (2014) *Music Therapy Social Skills Assessment and Documentation Manual (MTSSA): Clinical Guidelines for Group Work with Children and Adolescents.* London: Jessica Kingsley Publishers.

Heaton, P. (2009) 'Assessing music skills in autistic children who are not savants.' *Philosophical Transactions of the Royal Society B: Biological Sciences, 27,* 364, doi: 10.1098/rstb.2008.0327.

Hess, E. (2013) 'DIR®/Floortime™: Evidence based practice towards the treatment of autism and sensory processing disorder in children and adolescents.' *International Journal of Health and Human Development, 6,* 3, 267–274.

Hicks, P. J., Englander, R., Schumacher, D. J., Burke, A., *et al.* (2010) 'Pediatrics Milestone Project: Next steps toward meaningful outcomes assessment.' *Journal of Graduate Medical Education, 2,* 4, 577–584.

Hohmann, L., Bradt, J., Stegemann, T., and Koelsch, S. (2017) 'Effects of music therapy and music-based interventions in the treatment of substance use disorders: A systematic review.' *PLoS One,* doi: 10.1371/journal.pone.0187363.

Jackson, N. (2010) 'Models of response to client anger in music therapy.' *Arts in Psychotherapy, 37,* 1, 46–55.

Letule, N. (2016) 'An assessment model for the musical material produced during the course of music therapy.' *Casa Baubo. 2° Seminario Internacional de Jazz y Musicoterapia 2014,* 64–83.

Limbos, M. and Joyce, D. (2011) 'Comparison of the ASQ and PEDS in screening for developmental delay in children presenting for primary care.' *Journal of Developmental & Behavioral Pediatrics, 32,* 7, 499–511, doi: 10.1097/DBP.0b013e31822552e9.

Mariath, L. M., da Silva, A. M., Kowalski, T. W., Gattino, G. S., *et al.* (2017) 'Music genetics research: Association with musicality of a polymorphism in the AVPR1A gene.' *Genetics and Molecular Biology, 40,* 2, 421–429, doi: 10.1590/1678-4685-GMB-2016-0021.

Moreira, S., Gattino, G., Ferrari, K., Alcântara-Silva, T., Araujo, G., and Ortega, I. (2016) 'Assessment in music therapy: Strategies and applications to clinical practice in an international perspective.' *Nordic Journal of Music Therapy, 25,* 95, doi: 10.1080/08098131.2016.1180082.

New York University (2017) *Nordoff-Robbins Center for Music Therapy: Developments.* Retrieved 13/12/2017 from http://steinhardt.nyu.edu/music/nordoff/developments.

Raglio, A., Bellelli, G., Traficante, D., Gianotti, M., *et al.* (2008) 'Efficacy of music therapy in the treatment of behavioral and psychiatric symptoms of dementia.' *Alzheimer Disease & Associated Disorders, 22,* 2, 158–162.

Salokivi, M. (2012) 'The Individualized Music Therapy Assessment Profile as an Initial Assessment Tool of Social Emotional Functioning.' Unpublished master's thesis, Department of Music, Faculty of Humanities, University of Jyväskylä, Finland. Retrieved 13/12/2017 from https://jyx.jyu.fi/dspace/bitstream/handle/123456789/40439/URN:NBN:fi:jyu-201211273079.pdf?sequence=1.

Silverman, M. J. (2007) 'Evaluating current trends in psychiatric music therapy: A descriptive analysis.' *Journal of Music Therapy, 44,* 4, 388–414.

Spiro, N. and Himberg, T. (2016) 'Analysing change in music therapy interactions of children with communication difficulties.' *Philosophical Transactions of the Royal Society B: Biological Sciences, 371,* 1693, doi: 10.1098/rstb.2015.0374.

Twyford, K. and Watters, S. (2016) 'In the groove: An evaluation to explore a joint music therapy and occupational therapy intervention for children with acquired brain injury.' *Voices: A World Forum for Music Therapy, 16,* 1, doi: 10.15845/voices. v16i1.851.

Wheeler, B., Wagner, G., Summer, L., Madsen, C., Turry, A., and Eschen, J. (2012) 'Five international models of music therapy practice.' *Voices: A World Forum for Music Therapy, 12,* 1, doi: 10.15845/voices.v12i1.634.

Wigram, T. (2000) 'A method of music therapy assessment for the diagnosis of autism and communication disorders in children.' *Music Therapy Perspectives, 18,* 1, 13–22.

Wigram, T. P., Bonde, L. O., and Pedersen, I. N. (2002) *A Comprehensive Guide to Music Therapy.* London: Jessica Kingsley Publishers.

Yong, S. (2014) 'An Exploratory Inquiry into Music Therapy Assessment for Children with Special Needs.' Unpublished master's thesis, Seoul National University Graduate School, College of Education, Program of Special Education, South Korea.

CHAPTER 9

Event-Based Analysis

Tony Wigram and Stine Lindahl Jacobsen[1]

Tony Wigram is one of the legends in music therapy assessment. Even though he is no longer with us, the editors of the book got permission from Jessica Kingsley Publishers and Jenny Wigram to use Wigram's own writing about the assessment tool Event-Based Analysis (EBA) which has been used and implemented widely by music therapists in both research and clinical practice. The text is largely based on his descriptions and reflections and the second author primarily merged different publications, updated statements about research and literature, and ensured a natural flow and transitions between sections.

Setting and motivation

For many years, I have been concerned with eliciting evidence from a music therapy assessment to support a diagnostic formulation within

---

1   The text in this chapter is based on the following publications: Wigram, T. (2004) *Improvisation: Methods and Techniques for Music Therapy Clinicians, Educators and Students.* London: Jessica Kingsley Publishers; Wigram, T. (2007) 'Event-Based Analysis of Improvisation Using the Improvisational Assessment Profiles (IAPs).' In T. Wosch and T. Wigram (eds) *Microanalysis in Music Therapy – Methods, Techniques and Applications for Clinicians, Researchers, Educators and Students.* London: Jessica Kingsley Publishers; Wosch, T. (2007) 'Microanalysis of Processes of Interactions in Clinical Improvisation with IAP-Autonomy.' In T. Wosch and T. Wigram (eds) *Microanalysis in Music Therapy – Methods, Techniques and Applications for Clinicians, Researchers, Educators and Students.* London: Jessica Kingsley Publishers.

the field of child and adolescent psychiatry, which formed the basis for the development of the use of the Improvisation Assessment Profiles (IAPs) and EBA (Wigram 2007).

The fundamental rationale for diagnostic formulation in music therapy is the connection between musical material, pathological problems, and therapeutic process. When presenting the results of a music therapy assessment, or a period of music therapy, the documentation of musical material and the analysis of the musical experience that has been present during the session(s) with clients have specific connections to therapeutic issues including change or lack of change. Therefore, the analysis involves examining the "function" of the music in order to establish connections to pathological problems and therapeutic process (Wigram 2004).

One assessment procedure that focuses specifically on musical elements as the basis for analyzing change or lack of change in clients is IAPs (Bruscia 1987), and this is the tool I think is the most comprehensive and relevant way to explain the function of the music. Despite the fact that IAPs have been in the literature for some years, there is quite a limited use of this assessment method in its full format, perhaps because it is a complex, detailed, and extensive method of analysis. In the complete set of IAPs, Bruscia has defined six specific areas of potential analysis: autonomy, variability, integration, salience, tension, and congruence. Each profile provides criteria for analyzing improvisation, and the criteria for all the profiles form a "continuum of five gradients or levels, ranging from one extreme or polarity to its opposite" (Bruscia 1987, p. 406).

To use these profiles in an economic and effective way to analyze musical material, it is necessary to follow the recommendations and guidelines that Bruscia offers for using IAPs. Part of this process involves reducing the amount of material to be analyzed to that which is both pertinent and essential, and then choosing the appropriate profile(s) to apply. The practical application of IAPs can include both quantitative and qualitative analysis. I want to explain the method by which I apply this comprehensive assessment tool, describing both the decisions I take and the use of the parameters Bruscia has incorporated for analysis (Wigram 2007).

Theoretical background

Of Bruscia's six areas for analysis, the two profiles that I use most frequently for the analysis of musical material with children who have communication disorder are autonomy and variability (Wigram 1999, 2000), and so I will use these two for the purposes of explaining the method I use in this analysis. For the original and comprehensive text on IAPs, see Bruscia (1987).

> The autonomy profile deals with the kinds of role relationships formed between the improvisers. The scales within the profile describe the extent to which each musical element and component is used to lead or follow the other. (Bruscia 1987, p. 405)

> The variability profile deals with how sequential aspects of the music are organised and related. Scales within the profile describe the extent to which each musical element or component stays the same or changes. (Bruscia 1987, p. 404)

For the purposes of aiding diagnostic assessment, these two profiles are relevant and useful in differentiating between children who have autism (ASD), or some other variant of pervasive development disorder, such as Asperger syndrome (mild ASD) and pervasive developmental disorder not otherwise specified (PDDNOS), or communication disorder. Autonomy helps one look closely at the interpersonal events that are going on, particularly the readiness of a child to work with a therapist or another, take turns, share, and act as a partner. The profile also identifies style and quality of playing that demonstrates either resistance to suggestion, maybe an independent attitude, or conversely becoming extremely dependent and reliant. Variability can illustrate at an inter- and intramusical level a child's capacity for creativity, or evidence of a child's rigid or repetitive way of playing that might support a diagnosis on the autistic continuum. This profile is helpful for teasing out the quality of a child's play and, as the music therapy improvisational approach searches for and promotes creativity and expression as the medium for both social engagement and communication, the degree of variability helps identify a child's flexibility and creativity (Wigram 2007).

The Event-Based Analysis procedure

Two to three assessment sessions (20–40 minutes) are often necessary to get an idea of both the potential and challenges of the child and the potential of music therapy treatment. Sessions should preferably be video recorded as opposed to only audio recorded, but regardless of which method is used, consent and permission have to be established. The music therapy framework allows children potential for revealing pre-verbal and alternate communication systems that they have developed, where improvisation particularly leaves the child free to explore within an intermusical relationship.

The EBA sessions are different from regular music therapy sessions. The therapist has to explore the client and the client's music and it is therefore necessary to work at different levels using different approaches. You should not move too suddenly or unpredictably from one idea to the next. The session remains essentially a therapy session with subtle movement from one framework or scenario to another. If a child is easily engaged and enjoys close contact, the therapist can at some point in the session try to establish distance from the child, retreating from the engagement to see what happens. If the child is more responsive to structure and finds that approach easier, you can introduce a period of very free activity without rules or direction. It is important to create a careful balance between giving the child freedom to control what is happening in the session, and placing demands on the child. The therapist can thus explore the reactions when more demands are made (as when, for example, the child is encouraged to engage despite apparent resistance). You should have a wide range of instruments that children can use in therapy sessions as it is important to explore their potential using a wide range of instruments (Wigram 2000).

When using thematic improvisation or matching (Wigram 2004) together with the child, the therapist can find a starting point with a client by, for instance, using a short rhythmic, melodic, or harmonic theme which may be created by the therapist or the client at the beginning of an improvisation. Turn-taking is also very important to explore in the assessment improvisation, as the nature of music making between two people relies on timing, turn-taking, sharing, and creating—the essence of communication (Wigram 2000).

Selecting data

The first part of this method of EBA (Stage 1) involves following the recommendations and guidelines that Bruscia offers for using IAPs. Essentially one has to follow a process of reducing the amount of material to be analyzed to that which is both pertinent and essential, and then choosing the appropriate method within IAPs to do it.

Stage 1: Selection profiles and improvisational material

Step 1.1: Consider whether one is focusing on intramusical or intermusical events, or both.

Step 1.2: Choose the relevant profiles for analysis, related to either the focus of the therapy or the questions raised for the assessment.

Step 1.3: Review the entire session to be analyzed, and select sections or improvisations from the session that contain some of the most relevant material that will reap pertinent and valuable information when analyzed. (Bruscia 1987, pp. 418–421)

Steps 2 and 3 can be reversed (Step 3 and then Step 2). I have added to this some criteria that are particularly helpful in the process of diagnostic assessment, and also continue to reduce the amount of analysis that is necessary to produce some relevant information through which one can interpret and evaluate what is happening musically. Based on issues related to the referral or the child's behavior, and having reviewed musical events and the musical behavior of the child in this session, I choose the particular musical elements on the scale that are most relevant to use in the analysis. The scales are quite detailed and lengthy, and it may be beneficial to select out, for example, rhythm, volume, and phrasing as three particular elements that will be fruitful for analysis.

I use an event-charting system where, on looking at a video recording or listening to an audiotape, I search for musical events that can be categorized using the gradients of the profiles. I have generated a simple form for undertaking this analysis (Figure 9.1).

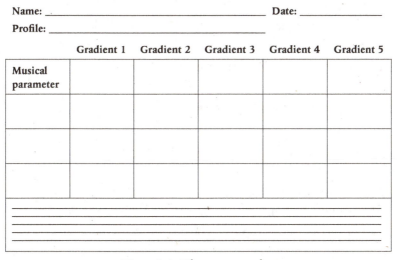

Figure 9.1: The raw score sheet

This form is the raw score sheet within which I place the gradients of the chosen profile, and the chosen musical parameters from Bruscia's scales. Then I record with a mark or a tick each time an event occurs. This can be applied through either video analysis or audio analysis. However, my method has exclusively involved video analysis. The lines underneath are a stave to write in musical motifs or fragments.

Before the analysis

The procedure for analyzing improvisation excerpts for the purpose of diagnostic assessment involves selecting two (or a maximum of three) improvisations that occurred within the session. Dependent on the length of the improvisations, a further reduction of data to be analyzed may be necessary, or not. This decision requires that the initial overview where the most fruitful and relevant selection is made is based on what is in focus for the analysis. Actually, choosing a longer or shorter excerpt of an improvisation to analyze may be influenced by a number of factors, including expectations regarding duration, frequency, consistency, and intensity of the musical events in focus. Consequentially, a "chicken-and-egg" decision process occurs over what comes first—the relevant section, or the relevant musical focus. I usually decide this based on diagnostic questions, therapeutic relevance, and individual needs.

The procedure then requires selecting the musical elements that are most in focus, and decisions about that depend on the child's use of musical equipment, media, and type of production. With many children, if they select to use unpitched percussion (drums, cymbals, wood-blocks, djembes, etc.), the elements on the scale are often tempo, rhythm, volume, timbre, and phrasing, while if they play on pitched percussion (keyboards or flutes, etc.), melody and harmony may become more relevant. This choice is based on clinical perspectives as well as musical ones. But one thing is important here—there should be a maximum of three musical descriptors.

Watching the sections I have chosen to analyze on video, often two to three times, I will score the number of events in the boxes where I can see, for example, variability in tempo. As mentioned previously, Bruscia provides a very rich resource in his descriptors and definitions of types of musical material that come under these gradients where he describes the five different levels of either variability or autonomy in his descriptions of IAPs (Bruscia 1987; Wigram 2007).

Data analysis

Stage 2: Event-Based Analysis

Stage 2 of the EBA involves a sequence of steps through which decisions are made and analysis is systematically undertaken by repeated video observation. For this to be realistic within the working timeframe of clinical practice, limiting the amount of material to be analyzed, and also selecting the parameters (musical elements for the scales) that are to be applied, need to be very carefully considered on the basis of what is relevant and essential. As the steps in both Stage 1 and Stage 2 are all necessary in order to do the analysis, there is no short form for clinical practice, but this two-stage analysis will be short enough if the constraints described above are applied.

> *Step 2.1:* Watch or listen to the extract from the improvisation and decide which musical/other parameters will be monitored from the profile (a maximum of three). The therapist may have already made this decision from a memory check of the relevant improvisation in the session.

> *Step 2.2:* Choose one musical parameter to begin with and watch the video again.

> *Step 2.3:* Events. Make a tick in the box *each time* an event occurs in the improvisation. Pause the video clip while doing so. For example, if the client changes tempo, and the therapist follows, and the client then remains stable for a few seconds in the new tempo, make a tick in a specific box:
>
> - Autonomy: rhythmic ground—*leader*
>
> - Variability: tempo—*variable* or *contrasting*

> *Step 2.4:* Where relevant, pause the video clip to notate any clear "leit-motifs/themes" as they occur in the stave at the bottom of the scoring sheet (Figure 9.1) for future reference in reports.

Step 2.5: When finishing this parameter, choose the second parameter and analyze the events again (Steps 2.2–4).

Step 2.6: Add up the events in each box, and put total scores onto the raw score table (Figure 9.1 under the column for the first improvisation or excerpt from an improvisation).

Step 2.7: Interpret the scores for this section of improvisation in relation to the aims of therapy or the diagnostic questions. Here, the therapist should already have established the pre-criteria for the analysis, in order that the evidence from the analysis either supports or does not support a diagnostic formulation. Also, for analyzing the process over time in therapy sessions, the analysis may reveal a shift in playing style and interpersonal/intermusical behavior.

Step 2.8: If another profile is to be applied, repeat the process from Steps 2.1–7. Depending on both the musical and the therapeutic situation, events can be identified by frequency alone, or by frequency and duration. In many cases, the complexity and multi-layered nature of the music in improvisations makes it quite difficult to identify the duration of an event. For example, you may note when a client (or therapist) has changed tempo, and if the other follows—but how long that new tempo remains stable (duration of the event) can be difficult to see when other related or unrelated events are occurring simultaneously. Therefore, for some purposes, it is enough to record a moment when an event starts.

Following recording of the scores during the analysis, the total scores for each musical element on each profile can be transferred to another form (Figure 9.2) to give an overview of what is occurring.

(Wigram 2007)

Patient's name: _____ Date: _____

Improvisation 1:

Improvisation 2:

Improvisation 3:

Automomy				Variability			
Dependent	1	2	3	Rigid	1	2	3
Follower				Stable			
Partner				Variable			
Leader				Contrasting			
Resister				Random			

Figure 9.2: Event-Based Analysis data sheet

Interpretation and EBA report

The best way to illustrate the use and interpretation of EBA data is to describe it through case material.

Ben was a 5-year-old boy referred to the clinic for a second opinion on a suggested diagnosis of ASD. He had the following characteristics:

- very limited and disordered speech

- echolalia

- obsessions with mechanical objects

- lack of interest in sharing activities

- enjoying self-chosen activities

- unstable cognitive ability as he was not able to engage in cognitive tests.

This profile of difficulties may suggest an ASD diagnosis, but can also be seen in the more severe end of the developmental disability population. Prior to the music therapy assessment, Ben had undertaken an art therapy assessment. During this he had demonstrated compliance and cooperation, but a lack of engagement with the therapist, except to echo the last words in a communication the therapist made to him. He was interested in the art materials, but not in engaging through them with the therapist. The music therapy assessment contained a number of improvisations, the most significant of which were in the opening improvisation. Ben played on two drums with two separate beaters and I played on the piano. During this section, Ben showed the ability to "control" the improvisation, by stopping and starting when he wished. He played mainly in a pulse, without much rhythmic variation, therefore Rhythmic ground/Tempo where relevant on the Autonomy and Variability profiles. Ben showed some differentiation in volume, so this was also scored on both profiles. Finally, as there was quite a lot of turn-taking and musical events where Ben followed me, Phrasing was also a relevant musical parameter for the Autonomy profile. In the second chosen short improvisation, Ben came and sat next to me on the piano in the treble position and we played together. The significant elements during this improvisation were the turn-taking and playing together. Therefore, the Autonomy profile was relevant in identifying events where Ben led, but more importantly where he also followed the therapist. Phrasing and Rhythmic ground/Tempo were the most significant musical elements.

Name: Ben   **Date:** _____

Profile: Autonomy

Musical parameter	Gradient 1 Dependent	Gradient 2 Follower	Gradient 3 Partner	Gradient 4 Leader	Gradient 5 Resister/ independent
Rhythmic ground		1111111111		111	1
Volume		111		1	11
Phrasing		11111111		111	1

Figure 9.3: Example of EBA data

Name: Ben   **Date:** _____

Profile: Variability

Musical parameter	Gradient 1 Rigid	Gradient 2 Stable	Gradient 3 Variable	Gradient 4 Contrasting	Gradient 5 Resister/ independent
Rhythmic ground	1	11	111111		
Volume	111	11	1111		
Phrasing		1111	1111111111		

Figure 9.4: Example of EBA data

Name: Ben   **Date:** _____

Profile: Variability

	Gradient 1	Gradient 2	Gradient 3	Gradient 4	Gradient 5
Musical parameter	Rigid	Stable	Variable	Contrasting	Random
Tempo	1	11	111111		
Phrasing		1111	11111111		

Figure 9.5: Example of EBA data

Name: Ben   **Date:** _____

Profile: Autonomy

	Gradient 1	Gradient 2	Gradient 3	Gradient 4	Gradient 5
Musical parameter	Dependent	Follower	Partner	Leader	Resister/ independent
Rhythmic ground		1111		1	
Phrasing		11111		1	

Figure 9.6: Example of EBA data

Figures 9.3–9.6 provide the raw sources for the analysis of events in both Improvisation 1 and Improvisation 2 of the selected samples from Ben's session. They show the results for the Autonomy profile (Figures 9.3 and 9.6) and for the Variability profile (Figures 9.4 and 9.5). Figure 9.7 shows the final scoring sheet where the cumulated scores for all gradients of the Autonomy and Variability profiles are entered for both selected improvisations.

Patient's name: Ben   Date: _____

Improvisation 1: Ben playing the drums, the therapist (Tony) on the piano

Improvisation 2: Ben and the therapist (Tony) playing on the piano

Automomy   **Variability**

Dependent	1	2	3	Rigid	1	2	3
Rhythmic ground	0	0	–	Tempo	1	1	
Volume	0	–	–	Volume	3	–	
Phrasing	0	0	–	Phrasing	0	0	
Follower				Stable			
Rhythmic ground	10	4	–	Tempo	2	2	
Volume	3	–	–	Volume	2	–	
Phrasing	8	7	–	Phrasing	4	4	
Partner				Variable			
Rhythmic ground	0	0	–	Tempo	6	6	
Volume	0	–	–	Volume	4	–	
Phrasing	0	0	–	Phrasing	10	8	
Leader				Contrasting			
Rhythmic ground	3	1	–	Tempo	0	0	
Volume	1	–	–	Volume	0	–	
Phrasing	3	1	–	Phrasing	0	0	
Resister				Random			
Rhythmic ground	1	0	–	Tempo	0	0	
Volume	2	–	–	Volume	0	–	
Phrasing	1	0	–	Phrasing	0	0	

Figure 9.7: Example of EBA data

The scores reported in Figure 9.7 show that Ben demonstrated good *follower* abilities during the first improvisation in Rhythmic ground and also in Phrasing, which was scored mainly from the turn-taking events. There were no *dependent* events in either improvisation, and a very small number of *rigid* events. The balance between *follower* events and *leader* events on all parameters (cumulated scores *follower* = 32; *leader* = 9) shows a tendency in these two improvisations to following behavior, unusual in ASD, but not necessarily in music therapy.

The *partner* events are actually difficult to score as events (as this needs to be considered much more over time), but are more represented through this balance between *follower* and *leader*. In terms of variability, Ben's scores certainly represent *variable* playing, with just a few events noted in the *rigid* gradient. There are some *stable* events, as would be expected. The scores here are closely linked to the Autonomy scores, as the greater the number of events where the child is following the therapist, the more likelihood there is for a variable and flexible playing style (assuming the therapist's improvising is variable, not rigid).

Previous results from this method of EBA have demonstrated how the scored events help identify characteristics in musical play that relate specifically to diagnosis, and have been reported in previous publications, in illustrating different profiles of children referred for diagnostic assessment (Wigram 1999, 2000, 2002, 2004).

EBA in training

In developing musical skills to use in clinical improvisation, music therapy students and qualified practitioners learn how the balanced and effective use of these elements can be made in a very sensitive and subtle way to assess, engage, and help patients. Some clients need the stability and safety of predictable music, for example people with psychotic disturbance, whose world is chaotic and disconnected. Others, for example patients with autism, learning disability, or anxiety neuroses, need to develop abilities to cope with an unpredictable world, and this can begin in developing adaptability to unpredictable musical experiences. Therefore, to use EBA in an ethical, valid, and meaningful manner you need music therapy training (Wigram 2004).

In several music therapy bachelor and master's programs, IAPs and EBA are taught as basic ways to understand improvisations and assessment. IAPs are a highly sophisticated descriptive tool for undertaking qualitative analysis. Bruscia (1987) stated that they were used extensively as a teaching tool (p. 410), and I would also like to reinforce this aspect, because they are so useful in getting students to listen to what is happening, and then being able to analyze it at a music level, before jumping to conclusions in psychological, intuitive, but sometimes impetuous interpretation. Bruscia emphasizes the importance of listening to and hearing what is happening in the improvised music, as he recommends the starting point for using IAPs is with the Salience profile. This profile helps identify which musical elements are most prominent, exert most influence over other elements, and can be used to analyze intramusical and intermusical events. I think that when you know what you want to look for, you don't necessarily have to start with establishing the salience of characteristics of the improvisation (Wigram 2007).

EBA/IAP research

The practical application of IAPs has been developed by various researchers and practitioners for both quantitative and qualitative analysis (Abrams 2007; Bellido 2000; Erkkilä 2000; Frederiksen 1999; Jacobsen 2012; McFerran and Wigram 2004; Scholtz, Voigt, and Wosch 2007; Stige 1996; Wosch 2007; Wosch and Erkkilä 2016). I would like to reflect on the potential for analyzing numerical or categorical data from a functional analysis of musical improvisation. The functional, quantitative use I have made of IAPs so far has involved scoring (counting) events in musical improvisation and assigning scores to predetermined categories (Wigram 1999, 2000, 2002). For example, having decided that I want to look specifically at changes in tempo as a musical indicator related to autonomy, I have counted the number of times one or other person in a client-therapist improvisation changed tempo, and what provoked it. Therefore, it is relatively easy to make a "judgement" about the initiative that was taken to change tempo—whether it was independent or dependent on another—and to identify the event as standing somewhere on the gradients of the Autonomy profile. This event, together with others within the same category (tempo/rhythmic ground), provides data that can be initially used for *descriptive statistics*. *Frequency data*, such as numbers of events (as described above), is ripe for analysis through descriptive statistics, and appropriate conclusions can be drawn from such analysis in single cases.

Neither the gradients in IAPs nor the scales can be scored using a *ratio* or *interval* scale, and therefore *parametric statistics* cannot be undertaken on a set of data if one is computing on the basis of equidistant points on a scale. However, *non-parametric* tests can be used. The value of non-parametric statistics is that rather than calculating the exact numerical difference between scores, and basing the statistical computation on this, non-parametric tests only take into account whether certain scores are higher or lower than other scores, effectively rank ordering the scores, as can be seen in a Wilcoxon Signed-Ranks Test, Mann-Whitney U,[2] a Friedman, or a Kruskal-Wallis (parametric equivalents: related t-test, unrelated t-test, one-way ANOVA related, or one-way ANOVA unrelated respectively). Less robust but applicable statistical tests are thus available should analysis comparing the number of scored events on an ordinal scale seem appropriate through rank ordering, and where the data is clearly not homogenous (Wigram 2001).

For a different type of analysis, categories can be developed and statistical tests applied (chi-square). The gradients on IAPs could be treated as categories, and the assignment of musical elements defined as a whole series of sub-categories, i.e. rhythmic ground follower, rhythmic ground leader, contrasting phrasing, rigid phrasing. The normal use of the chi-square is where the data is nominal and the subjects are assigned to one or more categories. In the case of IAPs, the musical events could be assigned to categories, as in the example above. One is therefore attempting to find out whether there is some significant difference between categories. A chi-square can compute a comparison of the observed frequencies by which a number of

2   Analysis for non-parametric statistics.

events will fall into different categories (cells) with the expected frequencies for each "category" if the differences are due to chance, as stated by the null hypothesis. It is important to note that a minimum number of at least 20 events (or subjects) is required to have enough allocated to each category (cell). The gradients on IAPs are ordinal data, but can also be described as categories of description, response, or interaction, and therefore could lend themselves well to this type of statistical analysis (Wigram 2001, 2004).

Discussion and summary

Musically structured or free improvisation provides a complex source of data for analysis, and the applied use of IAPs through EBA is effective in identifying music events that relate to therapeutic issues, as well as analyzing creativity and musical interaction. Children with autism demonstrate their pathology in their music, and from a diagnostic point of view can reveal aspects of behavior that set them apart from children with a language disorder who may present as autistic. The value of a music therapy assessment, particularly because of the freedom improvised music allows, is that besides identifying areas of difficulty, children often reveal unexpected abilities and potential. Depending on the client(s), the analysis of musical material can provide concrete evidence in the form of the events that take place on specific musical elements to identify important aspects relating to the direction, process, and outcome of therapy. It is necessary to make such an analysis in order to support and validate an intuitive understanding of a client's musical ability or creativity, without some of the significant and concrete events (Wigram 2004).

EBA can be used for analysis of improvisations in clinical work, and is effective in determining changes over time. The timeframe may be what changes occur in a single session or over a course of sessions. Bruscia comments on the differences of analyzing one or several improvisations. The insights gained from analyzing a single improvisation are quite different from those gained from comparing an entire set of improvisations. The reliability of the analysis of a single improvisation is established only through repeated occurrences within the same improvisation, but even this provides no evidence that the improvisation is typical of the individual, or that the individual's tendencies or style when improvising have been revealed (Bruscia 2001).

This comment on reliability tends to suggest a perspective where the characteristics of a client present in their musical "behavior" should recur enough in order to establish consistency of evidence, and is actually a supportive argument to EBA that is the method articulated in this chapter. EBA inevitably leads to an accumulation of events over time.

What also makes IAPs a remarkable tool for determining change over time is the bi-directional aspect of each of the profiles. Initially, a therapist might look for evidence that the client is playing in a way that matches the middle gradient on any one of these six profiles. Taking the Autonomy profile as an example, the mid-point (*partner*) can be perceived as a "healthy" position, while the gradients immediately either side of that mid-point (*leader* and *follower*) may denote either a "state," the behavior of a person in a certain period of time, or a personality "trait"—evidence of a consistent pattern of behavior. The potential of therapy, and of this profile to identify change over time, is that a client with a *follower*, perhaps *dependent*, way of behaving may be working in therapy in the direction of increasing their autonomy, making more decisions, taking the lead (*leader*), and even demonstrating "independence" (an alternative term to that of *resister*). Conversely, in the field of ASD, the pathology tends to present a person with a high level of autonomy, to the degree that everything that happens has to be on their terms, and attempts to elicit a response can be met with rejection and avoidance (*resister*). Here, the therapeutic direction, and the focus of the analysis, can be searching for examples over time where events in the music making showing the client as a *follower*, or even *dependent*, can denote a significant and important shift (or potential) in that client's readiness to engage with others.

Musically structured or free improvisation provides a complex source of data for analysis, and the applied use of IAPs is effective in identifying music events that relate to therapeutic issues, as well as in analyzing creativity and musical interaction. Depending on the client(s), the analysis of musical material through EBA can provide concrete evidence in the form of the events that take place on specific musical elements to identify important aspects relating to the direction, process, and outcome of therapy. It is necessary to make such an analysis both of single improvisations (microanalysis) and of a series of improvisations or sessions (session analysis) in order to support an intuitive understanding of a client's musical behavior (Wigram 2007).

References

Abrams, B. (2007) 'The Use of Improvisation Assessment Profiles (IAPs) and RepGrid in Microanalysis of Clinical Improvisation.' In T. Wosch and T. Wigram (eds) *Microanalysis in Music Therapy – Methods, Techniques and Applications for Clinicians, Researchers, Educators and Students.* London: Jessica Kingsley Publishers.

Bellido, G. (2000) 'IAPs revisited.' Online discussion forum on IAPs. *Nordic Journal of Music Therapy.* Retrieved from www.njmt.no.

Bruscia, K. (1987) *Improvisational Models of Music Therapy.* Springfield, IL: Charles C. Thomas.

Bruscia, K. (2001) 'Response to the discussion forum on IAP.' *Nordic Journal of Music Therapy.* Retrieved from www.njmt.no.

Erkkilä, J. (2000) 'A proposition for the didactics of music therapy improvisation.' *Nordic Journal of Music Therapy, 9,* 1, doi: 10.1080/08098130009477982.

Frederiksen, B. V. (1999) 'Analysis of Musical Improvisations to Understand and Work with Elements of Resistance in a Client with Anorexia Nervosa.' In T. Wigram and J. De Backer (eds) *Clinical Applications of Music Therapy in Psychiatry.* London: Jessica Kingsley Publishers.

Jacobsen, S. L. (2012) 'Music Therapy Assessment and Development of Parental Competences in Families Where Children Have Experienced Emotional Neglect: An Investigation of the Reliability and Validity of the Tool, Assessment of Parenting Competencies (APC).' Unpublished PhD thesis. Department of Communication and Psychology, Aalborg University.

McFerran, K. and Wigram, T. (2004) 'Articulating the dynamics of music therapy group improvisations: An empirical study.' *Nordic Journal of Music Therapy, 14,* 2, 33–46.

Scholtz, J., Voigt, M., and Wosch, T. (2007) 'Microanalysis of Interaction in Music Therapy (MIMT) with Children with Developmental Disorders.' In T. Wosch and T. Wigram (eds) *Microanalysis in Music Therapy – Methods, Techniques and Applications for Clinicians, Researchers, Educators and Students.* London: Jessica Kingsley Publishers.

Stige, B. (1996) 'Om Improvisational Assessment Profiles (IAP). Del II: Klinisk og forskningsmessig relevans.' *Nordic Journal of Music Therapy, 5,* 1, 3–12.

Wigram, T. (1999) 'Assessment methods in music therapy: A humanistic or natural science framework?' *Nordic Journal of Music Therapy, 9,* 1, 6–24.

Wigram, T. (2000) 'A method of music therapy assessment for the diagnosis of autistic and communication disordered children.' *Music Therapy Perspectives, 18,* 1, 13–22.

Wigram, T. (2001) 'Quantifiable data, statistical analysis and the IAPs: IAPs revisited.' Online discussion forum on IAPs. *Nordic Journal of Music Therapy.* Retrieved from www.njmt.no.

Wigram, T. (2002) 'Indications in music therapy: Evidence from assessment that can identify the expectations of music therapy as a treatment for autistic spectrum disorder (ASD). Meeting the challenge of evidence based practice.' *British Journal of Music Therapy, 16,* 1, 11–28.

Wigram, T. (2004) *Improvisation: Methods and Techniques for Music Therapy Clinicians, Educators and Students.* London: Jessica Kingsley Publishers.

Wigram, T. (2007) 'Event-Based Analysis of Improvisation using the Improvisational Assessment Profiles (IAPs).' In T. Wosch and T. Wigram (eds) *Microanalysis in Music Therapy – Methods, Techniques and Applications for Clinicians, Researchers, Educators and Students.* London: Jessica Kingsley Publishers.

Wosch, T. (2007) 'Microanalysis of Processes of Interactions in Clinical Improvisation with IAP-Autonomy.' In T. Wosch and T. Wigram (eds) *Microanalysis in Music Therapy – Methods, Techniques and Applications for Clinicians, Researchers, Educators and Students.* London: Jessica Kingsley Publishers.

Wosch, T. and Erkkilä, J. (2016) 'Microanalysis in Objectivist Research.' In B. L. Wheeler and K. Murphy (eds) *Music Therapy Research* (3rd edition). Dallas, TX: Barcelona Publishers.

CHAPTER 10

The AQR Tool

Assessment of the Quality of Relationship

Karin Schumacher, Claudine Calvet, and Silke Reimer

The history of the AQR Tool

Children with autism suffer from social, interactive, and communicative disabilities. The more severe the impairments, the more difficult it can be for caregivers and therapists to get in touch with these children. Interactions and interventions that require the ability to join in overstimulate children with autism who have not yet developed the capacity for interpersonal relationships. The first author of this chapter Karin Schumacher (KS), has found that, in music therapy, contact can develop even before an interpersonal relationship has been developed.

KS worked as a music therapist in an institution for children on the autism spectrum with eight children between the ages of 7 and 12 years. The children had not developed the ability for joint attention and couldn't speak, corresponding to a developmental age of less than one year. In the 1990s, there was no tool with which one could specifically analyze the developmental steps up to joint attention for a socio-emotional development level of less than one year. KS started a research collaboration in the early 1990s with developmental psychologist Claudine Calvet (CC), the second author of this chapter. We filmed eight children during their music therapy sessions and analyzed the videos.

First, we started with one child called Max and followed his development in music therapy (Schumacher 2017). Max was a 7-year-old non-speaking boy with an obsessive stereotypic behavior, difficult to reach, and without any interpersonal contact with other children or adults. For the development of the AQR Tool, we concentrated first on his contact with musical instruments. Based on his social-emotional development and his relationship to objects and the therapist, we developed a scale to assess the quality of relationship to instruments, called IQR (Instrumental Quality of Relationship). This is one of four scales of the AQR Tool.

Then we focused on Max's vocal pre-speech development. We started to research and compare how children normally develop in all their vocal pre-speech expressions, focusing on the question: What are the typical vocal pre-speech features and difficulties in children with autism? Our findings led to the development of a second scale: VQR (Vocal Pre-Speech Quality of Relationship). Then we filmed and analyzed other children with severe contact problems who attended this school, especially those who neither played on instruments nor vocalized. We started to think about a third scale, which would relate to their own bodies and physical-emotional expressions, asking: What can we read in their faces and body language? Can we also see a development without musical expression? A third scale was developed: PEQR (Physical-Emotional Quality of Relationship).

For us, a further important question was: Which interventions should the therapist apply in order to enable the ability for interpersonal relationships? What interventions are helpful if the child does not appear to react either to the therapist or to their interventions? We started to analyze the therapeutic interventions and developed the fourth scale of the AQR Tool. The TQR Scale describes the therapist and their interventions. We realized that a relationship can only develop when the intervention meets the child's level of development and if an appropriate music therapy intervention is applied. Through the film analysis, we could see how differently children with autism were developed in the various domains (object relationship, body and body awareness, vocal expression). The focus of our attention became increasingly the therapist, whose sensitivity and flexibility recognized the appropriate level of development (Ainsworth and Bell 1974; Ainsworth *et al.* 1978). Only in this way could over- and understimulation of the child be avoided and development be supported.

Theoretical background

All the children mentioned above did not yet have the ability to make contact with the therapist or to play with the therapist at the beginning of the music therapy sessions. Some also did not respond to the therapist or the music. From a developmental psychological point of view, the question arises as to how a person usually develops the ability to get in contact with other people and what experiences and developmental steps precede this ability. Looking from a developmental psychological perspective at the clinical picture of autism, the question concerns what abilities and experiences are missing that prevent the child with autism from relating to other people. The findings of developmental psychology are also helpful for identifying useful interventions. In particular, the recognition of over- and understimulation by the reference person is the basis of good development and determines the therapeutic intervention.

How, then, does the ability of interpersonal relationship/ intersubjectivity evolve, and how does the caregiver support this development? The main inspiration was Daniel Stern's knowledge about the pre-verbal time in the first year of the child's life (Stern 2000). As an infant researcher, Stern not only focused on the child's capacities, but also on the child's development in the context of the relationship with the caregiver.

Stern's so-called "layered model of development" (Stern 2000), in which he describes the experiences of infants and the development of intersubjectivity, gave the structure for the development of the AQR Tool. CC, as a developmental psychologist and specialist in early interaction disturbances in mother-child relationships (Calvet-

Kruppa 2001; Calvet-Kruppa, Ziegenhain, and Derksen 2005), addressed developmental psychological themes in the scale development. In the early 1990s, CC was especially influenced by Crittenden (Crittenden 1990; Crittenden, Partridge, and Claussen 1991), who first trained her in the "Care index" (Crittenden 1979–2005). This is a tool used in infancy to observe and assess the interaction between parents and children. Through Crittenden's teamwork with Bowlby (1969, 1979, 1998), Ainsworth *et al.* (1978), and Ainsworth and Bell (1974), the knowledge of attachment theory added an important element to our work.

Main's description of the disorganized type of attachment (Main and Salomon 1986) led us to thinking about the issue of trauma. The variety of clinical presentations of children who had been diagnosed with autism led us to ask if the AQR Tool could help to differentiate between early-inborn autism, socio-emotional deprivation (hospitalism), attachment disturbances, and trauma. Through further analysis of our clinical videos, a question emerged concerning the specific moments in music therapy which seemed to be especially beneficial.

The synchronous moment was recognized by Lenz (2000) in her work with screaming babies. A synchronous moment denotes the moment in which the exact correspondence of time structures of two or more people during a musical play occurs. An exact attunement of rhythm and intensity can be identified (Schumacher and Calvet 2008). Lenz's work brought us to the research results of the German brain researcher Hüther (2003, 2004). He raised our awareness that an emotionally positive interpersonal relationship has an influence on the development of the brain. He emphasized the important effect of a therapeutic relationship (Hüther 2003, 2004). The discovery that synchronous moments could positively change the quality of relationship, which can be analyzed with the AQR Tool, became another focus of our research. Therefore, a music theorist analyzed the synchronous moment in music therapy with a child and recorded this with graphic notation. The same sequence was analyzed by a dance therapist with Laban notation, which was developed for dancers. KS analyzed rehearsals with the conductor Herbert von Karajan and demonstrated how important the ability for synchronized playing also is for musicians. CC showed how important the experience of synchronization is for newborn babies. The results of the analysis showed that synchronous moments not only change the quality of the relationship, they even improve it (Schumacher and Calvet 2008).

The American researcher Sroufe (1997) helped us to understand pre-verbal, socio-emotional development with the themes of emotional development and affect regulation. In order to understand the ability for interpersonal relationships and their dynamics, we used the behavioral organization developed by Als (1986). She presented four systems of pre-natal development which are activated after birth and developed throughout life through the quality of interaction. The realization that interaction is only possible on the basis of a balanced, stable, vegetative, and motoric system had a decisive effect on the music therapy intervention. Using the AQR Tool for analysis demonstrated that stress signs that arose through over- or understimulation during music therapy could be understood on this basis. Specific music therapy interventions aim to regulate and stabilize the affects as the basis of the interaction.

Development of the AQR Tool

The AQR Tool focuses on the way relationships to oneself (body and voice), to objects (music instruments), and to others (the music therapist) are built. With the aid of specific characteristics, the quality of this ability for relationship can be assessed and therefore determined in a comprehensive way. The four lists of characteristics of the TQR, PEQR, VQR, and IQR Scales have already been published as a method for microanalysis in a short form (Schumacher and Calvet 2008). As shown in Figure 10.1, each scale contains the description of specific focuses of observation. For each scale, seven qualities of relationship, called modus 0 to modus 6, were described. Modus means the way in which the relationship is expressed. The order of the modi 0–6 was the same in each of the four scales, as they were in accordance with the socio-emotional development concepts of Stern (2000) and Sroufe (1997).

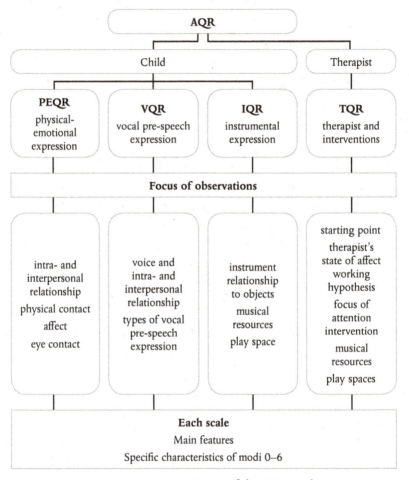

Figure 10.1: Organigram of the AQR Tool

Modus 0 Lack of contact / Contact refusal

The main characteristic is a lack of reaction. There seems to be either no awareness of the therapist's offer or it is rejected. The child is unapproachable—mostly stereotypic behavior can be observed. The therapist accepts the child in their "so-state." Music is offered with the intention of creating an atmosphere that makes a relationship possible without forcing it.

Modus 1 Sensory contact/Contact-reaction

The therapist concentrates on the sensory needs and/or the stereotypic movements of the child. The rhythm of the child's movement and its intensity are precisely taken up and made audible or the therapist rocks and swings the child and synchronizes this movement to their singing. The aim is to bring the sensory impressions of the child—feeling, seeing, hearing, and especially their body awareness—into attunement and to enable the child to have synchronized experiences. If this intervention is successful, short positive reactions can be observed.

Modus 2 Functionalizing contact

The child is very tense and their affect is in the foreground of the physical-emotional expression. Instruments are used for the affective needs of the child and are often destructively handled or played in a destructive way. The therapist regulates these affects with affect attunement and affect shaping so that the child can experience affect regulation through another.

Modus 3 Contact to oneself/Self-awareness

The child is attentive and calm. They are aware of their own body as the origin of activity and they explore instruments, their own voice, or their own body in order to perceive themselves in this self-effectiveness and authorship. The therapist supports this exploration by imitating and accompanying the child's expressions and actions.

Modus 4 Contact to another/Intersubjectivity

The child shows interest in the therapist and in the joint activity. The ability for inter-attentionality (joint attention) is developed and the child regulates their own affect through exchange of eye contact and through rests. The therapist meets the child's need for social referencing of their perception and feelings and has the experience of being included as a person by the child.

Modus 5 Relationship to others/Interactivity

The main characteristic is the ability to imitate. In the dialogical exchange of motifs, the mutual referencing, as well as the keeping of rests, becomes evident. The therapist takes up the child's motifs and experiences that the child answers.

Modus 6 Joint experience/Inter-affectivity

The relationship is firmly established and the joint expressive playing is accompanied by a positive emotional state in both players. The child and the therapist experience pleasure and fun together.

Teaching videos for training and the reliability control of the AQR Tool were developed (IQR: Schumacher 1999; VQR: Schumacher and Calvet-Kruppa 1999a; PEQR: Schumacher and Calvet-Kruppa 2001; TQR: Schumacher and Calvet-Kruppa 2005). The AQR Tool was published in a short form in English (Schumacher and Calvet-Kruppa 1999b) and the first complete version several years later (Schumacher and Calvet 2008). Together with the music therapist Silke Reimer, the third author of this chapter, the final revised German version was published in 2011 (Schumacher, Calvet, and Reimer 2013). The application of the AQR Tool in the practical work with an 11-year-old boy with autism and the function of music has also been described (Schumacher 2014). Schumacher and Calvet (2016) discuss the important focus on the body and the physical-emotional expression as the starting point in music therapy.

Reliability

The teaching videos mentioned above were used to educate 84 raters who were interested in testing the reliability of the AQR Tool. We organized working groups of students and music therapists in different cities (Berlin, Munich, Vienna, Sjoevig/Sweden). In cooperation with a statistician, the reliability of the AQR Tool was analyzed (Schumacher, Calvet, and Stallmann 2005). The results of the reliability analysis showed the following intra-class correlations (ICC) for the various scales.

Scale	ICC	95% confidence interval
PEQR	0.75	0.56–0.93
TQR	0.78	0.62–0.93
VQR	0.83	0.68–0.95
IQR	0.82	0.67–0.94

Application of the AQR Tool

Depending on the research question, a one- to three-minute scene should be filmed and assessed with the corresponding scales. We always begin with the question of what intervention the therapist chooses in this situation. This can be assessed with the help of the TQR (Therapeutic Quality of Relationship) Scale. Depending on whether the patient expresses themselves physically-emotionally, vocally, or instrumentally, the scene is assessed using one of three scales: the PEQR Scale for physical-emotional expression, the VQR Scale for vocal pre-speech expression, or the IQR Scale for instrumental expression. Only when the therapist's modus coincides with that of the patient can we expect a constructive course of therapy. If this is not the case, it is important to work out possible reasons for the therapist so that they can intervene in a more appropriate way. The time required for the assessment depends on the training and practice of the therapist.

Data analysis and results

A graphic representation of the assessment quickly reveals whether the therapist has intervened according to the needs of the child. For this purpose, the modi are entered as colored balls in a diagram (Figure 10.2).

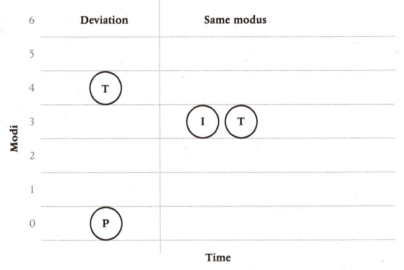

Figure 10.2: Results of the reliability analysis

If the child's expression and the therapist's intervention are rated as being in the same modus (e.g. as with the ratings of TQR and IQR in Figure 10.2), the therapist's intervention is appropriate to the needs and current emotional condition of the child. If the therapist's intervention deviates from the child's needs or conditions (e.g. as with the ratings of TQR and PEQR in Figure 10.2), the therapist has a working hypothesis that does not correspond to the child. The therapist is not providing an environment to support the child's development (Mössler *et al.* 2017).

Training

For many years, in addition to introductory courses providing information, a further educational course in the AQR Tool has been offered at various German, English, and French music therapy training centers. As of now, those places are: Berlin, Munich, Vienna, Zurich, and Lausanne. The goal is an independent application of the AQR Tool. The course includes five weekends (a total of 90 hours), and participants need to have completed music therapy training and have practical experience in music therapy work. This course, however, is not just about getting to know the AQR Tool with its intervention techniques—the developmental psychological theories underpinning the AQR Tool are also taught. These are applied in the analysis of video examples from each of the students and help to recognize the emotional-cognitive developmental level of the patient and the dynamics of the patient's development in music therapy. The course ends with a certificate exam, so that the participants are then given a certificate from the respective university. In addition, the particular value of this course is the discussion of individual perception and assessment in a group of experienced music therapists. Not only do therapists who work with children with autism participate in the courses, but others from different fields of work do as well. The common basis is the developmental psychological-oriented understanding of the difficulties and disorders of the patients. It is often necessary to adjust the scales for the various working fields so that they can be used with other populations. According to the areas of application, the previously certified participants of the courses were organized in groups to enable them to continue working locally.

Transference to further fields of application

Even in the courses of certification, it became clear that the AQR Tool had to be adapted to the respective field of application. Thus, for example, Baumann, who specializes in the field of neurology, showed that modus 0 (Lack of contact) and modus 1 (Sensory contact) must be more precisely characterized. The perception of observable characteristics, especially in these often minimally responsive patients, is the basis for assessing the quality of relationship (Baumann 2018). The AQR Tool helped to describe which qualities of relationship are threatened in patients with dementia and which qualities can be maintained longer with the help of music therapy (Muthesius *et al.* 2010). In music therapy with patients who are diagnosed with borderline personality disorder, especially in patients with attachment trauma, the importance of affect regulation (modus 2—Functionalizing contact) and the stabilization of self-efficacy (modus 3—Self-awareness) has been highlighted through AQR analysis by Kupski and Schulz-Venrath (2014, 2016).

Modus 2 also plays an important role in music therapy with adults with severe multiple disabilities, which appears here in the form of stereotypes, self-stimulation, and self-injurious behavior. Here, the correlation of these behaviors with the severity of bodily impairments and with overstimulation and understimulation, respectively, has been investigated. The description of music therapy interventions that helped the patient first to become calm and attentive, then to make contact with the therapist, was the aim of this study (Reimer 2016). In work with psychosomatic patients, the AQR Tool has been used as a diagnostic instrument. The results of the first session have been compared to another German diagnostic instrument, OPD-2 (Körber 2009). For patients with schizophrenia, a "body movement music score" has been developed and the AQR Tool has been evaluated for this area of application (Skrzypek 2017).

In addition to use with various populations, the AQR Tool was also used in the field of music education. Here, it was found that people who don't have the ability for joint attention cannot really benefit from the teacher's method (Salmon and Kallos 2010); therefore the teaching methodology for people with different abilities must take this factor into account. The course of therapy of children with mental disorders has also been assessed with the AQR Tool (Fragkouli 2012).

Research

The AQR Tool has not only been transferred to further fields of application, but has also been used in a large international research project conducted by the Grieg Academy Music Therapy Research Centre (Bergen, Norway) from 2013 to 2017 in collaboration with the Berlin University of the Arts. For the project, the AQR Tool was used as an outcome measure for therapy with children on the autism spectrum over five months to examine therapeutic relationship quality as a predictor of the development of social-emotional skills in children with autism spectrum disorder. The first results showed that a therapeutic relationship in which the therapist attunes to the child's expressions musically and emotionally seems to be an important mediator of generalized social skills. These findings were observed by independent, blinded assessors, as well as by parents in natural settings (Mössler *et al.* 2017).

Current projects and future plans

The translation of the AQR Tool into different languages is in preparation.[1] As the AQR Tool should be learned through practical courses, further education courses in the respective languages are important. The combination of the theoretical foundations with the practical experience must be developed for the respective fields of application. The main goal of a research project at the Orff Institute of the Mozarteum University Salzburg (Austria) is the adaptation of the AQR Tool for pedagogical use. The AQR Tool should be used as a guide to the pedagogical practice to show which interventions generate which effects, how the quality of relationship can be strengthened or changed, and which interventions are most suited to the respective development level of the children (Esterbauer, Salmon, and Schumacher 2018; Salmon 2012).

The fact that schools are changing towards inclusive teaching compels us to set new and different goals. At the University of Potsdam, a project has been initiated in which children's improvisations are analyzed with the help of the AQR Tool (Fröhlich 2018). Since only the pre-speech behavior can be assessed with the VQR Scale, a so-called "speech scale" is under development. For this purpose, a videographed therapy course over a ten-year period with a child on the autism spectrum has been analyzed (Jordan 2017). The question is whether the modus for non-verbal expressions can also be applied to verbal expressions.

---

1   English: G. Litwin, S. Salmon; Japanese: S. Suzuki-Kupski; French: Nicole Droin.

Therapeutic and pedagogical approaches often require that patients communicate, perform tasks, or perceive offers of social interactions. Many music therapists are trained to play together with their patients dialogically or to play for them to contribute to a development. But what if a patient cannot join in and imitate, or does not show positive reactions to the therapist or their offers? If the therapist then continues with intervention techniques which are exclusively aimed at the patient's reciprocal reaction to their interventions, this can be an overstimulation for the patient. The less a patient can relate to the therapist, the more the therapist has to base the interventions on the patient's physical-emotional state, and their utterances and actions. The AQR scales not only allow the therapist to assess the development of patients who do not yet possess the ability for intersubjectivity, but also allow the therapist to describe interventions that are effective and applicable before the development of intersubjectivity and particularly the capacity of joint attention. Thus, the AQR Tool is not only helpful for analysis of the patient's responses in therapy, but also as a guide in every therapeutic situation. To date, no other tool has been known in the field of music therapy which describes in such detail the developmental precursors of intersubjectivity and the corresponding interventions.

For research in music therapy, it is important not only to describe a patient's development but also to understand more and more precisely what the music therapist is doing and why they are using a particular intervention. The effectiveness of music therapy can only be measured when the interventions have been adapted to the clinical picture, the symptoms, and the individual needs of the patient.

Discussion

The question of therapists' interventions, their inner working model (Bowlby 1969), and their goals is an equally difficult and helpful question. In educational courses as well as in research projects, the perception of what happens in a video can be very individual. The discussion of different perceptions is not intended to lead to a judgement of "right" or "wrong," but to the extension of one's own capacity for observation and to an awareness of one's own actions. Finally, the patient's reaction, their socio-emotional development, and the resulting contact show whether the therapist's interventions are on a course that is helpful to the patient's development. The main purpose of the AQR Tool is to reach people whose ability for intersubjectivity is brittle or not yet developed on an emotional level. The music therapist's ability to create the prerequisites for synchronous moments (Schumacher and Calvet 2008) proved to be the driving force behind the development of the AQR Tool. Further attention should be paid to this phenomenon in the future.

References

Ainsworth, M. D. S. and Bell, S. M. (1974) 'Mother-Infant Interaction and the Development of Competence.' In K. Connolly and J. S. Brunner (eds) *The Growth of Competence*. London and New York, NY: Academic Press.

Ainsworth, M. D. S., Blehar, M. C., Waters, E., and Wall, S. (1978) *Patterns of Attachment: A Psychological Study of the Strange Situation*. Hillsdale, NJ: Erlbaum.

Als, H. (1986) 'A Synactive Model of Neonatal Behavioral Organization: Framework for the Assessment of Neurobehavioral Development in the Premature Infant and for Support of Infants and Parents in the Neonatal Intensive Care Environment.' In J. Sweeney (ed.) *The High-Risk Neonate: Developmental Therapy Perspectives*. New York, NY: Haworth Press.

Baumann, M. (2018) 'Musik im Übergang—Die Improvisation in der (Früh-) Rehabilitation Hirnverletzter.' In M. Nöcker-Ribaupierre (ed.) *Musik in Therapie und Medizin*. Wiesbaden: Reichert-Verlag.

Bowlby, J. (1969) *Attachment and Loss. Vol. 1: Attachment*. New York, NY: Basic Books.

Bowlby, J. (1979) *The Making and Breaking of Affectional Bonds*. London: Tavistock Publications.

Bowlby, J. (1998) *A Secure Base*. New York, NY: Basic Books.

Calvet-Kruppa, C. (2001) 'Feinfühligkeit als Interaktionsqualität. Ein Leitfaden entwicklungspsychologischer Intervention.' In O. Decker and A. Borkenhagen (eds) *Psychoanalyse, Texte zur Sozialforschung, 9*, 153–156.

Calvet-Kruppa, C., Ziegenhain, U., and Derksen, B. (2005) 'Kinder mit Down-Syndrom: Entwicklungspsychologische Elternberatung.' In Jürgen Kühl (ed.) *Autonomie und Dialog—Kleine Kinder in der Frühförderung*. München: Reinhardt.

Crittenden, P. M. (1979–2005) 'CARE-Index: Infant Coding Manual.' Unpublished manuscript, Miami, FL. Available from www.patcrittenden.com.

Crittenden, P. M. (1990) 'Internal representational models of attachment relationships.' *Infant Mental Health Journal, 11*, 259–277.

Crittenden, P. M., Partridge, M. F., and Claussen, A. H. (1991) 'Family patterns of relationship in normative and dysfunctional families.' *Development and Psychopathology, 3,* 491–512.

Esterbauer, E., Salmon, S., and Schumacher, K. (2018) 'Einschätzung der Beziehungsfähigkeit mit Hilfe des "EBQ-Instruments" im inklusiven Musikunterricht.' *Zeitschrift Diskussion Musikpädagogik.*

Fragkouli, A. (2012) 'Music Therapy for Children with Psychological Disorders in Special Education.' Unpublished PhD thesis, Department of Early Childhood Education, National and Kapodistrian University of Athens, Athens, Greece.

Fröhlich, C. (2018) 'Kind—Spiel—Musik—ein Mikrokosmos gegenseitiger Bezogenheit.' *Bildung Schweiz, 10,* 36–37.

Hüther, G. (2003) *Die Bedeutung emotionaler Sicherheit für die Entwicklung des menschlichen Gehirns.* DVD 437D. Auditorium.

Hüther, G. (2004) 'Ebenen salutogenetischer Wirkungen auf das Gehirn.' *Musiktherapeutische Umschau, 25,* 1, 16–26.

Jordan, A. K. (2017) 'Assessing the Quality of Relationship in Music Therapy Sessions with the Focus on Language.' Oral presentation at the ESCOM Conference in Gent, Belgium.

Körber, A. (2009) *Beziehungsqualität in der Musiktherapie mit Psychotherapiepatienten. Vergleichende Untersuchung interpersonalen Verhaltens (EBQ, OPD-2, IIP).* Saarbrücken, Germany: VDM Verlag Dr. Müller.

Kupski, G. and Schulz-Venrath, U. (2014) '"Let's beat the drum…" "Yes, but tell me how"— Interventionen in der Musiktherapie mit Borderline-Patienten aus Sicht des Mentalisierungsmodells.' *Jahrbuch Musiktherapie, 10, Mentalisierung und Symbolbildung in der musiktherapeutischen Praxis.* Wiesbaden: Reichert-Verlag.

Kupski, G. and Schulz-Venrath, U. (2016) 'Musiktherapie mit Borderline-Patienten aus Sicht des Mentalisierungsmodells.' In S. Leikert and A. Niehbur (eds) *Von der Musik zur Sprache und wieder zurück. Jahrbuch für Psychoanalyse und Musik, 1.* Gießen: Psychosozial-Verlag.

Lenz, G. M. (2000) 'Musiktherapie bei Schrei-Babys. Eine Pilotstudie zu frühen Interaktionsstörungen zwischen Mutter und Kind.' *Musiktherapeutische Umschau, 21,* 126–140.

Main, M. and Salomon, J. (1986) 'Discovery of an Insecure-Disorganized/Disoriented Attachment Pattern.' In T. B. Brazelton and M. N. Yogman (eds) *Affective Development in Infancy.* Norwood: Ablex Publishing Corporation.

Mössler, K., Gold, C., Assmus, J., Schumacher, K., *et al.* (2017) 'The therapeutic relationship as predictor of change in music therapy with young children with autism spectrum disorder.' *Journal of Autism and Developmental Disorders.* doi: 10.1007/s10803-017-3306-y.

Muthesius, D., Sonntag, J., Warme, B., and Falk, M. (2010) *Musik Demenz Begegnung: Musiktherapie für Menschen mit Demenz.* Frankfurt am Main: Mabuse-Verlag.

Reimer, S. (2016) *Affektregulation in der Musiktherapie mit Menschen mit schwerster Mehrfachbehinderung. Zeitpunkt musik.* Wiesbaden: Reichert-Verlag.

Salmon, S. (2012) 'Die Einschätzung der Beziehungsqualität bei Menschen mit Schwerstbehinderung in einem musikpädagogischen Setting.' In A. Langer and M. Oebelsberger (eds) *Reihe Musikpädagogische Forschung Österreich, 4*; G. Enser and M. Oebelsberger (eds) *Vernetzung als Chance für die Musikpädagogik*. Wien, Austria: Universal Edition.

Salmon, S. and Kallos, C. (2010) *"Between Freedom and Ritual." Means of Expression with Music and Movement for People with Disabilities*. Mozarteum University Salzburg/ Department for Music and Dance Education, Orff Institut. UNIMOZ-002.

Schumacher, K. (1999) *Musiktherapie und Säuglingsforschung. Zusammenspiel. Einschätzung der Beziehungsqualität am Beispiel des instrumentalen Ausdrucks eines autistischen Kindes*. Frankfurt am Main: Peter Lang.

Schumacher, K. (2014) 'Music Therapy for Pervasive Developmental Disorders, Especially Autism: A Case Study with Theoretical Basis and Evaluation.' In J. De Backer and J. Sutton (eds) *The Music in Music Therapy. Psychodynamic Music Therapy in Europe: Clinical, Theoretical and Research Approaches*. London: Jessica Kingsley Publishers.

Schumacher, K. (2017) *Musiktherapie bei Kindern mit Autismus. Musik, Bewegungs und Sprachspiele zur Behandlung gestörter Körper und Sinneswahrnehmung*. DVD in collaboration with C. Calvet and S. Reimer. Wiesbaden: Reichert-Verlag.

Schumacher, K. and Calvet, C. (2008) *Synchronisation/Synchronization. Musiktherapie bei Kindern mit Autismus/Music Therapy with Children on the Autistic Spectrum*. DVD box and booklet. Göttingen: Vandenhoeck and Ruprecht.

Schumacher, K. and Calvet, C. (2016) 'The body and the state of affect as starting points in music therapy.' *Tijdschrift voor muziektherapie*. Retrieved 18/09/17 from www.tijdschriftvoormuziektherapie.be/autisme/the-body-and-the-state-of-affect-as-starting-points-in-music-therapy-k-schumacher-c-calvet-2.

Schumacher, K., Calvet, C., and Reimer, S. (2013) *Das EBQ-Instrument und seine entwicklungspsychologischen Grundlagen*. Göttingen: Vandenhoeck and Ruprecht.

Schumacher, K., Calvet, C., and Stallmann, M. (2005) '"Zwischenmenschliche Beziehungsfähigkeit"—Ergebnisse der Reliabilitätsprüfung eines neu entwickelten Instrumentes zum Wirkungsnachweis der Musiktherapie.' In B. Müller-Oursin (ed.) *Ich Wachse, Wenn Ich Musik Mache. Musiktherapie mit chronisch kranken und von Behinderung bedrohten Kindern*. Wiesbaden: Reichert-Verlag.

Schumacher, K. and Calvet-Kruppa, C. (1999a) 'Musiktherapie als Weg zum Spracherwerb.' *Musiktherapeutische Umschau, 20*, 216–221.

Schumacher, K. and Calvet-Kruppa, C. (1999b) 'The AQR—an analysis system to evaluate the quality of relationship during music therapy.' *Nordic Journal of Music Therapy, 8, 2*, 188–192.

Schumacher, K., and Calvet-Kruppa, C. (2001) 'Die Relevanz entwicklungspsychologischer Erkenntnisse für die Musiktherapie.' In H.-H. Decker-Voigt (ed.) *Schulen der Musiktherapie*. München: Reinhardt.

Schumacher, K. and Calvet-Kruppa, C. (2005) '"Untersteh' Dich!"—Musiktherapie bei Kindern mit autistischem Syndrom.' In C. Plahl and H. Koch-Temming (eds) *Musiktherapie für Kinder. Grundlagen, Methoden, Praxisfelder*. Bern: Hans Huber.

Skrzypek, H. (2017) 'Körper, Bewegung und Musik als Partitur für künstlerische Psychotherapien.' Unpublished PhD thesis, University of Music, Augsburg.

Sroufe, L. A. (1997) *Emotional Development: The Organization of Emotional Life in the Early Years*. Cambridge: Cambridge University Press.

Stern, D. (2000) *The Interpersonal World of the Infant*. New York, NY: Basic Books.

Wosch, T. and Wigram, T. (2017) *Microanalysis in Music Therapy – Methods, Techniques and Applications for Clinicians, Researchers, Educators and Students*. London: Jessica Kingsley Publishers.

CHAPTER 11

The Music-Based Evaluation of Cognitive Functioning

Anne Lipe

Setting and motivation

In the early 1980s, the practice of music therapy with older adults was in its infancy. In general, music therapists working in nursing or healthcare facilities for frail older adults, including those with dementia or other cognitive impairments, were employed as part of the activities or recreation therapy staff. The primary goal of this service was to provide diversional activity; the professional literature was very limited in guiding the development of specific, goal-oriented treatment options. One notable exception was the work of music therapy pioneer Marian Palmer who established a music therapy program at Cedar Lake Home in West Bend, Wisconsin, in the 1970s. In an early article, Palmer described music-based interventions to address physical and cognitive needs among older adults in a comprehensive care setting, and shared case examples to illustrate the effectiveness of these techniques (Palmer 1977).

In 1981, when I began my work in a healthcare facility for older adults, I was fresh out of internship and excited about establishing a unique niche for music therapy within the facility. The first step was setting up group music therapy sessions once weekly on each of the facility's seven units. These were general living areas for individuals with a variety of care needs; special dementia care units did not exist at the time. While these groups were open to any resident who wanted to participate, their primary goal was to provide structured music experiences to benefit those whose functional limitations prevented them from successfully participating in many of the general activity programs. In the process of learning, observing, and adapting the musical experiences, I began to notice consistent responses among those with cognitive impairments: people with speech difficulties could correctly sing lyrics to familiar songs; with appropriate prompts, new songs which I introduced were recalled in later sessions; imitation of demonstrated rhythmic patterns was accurate; and many could sustain their attention to group tasks over a 30–40-minute time period. Questions arose: What do these responses mean? How is it that people with moderate or advanced cognitive impairments can still participate successfully in music experiences? What can these responses to musical tasks tell us about intact cognitive processes?

To address this question, I began to explore the role that assessment might play. At this time, formal, standardized assessments for use with older adults with cognitive impairments did not exist. Assessment in music therapy was informal and based on the needs of specific clinical situations (Wheeler 2013). This was consistent with my experience, in which referrals came informally from nursing staff or other members of the treatment team who had seen the positive results of music therapy. I began to realize that some type of formal, standardized assessment process would help to clarify the relationship between music ability and general cognition, and also might support music therapy as a recognized, unique service within this setting. Such a process also would provide a way of systematically organizing and communicating this information to other team members. Additionally, it might have the potential to aid the practitioner in identifying specific music tasks for each individual's needs and to track progress over time. During my doctoral study, I continued to explore possible relationships between music ability and general cognitive functioning, and to develop specific music tasks that might provide information about cognitive functioning in these individuals.

Theoretical background

A primary theoretical foundation for the evolution of the Music-Based Evaluation of Cognitive Functioning (MBECF) was classical test theory. This theory specifies assumptions and procedures for the development and refinement of instruments designed to identify and measure psychological constructs (Crocker and Algina 1986). A fundamental assumption of the theory is that a trait or attribute which can be quantified in an overall score (observed score) represents an underlying "true" trait or attribute plus random error (Cappelleri, Lundy, and Hays 2014). Statistical methods for evaluating an instrument's reliability and validity are employed in order to accurately depict the construct of interest. Central to the classical test theory, and to any discussion of assessment development, is an understanding of the importance of *constructs* and their relationship to observed behaviors. Constructs are defined as intangible psychological characteristics which cannot be measured directly, so their presence must be inferred through observed behaviors (Crocker and Algina 1986). In music therapy, a primary construct of interest is *music ability* or *musicality*, which has been defined in a number of ways (Lipe 2015). Since constructs cannot be observed or measured directly, a primary task in assessment development is to *operationalize* relevant constructs so that they can be measured. Initial development of the MBECF began with observations of responses to music that seemed inconsistent with other verbal or behavioral characteristics of individuals with moderate or severe dementia.

Concurrent with these observations was speculation regarding possible explanatory mechanisms for this phenomenon. Swartz *et al.* (1989) proposed five levels of perceptual ability ranging from a basic level at which general acoustic features are perceived to a complex level which recognizes complex forms and the transformation of thematic and rhythmic aspects of music. Musical perception is presumed to be intact at lower levels of perception if naming is not involved (Swartz *et al.* 1989, p. 154). Advanced musical training or education was hypothesized to slow deterioration at higher levels of perception. Aldridge and Aldridge (1992) hypothesized that hemis-pheric differences in the processing of language and music might explain the phenomenon, noting that music processing involves both hemispheres of the brain. They emphasized that the disorders of perception identified by Swartz and colleagues (1989) might represent disorders of audition rather than deficits in musical ability itself (Aldridge and Aldridge 1992, pp. 248, 252). This observation was further supported by a review of more recent literature which noted that much of what has been learned about music cognition among people with dementia has come from controlled experiments which used tasks requiring verbal responses (Lipe, York, and Jensen 2007). Aldridge and Aldridge (1992) emphasized the importance of using music production tasks to provide information on cognitive functioning in people with dementia. This discussion illustrates that the way in which constructs are defined and interpreted is based largely on the accuracy of the methods chosen to measure them.

Further examples of ways in which type of measurement influences the interpretation of constructs can be found in a brief examination of the principles underlying the development of mental status tests. These instruments are widely used as part of a diagnostic workup to differentiate normal cognitive changes associated with aging from those which may be symptomatic of disease. A brief history of the development of mental status tests shows that earlier approaches assumed that standard measures of intelligence such as the Wechsler Scale of Adult Intelligence could be useful in identifying pathological cognitive change, and this test was frequently used in construct validity testing of these instruments (Lipe 1994). Wechsler (1975) himself believed that while abilities such as reasoning and problem solving are important in defining "intelligence," this construct consists of non-intellective elements as well, the goal of which is to help an individual to successfully understand and cope with the world (Wechsler 1975). Albert (1984) identified five components of mental function which she believed should be part of these examinations: attention, language, memory, visuospatial ability, and conceptualization. Many variations on and interpretations of these components are evident in mental status instruments published between 1943 and the mid-1980s. Some tests were validated using clinical diagnosis, but the criteria used to make diagnoses were inconsistent or not reported. Many instruments were tested with hospitalized individuals, required verbal fluency, and rarely considered educational level and cultural background. Many tasks included in these instruments lacked ecological validity or relevance to an individual's everyday experiences (Lipe 1994).

In attempting to address the question of the relationship between music ability and cognitive functioning, test theory was useful in helping to flesh out how previous measures had defined and operationalized the construct of "cognitive functioning," and how limitations in the development of these measures might have led to an incomplete understanding of the construct of interest. Aldridge and Aldridge (1992) provided detailed examples of the ways in which music production tasks might be useful in assessing areas of cognitive functioning addressed in more traditional instruments and areas such as flexibility and intentionality, which might not be adequately addressed. Their table of comparisons of elements in medical and musical epistemologies served as a template for the development of the tasks for the MBECF, and their possible relationship to similar tasks contained in mental status tests.

Purpose of the MBECF

The MBECF is designed to assess cognitive abilities in older adults with dementia using music performance tasks. The assessment includes 19 tasks which require singing, melodic, rhythmic movement, and verbal responses. One listening task is included but is not scored. Tasks are scored on a scale from 0 to 3 points, with a total possible score on the assessment of 54 points. Practitioners administering this assessment are encouraged to structure it as much like a regular music therapy session as possible. Once invited to participate, the client should be seated directly across from the clinician. A list of equipment needed to conduct the assessment is included in the administration manual, which is available from the author. Also included in the manual are directions for implementing each task.

Development and procedure

The clinical observations and experiences described above provided a starting point for developing specific tasks for the evaluation. Additionally, research literature on the use of music and music therapy with older adults was consulted to examine which tasks or interventions had been most successful in achieving identified outcomes. For example, literature noted the importance of using preferred, familiar songs with these individuals (Gibbons 1977; Gilbert and Beal 1982; Lathom, Petersen, and Havlicek 1982). Prickett and Moore (1991) demonstrated that recall for sung words was higher than for spoken words alone, and that with prompts and practice, individuals with probable Alzheimer's disease could recall words to newly learned songs. Several studies documented positive responses to rhythm tasks, especially those using imitation and repetition. These responses were observed even among those with severe cognitive impairments (Clair 1991; Clair and Bernstein 1990a, 1990b).

The original protocol for the MBECF included two parts. Part I included a questionnaire completed by either the participant or a caregiver which gathered information on music training, background, and experiences with and attitudes about music. Part II was designed to be completed by the music therapist, and included 19 tasks to be administered in a format similar to an individual music therapy session. One listening task was administered at the beginning of the assessment, and was followed by four singing tasks and eight rhythm tasks interspersed with six short verbal tasks (usually questions). The listening task was not scored, but included a short checklist for the therapist to identify any observable behaviors elicited by the listening experience.

Following item analysis of the original instrument (Lipe 1994), one item in Part II was omitted, and several were revised to improve consistency in the scoring. Material in Part I was condensed and the music attitude component was reduced to one question about the meaningfulness of music in the individual's life. Questions about music preference also were included in both the original and revised versions of Part I. The revised version was used in subsequent research (Lipe *et al.* 2007).

Parts I and II of the MBECF may be administered separately, depending upon the cognitive status and energy level of the individual client. Since it gathers information on background and interests in music, Part I can be completed by a surrogate if the client is unable to complete it. Information in Part I is typically obtained through an interview, but can be submitted in writing if necessary. Part II of the evaluation takes approximately 30 minutes to complete and is conducted as a regular individual music therapy session.

Data collection and analysis

In Part I, data is collected on three components of music background. In the music experience category, a number of possible musical experiences are identified in a table which includes a stem—"Did you or do you…?"—and 15 possible options such as "sing in a choir or chorus." The interviewer checks a box "yes" and writes any details of the informant's response in a "Comments" column. One question asks about training in music and, if yes, what the major instrument of study was. One item asks, "How meaningful has music been in your lifetime?" Response options are arranged on a three-point Likert scale, where 3 stands for "very meaningful" and 0 stands for "not at all meaningful." Data on music preferences is collected via open-ended questions about favorite musical genres and songs. None of these items is scored; this information is designed primarily to assist the practitioner in structuring some of the tasks in Part II, and in building an overall musical profile of the client which might be useful during treatment.

Part II includes 18 performance tasks and one listening task.

With the exception of the listening task, responses to all other tasks are scored using a three-point scale. The scoring system of the MBECF is intended to be meaningful, to allow some degree of flexibility on the part of the practitioner, and to reflect genuine differences in musical/cognitive functioning between individuals at different stages of dementia. In general, a score of 3 represents responses which are both correct and offered independently. A level 2 score reflects responses which are partially correct (when multiple responses are necessary), or when prompts are required. In several tasks, a level 2 score indicates that the practitioner recognizes an organized attempt on the part of the client to comply with the *intent* of the task, even if the response lacks the precision required for a level 3 response. A level 1 score is intended to represent the abilities of those who may not have verbal skills but who demonstrate the ability to attend to and engage in music tasks at a very basic level. While guidelines for scoring each task are included in the evaluation administration manual, the musical, clinical, and intuitive skills of the therapist are also important for assigning the most appropriate score for any given task.

The listening task is offered first and provides an opportunity for the client to orient to the music experience. Two to three minutes of recorded ragtime piano music is recommended for this task, but other piano selections may be substituted by the practitioner based on information collected in Part I. This style of music is recommended based on its rhythmic regularity and repetitive structure; the use of piano music is recommended because two additional items (L1V, L2V) ask the client to recall the name of the instrument heard in the earlier task. Since the purpose of this task is to orient the client to the music experience, and to move from a "no music" to "music" environment (activation of music perceptual level 1—Swartz et al. 1989), this item is not scored. A checklist containing six possible behavioral responses to this task is included, and the practitioner may circle "yes" or "no" to indicate which responses, if any, were observed. A verbal task follows the listening experience in which the client is asked to provide the name of the instrument heard in the music. This task is scored on a three-point scale.

The listening task is followed by a series of eight singing and verbal tasks, two tasks involving melodic imitation and improvisation, and seven tasks requiring verbal, movement, and rhythmic responses, each of which is scored using the three-point scale described above. American folk songs are recommended for use on two of the singing tasks because of their repetition, structural simplicity, limited vocal ranges, and likely familiarity to many clients (Taylor 1997). However, substitutions may be made if the musical criteria and content of the substitutions reflect that of the recommended songs. For example, some clinicians substituted the refrain of "Goodnight Irene" for "Ev'ry Night When the Sun Goes In" for singing task S3 as it can be associated with the question asked in the verbal association task which follows. The verbal tasks are interspersed with those involving music production to examine the degree to which music engagement might prime any residual verbal ability and better facilitate recall (Prickett and Moore 1991).

Data interpretation, documentation, and report

Each series of tasks generates a subtotal score; these then are added together for a total score on the evaluation. Table 11.1 illustrates the range of possible scores on the original and revised versions of the MBECF as they relate to scores on the Mini-Mental State Exam (MMSE; Folstein, Folstein, and McHugh 1975).

TABLE 11.1: COMPARISON OF
MMSE AND MBECF SCORES

MMSE scores (N = 82)	MBECF scores[1] (N = 32)	MBECF(Rev) scores (N = 50)
23–30 (without dementia)	41–48	N/A
18–22 (mild impairment)	41–45	40–54
10–17 (moderate impairment)	29–42	30–43
Below 10 (severe impairment)	20–31	2–30

[1] N = 16 individuals with dementia; N = 16 individuals without dementia

In the first study on the MBECF (Lipe 1994), there was a general "ceiling effect" on the evaluation for individuals without dementia, which indicates that the tasks presented little cognitive challenge for this group. Individuals with mild degrees of impairment also scored above 40 on the MBECF; items requiring verbal recall of stimulus material presented some difficulty for these individuals. Those with moderate degrees of impairment generally displayed an inability to respond to verbal items and experienced some difficulty with those requiring singing responses. Severely impaired individuals demonstrated the ability to attend to the entire assessment, and generally performed successfully on items requiring rhythmic responses. A similar pattern was observed in the administration of the revised version (Lipe *et al.* 2007).

Included in the protocol is a separate scoring summary sheet which can be used informally by the clinician in writing up a general report on the results of the evaluation or can be placed directly into a client's permanent record. Documentation and reporting formats are left to the discretion of the clinician, and should be consistent with the policies and procedures of the facility or agency overseeing music therapy services. The MBECF is not designed to be used as a diagnostic tool; however, it may provide additional information on an individual's cognitive ability in order to confirm a diagnosis, especially for those with severe impairment who may be considered "untestable" using other tools. Its primary purpose is to serve as a baseline to identify and evaluate the effectiveness of music therapy interventions selected for an individual client's needs.

Training

The MBECF was designed to be user-friendly, and the manual contains directions for the overall administration of the evaluation plus directions for implementing and scoring each item. Numerous conference sessions and continuing music therapy education sessions (CMTEs) have been offered on the MBECF over the years, but no formal training or certification is necessary to use it. Since the scoring system utilizes clinical knowledge and intuition, the MBECF is designed to be administered by a credentialed music therapist. For example, several of the tasks requiring rhythmic responses require the therapist to determine when a client's playing is, in fact, *in rhythm*. Rather than providing detailed criteria for number of beats or a designated timeframe for these responses, it is left up to the therapist's intuitive musical and clinical judgement to assign the most appropriate score.

Research and psychometrics

Thirty-two older adult women participated in the research on the original MBECF. Sixteen participants had a diagnosis of dementia, while the other 16 did not; some lived in a skilled nursing facility and some attended an adult day center. Presence of dementia was determined by examination of the participant's medical record and confirmed by knowledgeable staff. Part II of the MBECF was administered twice to each individual, and administrations were 10–14 days apart. The investigator scored each evaluation as it was administered. Two trained raters separately viewed and scored videotapes of all of the administrations, and initial rater agreement between the raters and the investigator was .85. The investigator and the two raters met twice to review and resolve any cases in which rater agreement was below .80. Resolving these discrepancies resulted in an overall rater agreement of .92.

Cronbach's alpha analysis produced coefficients of .92 for Administration 1, .93 for Administration 2, and .95 for an average of both administrations, indicating strong internal consistency; a Pearson's correlation of .93 provided evidence of the evaluation's test-retest reliability (Lipe 1995). Criterion validity was demonstrated via Pearson correlations between total scores on the MBECF music performance tasks and scores on three standardized cognitive status measures: the MMSE (Folstein *et al.* 1975); the Brief Cognitive Rating Scale (BCRS; Reisberg *et al.* 1983); and the Severe Impairment Battery (SIB; Saxton *et al.* 1993). The MBECF music performance tasks correlated .93 with scores on the MMSE, −.83 with scores on the BCRS, and .98 with those on the SIB (Lipe 1994). In the BCRS, severity of dementia is represented by higher scores, whereas in the other two measures (and the MBECF) severity of impairment is represented by lower scores. Testing on the SIB was done only with the 16 participants with dementia. All correlations were significant at $p < .01$. A t-test for independent samples performed on total MBECF scores and a breakdown of scores on the verbal, singing, and rhythm tasks demonstrated that those without dementia scored significantly higher on all of these dimensions than did those with dementia. All t-values were significant at $p = .000$ (Lipe 1995).

As noted above, revisions to the MBECF were made based on the results of the original research. Fifty individuals with dementia (33 men and 17 women) participated in a follow-up study designed to examine the construct validity of the MBECF and the Residual Music Skills Test (RMST; York 1994). As in prior research, the MMSE was used to further confirm relationships between music ability and general cognition. Participants were drawn from the general community and from a variety of residential care settings. Cronbach's alpha analysis produced a score of .83 for the MBECF, further supporting the evaluation's internal consistency (Lipe *et al.* 2007). Pearson correlations of .89 between the MMSE and the MBECF, and .83 between the MBECF and the RMST, further supported the usefulness of the evaluation in assessing cognitive functioning in this population, and showed that even though the purpose of the two instruments differs, they are measuring similar aspects of music cognition (Lipe *et al.* 2007). A pattern of correlations examined possible relationships between the verbal, singing, and rhythm tasks on each instrument, and while all correlations between sub-scores were significant, several intriguing patterns emerged which are fully discussed elsewhere (Lipe *et al.* 2007). Regarding construct validity, it was concluded that "'music cognition' is a multidimensional construct comprised of rhythm, singing and melodic skills which can be uniquely identified, but which are not independent of each other" (Lipe et al. 2007, p. 381).

A Korean version (K-MBECF) has been the subject of two studies. The earlier study (Moon and Ko 2014) found that among a sample of 50 Korean older adults with dementia, the K-MBECF had strong internal consistency (Cronbach's alpha = .833), strong inter-rater reliability of 93 percent, and strong criterion validity when scores were compared with those on the K-MMSE (Pearson's r = .745). Scores also differentiated those in mild, moderate, and severe stages of dementia. In a later study, a short form of the K-MBECF was created by using Rasch analysis and Item Response Theory (IRT) to reduce item numbers from 18 to 10. A Content Validity Index (CVI) was used to verify the constructs that the K-MBECF claimed to measure (Moon and Ko 2017). A translation of the MBECF into Japanese has recently been completed (Imura 2017).

Future plans and discussion

Using criteria for evidence-based assessment recommended by Hunsley and Mash (2008), it is clear that use of larger samples and more sophisticated statistical procedures would strengthen the MBECF's psychometric characteristics. While the MMSE still is a widely used screening tool, it is recommended that further research compares MBECF scores to other standard mental status measures such as those described by Sheehan (2012) which are more sensitive to the overall progression of dementia. Recent research has documented the positive effects of music intervention on cognitive functioning in people with dementia (Chang *et al.* 2015; Lin *et al.* 2011), specifically the use of music as a mnemonic device for general content information (Simmons-Stern *et al.* 2012). However, minimal to no effects have been reported in other reviews (van der Steen *et al.* 2017; Zhang *et al.* 2017). The MMSE was the predominant outcome measure in most of the primary studies included in these reviews. Because it has been validated against the MMSE, the MBECF is likely to be useful in this type of research as it may be more sensitive to outcomes of interest to music therapy practitioners than the MMSE.

Given the psychometric information described above, it appears that the MBECF does provide useful information about both musical ability and general cognitive functioning among individuals at various stages of dementia. Music-based assessments are likely to be successful with this population because they focus on cognitive strengths instead of deficits. It is likely that positive associations with music may spark interest and motivate individuals to engage, thus leading to an increased sense of well-being. This was the approach taken in the development of the Music in Dementia Assessment Scales (McDermott, Orrell, and Ridder 2015). Music production tasks also have the advantage of allowing the practitioner to evaluate *process* as well as intent, two important aspects of cognition addressed by Aldridge and Aldridge (1992). For these reasons, the MBECF can be a useful resource for the music therapist providing services to individuals with dementia and their families.

References

Albert, M. (1984) 'Assessment of cognitive function in the elderly.' *Clinical Issues in Geriatric Psychiatry, 25,* 4, 310–317.

Aldridge, D. and Aldridge, G. (1992) 'Two epistemologies: Music therapy and medicine in the treatment of dementia.' *The Arts in Psychotherapy, 19,* 243–255.

Cappelleri, J. C., Lundy, J. J., and Hays, R. D. (2014) 'Overview of classical test theory and item response theory for the quantitative assessment of items in developing patient reported outcome measures.' *Clinical Therapeutics, 36,* 5, 648–662.

Chang, Y. S., Chu, H., Yang, C. Y., Tsai, J. C., *et al.* (2015) 'The efficacy of music therapy for people with dementia: A meta-analysis of randomised controlled trials.' *Journal of Clinical Nursing, 24,* 3425–3440, doi: 10.1111/jocn.12976.

Clair, A. A. (1991) 'Music Therapy for a Severely Regressed Person with a Probable Diagnosis of Alzheimer's Disease: A Case Study.' In K. Bruscia (ed.) *Case Studies in Music Therapy.* Phoenixville, PA: Barcelona Publishers.

Clair, A. A. and Bernstein, B. (1990a) 'A preliminary study of music therapy programming for severely regressed persons with Alzheimer's type dementia.' *The Journal of Applied Gerontology, 9,* 3, 299–311.

Clair, A. A. and Bernstein, B. (1990b) 'A comparison of singing, vibrotactile and nonvibrotactile responses in severely regressed persons with dementia of the Alzheimer's type.' *Journal of Music Therapy, 27,* 3, 119–125.

Crocker, L. and Algina, J. (1986) *Introduction to Classical and Modern Test Theory.* Fort Worth, TX: Holt, Rinehart & Winston.

Folstein, M. F., Folstein, S. E., and McHugh, P. R. (1975) '"Mini-Mental State": A practical method for grading the cognitive state of patients for the clinician.' *Journal of Psychiatric Research, 12,* 189–198.

Gibbons, A. (1977) 'Popular music preferences of elderly people.' *Journal of Music Therapy, 14,* 4, 180–189.

Gilbert, J. P. and Beal, M. R. (1982) 'Preferences of elderly individuals for selected music education experiences.' *Journal of Research in Music Education, 30,* 247–253.

Hunsley, J. and Mash, E. J. (2008) 'Developing Criteria for Evidence-Based Assessment: An Introduction to Assessments that Work.' In J. Hunsley and E. J. Mash (eds) *A Guide to Assessments that Work.* New York, NY: Oxford University Press.

Imura, S. (2017) 'Development of a Japanese Version of the Music-Based Evaluation of Cognitive Functioning (J-MBECF): Forward-Translation and Cultural Adaptation.' Unpublished master's thesis, Shenandoah University, Winchester, VA.

Lathom, W., Petersen, M., and Havlicek, L. (1982) 'Musical preferences of older people attending nutrition sites.' *Educational Gerontology, 8,* 155–165.

Lin, S. T., Yang, P., Lai, C. Y., Su, Y. Y., *et al.* (2011) 'Mental health implications of music: Insight from neuroscientific and clinical studies.' *Harvard Review of Psychiatry, 19,* 1, 34–46, doi: 10.3109/10673229.2011.549769.

Lipe, A. W. (1994) 'The Use of Music Performance Tasks in the Assessment of Cognitive Functioning among Older Adults with Dementia.' Unpublished doctoral dissertation, University of Maryland, College Park, MD.

Lipe, A. W. (1995) 'The use of music performance tasks in the assessment of cognitive functioning among older adults with dementia.' *Journal of Music Therapy, 32,* 3, 137–151.

Lipe, A. W. (2015) 'Music Therapy Assessment.' In B. L. Wheeler (ed.) *Music Therapy Handbook.* New York, NY: Guilford Press.

Lipe, A. W., York, E., and Jensen, E. (2007) 'Construct validity of two music-based assessments for people with dementia.' *Journal of Music Therapy, 44,* 4, 369–387.

McDermott, O., Orrell, M., and Ridder, H. M. (2015) 'The development of Music in Dementia Assessment Scales (MiDAS).' *Nordic Journal of Music Therapy, 24,* 3, 232–251, doi: 10.1080/08098131.2014.907333.

Moon, S. R. and Ko, B. S. (2014) 'The validity and reliability of the Korean version of the Music-Based Evaluation of Cognitive Functioning.' *Korean Journal of Music Therapy, 16,* 1, 49–63.

Moon, S. R. and Ko, B. S. (2017) 'The item analysis and the content validity for developing a short form of Korean version of the Music-Based Evaluation of Cognitive Functioning.' *Korean Journal of Music Therapy, 19,* 1, 73–92, doi: 10.21330/kjmt.2017.19.1.73.

Palmer, M. D. (1977) 'Music therapy in a comprehensive program of treatment and rehabilitation for the geriatric resident.' *Journal of Music Therapy, 14,* 4, 190–197.

Prickett, C. A. and Moore, R. S. (1991) 'The use of music to aid memory of Alzheimer's patients.' *Journal of Music Therapy, 28,* 2, 101–110.

Reisberg, B., Schneck, M. K., Ferris, S. H., Schwartz, G. E., and deLeon, E. D. (1983) 'The Brief Cognitive Rating Scale (BCRS): Findings in primary degenerative dementia (PDD).' *Psychopharmacology Bulletin, 19,* 1, 47–51.

Saxton, J., McGonigle, K. L., Swihart, A. A., and Boller, F. (1993) *The Severe Impairment Battery (SIB) Manual.* Pittsburgh, PA: The University of Pittsburgh, of the Commonwealth System of Higher Education.

Sheehan, B. (2012) 'Assessment scales in dementia.' *Therapeutic Advances in Neurological Disorders, 5,* 6, 349–358, doi: 10.1177/1756285612455733.

Simmons-Stern, N. R., Deason, R. G., Brandler, B. J., Frustace, B. S., *et al.* (2012) 'Music-based enhancement in Alzheimer's disease: Promise and limitations.' *Neuropsychologia, 50,* 3295–3303.

Swartz, K. P., Hantz, E. C., Crummer, G. C., Walton, J. P., *et al.* (1989) 'Does the melody linger on? Music cognition in Alzheimer's disease.' *Seminars in Neurology, 9,* 2, 152–158.

Taylor, D. B. (1997) *Biomedical Foundations of Music as Therapy.* St. Louis, MO: MMB Music, Inc.

van der Steen, J. T., van Soest-Poortvliet, M. D., van der Wouden, J. C., Bruinsma, M. S., *et al.* (2017) 'Music-based therapeutic interventions for people with dementia (review).' *Cochrane Database of Systematic Reviews, 5,* Art. No.: CD003477; doi: 10.1002/14651858.CD003477.pub3.

Wechsler, D. (1975) 'Intelligence defined and undefined: A relativistic approach.' *American Psychologist, 30,* 135–139.

Wheeler, B. (2013) 'Music Therapy Assessment.' In R. F. Cruz and B. Feder (eds) *Feder's The Art and Science of Evaluation in the Arts Therapies.* Springfield, IL: Charles C. Thomas.

York, E. (1994) 'The development of a quantitative music skills test for patients with Alzheimer's disease.' *Journal of Music Therapy, 31,* 4, 280–296.

Zhang, Y., Cai, J., An, L., Hui, F., *et al.* (2017) 'Does music therapy enhance behavioral and cognitive function in elderly dementia patients? A systematic review and meta-analysis.' *Ageing Research Reviews, 35,* 1–11.

CHAPTER 12

Residual Music Skills

Elizabeth York

Setting and motivation

It has been my experience that research questions arise while involved in clinical work. In 1988, I began to provide music therapy sessions in Atlanta, Georgia (USA), for a group of physically healthy elders who had recently been discharged from Georgia State Hospital, a large inpatient psychiatric facility in Milledgeville, Georgia. The arts-based work, made possible through a grant from the Dekalb County Arts Council, resulted in a performance piece entitled "I Heard the Angels Singing," performed by the participants at the facility. These elders, some in their eighties, had been institutionalized for many years and were now members of a day program where they learned daily living skills (including leisure pursuits), with the goal of living as independently as possible within their community. I was introduced to a group of primarily African Americans with whom I had little in common. As a white woman growing up in the segregated South, I had few interactions with the black community. Other than songs I had learned in school, and on my grandmother's knee, I knew only a few spirituals and work songs that might help me to forge a trusting relationship with this group of elders.

When I first met them they were quiet, and, I imagined, skeptical of what a white woman with a guitar might have to offer. The first song I sang was a lullaby first sung to me by my grandmother called

"Go to Sleep." As I finished my version of the song, Elnora began to sing additional lyrics that I had never heard: "And one'll be black, and one'll be blue, and one'll be the color of your Grandpa's shoes." After that memorable beginning, I decided on a theme-based approach to our music sessions that, I intuited, might evoke memories of their lives before they were hospitalized: sessions devoted to mothers, church, holidays, and cooking. Over three months, at each weekly session, I began with a song related to the theme of the day (a song I remembered). They sang songs from their childhood, songs that their mothers had taught them, songs sung with their bare feet pounding out rhythms on wooden floors because there were no pianos or other instruments in their churches. They talked about favorite foods and how to cook them: sweet potatoes, collard greens, corn bread ("Mama's little baby loves shortnin', shortnin'. Mama's little baby loves shortnin' bread"). I recorded each session and transcribed what I heard, much like an ethnomusicologist might when researching music from another culture.

The wealth of stories and songs contained in the memories of those individuals (some hospitalized for up to 30 years) moved me and led me to pursue graduate school in 1990 at the University of Miami (UM), Florida. I was fascinated by the ability of "the right music" to stimulate memories, not only spoken stories, but retrieving lyrics and melodies of meaningful songs from the past. I hypothesized that musical memory must be robust when I assessed and accessed familiar songs. My first year of graduate school was also the year of the first Senate Hearing on Music and Aging (1992). The hearing resulted in funding eight research projects of music therapists across the country who were working with older adults. Dr. Ted Tims, my mentor at UM, received one of those grants along with his colleague Dr. David Loewenstein from the University of Miami Center of Adult Development and Aging. Their study explored the physiological effects of music therapy with persons with probable Alzheimer's disease. My dissertation research devoted to assessment of the subjects piggy-backed onto their project. Shawn Buller, Gary

Verhagen, and I served as graduate research assistants. We developed and implemented the music therapy protocol. They served as independent raters in my study.

Dr. David Boyle, head of music education at UM at the time, was an expert on musical assessment along with his colleague Dr. Rudy Radocy from the University of Kansas. Together they published *Measurement and Evaluation of Musical Experiences* (1987) and I was fortunate to take Dr. Boyle's class. Much of the content was devoted to measures that had been developed to assess music perception, aptitude, and learning from a music educator's perspective (Bentley 1966; Gordon 1965, 1979; Seashore, Lewis, and Saetveit 1960). Most of these tests contained aural discrimination tasks folded within musical domains of pitch, rhythm, melody, timbre, and harmony. For example, tasks required the listener to determine highness or lowness of pitch, "same or different" melodic fragments, or recall/ identify rhythmic patterns. Gibbons (1982, 1983a, 1983b) was the only music therapist at the time who had used the Music Aptitude Profile (MAP) and Primary Measures of Music Audiation (PMMA) to investigate aural discrimination in healthy older adults and found that scores did not necessarily diminish with age. Those findings led me back to my original fascination with the preservation of musical memories and behaviors that I had observed with the African American clients with whom I had worked in Atlanta, Georgia.

Theoretical background

At the time of my original study, a small body of music therapy literature found clinical evidence of the preservation of musical memory in individuals with Alzheimer's disease (Aldridge and Aldridge 1992; Lipe 1991; Olderog-Millard and Smith 1989; Prickett and Moore 1991). Other researchers suggested that preservation of musical memory in patients with Alzheimer's disease might be due to the use of alternative cognitive, memory, and other neural mechanisms when presented with auditory and musical stimuli (Crystal, Grober, and Masur 1989; Walton et al. 1988). These authors supported my clinical observations that the musical behaviors of older individuals, even those with dementia, appear to be maintained while other cognitive functions decline.

Early in my graduate studies I conducted a case study with a 79-year-old woman in the middle stages of Alzheimer's disease (AD) at the Miami VA (Veterans Administration) Medical Center. She had been terminated from speech therapy due to severe expressive aphasia. Nevertheless, she continued to play an Orff xylophone in perfect rhythm as I sang a medley of songs from her youth, and, much to my surprise, read song lyrics out loud when she could not initiate spontaneous speech (York 1990). Lipe (1991) had published a similar case study of music therapy with an Alzheimer's patient. She identified the need for "standardized assessment and evaluation measures which are sensitive to the cognitive strengths of individuals with severe impairment" (p. 104). Her research questions were similar to my own. Could I create a scored assessment that included a sequence of active musical tasks which might reveal and quantify the preservation of musical behaviors in patients with AD? Was it possible to meet the criteria developed for standardized assessment tools in other professions? I could only do this by delving into the formidable world of psychometrics.

I explored standardized screening instruments that had been developed to identify cognitive decline and mental status in older adults. (A thorough treatment of many widely used tests may be found in a review by MacDougall (1990).) One was an extensive research tool, the Luria-Nebraska Neuropsychological Battery (LNNB; Golden *et al.* 1980), a neuropsychological test shown to be effective in discriminating among individuals with lateralized or localized injuries of the brain. The LNNB contained 12 musical items in its Rhythm subtest, including active musical tasks such as motor production of rhythmic patterns and the ability to sing a familiar song, and receptive tasks such as aural discrimination of melodic stimuli.

The other relevant tool was the Mini-Mental State Examination (MMSE; Folstein, Folstein, and McHugh 1975), a short, scored cognitive test that was determined to be a reliable and valid tool to identify cognitive impairment. Scores of 23 or below are considered indicators of dementia (Cockrell and Folstein 1988). The MMSE had been recognized by the National Institute of Neurological and Communicative Disorders and Stroke, and the Alzheimer's Disease and Related Disorders Association work group, as a quantitative aid in the clinical examination for AD (McDougall 1990). While the MMSE cannot diagnose AD, it has been shown to have concurrent validity with other, more comprehensive, neuropsychological instruments (Giordani et al. 1990). The popularity of the MMSE can be attributed to its ease of administration (5–10 minutes), which is helpful to clinicians working with dementia patients with attentional deficits (York 1994).

Description of the Residual Music Skills Test

The Residual Music Skills Test (RMST) is a quantitative tool designed to identify and measure "residual music skills" which I operationally defined as "music behaviors acquired over a lifetime without the benefit of formal musical training" (York 1994, p. 283). In other words, these were the musical skills acquired via enculturation. The test was specifically designed for older adults with possible/probable AD, but, I believe, has potential to be used for adults with other forms of cognitive impairment. Because a small body of clinical evidence has indicated that persons with probable AD may retain certain aspects of music cognition (remembering words to familiar songs, the ability to maintain a steady beat, for example), the clinical assessment and identification of these skills offers the music therapist and caregiver an additional means of communicating and interacting with a person with probable Alzheimer's type dementia. Since the RMST measures only musical skills and behaviors, it cannot be considered as a traditional music therapy assessment which typically measures non-musical domains such as social interaction, physical and emotional responses, and attentional attributes. However, if patients score high on the RMST (maximum score is 80), indicating the preservation of musical behaviors, they may be presumed to be good candidates for music therapy. Additionally, since the test provides scores on subtests and an overall score, it is possible to determine reliability and validity using the rigorous statistical analysis required to meet psychometric standards (i.e. required for standardization of any scored instrument).

Test construction and content validity

Initially, the content of the RMST was loosely modeled after the format of Folstein's MMSE. Test items generally reflected active and passive tasks that might be encountered in a music therapy session, and musical items that would correspond to non-musical items in the MMSE. Content validity was also supported by music objectives at the age 9 level to control for musical training (Norris and Bowes 1970). These included:

- singing words to a familiar song with and without a musical cue

- speaking the title of a familiar song with a musical cue

- identification of individual popular instruments by sound

- spontaneous rhythmic behaviors in response to a piece of recorded music

- performance of just previously heard rhythmic patterns

- two tasks involving the vocal repetition of just previously heard melodic patterns and previously heard instrumental sounds.

Short-term memory tasks, and one task that asked the subject to read and carry out a verbal command, were informed by the LNNB (Golden et al. 1980).

The initial version of the RMST (1991) was piloted with eight subjects diagnosed with probable AD at Vanderbilt University and the Miami VA Medical Center. Revisions were made to test items and scoring after that initial administration. Subtests in the revised RMST (1994) include: Recall of Song (1 item, 31 points); Instrument Identification (1 item, 6 points); Tonal Memory/Pitch Discrimination (1 item, 10 points); Short-Term Recall of Instrument Name and Song (2 items, 8 points); Musical Language (3 items, 12 points); and Rhythm Tasks (3 items, 13 points). The Musical Language tasks are musical measures of long-term memory as well as indicators of word retrieval and expressive language functioning. Short-term recall tasks are musical measures of short-term memory. Subjects were given numerical credit for a wide range of possible responses, giving subjects as many points as possible for each task. Total maximum score is 80 points.

A revised version of the RMST was subsequently field tested with 37 subjects in two-day treatment programs for AD patients in Atlanta, Georgia (York 1994). Preliminary data was obtained to analyze items, assess internal consistency, and determine inter-rater reliability using two independent raters. An attempt was made to explore relationships between the RMST and Folstein's MMSE (York 1994). All these steps utilized psychometric analysis required for the standardization of quantitative tests, including Pearson's Product Moment Correlation, Cronbach's alpha, and the Spearman Brown prophecy formula.

Reliability analysis

INTER-RATER RELIABILITY

In the 1994 study, two independent raters simultaneously scored each subject and inter-rater reliability was found to be high (r = .96). Subsequent inter-rater reliability analysis undertaken as a component of my dissertation research revealed an r > .90 at four data collection points taken at baseline, pre-test, post-test, and six-week follow-up (York 1995).

INTERNAL CONSISTENCY

Cronbach's alpha reliability analysis resulted in a coefficient of .66. Item discrimination analysis conducted on the RMST revealed strong positive correlations between Musical Recall (singing), Musical Language tasks, and overall test scores ($r = .87$ and $r = .82$). The results from the item discrimination procedure indicate strong relationships between scores on items that require singing (Items 1, 3, 6, 9). This suggests residual expressive language preservation in those individuals who scored highest on the RMST.

TEST-RETEST RELIABILITY

High test-retest reliability was found in a sample of 95 subjects in Utah diagnosed with possible and probable AD ($r = .92$). In this study, subjects were administered the RMST initially and retested 14 days after the initial administration (York 2000).

Validity analysis

CONSTRUCT VALIDITY

In the Atlanta study (York 1994), comparisons were made between RMST scores and scores from Folstein's MMSE (1975). Correlations between total scores of both tests were positive, but not strong ($r = .61$), indicating that the two tests were measuring very different aspects of cognitive functioning. Language sub-scores of the RMST and the MMSE were more highly correlated ($r = .72$).

Lipe and her colleagues (Lipe, York, and Jensen 2007) found additional evidence for construct validity between her tool, the Music-Based Evaluation of Cognitive Functioning (MBECF; Lipe 1995), the RMST (York 1994), and Folstein's MMSE (1975). Correlations were stronger between the MBECF and the MMSE ($r = .89$) compared to the RMST and the MMSE ($r = .76$). I conclude that the differences can be attributed to the intention of the RMST to identify music skills as opposed to the MBECF which uses musical tasks to assess general cognition. However, the fact that a correlation of .83 was obtained between the total scores of the MBECF compared to the total scores on the RMST indicates that both assessments measure similar aspects of music cognition.

Administration

The RMST is designed to be administered individually. Completion of the test takes approximately 15–20 minutes, although there is no set time limit. The test should be administered in a room with adequate lighting, minimal distractions, and a table and chairs for the subject and therapist. The individual to be assessed is positioned facing the therapist sitting across from the table. Please refer to the complete RMST administration procedures at the end of this chapter.

The following materials are needed to administer the RMST:

- a high-quality CD player (or other digital music player, MP3, iPhone) positioned within one meter of the subject. Recorded materials include:

  ◦ instrumental version of "You Are My Sunshine" (Davis 1937)

  ◦ sounds of a drum, guitar, and piano

  ◦ instrumental versions of:

    • "Happy Birthday" (public domain)

    • "Star Spangled Banner" (public domain)

    • "Chattanooga Choo Choo" (Warren and Gordon 1941).

  These songs can be recorded on piano with the exception of "Chattanooga Choo Choo," which is the original big band version by the Glenn Miller Orchestra.

- two maracas

- four laminated 8"×11" pictures of a piano, a guitar, a trumpet, and a drum

- a laminated 8"×11" sign that reads in bold letters, "Clap Your Hands"

- two tone bars (C and G) to provide pitches for a five-note scale and first phrase of "Zip-a-Dee-Doo-Dah" (Wrubel and Gilbert 1946)

- copy of the RMST with embedded script/instructions.

Interpretation of scores

The most accurate interpretation of a score on the test is that those with higher scores retain more residual music skills than those with lower scores. A close examination by the music therapist of the pattern of responses to individual items will provide guidance in the development and measurement of specific treatment goals and objectives for individual patients. No testing has been conducted to determine "norms" for residual music skills in this population. If scores with a sample of normal adults without dementia were compared with patients with dementia, we might find significant differences. Comparing scores on the RMST with persons in varying stages of AD might be useful. Until more studies are conducted, we don't know what might characterize "decline" in residual music skills reflected in test scores over time.

Limitations and assets

I acknowledge that the RMST was developed in the southern United States. Several songs are typically associated with southern culture and relevant to songs typical of the age group with whom I worked in 1992–95. Updating those songs may be necessary as a new generation of Alzheimer's patients comes of age who live in different parts of the United States. An attempt has been made to translate the test into Japanese (Okazaki 1999). Items were adapted to correspond to Japanese culture (instrument sounds and familiar songs). Pilot testing with 20 older adults in Japan revealed that the RMST could be adapted within a different cultural context without difficulty. Future studies conducted internationally might explore whether "residual music skills" are consistent across cultures.

The studies on the construction and psychometric properties of the RMST have been conducted with small samples with the exception of the test-retest reliability study (York 2000). Further research on the RMST will benefit from the use of larger samples. A study examining test scores with healthy older adults would provide the normative data useful in comparisons between patients with dementia and normal older adults. Singing tasks were found to be highly correlated with overall test scores of the RMST. Therefore, scoring and weight of those items that require singing may need to be re-evaluated. However, since expressive aphasia is characteristic of persons in mid-to-late stages of the disease, items requiring musical language (especially sung words to familiar songs) may be early indicators of cognitive decline. Alternatively, demonstration of singing skills over time may confirm anecdotal clinical reports that musical language is unique and can be accessed by the patient with cognitive deficiencies even when spoken language is declining. Studies using an experimental design with the RMST might explore the effects of music therapy interventions on comparing pre-post test scores; it will also be possible to compare scores over time to determine if musical language changes are parallel with changes in spoken language and how these changes affect total scores as well as sub-scores within the test. The RMST might also be field tested with patients with cognitive impairments due to traumatic brain injury and other dementias.

Conclusion

Radocy doubted whether psychometrically valid tests could be created for music therapy because the profession was so diverse (Radocy 1999). Cuddy and Duffin (2005) noted that the "efforts of test developers to design reliable, quantitative, music memory tests for AD patients should be supported" (p. 233). They insisted that evidence of the preservation of musical memory in Alzheimer's dementia is still primarily anecdotal. The RMST was created just for this purpose. It has been found to be suitable for administration to individuals with a clinical diagnosis of possible or probable AD. Not only was the test simple to administer, but it appeared that, for most subjects, taking the test was a non-stressful experience, based on the observation of positive affective responses and unsolicited musical responses during testing. This is a positive outcome, given the short attention span and distractibility during evaluation of persons with severe cognitive impairment.

The RMST may serve to enhance existing qualitative facility-based behavioral assessments currently used in residential care, since reliability and validity have been determined. Administering the test over time may produce useful information as to the decline in music cognition versus the decline of other cognitive functions. Its use in treatment facilities for Alzheimer's patients may help to identify individuals who might benefit from music therapy treatment and provide an indication of how music might enhance the quality of life for both AD patients and their caregivers. Lipe and York have continued to advocate for evidence-based assessment approaches that would lead to targeted treatment goals and objectives and best practice decisions (Lipe 2015; Lipe and York 2000). We who have pioneered in developing quantitative tests suitable for specific client populations have met the challenge from those who doubted that it was possible. Its usefulness has yet to be determined in clinical settings, and my fervent wish is that this publication will lead to the use of the RMST in clinical practice.

References

Aldridge, D. and Aldridge, G. (1992) 'Two epistemologies: Music therapy and the treatment of dementia.' *The Arts in Psychotherapy, 19,* 243–255.

Bentley, A. (1966) *Music Ability in Children and its Measurement.* New York, NY: October House, Inc.

Boyle, J. D. and Radocy, R. E. (1987) *Measurement and Evaluation of Musical Experiences.* New York, NY: Shirmer.

Cockrell, J. R. and Folstein, M. F. (1988) 'Mini-Mental State Examination.' *Psychopharmacology Bulletin, 24,* 689–692.

Cuddy, L. L. and Duffin, J. (2005) 'Music, memory, and Alzheimer's disease: Is music recognition spared in dementia, and how can it be assessed?' *Medical Hypotheses, 64,* 229–235.

Crystal, H., Grober, E., and Masur, D. (1989) 'Preservation of musical memory in Alzheimer's disease.' *Journal of Neurology, Neurosurgery, and Psychiatry, 52,* 1415–1416.

Davis, J. (1937) 'You Are My Sunshine.' Decca Records.

Folstein, M. F., Folstein, S. E., and McHugh, P. R. (1975) 'Mini-mental state: A practical method for grading the cognitive state of patients for the clinician.' *Journal of Psychiatric Research, 12,* 189–198.

Gibbons, A. C. (1982) 'Musical Aptitude Profile scores in a non-institutionalized elderly population.' *Journal of Music Therapy, 30,* 23–29.

Gibbons, A. C. (1983a) 'Item analysis of the Primary Measures of Music Audiation in elderly care home residents.' *Journal of Music Therapy, 20,* 201–210.

Gibbons, A. C. (1983b) 'Primary Measures of Music Audiation scores in an institutionalized elderly population.' *Journal of Music Therapy, 20,* 21–29.

Giordani, B., Boivin, M. J., Hall, A. L., Foster, N. L., *et al.* (1990) 'The utility and generality of the Mini-Mental State Examination scores in Alzheimer's disease.' *Neurology, 40,* 1894–1896.

Golden, C. J., Sweet, J., Hammeke, T., Purisch, A., Graber, B., and Osman, D. (1980) 'Factor analysis of the Luria-Nebraska Neuropsychological Battery: I. Motor, rhythm and tactile scales.' *International Journal of Neuroscience, 11,* 91–99.

Gordon, E. E. (1965) *Music Aptitude Profile.* Boston, MA: Houghton Mifflin.

Gordon, E. E. (1979) *Primary Measures of Music Audiation.* Chicago, IL: GIA Publications.

Lipe, A. (1991) 'Using music therapy to enhance the quality of life in a client with Alzheimer's dementia: A case study.' *Music Therapy Perspectives, 9,* 102–105.

Lipe, A. (1995) 'The use of music performance tasks in the assessment of cognitive functioning among older adults with dementia.' *Journal of Music Therapy, 32,* 137–151.

Lipe, A. (2015) 'Music Therapy Assessment.' In B. L. Wheeler (ed.) *Music Therapy Handbook.* New York, NY: Guilford Press.

Lipe, A. and York, E. F. (2000) 'Guest editorial: Special issue on assessment in music therapy.' *Music Therapy Perspectives, 18,* 11–12.

Lipe, A., York, E. F., and Jensen, E. (2007) 'Construct validation of two music-based assessments for people with dementia.' *Journal of Music Therapy, 54,* 369–387.

McDougall, G. J. (1990) 'A review of screening instruments for assessing cognition and mental status in older adults.' *Nurse Practitioner, 15,* 18–28.

Norris, E. L. and Bowes, J. E. (1970) *National Assessment of Educational Progress: Music Objectives.* Ann Arbor, MI: National Assessment Office.

Okazaki, K. (1999) 'A Japanese adaptation of the Residual Music Skills Test.' Unpublished manuscript.

Olderog-Millard, K. A. and Smith, J. M. (1989) 'The influence of group singing therapy on the behavior of Alzheimer's disease patients.' *Journal of Music Therapy, 26,* 58–70.

Prickett, C. A. and Moore, R. S. (1991) 'The use of music to aid memory of Alzheimer's patients.' *Journal of Music Therapy, 28,* 101–110.

Radocy, R. (1999) 'Measurement Traditions: May They Facilitate Music Therapy Assessments?' In B. Wilson and E. York (eds) *Proceedings of the Institute on Music Therapy Assessment, 4–8.* Washington, DC: World Congress of Music Therapy.

Seashore, C. E., Lewis, L., and Saetveit, J. G. (1960) *Seashore Measures of Musical Talents.* New York, NY: The Psychological Corporation.

Senate hearings (1992) 'Forever Young: Music and Aging. Hearing before the senate special committee on aging.' *Music Therapy Perspectives, 10,* 45–61.

Walton, J. P., Frisina, R. D., Swartz, K. P., Hantz, E., and Crummer, G. C. (1988) 'Neural basis for music cognition: Future directions and biomedical implications.' *Psychomusicology, 7,* 127–138.

Warren, H. (composer) and Gordon, M. (lyricist) (1941) 'Chattanooga Choo Choo.' [Recorded by Glenn Miller AAF Orchestra.] On Sun Valley serenade [audio recording]. Camden, NJ: Bluebird Records (May 7, 1941).

Wrubel, A. and Gilbert, R. (1946) 'Zip-a-Dee-Doo-Dah.' Anaheim, CA: Disney Productions.

York, E. F. (1990) 'A Music Therapy Assessment of a Patient Diagnosed with Alzheimer's Type Dementia.' Unpublished manuscript, University of Miami.

York, E. F. (1994) 'The development of a quantitative music skills test for patients with Alzheimer's disease.' *Journal of Music Therapy, 31,* 280–296.

York, E. F. (1995) 'The Effects of Music Therapy Interventions on Naming and Verbal Fluency in Persons with Probable Alzheimer's Disease.' Unpublished PhD dissertation, University of Miami.

York, E. F. (2000) 'A test-retest reliability study of the Residual Music Skills Test.' *Psychology of Music, 28,* 174–180.

Residual Music Skills Test (RMST)

Introduction

"[Name], I'd like to ask you some questions about music today. Do you like music?" (Wait for reply.) "I hope this will be enjoyable. If you get tired, just let me know, and we'll rest for a while."

Recall of song (31 points)

"I'm going to play a song that might be familiar to you. If you can, I want you to sing along with the recording. Try to sing as many words as you remember."

(Score 1 point per word. Circle each word sung.)

You are my sunshine, my only sunshine

You make me happy when skies are grey.

You'll never know dear, how much I love you.

Please don't take my sunshine away.

Davis, 1937, Decca Records

"Do you remember the name of that song?"

_____ Score 1 point if person remembers name of song.

_____ Score 0 points if person does not remember.

Recall of song sub-score _____

Instrument identification (6 points)

Show pictures of four instrument cards.

"Here are some pictures of common musical instruments. I am going to play you the sounds of three musical instruments. I want you to *point* to the instrument that you hear after you have heard each one."

Recorded sounds are played one at a time. *Score 2 points for each correct answer.* After each attempt, say the name of the instrument. Repeat until the person can say all three.

_____ Drum _____ Piano _____ Guitar

Instrumentation identification sub-score _____

Tonal memory/pitch discrimination (10 points)
"Now I want you to sing this after me: la la la la la." (Reference C on tone bar and sing first five notes in a C major scale sung a cappella in moderate 4/4 time.)

_____ *Score 2 points for each note sung in tune.*

_____ *Score 1 point for each approximated pitch.*

_____ *Score 0 points if person is unable to complete task.*

Tonal memory/pitch discrimination sub-score _____

Short-term recall of instrument names and song (8 points)
Show pictures of music instruments again.

"I played three musical instrument sounds for you a few minutes ago. Can you point to the musical instruments you heard?"

Score 2 points for each correct answer.

_____ Drum _____ Piano _____ Guitar

"I played a song for you a few minutes ago. Can you tell me the name of that song?"

_____ *Score 2 points for correct answer ("You Are My Sunshine").*

Short-term recall sub-score _____

Musical language (12 points)
"Now I am going to play two more songs that you might know."

Play instrumental versions of "Happy Birthday" and "Star Spangled Banner."

After each song is played, ask the song's name.

Score 1 point for the following behaviors while songs are played.

Humming _____ Whistling _____ Singing words _____ ("Happy Birthday")

Humming _____ Whistling _____ Singing words _____ ("Star Spangled Banner")

Score I point for each correct name.

_____ "Happy Birthday" _____ "Star Spangled Banner"

"Now I want you to sing exactly what I sing. Listen first, and then YOU sing." (Reference G tone bar. Sing first five notes of "Zip-a-Dee-Doo-Dah" (Wrubel and Gilbert, 1946, Disney Productions).)

_____ *Score I point if person matches pitches exactly.*

_____ *Score I point if person imitates contour of melody.*

_____ *Score I point if person sings syllables correctly.*

"Now I would like you to sing a line from any song that you know."

_____ *Score I point if person completes task.*

_____ *Score I point if person is unable to complete task.*

Musical language sub-score _____

Rhythm tasks (13 points)

"I want to show you this instrument." (Show maraca.) "It's called a maraca, and here's how you play it." (Demonstrate in a moderate 4/4 tempo.) "I'd like you to play a maraca with me." (Hand person another maraca.) "You play when I start. Ready? GO!"

_____ *Score 3 points if person plays evenly with therapist.*

_____ *Score 2 points if person plays randomly.*

_____ *Score I point if person holds instrument but does not play.*

_____ *Score 0 points if person does not hold instrument.*

"Now I am going to show you a sign. I want you to read the sign and do what the sign tells you to do." (Show CLAP YOUR HANDS sign, written in large, bold letters.)

_____ *Score 3 points if person claps more than once, evenly, in rhythm.*

_____ *Score 2 points if person claps more than once randomly.*

_____ *Score 1 point if person claps once.*

_____ *Score 0 points if person is unable to complete task.*

"Now I'm going to play some music for you that I hope you'll enjoy. Feel free to do anything you want while the music is playing." (Play instrumental version of "Chattanooga Choo Choo" (Warren and Gordon, 1941, Bluebird Records).)

Score 1 point for each of the following rhythmic behaviors:

_____ Clapping _____ Tapping feet _____ Nodding head

_____ Swaying in chair _____ Tapping fingers on table

_____ Dancing   Other: _____

Rhythm sub-score _____

Total score: _____ *(maximum score: 80 points)*

Comments:

_____

_____

_____

_____

_____

CHAPTER 13

The Interpersonal Music-Communication Competence Scales

Søren Hald

Setting and motivation

After finishing my master's degree in music therapy, I started working within the field of neurological rehabilitation with people suffering from acquired brain injury (ABI). Clients suffering from an ABI can have a wide range of individual rehabilitation needs (e.g. physical, cognitive, psychological, and social needs/problems). However, since the brain is the mediator of all types of interactions, I realized that almost all my clients suffering from ABI had problems with interpersonal communication. In addition, I experienced that music therapy was able to change my clients' ability to communicate. After some years of clinical work, I felt the urge to describe, quantify, and structure my experiences, and this specific motivation led to my PhD study.

People with ABI display reduced interpersonal communication competencies. Often they experience difficulties in engaging in conversation due to difficulties in topic maintenance, memory, self-expression and clarity (verbal and non-verbal), initiative, understanding of social rules (inappropriate behavior), perseveration, and sensitivity to communication partners (Bateman *et al.* 2010; Kay *et al.* 1992; Struchen *et al.* 2008). In addition, music therapy has been found to enhance interpersonal communication abilities in people with ABI (Barker and Brunk 1991; Gilbertson and Aldridge 2008; Jeong and Kim 2007; Nayak *et al.* 2000; Purdie 1997).

For the above reasons, I began my PhD study with an emphasis on the effect of music therapy on interpersonal communication competencies in people suffering from ABI, both in music and in everyday life. As there were no usable standardized measures of interpersonal communication competencies available at the time, I developed my own assessment instrument. In-depth information on the theory, analysis, and research results of the Interpersonal Music-Communication Competence Scale (IMCCS) is available in several publications (Hald 2012; Hald, Baker, and Ridder, 2015, 2017).

Theoretical background

In the literature, definitions of interpersonal communication are very diverse. Sias and Jablin (2001) state in their review of communication competencies: "There are almost as many definitions of communication competence as there are researchers interested in the construct" (p. 820). Their statement is supported by communication expert Spitzberg (2003), who states: "Few characteristics are more important to the everyday quality of life as the skill with which interpersonal communication is negotiated, yet few concepts are as difficult to define and assess as interpersonal skills" (p. 93). Interpersonal communication competencies are defined here as a combination of communication skills (which are the exchange of messages) and interpersonal skills (which are essentially relational and process oriented) (Duffy *et al.* 2004).

The purpose of spoken communication is semantic interchange, whereas the purpose of non-verbal communication is often seen as complementing the spoken word (Hargie and Dickson 2004). Burgoon and Bacue (2003) write about the importance of non-verbal communication:

> Far too often, however, theoretical and practical conceptions of communication skill emphasize the role of verbal cues while discounting the importance of nonverbal behaviors in actualization of this endeavour. This is particularly alarming given estimates that upwards of 60% of the meaning in any social situation is communicated nonverbally…and research indicating that nonverbal cues are especially likely to be believed when they conflict with verbal messages. (Burgoon and Bacue 2003, p. 179)

Interpersonal communication is a continuous process of signaling to and receiving signals from others. Neurologically, the communicative modus is a continuous process of sensory input, integration, and motor output. The communicating self is composed of many relatively separate, but interdependent, neural systems that function as a coherent self-system (Hart 2006). Neurologist Damasio (2010) emphasizes that the communicating "self" is neurological, stemming from a complex network of systems in body and brain.

ABI and interpersonal communication

Living a meaningful life with interpersonal interaction is often compromised when people acquire a brain injury. Even though the literature emphasizes that ABI is often accompanied by social and interpersonal problems, there are only a limited number of empirical studies that investigate this (Struchen 2005). In Table 13.1, a synthesis of information about common cognitive and behavioral changes seen after ABI is presented (Struchen 2005). In the left column, the cognitive and behavioral changes are listed, and in the right column the impact on social communication abilities is explained.

TABLE 13.1: EXAMPLES OF COMMON COGNITIVE/ BEHAVIORAL CHANGES SEEN AFTER ABI

Cognitive/behavioral changes due to traumatic brain injury	Possible impact on social communication abilities
Attention/concentration	
Poor concentration	Difficulty maintaining a topic, difficulty keeping track of conversation in presence of distractions
Difficulty shifting attention	Difficulty switching topic, problems in shifting between speaker and listener roles
Slowed processing speed	Long pauses in speaking, slowed-down speaking rate, difficulty comprehending others when speaking at normal rate
Learning and memory	
Poor immediate memory	Repeats self, loses track of conversation topic
Intrusions, susceptibility to interference	Mixes up instructions or messages, has difficulty staying on topic
Poor organization of learning/recall	Disorganized speech, rambling
Executive functioning	
Difficulty with integration	Difficulty reconciling conflicting verbal/non-verbal information
Reduced initiation	Reduced initiation of conversation, apparent lack of interest in others
Poor self-monitoring	Poor use of feedback, poor recognition of errors
Poor planning/organization	Poor sequencing in giving directions, poorly organized speech

Egocentricity	Interrupts, excessive talking, difficulty taking others' perspectives
Perseveration	Difficulty changing topic, stereotyped responses
Poor regulation of emotion/behavior	Unpredictable social behavior, inappropriate laughter, excessive expression of anger
Poor self-awareness	Described unrealistic goals or life situations, lack of credibility, poor use of compensatory strategies

(Struchen 2005, p. 90)

Most of these problems become apparent in musical interactions with people suffering from ABI as well. The music therapy setting offers a scene where these problems can be rehabilitated. People with ABI in the music therapy setting are offered the possibility to rehearse communicative musicality abilities such as pulse, quality, and narratives. Further, interpersonal communication competencies such as attentiveness, empathy, self-disclosure, self-awareness, tone of voice, and turn-taking can be rehearsed. The aim is that the rehearsed interpersonal communication competencies can transfer from musical interactions via "ways of being with others" (Stern 2000) into everyday interactions, affecting general interpersonal communication competencies.

Interpersonal communication and music therapy

Music therapists often describe musical improvisation with clients as communication in sound (Pavlicevic 2000) and there seems to be a clear parallel between how the clients communicate in music and in everyday life interactions (Smeijsters 2003). Mithen (2006), who sees musical communication as an evolutionary early stage of verbal communication, supports this notion. In addition, there seem to be overlapping brain networks involved in verbal and musical (improvisation) communication (Lopez-Gonzalez and Limb 2012; Vuust 2007). Furthermore, studies have shown that there is a clear parallel in how jazz musicians communicate musically in dyads and how mothers and infants communicate using sounds (Schögler 1998). The musical competencies involved in pre-verbal (and jazz) communication originate in rhythm and involve synchronization, phrasing (narratives), and dynamics (Malloch and Trevarthen 2009; Schögler 1998).

The resemblance between musical communication and everyday life communication has led to the concept of "communicative musicality" (Malloch and Trevarthen 2009), a theory grounded in the interpersonal theories of Daniel Stern (1985). Communicative musicality is not restricted to musical interaction but is rooted in how (and not what) we communicate. Communicative musicality is developed through actions and states such as joint attention, mirroring/copying, empathy, turn-taking, dynamics, non-verbal expressions, quality, phrases, and so on. According to Stern (1985), these non-linguistic features of communication evolve during the first two years of our life while interacting with primary caregivers. These underlying "communicative competencies" can be rehearsed through musical interactions within the music therapy setting (Bonde, Nygaard Pedersen, and Wigram 2001) and can be transferred from "musical interactions" via the ways-of-being-with-others concept (Stern 1985) into everyday interactions.

Assessing interpersonal communication

Assessing the development in clients' interpersonal communication competencies may be carried out as a measurement of the effect either inside or outside the music therapy setting. Measuring the transference or multi-modal effect (the effect outside the music therapy setting) is a key factor in evidence-based practice. However, it must be considered that there is some development happening within the therapy setting that cannot be measured outside the setting, and that some effects will not be measurable before a certain timespan. Several outcome measures have been used to assess the effect of music therapy on communication competencies outside the music therapy setting of people with ABI. Jeong and Kim (2007) used the Relationship Change Scale, which measures eight features of relationship (Leading-advising, Self-enhancing-competitive, Aggressive-rejecting, Resisting-distrustful, Self-effacing-submissive, Docile-dependent, Cooperative-friendly, Accepting-assisting (Shannon and Guerney 1973), and the Neurobehavioral Rating Scale (Levin *et al.* 1987), which assesses ABI-specific problems in relation to executive/cognitive function, positive symptoms, negative symptoms, and mood/affect.

Several quantitative tools have been developed to analyze the interactions performed during musical improvisation, such as the Individualized Music Therapy Assessment Profile (IMTAP) by Baxter *et al.* (2007), the Improvisation Assessment Profiles (IAP) by Bruscia (1987), and the Musical Interaction Rating (MIR) by Pavlicevic and Trevarthen (1989). However, none of these tools is designed to assess the full spectrum of communicative competencies and they are not psychometrically validated for assessing people with ABI. There is, to the best of my knowledge, no available, easy-to-use, appropriate, reliable, and valid assessment tool that focuses on interpersonal competencies of music communication for people with ABI, as well as a parallel measure of interpersonal communication competencies in everyday life. In order to meet the need for such a tool, I therefore decided to construct a scale designed to measure interpersonal music communication in people with ABI based on the Interpersonal Communication Competence Scale by Rubin and Martin (1994).

The Interpersonal Communication Competence Scale

Spitzberg (2003) identified four general models/measures of interpersonal communication:

1. The Interpersonal Communication Competence Scale, ICCS (Rubin and Martin 1994; Rubin *et al.* 1993).

2. The Mediational Model of Men's Interpersonal Competence (Bruch, Berko, and Hasse 1998).

3. A combination of three scales (the Attributes Questionnaire SF, the Interpersonal Competence Scale, and the Relationship Satisfaction Scale) (Lamke *et al.* 1994).

4. Model of the Perceived Competence of Conflict Strategies (Canary and Spitzberg 1989).

Of these four models/measures, the ICCS is the only model of communication that is not population specific. It is unique in that it incorporates a resource-oriented perspective by evaluating people's competencies rather than their communication deficits.

The ICCS had not formerly been applied in ABI research but has been successfully implemented in other studies focusing on communication (Macik-Frey 2007), attention problems (Fields 2008), attachment style (Anders and Tucker 2000), and leadership training (Chan 2003). The ICCS was selected because its items deal with everyday life situations where the interaction taking place is both verbal and non-verbal. As stated earlier, there are clear parallels between the competencies used in music interactions and those used in non-verbal interactions.

The ICCS consists of 30 Likert-scale items, grouped into ten subscales representing ten domains of interpersonal communication: Self-disclosure, Empathy, Social relaxation, Assertiveness, Interaction management, Altercentrism, Expressiveness, Supportiveness, Immediacy, and Environmental control.

In my PhD study, the original ICCS was slightly modified into a version where the items were easier to understand for people with ABI. This was done in order to assess the participant's interpersonal communication competencies in everyday life—see Hald *et al.* (2015) for more information. Further, a music-communication version of the ICCS was developed for the PhD study.

Interpersonal Music-Communication Competence Scale

The original ICCS was developed by Rubin and Martin (1994) in order to assess general communicative competencies with subscales that are predominantly focusing on non-linguistic aspects of everyday communication. The everyday interactions of the ICCS were adjusted into music interactions by letting the items relate directly to four dyadic musical improvisations that had just been performed.

Procedure

The musical improvisations that form the foundation of the IMCCS consists of four dyadic musical exercises: (1) Dialogue, (2) Follow, (3) Maintain phrase, and (4) Free expression. The exercises are designed to provide opportunities for the various interpersonal music-communication competencies to emerge. The timeframe for all four exercises is approximately 15 minutes, and therapist and participant rate the IMCCS individually right after the last exercise. The four improvisational exercises that were designed to create opportunities for the interpersonal music-communication competencies to be displayed were based on pre-existing improvisational activities (Bruscia 1987; Wigram 2004).

Exercise 1: Dialogue

Dialogue on self-chosen instrument. During this exercise, the participant is instructed to engage in a musical conversation with the therapist on an instrument of their choice. The therapist ensures that the improvisation begins with turn-taking, followed by the therapist musically motivating the participant to be creative and, if possible, simultaneously having a dialogue with the therapist. According to Bruscia (1987, p. 290), the music therapy techniques commonly used in dialogues include imitation, repetition, variation, exaggeration, and modeling. The goal of the exercise is not to facilitate therapeutic development, but rather to make the participant communicate to their highest potential in the music. The activity is designed to illuminate the following abilities of the participant: self-disclosure, empathy, altercentrism, interaction management, and environmental control in music.

Exercise 2: Following

Following the therapist on piano/keyboard. During this activity, the participant is instructed to musically follow the expressive state of the therapist's music. The instructions are not to play the exact same notes as the therapist, but to match the therapist's music. The therapist's improvisation will start in one emotional state before moving to another (e.g. from sad to happy, or angry to tender). The exercise is designed to assess the participant's ability to be empathic, and match and follow musical expression (Bruscia 1987; Wigram 2004). Further, the exercise enables assessment of the participant's expressiveness and immediacy in music.

Exercise 3: Maintain phrase

Maintaining playing a phrase on self-chosen instrument while the therapist interrupts. During this activity, the participant is instructed to play a short melodic or rhythmic phrase and then to continue to repeat this phrase until otherwise instructed to stop. After the therapist and participant have played several repetitions of the phrase together, the therapist will begin to challenge the participant by, for example, increasing/decreasing tempo or playing off-scale notes. This exercise is designed to assess the participant's musical independence, autonomy, and assertiveness as described by Bruscia (1987). Further, the exercise enables assessment of the participant's social relaxation (ability to deal with a stressful situation) and altercentrism (ability to be focused) in music.

Exercise 4: Free expression

Free improvisation on self-chosen instrument. Free shared music making is a technique used in almost all music therapy approaches (Bruscia 1987; Wigram 2004). The goal is to offer opportunities for the participant to display their capacity to be expressive and present in music and communication. The participant is instructed to musically express how they feel in the present situation. The therapist has a supportive role in the improvisation. If the music becomes rigid for more than two minutes, the therapist will musically motivate transitions. This exercise can potentially give information on all interpersonal music-communication competencies.

The music therapist is instructed to initiate music communication in Exercises 1 and 4 only in order to be able to assess the participant's communicative performance. Communicative initiatives involve clear pausing after a phrase, offering a response to a call, and developing the participant's phrases. The music therapist's support in Exercise 4 involves improvisational techniques such as supporting, mirroring, and holding (Wigram 2004). If the exercises are to be rated by an external rater, the four assessment exercises need to be video recorded and edited to start just before the first note and finish right after the last note. The improvisations may last a couple of minutes, and the music therapist will prompt an ending at five minutes. After the improvisation exercises, both therapist and client rate their experience of the music making using the IMCCS.

Different raters and versions

In order to increase validity of the IMCCS, it was found necessary not only to develop a music therapist version of the scale, but also to develop a version that the participant would be able to score. With a self-rater version, information about how the participant views their own competencies is obtained. Further, it is possible to converge these findings. In order to use the scale in objectivistic research, it was decided to develop a blind-rater version to be scored from video data. Therefore, the following three versions of the IMCCS were developed: a music therapist version (IMCCS-Therapist), a music therapy participant version (IMCCS-Participant), and a music-communication rater version (IMCCS-Rater).

The 30 items in the original ICCS on everyday communication competencies were converted into 30 items on music-communication competencies relating to the four musical improvisations just performed. This was done by focusing on the sub-group competency and how the competency would appear in music. As an example, the ICCS item 1) "I allow friends to see who I really am" was converted into: "Did your music express how you felt?" In Table 13.2, the original ICCS items as well as the converted IMCCS-Therapist items are shown.

Because the participant and therapist IMCCS evaluations are performed immediately following the four exercises, the ICCS Likert scale was changed from a "how often" interval to a degree interval. In this way, asking a music therapy participant who performs an improvisation for the first time "how often" they generally reveal emotions in music was avoided. The answer would inevitably have been "not often." Consequently, the Likert scale was changed into: 5) Highest degree, 4) Greater degree, 3) Medium degree, 2) Less degree, and 1) Minimum degree. In this way, not only the items but also the Likert scale related to the four music improvisations just performed (see Table 13.2 for details on the IMCCS-Therapist items) The music therapy participant version (IMCCS-Participant) is very similar to the therapist version (IMCCS-Therapist).

TABLE 13.2: CONVERTING THE ICCS ITEMS INTO THE IMCCS-THERAPIST ITEMS

Item	ICCS (Rubin and Martin 1994)	IMCCS-Therapist version
	Self-disclosure	**Self-disclosure in music**
1	I allow my friends to see who I really am	Did the participant's music authentically express their identity?
2	Other people know what I'm thinking	Can you make sense of the participant's music?
3	I reveal how I feel to others	Did the participant express emotions in the music?
	Empathy	**Musical empathy**
4	I can put myself in others' shoes	Did the participant (appear to?) understand the emotion you played?
5	I don't know exactly what others are feeling (Reversed)	Did the participant have difficulty understanding the feelings you expressed in the "following" exercise? (R)
6	Other people think that I understand them	Did the participant make an effort to be empathic in the music?
	Social relaxation	**Social relaxation in music**
7	I am comfortable in social situations	Was the participant comfortable playing music together with you?
8	I feel relaxed in small groups	Was the participant relaxed when you played music together?
9	I feel insecure in groups of strangers (Reversed)	Was the participant uncomfortable playing music with an unfamiliar person? (R)

cont.

	Assertiveness	Assertiveness in music
10	When I've been wronged, I confront the person who wronged me	Did the participant react musically to things that were annoying in the music?
11	I have trouble standing up for myself (Reversed)	Did the participant have difficulty being autonomous in the music? (R)
12	I stand up for my rights	Did the participant create their own musical space?
	Altercentrism	**Altercentrism in music**
13	My conversations are pretty one-sided (Reversed)	Did the participant play more than listen? (R)
14	I let others know that I understand what they say	Did the participant's music complement your music?
15	My mind wanders during conversations	Was the participant focused in their playing?
	Interaction management	**Interaction management in music**
16	My conversations are characterized by smooth shifts from one topic to the next	Was the participant's music flexible and varied?
17	I take charge of conversations I'm in by negotiating what topics we talk about	Did the participant give space and lead in to the music?
18	In conversations with friends, I perceive not only what they say but what they don't say	Did you notice something that was not expressed in the music?
	Expressiveness	**Expressiveness in music**
19	My friends can tell when I'm happy or sad	Could you recognize how the participant was feeling based on their musical expression?
20	It's difficult to find the right words to express myself (Reversed)	Was it difficult for the participant to musically communicate and express how they feel? (R)

21	I express myself well verbally	Was the participant accurate in their musical expression?
	Supportiveness	**Supportiveness in music**
22	My communication is usually descriptive, not evaluative	Did the participant match your musical ideas?
23	I communicate with others as though they're equals	Did you and the participant maintain an equal (musical?) relationship?
24	Others would describe me as warm	Did you sense compassion and warmth in the participant's music?
	Immediacy	**Immediacy in music**
25	My friends truly believe that I care about them	Did you feel the participant cares about you and your musical contributions?
26	I try to look others in the eye when I speak to them	Did the participant adapt their music to your music?
27	I tell people when I feel close to them	Did you experience closeness from the participant?
	Environmental control	**Environmental control in music**
28	I accomplish my communication goals	Did the participant express what they wanted in the music?
29	I can persuade others to my position	Did the participant influence you to follow their musical ideas?
30	I have trouble convincing others to do what I want them to do (Reversed)	Did the participant have problems drawing you into their own musical space? (R)

Items and results

In the IMCCS-Rater, the items were changed into observable parameters in order to enable the rating procedure. Thus, most of the IMCCS-Therapist items were rephrased in the IMCCS-Rater. For example, item two regarding the therapist's understanding of the participant's music was rephrased into whether the rater experienced clarity/focus in the music. Further, in the IMCCS-Rater, the Likert scale shows a time/amount focus: 5) Almost all the time (>90%), 4) A lot of the time (60–90%), 3) Some of the time (40–60%), 2) Little of the time (10–40%), and 1) Almost none of the time (0–10%). In order to ease the rating procedure, the items in the IMCCS-Rater are divided into four groups linked to each of the four improvisational assessment exercises. The rater is to rate the "Dialogue" exercise using items 2, 6, 9, 13, 14, 16, 17, 28, 29, and 30 from the IMCCS-Rater. Then the "Following" exercise using items 4, 5, 20, 21, 25, and 26, the "Maintain phrase" exercise using items 8, 10, 11, 12, and 15, and last the "Free expression" exercise using items 1, 3, 7, 18, 19, 22, 23, 24, and 27 from the IMCCS-Rater.

Each subscale and total score is accumulated by the Likert scale answers, where items 5, 9, 11, 13, 20, and 30 are reversed. This results in a total score ranging from 30 to 150 and subscale scores ranging from 3 to 15.

Research and psychometrics

The three IMCCS scales (therapist, participant, and rater) were psychometrically tested on 15 participants with medium-to-severe ABI (ages 22–65, mean 48 years; eight men, seven women). The participants' communicative competencies in music were assessed before and after a 20-session group music therapy program using the described assessment procedure.

For the statistical analyses, internal consistency tests using Cronbach's alpha were performed on all three IMCCS scales. In addition, the raters' agreements on the IMCCS-Rater were calculated using a Pearson correlation and Cohen's kappa coefficient. The quadratic weighted kappa was chosen because the difference between scores should be weighted proportionally, and according to Maclure and Willett (1987), the quadratic approach is most common.

The participants' scores on IMCCS-Participant were correlated with their scores on everyday interpersonal communication competencies (both self-rated and staff-/relative-rated ICCS measures). Data on IMCCS-Therapist and IMCCS-Participant was collected using the Danish versions of the scales, whereas the IMCCS-Rater version was administered in English.

One experienced music therapist and two raters assessed the participants' communicative competencies in music using the IMCCS-Therapist and the IMCCS-Rater. Further, two slightly adapted (and translated into Danish) versions of the original ICCS scale (one for the participants and one for staff and relatives) were administered before the music therapy in order to retrieve information on the participants' everyday interpersonal communication competencies (for the psychometric evaluation of these scales, see Hald *et al.* 2015). The assessment took place before and after 20 group music therapy sessions. Due to dropout, only 28 out of 30 assessment sessions were completed, resulting in 112 improvisation exercises lasting from 54 seconds up to 5 minutes and 46 seconds.

Reliability

The overall Cronbach's alphas on the three scales range from .89 to .93, which indicates good-to-excellent internal consistency. A two-tailed Pearson correlation and Cohen's kappa was calculated in order to reveal how well the two blinded raters agreed on their assessment of the musical exercises using the IMCCS-Rater. The analysis revealed a significant correlation between the two raters' total scores and subscale scores. Since Pearson is not a robust indication of rater correlation, Cohen's kappa was used to calculate how well the two raters agreed on each item in the IMCCS-Rater. The overall Cohen's kappa for the IMCCS-Rater was .597.

A two-tailed Pearson correlation analysis was performed on the assessment of interpersonal communication competencies in everyday communication rated by staff/relatives and self-rated, and the musical-communicative competencies evaluation by music therapist, participant, and raters. Table 13.3 illustrates that the music therapist's scorings had the most positive correlation with the other measures. Furthermore, the participants' own evaluations of interpersonal communication competencies in everyday life had the least correlation with the other measures. As also seen in Table 13.3, staff and relatives' evaluation of the participants' interpersonal communication competencies in everyday life correlated significantly with the music therapist's evaluation of this. Further analysis reveals a significant correlation on five subscales (Empathy, Assertiveness, Altercentrism, Expressiveness, and Supportiveness). These results indicate that there is a parallel in interpersonal communication competencies on some aspects of musical and everyday life communication competencies. The total score of staff and relatives' evaluation of interpersonal communication competencies in everyday life correlated with the blinded raters' evaluation of interpersonal music-communication competencies with a significance level. The IMCCS-Rater and ICCS-Staff/Relatives scores correlated significantly on only one subscale: Expressiveness. On the remaining nine subscales, the correlation significance level was low. These results indicate a modest relationship in interpersonal communication competencies in musical and everyday life interaction.

TABLE 13.3: TWO-TAILED PEARSON CORRELATION ANALYSIS OF THE ICCS AND IMCCS

	IMCCS-Therapist	IMCCS-Participant	IMCCS-Rater	ICCS-Self-rated	ICCS-Staff-Relatives
IMCCS-Therapist		$r = .622$ $p = .007$	$r = .636$ $p = .005$	$r = -.057$ $p = .420$	$r = .766$ $p = .000$
IMCCS-Participant			$r = .619$ $p < .01$	$r = -.391$ $p = .075$	$r = .376$ $p = .084$
IMCCS-Rater				$r = -.215$ $p = .221$	$r = .408$ $p = .066$
ICCS-Self-rated					$r = .335$ $p = .111$

Interpretation and report

The IMCCS gives a total score on interpersonal music-communication competencies, which can be used to inform about clients' progression in communication competencies in general. The subscales give information on specific elements of the clients' communication competencies and can be used to inform about progression and/or domains to focus the music therapy.

The subscale "Self-disclosure in music" reveals information on clients' openness in music, and their ability to reveal themselves in the music. Bruscia (1987, p. 561) described different areas of self-disclosure in improvised music, stating that improvised music may reveal information on physical, emotional, intellectual, or social aspects of the self. When rating self-disclosure in the improvised music, the rater's focus should be on the "dialogue" and "free expression" exercises. When rating self-disclosures using the IMCCS-Rater, the rater has to rely on their sense of the participant, focusing on consistency (or discrepancy) between the musical statements, emotional indicators, social context, and bodily language.

The subscale "Musical empathy" gives information on the participants' ability to musically feel with the music therapist—decoding and responding to the emotional expression of the music therapist. When rating musical empathy, the rater's focus should be on the exercises "following" and "dialogue." The rating will give information on how well the participant is able to match the therapist's music, the overall expression, and the participants' ability to follow musical changes.

The subscale "Social relaxation in music" gives information on the participants' level of anxiety and feeling of comfort while playing music. When rating the participants' social relaxation, the rater's attention should be on "free expression" and "dialogue." The rater should notice if the participants' bodily expressions are tense, free, relaxed, and so on.

The subscale "Assertiveness in music" gives information on the participants' ability to produce music while being disturbed by the music of the therapist. When assessing assertiveness in the improvised music, the rater should primarily evaluate the "maintain phrase" improvisation. The rater is to focus on the participants' ability to establish stable melodic or rhythmical phrases and the participants' enjoyment of having musical independence.

The subscale "Altercentrism in music" has to do with interest in the other, attentiveness, and responsiveness to the music. When assessing altercentrism in the improvised music, the rater needs to focus on the "maintain phrase" and "dialogue" improvisations.

The subscale "Interaction management in music" reveals information on the participants' ability to engage in ritualistic procedures like taking turns, phrasing, and starting and ending improvisations. When assessing interaction management in the improvised music, the rater is primarily to evaluate the "dialogue" and "free expression" improvisations, focusing on the participants' ability to take turns, and start and end the music. In addition, the participants' ability to play in a flexible and varied way, come up with ideas in the musical dialogue, and perceive changes in the music should be noted.

The subscale "Expressiveness in music" has to do with communicating state of mind non-verbally. When rating, the rater's focus should be on "free expression" and "following." Musically, expressiveness has to do with dynamics, tonal/melodic language, tempo, and bodily expressions, which should also be noted when rating expressiveness in music.

The subscale "Supportiveness in music" has to do with the ability to support the music of the other. When assessing supportiveness in the improvised music, the rater's focus should be on the "free expression." Being supportive in music has to do with being spontaneous, empathic, and egalitarian. When assessing supportiveness in music, the rater should primarily evaluate the role of the participant—soloist or accompanist. In addition, the rater is to sense the participant's interpersonal warmth.

The subscale "Immediacy in music" has to do with being approachable and available for musical interaction. When assessing immediacy in the improvised music, the rater should focus on the "free expression" and "following" improvisations. When assessing immediacy, the rater is to look at eye contact, the ability to adopt an open stance, having a pleasant facial expression, leaning forward, and so on. On a more subtle level, immediacy has to do with conveying feelings of interpersonal warmth, closeness, and affiliation. On a concrete musical level, it has to do with responding to musical "questions" and having a focused attention.

The subscale "Environmental control in music" has to do with archiving predetermined goals and satisfying needs. When assessing environmental control in the improvised music, the rater is to primarily evaluate the "dialogue" improvisation. Environmental control in music involves gaining compliance from others, and the ability to solve disruptions in a cooperative manner. In the improvisations, the rater is to assess the participants' ability to signal intentions and satisfaction with their own output.

Discussion and summary

The IMCCS-Therapist Cronbach's alpha value indicated a good internal consistency, and the IMCCS-Participant Cronbach's alpha value indicated an excellent internal consistency. These high Cronbach's alphas suggest that the IMCCS is a reliable self-rating and therapist rating scale of interpersonal music-communication competence. On the IMCCS-Rater, Cronbach's alpha indicated an excellent consistency. Cronbach's alphas exceed .9 in both the IMCCS-Participant and IMCCS-Rater, suggesting that some items might be unnecessary. However, a removal of items would alter the construct of the scales, making correlation and comparison problematic. Cohen's kappa coefficient on the overall IMCCS-Rater score indicated a moderate (almost substantial) agreement between the raters. There are substantial correlations between the scales indicating a relationship between the ratings and the scales. In addition, a possible correlation between everyday life and musical-communicative competencies was found. The scales are not fully validated yet. They need to be correlated with other scales measuring almost the same thing, such as the IMTAP, MIR, and IAP. There are, however, at present no such plans.

The music therapist's evaluation of the participants' interpersonal communication competencies in music provides a first-hand report on the interactions that occurred during the four exercises. From a clinical perspective, the IMCCS-Therapist provides a structured method of measuring the participants' interpersonal communication competencies in music. The high correlation between the therapist's and blinded raters' evaluation indicates that the tool is reliable. Feedback from the music therapist performing the assessments indicates that the IMCCS-Therapist tool was fast and easy to complete, and as such not burdensome to include as part of standard clinical monitoring. However, it must be assumed that the non-musical interaction between the musical improvisations affected the music therapist's ratings and therefore the therapist might have rated non-musical competencies as well. In addition, the music therapist performing the assessments knew the participants from the everyday life setting, which may have affected her ratings of participants' interpersonal communication competencies in music.

By using the constructs embedded in the ICCS, the three measurements of the IMCCS can be compared with everyday communicative competencies measured with the ICCS.

The IMCCS scales are, compared with the other improvisation assessment tools (IMTAP, MIR, and IAP), more rigid, focusing only on interpersonal communication competencies in music. This can be viewed as a strength since it enables a more focused and comparable assessment of clients' communicative competencies. At the same time, this rigidness is the greatest limitation of the IMCCS tools since the assessing therapist will have to leave out other observations and eventual areas of concern.

Clinical application of the IMCCS

The IMCCS scales can be used in both research and practice. The IMCCS-Therapist is easily administered by the music therapist and can bring information to the clinician about the client's strengths. The more time-consuming and comprehensive assessment using blinded raters is primarily for use in research. The combination of the IMCCS and the ICCS offers a method of measuring interpersonal communication competencies across settings (daily life and music) that may be an important tool to apply for other populations as well. A relevant future study would be to make a norm-score of the IMCCS for non-ABI groups (adolescents, adults, psychiatric patients, etc.). In addition, applying both the ICCS and IMCCS on a non-clinical population would reveal whether the correlation of interpersonal communication competencies in music and daily life, as revealed in this study, can be generalized to a population not suffering from ABI. Such a study could reveal whether the lack of correlation on some of the subscales was due to the cognitive deficits of participants. When applying the IMCCS in future studies, other scales measuring similar aspects should be applied as well. This will enable further validation of the scale.

References

Anders, S. L. and Tucker, J. S. (2000) 'Adult attachment style, interpersonal communication competence, and social support.' *Personal Relationships, 7,* 4, 379–389.

Barker, V. L. and Brunk, B. (1991) 'The role of creative arts group in the treatment of clients with traumatic brain injury.' *Music Therapy Perspectives, 9,* 26–31.

Bateman, A., Braithwaite, B., Bromley, D., Evans, J., *et al.* (2010) *The Brain Injury Handbook.* Glasgow: Rehab Group.

Baxter, H. T., Berghofer, J. A., MacEwan, L., Nelson, J., Peters, K., and Roberts, P. (2007) *The Individualized Music Therapy Assessment Profile: IMTAP.* London: Jessica Kingsley Publishers.

Bonde, L. O., Nygaard Pedersen, I., and Wigram, T. (2001) *Musikterapi: Når ord ikke slår til.* Århus: Forlaget Klim.

Bruch, M. A., Berko, E. H., and Haase, R. F. (1998) 'Shyness, masculine ideology, physical attractiveness, and emotional inexpressiveness: Testing a mediational model of men's interpersonal competence.' *Journal of Counseling Psychology, 45,* 1, 84–97.

Bruscia, K. E. (1987) *Improvisational Models of Music Therapy*. Springfield, IL: Charles C. Thomas.

Burgoon, J. K. and Bacue, A. E. (2003) 'Nonverbal Communication Skills.' In J. O. Greene and B. R. Burleson (eds) *Handbook of Communication and Social Interaction Skills*. New York, NY and London: L. Erlbaum Associates.

Canary, D. J. and Spitzberg, B. H. (1989) 'A model of the perceived competence of conflict strategies.' *Human Communication Research, 15,* 4, 630–649.

Chan, D. W. (2003) 'Leadership skills training for Chinese secondary students in Hong Kong: Does training make a difference?' *Prufrock Journal, 14,* 3, 166–174, doi: 10.4219/jsge-2003-427.

Damasio, A. R. (2010) *Self Comes to Mind: Constructing the Conscious Brain*. New York, NY: Pantheon Books.

Duffy, F. D., Gordon, G. H., Whelan, G., Cole-Kelly, K., and Frankel, R. (2004) 'Assessing competence in communication and interpersonal skills: The Kalamazoo II Report.' *Academic Medicine, 79,* 6, 495–507.

Fields, A. D. (2008) 'Recognition of Facial Affect on Adults with Attention Problems.' PhD, George Mason University, Fairfax, Virginia.

Gilbertson, S. and Aldridge, D. (2008) *Music Therapy and Traumatic Brain Injury: A Light on a Dark Night*. London: Jessica Kingsley Publishers.

Hald, S. (2012) 'Music Therapy, Acquired Brain Injury and Interpersonal Communication Competencies.' PhD, Aalborg University, Aalborg.

Hald, S. V., Baker, F. A., and Ridder, H. M. (2015) 'A preliminary psychometric evaluation of the Interpersonal Communication Competence Scale for aquired brain injury.' *Brain Injury, 1–8,* doi: 10.3109/02699052.2015.1024740.

Hald, S. V., Baker, F. A., and Ridder, H. M. (2017) 'A preliminary evaluation of the Interpersonal Music-Communication Competence Scales.' *Nordic Journal of Music Therapy, 26,* 1, 40–61, doi: 10.1080/08098131.2015.1117122.

Hargie, O. and Dickson, D. (2004) *Skilled Interpersonal Communication* (4th edition). London: Routledge.

Hart, S. (2006) *Hjerne, samhørighed, personlighed*. Copenhagen: Reitzels.

Jeong, S. H. and Kim, M. T. (2007) 'Effects of a theory-driven music and movement program for stroke survivors in a community setting.' *Applied Nursing Research, 20,* 3, 125–131, doi: 10.1016/j.apnr.2007.04.005.

Kay, T., Newman, B., Cavallo, M., Ezrachi, O., and Resnick, M. (1992) 'Toward a neuropsychological model of functional disability after mild traumatic brain injury.' *Neuropsychology, 6,* 4, 371–384, doi: 10.1037/0894-4105.6.4.371.

Lamke, L. K., Sollie, D. L., Durbin, R. G., and Fitzpatrick, J. A. (1994) 'Masculinity, femininity and relationship satisfaction—the mediating role of interpersonal competence.' *Journal of Social and Personal Relationships, 11,* 4, 535–554.

Levin, H. S., High, W. M., Goethe, K. E., Sisson, R. A., *et al.* (1987) 'The Neurobehavioural Rating Scale: Assessment of the behavioural sequelae of head injury by the clinician.' *Journal of Neurology, Neurosurgery, and Psychiatry, 50,* 183–193.

Lopez-Gonzalez, M. and Limb, C. J. (2012) 'Musical creativity and the brain.' *Cerebrum, 2.* Retrieved 26/02/2018 from http://dana.org/news/cerebrum/detail.aspx?id=35670.

Macik-Frey, M. (2007) 'Communication-Centered Approach to Leadership: The Relationship of Interpersonal Communication Competence to Transformational Leadership and Emotional Intelligence.' Unpublished PhD thesis, University of Texas, Arlington. Retrieved 12/12/2017 from http://dspace.uta.edu/bitstream/handle/10106/557/umi-uta-1743.pdf?sequence=1.

Maclure, M. and Willett, W. C. (1987) 'Misinterpretation and misuse of the kappa-statistic.' *American Journal of Epidemiology, 126,* 2, 161–169.

Malloch, S. and Trevarthen, C. (2009) *Communicative Musicality: Exploring the Basis of Human Companionship.* Oxford; New York, NY: Oxford University Press.

Mithen, S. J. (2006) *The Singing Neanderthals: The Origins of Music, Language, Mind and Body.* London: Weidenfeld & Nicolson.

Nayak, S., Wheeler, B. L., Shiflett, S. C., and Agostinelli, S. (2000) 'Effect of music therapy on mood and social interaction among individuals with acute traumatic brain injury and stroke.' *Rehabilitation Psychology, 45,* 3, 274–283.

Pavlicevic, M. (2000) 'Improvisation in music therapy: Human communication in sound.' *Journal of Music Therapy, 4,* 269–285.

Pavlicevic, M. and Trevarthen, C. (1989) 'A musical assessment of psychiatric states in adults.' *Psychopathology, 22,* 6, 325–334.

Purdie, H. (1997) 'Music therapy with adults who have traumatic brain injury and stroke.' *British Journal of Music Therapy, 11,* 2, 45–50.

Rubin, R. B. and Martin, M. M. (1994) 'Development of a measure of interpersonal communication competence.' *Communication Research Reports, 11,* 1, 33–44.

Rubin, R. B., Martin, M. M., Bruning, S. S., and Powers, D. E. (1993) 'Test of a self-efficacy model of interpersonal communication competence.' *Communication Quarterly, 41,* 2, 210–220.

Schögler, B. (1998) 'Music as a tool in communications research.' *Nordisk Tidsskrift for Musikkterapi, 7,* 1, 40–49, doi: 10.1080/08098139809477919.

Shannon, J. and Guerney, B. (1973) 'Interpersonal effects of interpersonal behavior.' *Journal of Personality and Social Psychology, 26,* 1, 142–150.

Sias, P. M. and Jablin, F. M. (2001) 'Communication Competence.' In L. L. Putnam and F. M. Jablin (eds) *The New Handbook of Organizational Communication: Advances in Theory, Research, and Methods.* Thousand Oaks, CA: Sage Publications.

Smeijsters, H. (2003) 'Forms of feeling and forms of perception: The fundamentals of analogy in music therapy.' *Nordic Journal of Music Therapy, 12,* 1, 71–85.

Spitzberg, B. H. (2003) 'Methods of Interpersonal Skill Assessment.' In J. O. Greene and B. R. Burleson (eds) *Handbook of Communication and Social Interaction.* London: Routledge.

Stern, D. (1985) *The Interpersonal World of the Infant: A View from Psychoanalysis and Developmental Psychology.* New York, NY: Basic Books.

Stern, D. (2000) *The Interpersonal World of the Infant.* New York, NY: Basic Books.

Struchen, M. A. (2005) 'Social Communication Intervention.' In W. M. High (ed) *Rehabilitation for Traumatic Brain Injury.* New York, NY: Oxford University Press.

Struchen, M. A., Clark, A. N., Sander, A. M., Mills, M. R., Evans, G., and Kurtz, D. (2008) 'Relation of executive functioning and social communication measures to functional outcomes following traumatic brain injury.' *Neurorehabilitation, 23,* 2, 185–198.

Vuust, P. (2007) 'Musikkens sprog.' *Musik og Psykologi,* 186–209.

Wigram, T. (2004) *Improvisation: Methods and Techniques for Music Therapy Clinicians, Educators, and Students.* London: Jessica Kingsley Publishers.

CHAPTER 14

The Assessment of Parent-Child Interaction

Stine Lindahl Jacobsen

Setting and motivation

Almost ten years ago during a four-month internship at a family care center in Denmark, I started to investigate how I could assess parent-child interaction as a music therapist on a multidisciplinary team. The families were often very frustrated and anxious when they arrived at the center and they had difficulties interacting typically. Some might try to "put on a show," and some might only show their weaknesses due to their anxiousness. In spite of these circumstances, music therapy seemed to make the families relax and sometimes even have fun together. Meanwhile, it was possible for me to observe, encounter, and assess parent-child interactions and the parental capacity in the family. In continuation of my internship as part of my master's thesis, I therefore developed the first version of the tool, Assessment of Parenting Competences (APC; Jacobsen and Wigram 2007). After three years at the family care center, and as part of my doctoral work, I wanted to further strengthen the tool by quantifying it and performing psychometric analysis to explore validity and reliability. My motivation for further developing the APC was to ensure the ethical and objective investigation of the families to give them a fair chance and to enable them to get the best possible help.

It can be difficult to witness children who have experienced emotional neglect trying to survive in the world, and sadder still to see a parent struggling to make it better. Sometimes the best solution is to take the child away from the family, and sometimes it is not. Regardless, it is crucial that the decision be based on objective data and that the family or parents understand this decision.

Those working with families know the importance of keeping track and improving emotional communication between parent and child. In a recent systematic review, Colegrove and Havighurst (2016) specifically highlight the importance of non-verbal communication between parent and child. Non-verbal processes are crucial to parent-child communication, but are seldom the focus of therapeutic intervention once a child is over 12 months of age. They further state, "Given the importance of nonverbal communication for effective parenting and parent–child communication, we recommend that nonverbal communication is assessed and addressed explicitly as a core part of parent–child intervention, development and evaluation" (Colegrove and Havighurst 2016, p. 1).

Theoretical background

According to Schore and Schore (2008), supporting the child's ability to regulate emotions and thus the ability to be emotionally stable is one of the core aspects of parental capacity. Self-regulation is mainly developed in early childhood through sensitive emotional communication between mother and infant also known as affect attunement and intersubjectivity (Snyder, Shapiro, and Treleaven 2013; Stern 2000). But how can we evaluate the emotional and non-verbal communication between parent and child?

Developmental psychology involves many theories of "good parenting" in relation to the emotional needs of the child. The theories of Winnicott (1971) and Stern (1995, 2000, 2010a, 2010b) include music and play as important features, and these theories are commonly used in both psychotherapy and music therapy literature and research. Attunement in music therapy is of particular interest because it addresses non-verbal communication using musical parameters such as rhythm, pitch, and dynamics (Kim, Wigram, and Gold 2009; Pavlicevic 2002; Trondalen and Skårderud 2007; Bonde, Pedersen, and Jacobsen 2019). Trondalen and Skårderud explored affect attunement within the frame of musical improvisation and argued that interactive experiences in musical interplay are a non-verbal analogy to real life, where sharing is part of intersubjective behavior. This is in line with the concept of communicative musicality described by Mallock and Trevarthen (2009) and music therapist Holck (2008). Conversation analysis and descriptions of healthy, non-verbal communication between mothers and infants are useful in building theory and understanding the reciprocity of taking turns between parent and child as a part of parent-child interaction in music therapy (Holck 2004; Knapp and Hall 2009).

Modern attachment theory explains how early experiences of emotional communication and interaction, affect attunement, and intersubjectivity may be regulated or dysregulated, resulting in secure or insecure attachments (Schore and Schore 2008). Early attachment patterns can affect the individual throughout life and the communication skills parents use when displaying the complexity of interaction, relation, and attachment between child, parent, and possibly grandparents.

Many research studies have focused on linking a child's level of vulnerability and different types of child temperament with the parental behavior. When a parent becomes exhausted from child interactions resulting from difficulties with feeding, sleeping, poor adaptive skills, or perceived excessive independence, it can lead to a vicious circle where the parent expects problems and creates aversive interaction, and the child becomes more demanding and attention-seeking (Iwaniec 1995). However, building on decades of research, there is a consensus among researchers, clinicians, and theorists that four main types of attachment pattern strategies are displayed by children (and adults) (Ainsworth et al. 1978; Killén 2012).

Children who experience sensitive, predictable, and available caregivers tend to develop secure attachment (type B), which reveals itself through healthy independence and healthy self-regulation. Children who experience insensitive, unpredictable, and either controlling or withdrawn caregivers tend to develop insecure avoidant attachment (type A), which also manifests as seemingly independent behavior in children. Insensitive, inconsistently available caregivers tend to yield development of insecure ambivalent attachment (type C) in children, which can reveal itself through highly dependent and clingy behavior or aggressive and resisting behavior in the child. Attachment behavior is considered a coping strategy where the child finds a way to get a sense of control over the interaction and finds a way to gain access to their caregivers. Disorganized attachment (type D) is considered a non-functioning strategy where the child experiences an inconsistent and contradicting parent who is often hostile or helpless, frightening, extremely insensitive, and/or violent (Killén 2012). The parent, whom the child needs for comfort and protection, is the parent the child is afraid of (Juffer, Bakermans-Kranenburg, and van IJzendoorn 2005).

The fundamental purpose of assessing parental capacity is to shield the child from challenged parenting, including neglect and abuse. There are also other advantages to assessing parents besides ensuring the welfare of the child. These include therapeutic benefits of the assessment process (e.g. as a springboard for further intervention techniques) and increased parental insight, revealing strengths and needs, empowering parents, and increasing much-needed self-esteem (Wolf and Peregoy 2003).

All arts therapy clinical measurements are faced with the challenge of assessing a process in which abstract concepts are linked to empirical indicants. Interpretation of art is often considered highly subjective, and it may be difficult to maintain objectivity. However, Deacon and Piercy (2001) described arts therapies as having a particular advantage in gathering information. Activities in the art therapies can both serve as an assessment technique for the therapist and as a therapeutic experience for clients. Clients are usually less anxious when they express themselves through an arts medium.

Activity shifts the focus from problem to product (in the clients), and this allows the family to both enjoy the process and connect positively to each other. Many family members may fear being too verbally direct, thereby hurting other family members' feelings. However, when asked for metaphors, families often tend to be less defensive and more able to express themselves in symbolic ways. Furthermore, arts activities can include family members of various ages and abilities and encourage a more egalitarian and less intrusive role for the therapist (Deacon and Piercy 2001).

Music therapy is particularly relevant in assessing parent-child interaction due to its ability to reveal emotional communication, power struggles and levels of autonomy, symptoms of dysfunction, cooperation, turn-taking, and other components of interaction. Music therapy techniques can be used to assess parents and their capacity to meet their children's needs through how they communicate and interact (Oldfield and Flower 2008). Through music therapy assessment, aspects of communication, dynamics, and relationships are often strikingly apparent to both staff and the families themselves, including non-verbal events such as eye contact, attending, listening, and mirroring (Molyneux 2008). If the family are given general tasks, the balance of power can be assessed through observation of their way of completing the tasks. Unstructured musical tasks of interaction can show the particular function and style of communication for each family member. Imbalances of power and diffuse boundaries become evident (Miller 1994). Jacobsen and Wigram (2007) observed how assessment of parenting competencies for parents of children potentially in need of care included an evaluation of the parent's relationship with the child and the interaction that underpins that relationship.

The Assessment of Parent-Child Interaction

Procedure and population

The Assessment of Parent-Child Interaction (APCI) is a dyadic observational assessment tool consisting of a specific assessment protocol where the video-recorded exercises are designed and chosen to investigate the quality of the relationship and non-verbal communication skills between parent and child and to evaluate the parent's emotional response to the child in the field of child protection. The protocol consists of two identical assessment sessions with four fixed improvisational exercises that differ in levels of structure. The session starts with the family exploring the room followed by an easy, familiar greeting song, and ends with a similar closing farewell song. The music therapist together with the family dyad first models three exercises before the dyad performs the exercises alone. From the same selection of musical instruments, family members choose their instruments freely for each exercise. The first exercise consists of playing soft, loud, and then soft again. The second exercise consists of the parent and child taking turns in playing their self-chosen musical instrument. In the third exercise, the parent and child take turns in leading the improvisation, and the fourth exercise is a free play improvisation together with the music therapist. The exercises are videotaped and the first two minutes (or as long as the exercise lasts, whichever is shorter) are later scored by a trained music therapist.

The participants need to be able to understand the instructions (cognitive level of a 4-year-old), and therefore this limits the usage of the APCI in the current form. The APCI has so far successfully been used within the field of child protection, refugee families, adoption, families with children with mild developmental disorders, and families and adolescents. It is considered highly relevant to investigate modifications of the APCI to be able to assess families with children with special needs, including autism spectrum disorder.

Data analysis and results

The APCI produces three main scores (Mutual Attunement, Nonverbal Communication, Emotional Parental Response), 16 different profiles, and in-depth qualitative descriptions and recommendations made by the therapist. The development of these scores is based on a comparison of numerical data from both clinical and non-clinical families, including several statistical analyses of significant differences between clinical and non-clinical groups. The scores were never meant to stand alone in a report on parent-child interaction but were meant to be as important as descriptions of both observations and scores (Jacobsen and Killén 2015).

Mutual attunement

This score evaluates how attentive and attuned a child and a parent are towards each other regarding non-verbal and musical interactions. The analysis is based on three exercises from the assessment session and is analyzed using Bruscia's (1987) Improvisation Assessment Profiles and Wigram's (2004, 2007) Event-Based Analysis. The relationship between following and leading behavior during the improvisations is the main focus and reveals aspects of the emotional communication capacity of both parent and child—specifically how well attuned the parent is to the child's play and how well the parent follows or matches the child. It also reveals the child's emotional communication toward the parent, thus providing information on the equality between leading and following events in each individual and the equality in autonomy between parent and child.

Nonverbal communication

The Nonverbal Communication score assesses the dyad's capacity to effectively communicate non-verbally in terms of both displaying and understanding non-verbal cues and signals. Both the parent and child are instructed to take turns playing during one specific exercise in the APCI assessment protocol, and the score is based on a turn-giving analysis of how the parent or child yields their turn in terms of musical, gestural, and confusing turn-givings (ambiguous signals). Furthermore, frequency of pure and interruptive turn-takings is integrated into the Nonverbal Communication score. The clinical relevance of the score revolves around evaluation of the turn-organization of the family and effective non-verbal communication in terms of providing clear signals. The non-verbal score is an indicator of how clearly the parent and child encode and decode non-verbal communication (Jacobsen and Killén 2015).

As described earlier, non-verbal communication capacity and the understanding of social communication are established based on proper non-verbal feedback from caregivers or parents in early and later childhood. Poor non-verbal communication in the parent increases the risk of poor non-verbal communication in the child. In cases of neglect and lack of availability, the child might be a good decoder but still have poor encoding skills, meaning that the child understands non-verbal signals but is not able to display them. The score itself does not reveal such valuable details, even though it would yield a score below the assumed cut-off (the percentile norms are currently based on a sample of 99 families), and therefore an added interpretative description is necessary. The score *alone* does not tell you everything about a child's ability to understand non-verbal signals but it can be indicative of a child's capacity and should be considered in the context of other assessment data (e.g. records, interviews, and/or observations). Refer to Figure 14.1 to see how the scores for mutual attunement and non-verbal communication are visually presented in a graph meant to indicate the relevant clinical focus for possible future treatment.

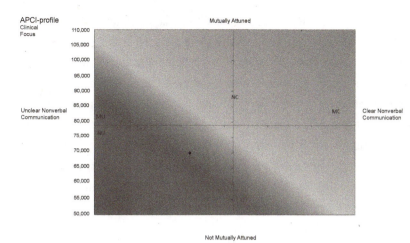

Figure 14.1: APCI Graph - Indication of Attachment

Emotional parental response

The Emotional Parental Response score evaluates how well the parent accommodates and meets the emotional needs of the child. Six general types of parental response from the music therapy, developmental psychology, and sociology literature are used as predefined categories, which include rejecting, dominating, over-involved, passive, supportive, and emotionally exchanging. These categories are scored in four of the five exercises during the APCI. The analysis of parent response aims to reveal how the parent acts toward the child's individual needs and gives additional information on parental behavior. The Emotional Parental Response score consists of the positive response types (supportive and emotionally exchanging), whereas the negative response types (rejecting, dominating, over-involved, and passive) are only reported in qualitative descriptions (Jacobsen and Killén 2015). The three categories of negative response type—rejecting, dominating, and over-involved parental response—indicate possible abuse, while passive parental response is an indicator of neglect. The Emotional Parental Response score is related to attachment behavior type, where clear and predictable lack of support and a passive or controlling (dominating/over-involved) non-available parent most likely result in unsecure avoidant type A attachment in the child (Jacobsen and Killén 2015). An unpredictable, over-involved, slightly supportive, and passive parent might indicate unsecure ambivalent type C attachment in the child. Attachment type D in the child could be indicated by an unpleasant combination of a rejecting, dominating, and passive parent, while sufficient and predominantly supportive and emotionally exchanging parenting most likely would be an indicator of secure attachment type B in the child. Refer to Figure 14.2 to see how emotional response and child autonomy (based on Event-Based Analysis) are visually presented in a graph meant to indicate attachment behavior portrayed between parent and child in the session.

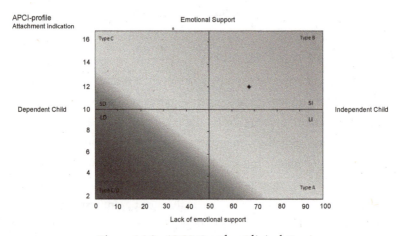

Figure 14.2: APCI Graph - Clinical Focus

Interpretation and APCI report

The APCI yields 16 different profiles where the scores are considered continuums, which further aids the interpretation of the results. The APCI can thus be used for screening the level of emotional neglect (and possible abuse) by looking at 16 different profiles based on different combinations of continuums of mutual to non-mutual attunement, clear to unclear non-verbal communication, emotional support to lack of emotional support, and finally how dependent or independent the child is, as this aids the understanding of attachment behavior in the child and between the parent and the child (Jacobsen and Killén 2015). The profiles are named with four capital letters indicating where in the four continuums they are placed, ranging from MCSI (Mutual attunement, Clear non-verbal communication, Support, and Independent child) to NULD (Not mutually attentive, Unclear non-verbal communication, Lack of support, and Dependent child) (see Table 14.1). The profiles are based on preliminary norm calculations, which require further study using a larger sample of families. However, some indication of clinical application and use can still be addressed. Table 14.1 shows how the APCI profiles can be interpreted in terms of level of neglect, ranging from good enough to at risk and possible neglect/abuse.

TABLE 14.1: SIXTEEN APCI PROFILES

	APCI profile	Good enough	At risk	Neglect/abuse
1	MCSI	x		
2	MCSD	x		
3	MUSI	x		
4	MUSD	x		
5	NCSD	x		
6	NCSI	x		
7	MCLI		x	
8	MULD		x	
9	MCLD		x	
10	MULI		x	
11	NUSI		x	
12	NCLD		x	
13	NCLI		x	
14	NULI			x
15	NUSD			x
16	NULD			x

When writing a report on APCI results, it is important to explain the level of skills without referring to a number or an analysis but by referring to observations and specific events. The different scores must be separated and so must observations from interpretations. A vital part of the report is the voice of the parent who has to be presented with the result/report and give a comment. The report is preferably two or three pages long and ends with a summary and clinical recommendation.

Training

Training and certification are needed to ensure standardized and ethical use of the APCI. Music therapists with entry-level training at minimum diploma degree are eligible for certification following three full days of training on administering the measure, analyzing the data, interpreting the results, and writing a report. For certification, the music therapist must administer the APCI outside the training, submit data from five non-clinical families, and participate in a follow-up one-day course. Here, course participants discuss and share experiences, code data from an additional family, learn how to give feedback to the parents, and finalize reports.

Research and psychometrics

An investigation of the robustness of the APCI was performed in 2012 that included 51 dyads, 18 of whom lived in residential care and 33 of whom functioned as a non-clinical comparison (children aged 5–12) (Jacobsen and McKinney 2015). All dyads underwent two video-recorded music therapy assessment sessions. Video analyses focused on autonomy relationship, turns, and parental response types, which produced scores for Mutual Attunement, Non-verbal Communication Skills, and Emotional Parental Response. The results of the psychometric analyses of the APCI included inter-rater reliability ($r = .73–.89$), test-retest reliability ($r = .70–.89$), and internal consistency (Cronbach's alpha $= .93$). A split-plot factorial design was used to test the reliability and validity of the APCI. To examine concurrent validity and criterion validity, correlations between scores from the Parenting Stress Index (PSI) and Parent-Child Relationship Inventory (PCRI) and the developed APCI were computed. Construct validity was examined by determining whether APCI scores could distinguish between clinical and nonclinical groups using ANOVA. In examining concurrent validity, the study employed a correlational design with correlations between developed APCI scores and standardized questionnaire scores. Pearson's correlation coefficient was used to examine reliability as the scores of the APCI, PSI, and PCRI all are numerical and continuous. The psychometric analysis suggested that the APCI produced reliable and valid scores, which adds to the existing observational instruments of parent-child interaction (Jacobsen and McKinney 2015).

Jacobsen, McKinney, and Holck (2014) investigated the effect of a dyadic music therapy intervention on parent-child interactions using the APCI scores (i.e. Mutual Attunement, Nonverbal Communication, and Emotional Parental Response) as outcomes, and self-reported parenting stress and parent-child relationship in families with emotionally neglected children, aged 5–12 (Jacobsen et al. 2014). As a randomized controlled trial study, conducted at a family care center in Denmark, 18 parent-child dyads were randomly assigned to receive ten weekly music therapy sessions with a credentialed music therapist (n = 9) or treatment as usual (n = 9). Observational measures for parent-child interaction and self-reported measures for parenting stress and parent-child relationship were completed at baseline and four months post-baseline assessment. Results showed that dyads who received music therapy evidenced significant improvement in their non-verbal communication and mutual attunement. Similarly, parents who participated in dyadic music therapy reported less parenting stress and significantly improved parent-child interactions with regard to talking to and understanding their children compared with parents who did not receive music therapy.

The APCI was used to show how dyadic music therapy intervention with families at risk and families with emotionally neglected children could improve the emotional communication between parent and child and interaction (Jacobsen *et al.* 2014). Recent research has focused on the experiences of clinicians administering the APCI and parents undergoing the APCI. Preliminary evidence from this exploratory study, which includes analyses of dialogues with trainees during training and questionnaires filled out by therapists and parents, is promising. All 32 certified music therapists (twelve from the UK, ten from Denmark, four from Austria, two from Switzerland, one from Iceland, one from Australia, one from Sweden, and one from Germany) agree that the tool is manageable, understandable, and easy to implement. The analyses make sense and provide unique and valuable information and insights into the family and parent-child interaction. Qualitative feedback included descriptions on how the APCI noticed unexpected ASD traits in the child only revealed to the therapist in hindsight. The parents participating also all agreed that the APCI sessions were engaging, easy, and motivating for their children. Qualitative feedback included comments on enjoying seeing their children being creative, enjoying a fun experience together, and the sessions being much more engaging and manageable than other assessment tools the family tried.

Future plans

Future study aims to establish a complete standardized norm for the APCI. This will require 500–1000 participating families, preferably from separate countries in Europe, randomly recruited to serve as a representative sample of the population. Internationally certified APCI music therapists will need to perform the APCI and collect and analyze data. Furthermore, investigations of modifications of the APCI to include families with children with special needs are also currently being considered.

Discussion and summary

When compared with other tools, the APCI is based on comparison between clinical and non-clinical samples and offers unique measures for the assessment of care and attachment in families at risk. The APCI includes structured observations of joint parent-child non-verbal interactions in music (George, Kaplan, and Main 1995; Green *et al.* 2000). The APCI is developed for children in the age range of 5–12 years. Attachment assessment is most often conducted from 0 to 5 years old, as these years are crucial for a child's healthy development. However, for some families, problems do not reveal themselves before the child is perceived as being more demanding, and we need to be able to assess older children also. Children of this particular age range (5–12 years) and their parents can be difficult to assess in terms of emotional interaction and attachment behavior because of the predominantly verbal communication between parent and child, which complicates the assessment of valuable nuances and subtleties indicative of emotional neglect and attachment type. The APCI is based on non-verbal interactions in music, thereby bypassing the verbal complexity of older children and providing a nuanced and resourceful assessment of parent-child interactions and parenting competencies.

Research shows how music therapy assessment is motivating and fun for families to participate in because the focus on play and non-verbal interaction makes them relax and possibly show their true potential (Jacobsen and McKinney 2015). Simultaneously, it is difficult for the families to portray inauthentic interaction patterns because they do not know what is expected of them in this setting where the focus is on form and not content.

Besides being administered in a consistent and stable manner, with standard procedures and good psychometric properties, the APCI can provide treatment-relevant information on the emotional interaction between parent and child, including mutual attunement, non-verbal communication, and parental emotional response. According to Schore and Schore (2008), attunement and non-verbal communication are highly significant for a child to develop healthy and dynamic emotion regulation skills. With information on parental emotional support and child autonomy, the APCI profiles can indicate the level of emotional neglect and attachment type, which can guide the treatment plan for the family. Through the APCI's use of music and non-verbal activities, it is possible to observe and assess the emotional communication between parent and child. The APCI can contribute to the assessment process by providing sensitive and valuable information to a multidisciplinary team in situations where it can be difficult to obtain in-depth detail on the parent-child interaction and parenting competencies.

References

Ainsworth, M. D. S., Blehar, M. C., Waters, E., and Wall, S. (1978) *Patterns of Attachment: A Psychological Study of the Strange Situation.* Hillsdale, NJ: Lawrence Erlbaum Associates Publishers.

Bonde, L. O., Pedersen, I. P., and Jacobsen, S. L. (eds) (2019) *Comprehensive Guide to Music Therapy* (2nd edition). London: Jessica Kingsley Publishers.

Bruscia, K. E. (1987) *Improvisational Models of Music Therapy.* Springfield, IL: Charles C. Thomas.

Colegrove, V. M. and Havighurst, S. S. (2016) 'Review of nonverbal communication in parent-child relationships: Assessment and intervention.' *Journal of Child Family Studies,* doi: 10.1007/s10826-016-0563-x.

Deacon, S. and Piercy, F. (2001) 'Qualitative methods in family evaluation: Creative assessment techniques.' *The American Journal of Family Therapy, 29,* 255–273.

George, C., Kaplan, N., and Main, M. (1995) 'The Adult Attachment Interview.' Unpublished manuscript, University of California at Berkeley.

Green, J. M., Stanley, C., Smith, V., and Goldwyn, R. (2000) 'A new method of evaluating attachment representations in young school-age children: The Manchester Child Attachment Story Task.' *Attachment & Human Development, 2,* 42–64.

Holck, U. (2004) 'Turn-taking in music therapy with children with communication disorders.' *British Journal of Music Therapy, 18,* 45–53.

Holck, U. (2008) 'Kommunikativ musikalitet. Kognition & pædagogik.' *Tidsskrift om den gode Læring, 18,* 70–79.

Iwaniec, D. (1995) *The Emotionally Abused and Neglected Child: Identification, Assessment, and Intervention.* Chichester, NH: John Wiley & Sons.

Jacobsen, S. and Wigram, T. (2007) 'Music therapy for the assessment of parental competences for children in need of care.' *Nordic Journal of Music Therapy, 16,* 129–142.

Jacobsen, S. L. and Killén, K. (2015) 'Clinical application of music therapy assessment within the field of child protection.' *Nordic Journal of Music Therapy, 24,* 2, 148–166.

Jacobsen, S. L. and McKinney, C. H. (2015) 'A music therapy tool for assessing parent-child interaction in cases of emotional neglect.' *Journal of Child and Family Studies, 24,* 2164–2173.

Jacobsen, S. L., McKinney, C., and Holck, U. (2014) 'Effects of a dyadic music therapy intervention on parent-child interaction, parent stress, and parent-child relationship in families with emotionally neglected children: A randomized controlled trial.' *Journal of Music Therapy, 51,* 4, 310–332.

Juffer, F., Bakermans-Kranenburg, M. J., and van IJzendoorn, M. H. (2005) 'Enhancing Children's Socioemotional Development: A Review of Intervention Studies.' In M. T. Douglas (ed.) *Handbook of Research Methods in Development Science.* Oxford: Blackwell Publishers.

Killén, K. (2012) *Barndommen Varer i Generationer. Forebyggelse af Omsorgssvigt.* Copenhagen: Hans Reitzels Forlag.

Kim, J., Wigram, T., and Gold, C. (2009) 'Emotional, motivational and interpersonal responsiveness of children with autism in improvisational music therapy.' *Autism, 13,* 389–409.

Knapp, M. and Hall, J. (2009) *Nonverbal Communication in Human Interaction: International Edition.* Boston, MA: Wadsworth Cengage Learning.

Malloch, S. and Trevarthen, C. (2009) *Communicative Musicality: Exploring the Basis of Human Companionship.* London: Oxford University Press.

Miller, E. M. (1994) 'Musical intervention in family therapy.' *Music Therapy, 12,* 39–57.

Molyneux, C. (2008) 'Music Therapy as Part of a Multidisciplinary Family Assessment Process.' In K. Twyford and T. Watson (eds) *Integrated Team Working.* London: Jessica Kingsley Publishers.

Oldfield, A. and Flower, C. (2008) *Music Therapy with Children and Their Families.* London: Jessica Kingsley Publishers.

Pavlicevic, M. (2002) 'Dynamic interplay in clinical improvisation.' *Voices: A World Forum for Music Therapy, 2.* Retrieved 26/02/2018 at https://normt.uib.no/index.php/voices/article/view/88/70.

Schore, J. and Schore, A. (2008) 'Modern attachment theory: The central role of affect regulation in development and treatment.' *Clinical Social Work Journal, 36,* 9, 9–20.

Snyder, R., Shapiro, S., and Treleaven, D. (2013) 'Attachment theory and mindfulness.' *Journal of Child and Family Studies, 21,* 709–717.

Stern, D. (1995) *The Motherhood Constellation.* New York, NY: Basic Books.

Stern, D. (2000) *The Interpersonal World of the Infant.* New York, NY: Basic Books.

Stern, D. (2010a) 'The issue of vitality.' *Nordic Journal of Music Therapy, 19,* 88–102.

Stern, D. (2010b) *Forms of Vitality.* Oxford: Oxford University Press.

Trondalen, G. and Skårderud, F. (2007) 'Playing with affects: And the importance of "affect attunement."' *Nordic Journal of Music Therapy, 16,* 100–111.

Wigram, T. (2004) *Improvisation.* London: Jessica Kingsley Publishers.

Wigram, T. (2007) 'Event-Based Analysis of Improvisation Using the Improvisational Assessment Profiles (IAPs).' In T. Wosch and T. Wigram (eds) *Microanalysis in Music Therapy – Methods, Techniques and Applications for Clinicians, Researchers, Educators and Students.* London: Jessica Kingsley Publishers.

Winnicott, D. (1971) *Play and Reality.* New York, NY: Basic Books.

Wolf, C. and Peregoy, J. (2003) 'Assessing Parenting Capability.' In K. Jordan (ed.) *Handbook of Couple and Family Assessment.* New York, NY: Nova Science Publishers.

CHAPTER 15

The Music Therapy Toolbox

Jaakko Erkkilä and Thomas Wosch

Setting and motivation—a short history of the MTTB

The Music Therapy Toolbox (MTTB) is based on the MIDI toolbox (Eerola and Toiviainen 2004a, 2004b), which was created for extracting several musical features from composed music. In a research project, Intelligent Music Systems in Music Therapy (2003–2006, Academy of Finland), a group of researchers started to develop the MIDI toolbox for music therapy usage, for extracting musical features from clinical improvisations. The project aimed to create a new toolbox (MTTB) (Erkkilä 2007; Erkkilä, Ala-Ruona, and Lartillot 2014; Erkkilä *et al.* 2004, 2005) and empirically test it for its ability to analyze clinical improvisations created by individuals with mental retardation and their music therapists. The group found that certain musical features (or musical behavior) predict the severity of mental retardation (Luck *et al.* 2006). Another interesting finding was that clinical improvisations do not often sound like "real music" and may give a random, or chaotic, impression. At least some of the meanings of clinical improvisation can be explained by using a combination of concepts taken from traditional music analysis, psychoacoustics, and mainstream psychology (Luck *et al.* 2008). In brief, the series of empirical investigations showed that, in clinical improvisations, certain anthropological and psychological mechanisms and meanings still exist even when the client is severely retarded.

Theoretical background and development of assessment tool

Daniel Stern's concept of microanalysis played an important role in understanding musical interaction in music therapy. Moreover, early mother-child interactions, communication, and relationship were a main subject of Stern's research (Stern 1971, 2004). Stern described his microanalysis research method and its objectives in 1971:

> Using a method frame-by-frame film analysis, we have studied in detail an example of "controlling" and "overstimulating" maternal behavior. We have attempted to identify some of the specific infant behaviors which are significantly influenced by, and in turn influence, such an interaction. We have conceptualized and analyzed this interaction in terms of the behaviors of mother and infant which maintain, terminate, avoid, and initiate social contact and stimulation. (Stern 1971, p. 502)

The context of these observations was non-verbal relationship and interaction. Kenneth Bruscia (1987) developed the Improvisation Assessment Profiles (IAPs) beginning in the early 1980s to assess clinical improvisations as one dimension of the non-verbal context and interaction. Regarding the use of the IAPs, Bruscia wrote: "They are intended to provide a model of client assessment based upon clinical observation, musical analysis, and psychological interpretation of the client's improvisation" (Bruscia 1987, p. 403).

The IAPs contain six profiles. These are Integration, Variability, Tension, Congruence, Salience, and Autonomy. Almost all the profiles assess the music made by clients in clinical improvisation. For the clinical assessment of children with communication disorders, Tony Wigram focused on the profiles Autonomy and Variability (Wigram 1999, 2007). Wosch (2007) focused on the profile Autonomy for a micro-assessment of adults with mental disorders and developed a second-by-second assessment of the "intermusical or interpersonal relationship" (Bruscia 1987). The musical analysis in the profile Autonomy contains the following musical scales.

Rhythmic ground

1. Rhythmic figure

2. Tonal/melodic

3. Harmonic

4. Textural

5. Phrasing

6. Volume

7. Timbre

8. Program/lyrics. (Bruscia 1987)

In each scale, with the exception of the last scale of program/lyrics, the "role relationship" (Bruscia 1987) of the client is assessed musically. The Autonomy-scale rhythmic ground includes tempo, meter, and subdivision (Bruscia 1987). The Autonomy-scale timbre is used to "determine the medium, instrument, production technique, and sound vocabulary" (Bruscia 1987, p. 403) of the client's improvisation. The Autonomy-scale tonal/melodic contains tonality and melody.

Finally, there are the following levels of intermusical relationship in the profile Autonomy.

Dependent

1. Follower

2. Partner

3. Leader

4. Resister. (Bruscia 1987)

Julia Scholtz and colleagues expanded the level of *resister* to include the level of *independent* in the assessment of children with developmental disorders (Scholtz, Voigt, and Wosch 2007). All these levels are assessed in each musical scale of the profile Autonomy (Wosch 2007). One example is that the therapist changes the tempo (musical scale, rhythmic ground) and the client follows this change by also changing the tempo. Here the therapist is the *leader* in rhythmic ground and the client is the *follower* in this moment of the clinical improvisation.

In Stern's comprehensive video analysis, the early non-verbal interaction patterns "which maintain, terminate, avoid and initiate social contact" (Stern 1971, p. 502) included gestures, mimic, voice, and so on, and can be compared with the musical role relationships of *follower*, *resister*, and *leader* described by Bruscia. This microanalysis of interaction (Bruscia 1987; Wosch 2007) is limited to musical behavior and is missing all motor activities, mimic, and more dimensions of behavior. However, in a survey of British music therapists, Elaine Streeter (2010) found that 91 percent of the clinicians were interested first of all in the "identification and quantification of interaction episodes," including musical interaction for future software assessment. The microanalysis version of IAP Autonomy (Wosch 2007) is very time consuming and has been applied so far solely in music therapy research. An automatized version is needed for clinical practice. The MTTB is very close in its automatized measurement of music features to the basic paradigm of musical role relationships of IAP Autonomy.

Procedure, data collection, data analysis, and interpretation

The first version of the MTTB only reads and handles MIDI (Musical Instruments Digital Interface) data. It is a protocol, where the key elements of musical information are presented as numbers and not as real music (Erkkilä *et al.* 2014). This means that in order to analyze musical data it must be first played by MIDI instruments or turn to MIDI from digital audio. The second version of the MTTB enables analyzing digital audio as well. Though challenging for musical feature extraction, digital audio brings certain important possibilities such as timbre-related features (not possible with MIDI data). The MTTB allows for the creation of a graphical notation of music consisting of user-selected musical features and interaction between client and therapist.

The musical features of the complete MTTB MIDI version are:

- density

- mean duration

- mean pitch

- standard deviation of pitch

- mean velocity

- pulse clarity

- tonality

- articulation

- tempo

- dissonance

- synchronicity. (Erkkilä 2007)

All these features are calculations from musical data. Two examples are given here for these calculations. Density is the "number of notes in the window divided by the length of the window" (Erkkilä 2007, p. 37). In the first version of the MTTB, the time-window was six seconds. In the second version of the MTTB, used in microanalysis, it is one second. Articulation is "the proportion of short silence in the window. Values close to zero indicate *legato* playing, while values close to one indicate *staccato* playing" (Erkkilä 2007, p. 37). For access to the MTTB, contact the Music Therapy Department, University of Jyväskylä. We are working on providing access to an MTTB download via a webpage.

Application of the MTTB

In MTTB analysis there are a few starting points that must be taken into account when producing clinical improvisations. With MIDI data, it is important that each improviser's music is sent on separate MIDI channels. If they are on the same channel, the MTTB understands the improvisation as a product of one improviser, which is not appropriate. With digital audio, it is also important to be able to separate the channels for the same reason. The current version of the MTTB reads a stereo file where the improvisers are panned on the left and right channels. When working with audio, recorded by microphones, it is important to prevent leaking between the microphones in order to have the sound as "clean" as possible on each of the channels. There are different kinds of microphones available, which largely only detect the source signal and not too many surrounding sounds. Recording improvisations in MIDI and/or audio formats can nowadays be done with relatively cheap, small-sized, and even transportable equipment. One needs a computer (a laptop, for instance), recording software installed (for recording MIDI and digital audio), MIDI and audio interface (separately or combined in the same gear), two microphones for recording the audio signal (from two djembe drums, one for the client and one for the therapist, for instance), and MIDI outputs on the instruments sending MIDI data (MIDI inputs and outputs are standard for most of the digital music instruments today). If one already has a computer, two djembe drums, and two digital keyboards, the investment starts from 1000 euros (even less) for the additional gear. In Table 15.1, some basic consequences for MTTB analysis are described depending on the setup and starting point.

TABLE 15.1: CURRENT PRECONDITION
FOR APPLICATION OF THE MTTB

	YES	NO
Identical instruments for both improvisers	The data is fully comparable between the improvisers in terms of the expressive possibilities	The data is not fully comparable between the improvisers, and the different expressive possibilities must be taken into account in the analysis
Identical sounds (e.g. piano) for both improvisers	The data is fully comparable between the improvisers when the sound does not affect the way of playing	The data is not fully comparable between the improvisers because different sounds affect the way of playing
Identical instruments and sounds in sequential sessions	Improvisations can be compared longitudinally for possible expressive or interactive changes, for instance	Comparing improvisations longitudinally is challenging or impossible, and affected by different setups
Identical instruments and sounds for all the clients	Opens possibilities for group-based analysis for finding patterns typical of a certain subgroup, for instance	Comparison between subjects is not very relevant or appropriate

A current challenge with the MTTB is that it only runs on *MatLab* engineering software. This means that hospitals, private practice, or university hospitals have to have *MatLab* software or need to buy access. Individual access currently starts at 2000 euros. However, we plan to work on a stand-alone version of the MTTB without *MatLab*.

Data collection and selection

There are various strategies to choose the improvisations to be used for MTTB analysis. Because MTTB analysis as such is a quick process, after the improvisations have been properly saved, the number of improvisations to be analyzed at a time is not the most critical question from the MTTB point of view. However, data reduction may be relevant for other reasons, such as the clinical relevance of an improvisation. When an improvisation is meaningful in a specific way, it may trigger strong emotions, images, associations, and so on, and this may be a reason to analyze just this improvisation and not others. In particular, in everyday clinical practice, it is a good idea to keep a diary where the therapist keeps track of the improvisations and evaluates their clinical meaning. To specifically focus on improvisation comparison in the course of time, one may want to develop a particular improvisational task with a more or less pre-planned procedure for increasing comparability between the improvisations created in different sessions. An example of such a task is to create an improvisation based on a fixed amount of time where the therapist always follows the same basic starting point— such as creating a simple accompaniment on a stable tempo based on rhythmic and tonal ideas—which remains the same between the sessions. When that task is repeated every now and then, there is a strong basis for comparison when the client's play can change. The basic rule is that the more differences between the contexts and starting points of the improvisations, the harder it is to make relevant comparison between them. Examples will be described in three cases in the following section about analysis data.

Data analysis and interpretation

Before using the MTTB for analysis and assessment of clinical improvisations, one has to carefully consider the added value of it and whether the clinical approach is suitable for its use. In principle, the MTTB does the analysis regardless of instruments and how they are played. Basically, the MTTB only offers an objective way to look at the clinical improvisation based on certain musical features extracted through mathematical algorithms. When it is possible to look separately at the client's and therapist's music in terms of each of the musical features, various aspects of interaction between the improvisers can be considered as well. With the MTTB, many fundamental elements of music (such as rhythm, register, timbre, tonality, etc.) can be considered. After that, it is up to the clinician or researcher to try to interpret what it means when the client, for example, first mostly improvises on a lower register, then in the course of the therapeutic process gradually expands the use of register.

One may want to look at music psychology literature and research to know how low and high musical registers are understood from a music psychology perspective (for example, are they sad or happy?). In music therapy literature and research, we have different models for interpreting certain musical phenomena as well. Analyzing improvisations as such, without rationale or a clear idea for improvisational work, is perhaps not too rewarding. But if there is any aspect of interaction or expression, based on musical behavior between the client and therapist, the MTTB may be worth applying. Furthermore, if there is anything that remains the same between improvisations within a music therapy process in terms of improvisational task, instruments employed, and so on, there is room for comparison. Three applications and dimensions of the MTTB in the assessment of musical interaction in clinical improvisations will be described in the following sections.

ASSESSMENT OF SYNCHRONICITY

De Backer (2008), who has specialized in clinical improvisation with psychotic patients, defines musical synchrony (in clinical improvisation) as shared sensations of common pulse and rhythm between the client and therapist with some moments of timbre-related interweaving as well. He also mentions single musical initiatives, dynamic features and endings of musical events, which give an impression of sharing.

In terms of the MTTB, synchrony can only be investigated by looking at what objectively happens in music concerning different musical features. In practice, the MTTB synchrony means simultaneity or interconnectivity of reciprocal musical behavior regarding certain musical features or feature combinations. Thus, synchrony may appear on a rhythmic level, which can be seen in a single musical feature, pulse clarity, or it can be a more complex phenomenon, for instance activity or strength (see the following regarding the client-therapist relationship), which is a combination of several musical features. Whether the question really is about experienced synchrony in a psychotherapeutic sense, such as empathy or rapport, is outside the MTTB's capacity. Therefore, to gain a richer picture on the synchrony, it is important to combine different data sources such as MTTB results and the real experiences of the improvisers. This fits the reasoning of Bruscia regarding the IAPs, which states that client assessment is based not only on music analysis but also on clinical observation and on psychological interpretation (Bruscia 1987).

In principle, there is also a phenomenon called "fake synchrony." It is the therapist's capacity and desire for musical synchrony, which may lead to a one-sided experience of synchrony. An example of this is when a clinician is improvising with an ASD client with limited skills for interaction. The therapist may unconsciously connect to the client's music without real responsiveness on the client's side. In other words, the client is just playing their own, internal music, hardly recognizing the other, but the therapist may have a feeling of synchrony due to the fact that they are very sensitively responding to the client's music. By using the MTTB, it is possible to analyze this phenomenon. The crucial concept here is timing. On the MTTB graph, it is possible to roughly check whether it is the therapist who always imitates the client's musical behavior. In Figure 15.1, one example of the synchronicity of the therapist can be seen in the musical feature of mean velocity (mean vel). In the upper graph, the client's line begins. The therapist joins in in the third second. The therapist adapts very closely to the client's line. With this, the lighter color increases in the upper part of the mean velocity graph.

This upper part identifies the therapist's activity and the lower part the client's activity. Another possibility is to apply the MTTB function called the imitation diagram, which shows who of the improvisers does something first and whether there is a pattern concerning this.

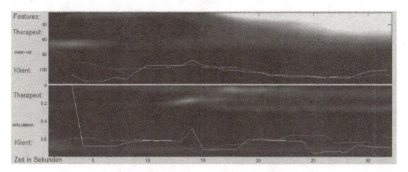

Figure 15.1: Synchronicity feature in MTTB basic musical features of mean velocity (version MTTB-B)
(white line = client, grey line = therapist)

In summary, the MTTB shows objective and precise similarity and simultaneity in music and provides a tool for tracing possible "fake synchrony." However, it is always a good idea to pay attention to other data sources as well, such as bodily synchrony (body movements, facial expression, etc.) and psychological experiences (experienced togetherness, empathy, rapport), and to look at the overall picture.

ASSESSMENT OF THE INTERMUSICAL RELATIONSHIP USING THE PROFILE AUTONOMY

In 2010 and 2011 a research and development group at the University of Applied Sciences, Würzburg-Schweinfurt, started the development of the MTTB in the assessment of role relationship of Bruscia's IAP Autonomy between client and therapist in clinical improvisations (Jonscher, Gruschka, and Scheder-Springer 2010). In Figure 15.2 an example for *resister* (second 38–40, see time-baseline) can be seen. In this case, the musical features density and pulse clarity for client (top line) and therapist (bottom line) move in opposite directions away from each other.

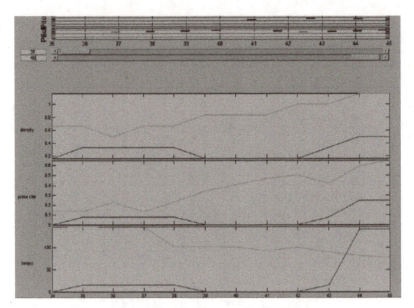

Figure 15.2: Example of resister in MTTB features
(top line = client; bottom line = therapist; second 38–40
shows the resisting behavior of the client)

Figure 15.3 shows an example of *independent* (middle box) using the musical feature tempo. Here, the client (light grey) plays similarly to the therapist (dark grey) but sometimes a little faster (above the therapist) and sometimes a little slower (below the therapist).

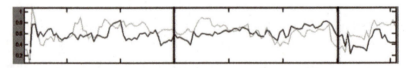

Figure 15.3: Example of independent in MTTB
feature tempo (dark grey line = client; light grey line = therapist; the
dark grey box shows the independent behavior of the client)

However, these levels of intermusical relationship or role relationship are not calculated yet in algorithms. Using the definitions of the six levels, the music therapist can detect these levels in the MTTB graphs. The next step of development can be the detection of the levels of *leader* and of *follower*. The calculation of these roles includes higher numbers for the *leader* and lower numbers for the *follower*. At the same time, with this distance between the *leader's* and *follower's* curves in the MTTB graph, synchronicity takes place. The *follower* follows the *leader*. In Figure 15.4 one can see that in the musical feature density the therapist (dark grey line) follows the client (light grey line) in second 80 (see time-baseline). In second 90, this changes. The therapist leads and the client follows during the next 10 seconds.

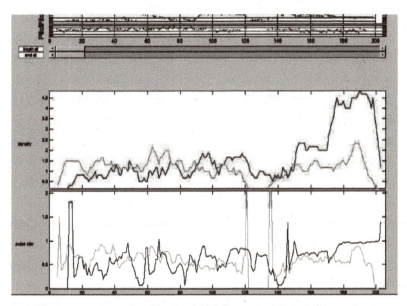

Figure 15.4: Example of leader and follower in MTTB feature density

An example of changes of role relationship between client and therapist in clinical improvisation can be seen in Figure 15.5. The music therapist marked the levels in the MTTB graph here. The color of the level defines whether this role belongs to the client (bottom line) or the therapist (top line). In determining leading and following, it is very important to note who begins the change or keeps the musical feature of main velocity and who follows this change afterwards.

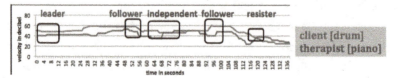

Figure 15.5: Change in role relationship in MTTB feature mean velocity
(Jonscher and Wosch 2012; Magee and Wosch 2017)

The interpretation of this MTTB assessment will be described in two different contexts of clinical practice. The first context is the clinical practice of individual music therapy for children with developmental disorders. In a case example of a client with developmental delays in motor activities, language, and cognitive capabilities, music therapy focused on additional social behavior symptoms. The MTTB assessment of six levels of role relationship was used here for assessing the role relationship of the client. In most of the musical features of the MTTB, the role of *leader* was assessed in the first clinical improvisations with this client. However, the role of *resister* could not be identified. This led to the interpretation that the client had social needs. Moreover, in the musical feature of pulse clarity, the client was assessed continuously in the role of *follower*. In the musical feature of tempo, the client was assessed also in the role of *independent* (see Figure 15.3). These two resources did increase in individual music therapy for this client according to this assessment. Within the context of developmental disorders, independence is an important resource. The assessment of *follower* is very important for role flexibility as a social skill of the client within the context of the main role of *leader*. The assessment of these resources in the rhythmic ground features of pulse clarity and tempo guided the music therapist in her clinical improvisation. Focusing on the rhythmic features of clinical improvisation supported the therapy of social behavior symptoms.

Another context of clinical practice is the use of the MTTB assessment in individual music therapy for adults with affective disorders. In one case, a client with a major depression worked in a symbolic way in the process using clinical improvisation in relationship with a primary object. At the beginning of this therapy, the MTTB assessment assessed a role change of the client from *leader* to *follower*, for example in the musical feature of density (see Figure 15.4). At the end of this psychodynamic music therapy treatment, the MTTB assessment assessed the continuous role of the client in the role of *leader* in clinical improvisation. In the verbal reflection on this individual music therapy, the client talked about change of relationship in everyday life. Moreover, the intensity of density (higher numbers) increased when the role of *leader* was assessed. In this case, within the context of a psychodynamic paradigm, *leader* and *follower* had an individual meaning for the client. Here, the assessment and treatment of the intermusical relationship are an assessment and treatment of the interpersonal relationship of the client. The MTTB assessment could illustrate this understanding musically.

ASSESSMENT OF CLIENT-THERAPIST RELATIONSHIP

A strong feature of the MTTB is that it shows objectively and exactly what happens in music based on its own logic and algorithms. We shall now extend and deepen the meaning of MTTB features within relationship, going beyond synchronicity and the Autonomy levels. There is a need for theorizing these kinds of objective findings—that is, trying to understand their meaning from the therapeutic relevance point of view. In a study by Luck *et al.* (2008), listeners (undergraduate students) were asked to provide ratings of perceived emotional content of clinical improvisations, created by mentally retarded clients together with their music therapists. By using the MTTB, a total of nine musical features were extracted from the improvisations. In addition to other findings, the researchers found that the experienced *activity* was best predicted by high note density and high pulse clarity, *pleasantness* by low note density and high tonal clarity, and *strength* by high mean velocity and low note density. This is an example of how raising the level of abstraction may help in understanding the core meaning of a musical feature or, as in this study, feature combinations. In terms of the client-therapist relationship, looking at improvisers' musical activity, strength, or pleasantness may make more sense than to keep an eye on a single, perhaps less communicative feature such as musical density or sensory dissonance. This use of the MTTB has to be further developed in music therapy research for final application in the assessment of clinical practice.

Music therapy approaches, client groups, and limitations

As the IAPs are not limited in specific music therapy approaches and methods, so the MTTB can be used in different theoretical and clinical contexts. The aim and theoretical orientations of the IAPs are described by Bruscia:

> Their aim is to enhance the therapist's understanding of the client through objective methods of data collection, while also stimulating interpretations of the data according to pertinent psychological theories... The intent has been to keep the content and vocabulary of the IAPs free from a specific theoretical orientation. (Bruscia 1987, p. 411)

The IAPs and the MTTB can only analyze and assess clinical improvisations, but all approaches and methods of music therapy using clinical improvisation can be assisted with analysis and assessment using the MTTB. Another limitation besides clinical improvisation is the focus on musical analysis. If behavior other than the musical behavior of the client is important and of interest for analysis and assessment, other assessment tools are needed, for example those based on video analysis. One example may be music therapy for severe developmental disorders and severe learning disabilities. In these cases, multisensory data about the client is needed, including motor activities, mimic, gaze, and vocal expression, beyond musical activities and interaction. So far, the MTTB has been applied in music therapy for major depression (Erkkilä et al. 2014; Wosch and Erkkilä 2016), for mental retardation (Luck et al. 2006), and for developmental disorders (Jonscher and Wosch 2012; Magee and Wosch 2017). In music therapy for major depression, clients did stay with the same instrument.

Finally, the following limitations of the MTTB are based on the current "state of the art" of the MTTB. There are a number of background factors that affect MTTB results and interpretation, including the client-therapist relationship. Some of them are described here.

Instrumentation

A musical instrument strongly affects the way of playing. If client and therapist have different instruments, with different sounds and musical capacity, it affects greatly the interpretation of MTTB results. This must be taken into account in interpretation in cases of use of more than one musical instrument.

Using various instruments or sounds over the course of therapy

Longitudinal considerations are challenging and are valid only if improvisations compared over time are based on usage of the same instruments and sounds.

Philosophy of therapeutic approach

There are music therapy models where instrumentation and musical roles are more or less fixed for the therapeutic approach. If a typical setting is piano (therapist) and percussion instruments (client), various aspects of MTTB analysis must be considered and many features of it cannot be utilized at all. Even if the client and therapist share an instrument, let's say piano, where a typical arrangement is the therapist sitting on the left side (lower register is approximately equal to accompaniment), the arrangement predetermines both the possible musical behaviors and MTTB analysis (and interpretation). However, this kind of arrangement can be therapeutically highly relevant and theoretically reasonable.

Understanding of clinical improvisation

Depending on the model and clinicians' personal preferences, clinical improvising can be highly spontaneous and free from any givens— or almost opposite to that. This may vary even within a single music therapy process, where improvisations may first be relatively structured (e.g. for holding and support-related reasons) and later on freer. Furthermore, professional musical interventions by the therapist play their own role in improvisational work. Naturally, these starting points and principles affect MTTB analysis and must be taken into account when interpreting the results.

Training

Training clinicians in using MTTB software is not the most crucial task. The MTTB is a computer application and people are used to working with many kinds of applications. One of the challenges with the MTTB currently is that there is no commercial version of it available. So, getting it working and having access to *MatLab* is a challenge for many.

An even bigger challenge is to connect the MTTB with clinical models and working styles. Improvisational music therapy is very divergent and we do not have too many clearly defined models in terms of musical interventions and techniques and their therapeutic dimensions. In addition, music therapists tend to favor various clinical methods, instruments, and working styles as a natural part of their therapeutic philosophy, which produces new challenges in terms of using the MTTB. With the Integrative Improvisational Music Therapy (IIMT) model, we are currently piloting the training for Finnish music therapists where understanding and using the MTTB is also a part of the skills to be acquired (based in the University of Jyväskylä). After finishing these pilots and gaining some new understanding on how to further synchronize the IIMT and MTTB, there might be room for starting training in other contexts as well. Moreover, in graduate and post-graduate research projects in Germany, the MTTB was synchronized in the first steps with Orff

Music Therapy and Improvisational Psychodynamic Music Therapy (based at the University of Applied Sciences, Würzburg-Schweinfurt, in collaboration with the University of Jyväskylä).

Research, psychometrics, and future plans

Research of the MTTB in musical analysis, microanalysis, and assessment of clinical improvisations has been named and described in previous sources (Erkkilä 2007; Erkkilä et al. 2004, 2005, 2014; Jonscher and Wosch 2012; Jonscher et al. 2010; Luck et al. 2006, 2008; Magee and Wosch 2017; Wosch and Erkkilä 2016).

The psychometrics of the MTTB as an assessment tool for clinical practice do not exist. The psychometrics of the MTTB assessment for clinical practice must be developed and implemented. With regard to the feature of synchronicity, this validation could include somatic measurements of heart rate and breathing. The use of these measures is based on rhythmic entrainment research (Trost, Labbé, and Grandjean 2017). However, validation regarding role relationship levels must include standardized observations of social behavior, relationship, and communication. In all cases, changes observed in the MTTB must be correlated with relevant outcome measurements. Another relevant analysis is the validation of MTTB assessment regarding the musical emotions of the client and the therapist in clinical improvisation (Jonscher and Wosch 2012). The change of musical emotions within a clinical improvisation has been calculated and assessed during the first steps of research. Although the results are promising, the validation of this assessment has not been carried out yet.

There are more future plans for the MTTB. One possibility is to export a data sheet consisting of numbers to be further analyzed by statistical software. This function is more for improvisation research. In addition, there is no continuous data on the data sheet but compressed values (mean, standard deviation, etc.) for each of the features. Thus, microanalysis is not possible based on data sheet values. However, it is possible to segment the improvisation into many parts, which is a way to get more detailed information from improvisations.

Moreover, IAP Autonomy Micro Method cluster analysis was used successfully for automatized calculation of improvisation segments (Wosch and Erkkilä 2016).

So far, the MTTB has only been applied to the individual setting (therapist-client improvisations) and more coding is necessary before it can be applied to the group context. Previous research in the MTTB and the IAPs' Autonomy profile showed differences between human assessment with the Autonomy profile and the automatized assessment with the MTTB. Two differences were flexibility in timeframes and in the assessed items. The MTTB calculates each musical feature in standardized timeframes. A future perspective in terms of timeframe is programming a flexible timeframe that adapts to changes within each musical feature.

The final future perspective for the further development of the MTTB is the development of a new feature of *leader* and *follower* as a new algorithm, based on the synchronicity feature of the MTTB. This can be extended to include more of the Autonomy levels.

The MTTB can be applied to everyday clinical work when a clinician finds the graphic notation mode practical and appropriate. It enables microanalytic (second by second) consideration and in addition saves the music therapist time, because instead of listening to the improvisation, one can see it visualized. After learning, reading, and interpreting the graphs, one can quickly compare different improvisations based on MTTB visualizations.

Acknowledgement

The authors wish to thank Melanie Voigt for assistance with the English in this chapter.

References

Bruscia, K. E. (1987) *Improvisational Models of Music Therapy*. Springfield, IL: Charles C. Thomas.

De Backer, J. (2008) 'Music and psychosis.' *Nordic Journal of Music Therapy, 17*, 2, 89–104.

Erkkilä, J. (2007) 'Music Therapy Toolbox (MTTB) – An Improvisation Analysis Tool for Clinicians and Researchers.' In T. Wosch and T. Wigram (eds) *Microanalysis in Music Therapy – Methods, Techniques and Applications for Clinicians, Researchers, Educators and Students.* London: Jessica Kingsley Publishers.

Erkkilä, J., Ala-Ruona, E., and Lartillot, O. (2014) 'Technology and Clinical Improvisation – From Production and Playback to Analysis and Interpretation.' In K. Stensæth (ed.) *Music, Health, Technogy and Design.* Oslo: Centre for Music and Health, University of Oslo.

Erkkilä, J., Lartillot, O., Luck, G., Riikkilä, K., and Toiviainen, P. (2004) 'An Overview of the Research Project Concentrating on Computer Aided Improvisation Analysis in Music Therapy Context.' The Commission on Music in Special Education, Music Therapy and Music Medicine, Vitoria, Spain.

Erkkilä, J., Lartillot, O., Luck, G., Riikkilä, K., and Toiviainen, P. (2005) 'Intelligent music systems in music therapy.' *Music Therapy Today, 6,* 4. Retrieved 13/11/2018 at www.musictherapyworld.net.

Eerola, T. and Toiviainen, P. (2004a) *MIDI Toolbox: MATLAB Tools for Music Research.* Finland: University of Jyväskylä.

Eerola, T. and Toiviainen, P. (2004b) *MIDI Toolbox: MATLAB Tools for Music Research.* Finland: University of Jyväskylä.

Jonscher, A. and Wosch, T. (2012) 'Computergestützte Musiktherapeutische Diagnostik zu Emotion und Interaktion,' 24th Werkstatt für musiktherapeutische Forschung. Augsburg: University of Augsburg.

Jonscher, A., Gruschka, K., and Scheder-Springer, N. (2010) 'Businessplan MicroEmotionMusic.' Hochschule für angewandte Wissenschaften Würzburg-Schweinfurt. Unpublished manuscript.

Luck, G., Riikkilä, K., Lartillot, O., Erkkilä, J., Toiviainen, P., Mäkelä, A., and Värri, J. (2006) 'Exploring relationships between level of mental retardation and features of music therapy improvisations: A computational approach.' *Nordic Journal of Music Therapy, 15,* 1, 30–48.

Luck, G., Toiviainen, P., Erkkilä, J., Lartillot, O., Riikkilä, K., Mäkelä, A., and Värri, J. (2008) 'Modelling the relationships between emotional responses to, and musical content of, music therapy improvisations.' *Psychology of Music, 36,* 1, 25–45.

Magee, W. and Wosch, T. (2017) 'Technology Developments in Music Therapy.' In S. Federici and M. Scherer (eds) *Assistive Technology Assessment Handbook* (2nd edition). Boca Raton: CRC Press.

Scholtz, J., Voigt, M., and Wosch, T. (2007) 'Microanalysis of Interaction in Music Therapy (MIMT) with Children with Developmental Disorders.' In T. Wosch and T. Wigram (eds) *Microanalysis in Music Therapy – Methods, Techniques and Applications for Clinicians, Researchers, Educators and Students.* London: Jessica Kingsley Publishers.

Stern, D. N. (1971) 'A micro-analysis of mother-infant interaction: Behavior regulating social contact between a mother and her 3 1/2-month-old twins.' *Journal of the American Academy of Child Psychiatry, 10,* 3, 501–517.

Stern, D. N. (2004) *The Present Moment in Psychotherapy and Everyday Life.* New York, NY: W.W. Norton & Company.

Streeter, E. (2010) *Computer Aided Music Therapy Evaluation: Investigating and Testing the Music Therapy Logbook Prototype 1 System.* York: University of York. Retrieved 03/08/2018 at http://etheses.whiterose.ac.uk/1201.

Trost, W., Labbé, C., and Grandjean, D. (2017) 'Rhythmic entrainment as a musical affect induction mechanism.' *Neuropsychologia, 96,* 96–110, doi: 10.1016/j.neuropsychologia.2017.01.004.

Wigram, T. (1999) 'Assessment methods in music therapy: A humanistic or natural science framework?' *Nordic Journal of Music Therapy, 8,* 1, 6–24.

Wigram, T. (2007) 'Event-Based Analysis of Improvisations Using the Improvisation Assessment Profiles (IAPs).' In T. Wosch and T. Wigram (eds) *Microanalysis in Music Therapy – Methods, Techniques and Applications for Clinicians, Researchers, Educators and Students.* London: Jessica Kingsley Publishers.

Wosch, T. (2007) 'Microanalysis of Processes of Interactions in Clinical Improvisation with IAP-Autonomy.' In T. Wosch and T. Wigram (eds) *Microanalysis in Music Therapy – Methods, Techniques and Applications for Clinicians, Researchers, Educators and Students.* London: Jessica Kingsley Publishers.

Wosch, T. and Erkkilä, J. (2016) 'Microanalysis in Objectivist Research.' In B. L. Wheeler and K. Murphy (eds) *Music Therapy Research* (3rd edition). Dallas, TX: Barcelona Publishers.

CHAPTER 16

The Voice Assessment Profile

Sanne Storm

Setting and motivation

My interest and inspiration in applying the human voice as a primary instrument within the context of therapy was encouraged by personal key voice work experiences as a music therapy student. These experiences enabled me to hear how my voice opened up and suddenly sounded fuller, richer, and more alive. At the same time, I felt my body vibrating; I felt empowered and full of renewed vitality. I had an experience of mind and body being strongly connected in a simple and clear way and had an experience of *singing myself* more *alive*. Gradually, over the years, I developed a clinical approach, referred to as psychodynamic voice therapy, where body and voice function as primary instruments in music therapy (Storm 2007, 2017).

The disseminative challenge of describing music therapy has also been an ongoing inspiration to me and has motivated me to develop the Voice Assessment Profile (VOIAS) as the purpose of the assessment tool is to communicate important observations of the human voice in music therapy. The aim for VOIAS is to be comprehensible for interdisciplinary teams as well as for clients, including clarifying how musical activities can support individual therapeutic processes. In other words, VOIAS provides a "language" which can connect music therapists and other interdisciplinary team members and establish a shared understanding of clients.

Theoretical background

In order to understand psychological interpretations of client voice expression, VOIAS involves both theoretical and practical approaches. In this section, I present my understanding of the human voice and the theoretical background of my clinical approach.

The human voice

My understanding of the human voice is holistic. The human voice is the instrument we are born with, and it is an essential part of how we communicate and express our needs, emotions, and state of being in the meeting with others and the world. When the human voice is applied as a primary instrument in music therapy, the therapeutic process can be described as a "bottom-up," non-verbal approach including sensory stimulation of the body (Bonde 2009; Hart 2012; Panksepp and Trevarthen 2009). The purpose is to support the client's ability to distinguish cognitive reactions from affective reactions, and regulate arousal levels by consciously self-soothing actions through sensory motoric work.

When we use our voice, we create sound to express our emotions and basic needs. Infants use their entire body and total voice range to express their basic needs and state of being (Stern 2000; Trevarthen and Malloch 2000, 2009). Using the *human voice* as a primary instrument in music therapy is connected with the polarity of the *lived body* and the *corporeal body* as described by the French phenomenological philosopher Merleau-Ponty. Merleau-Ponty (2002) focuses on the body and the embodied being-in-the-world, and according to him, you act through the body, perceive and exist through it, even without explicitly reflecting on it. Therefore, from an ontological point of view, body and mind are not separated, but one and the same—*a lived body*. In other words, the voice displays a human being *in balance* or *out of balance* and can be understood as a representation of the human state of balance, as the human voice dynamically changes according to emotional states. Our psychological (mind) and physiological (body) state of being as well as our "way of life" is reflected in the quality of our voices. One example of this is how a person suffering from severe depression often presents a cracked, rusty, thin, flat, inharmonic, or out-of-balance voice. Through voice work the client is *living* a path towards recovery and wholeness, and the sound of the voice reflects the client's process in how the voice grows. A full, harmonic, or balanced sound usually reflects a vital and balanced state of the patient (Storm 2013).

Arousal, dynamics, and forms of vitality

The arousal system is important as it supports the human being to think, feel, perceive, or move voluntarily and dynamically. Stern writes:

> To be aroused is "to be put into motion" or "stirred up" or "excited into activity," physically, mentally, or emotionally. It is synonymous with "to animate." In more scientific terms, it is the force behind the initiation, the strength, and the duration of almost everything we do. (Stern 2010, p. 58)

Body and mind are in a constant act of movement, and in the same way there is a constant ebb and flow of emotions where change happens in the intensity and duration of the movement. Arousal is the fundamental force in sensory stimulation and the basis of the feelings, creating a sensation of *vitality, empowerment, energy*, or a manifestation of *being alive* (Damasio 1999; Stern 2010). Vitality therefore can be described as an inner power and strength which expresses and provides a sensation of a person's urge and energy to live and actualize oneself, and therefore also an expression of being alive. Stern writes:

> Vitality is a whole. It is a gestalt that emerges from the theoretically separate experiences of movement, force, time, space and intention. It is not analyzed in any conscious way piece by piece, any more than a familiar face is, even though each separate element could be taken aside and studied in isolation. (Stern 2010, p. 5)

According to Stern (2010), the way energy, strength, and power take form in a movement is defined as "dynamic forms of vitality." These forms can best be described and explained using kinesthetic terms like surging, relaxing, gliding, tense, accelerating, weak, fluttering, and so on. The vocal gestalt is a complex phenomenon of many parameters, which include duration, range, frequency, volume, resonance, compression, timbre, intensity, and active overtones (Storm 2013). My research suggests that selected vocal parameters can describe and evaluate vocal sound and its expression, including evaluating the dynamic forms of vitality present, and provide relevant information about the client's state of being (Storm 2013). In depressive states, the arousal level is often low (Stern 2010) and one can describe such states as having a lack of body resonance and desynchronization (Fuchs 2005, 2009). This lack of body resonance is equivalent to lacking the ability to feel and sense, which often creates a sensation of lack of emotional quality and partial loss of self in the client (Fuchs 2005, 2009).

The physics of sound

Sound is a mechanical product of a resonating body. Sound waves are longitudinal, propagating via a series of compressions and rarefactions in a medium, and can move through all forms of matter such as air, gases, liquids, solids, and plasmas. The matter that supports the sound is called the medium (Howard and Angus 2006). The air molecules are set in motion by the density of air, and when the air molecules meet other molecules they try to push them out of the way, which basically means that the sound waves can set other molecules in motion and make the resonating object vibrate. When the music therapist and the client vocalize together, sound waves meet the body, and molecules in the body are set in motion and make the body vibrate and resonate. The basic conditions of the body influence how sound creates vibration or resonance and is reflected in the sound quality of the voice. Therefore, sound can be described as a sensory stimulation of the body (Bonde 2009; Howard and Angus 2006; Panksepp and Trevarthen 2009).

Listening perspectives

With the human voice as a primary instrument, the therapist provides or suggests vocal exercises, which support the client and the therapist to meet in an inter-subjective space, the *sounding space*.[1] To give sound is both something subjective and objective: subjective, because it reflects the inner life, feelings, thoughts, and experiences of the sounding person—a space of existence, of being and living; and objective, because the sound created by the human becomes an external object. The sounding space is a resource pool for the client and the therapist (Kenny 2006). The listening approach gives access to this pool of sound in different ways and aims to meet with the client, to listen to and use the resource pool of sound with respect and wisdom. The therapist is a facilitator in this process, and I consider *listening* a holistic phenomenon representing both objective and subjective elements. The listening perspective is shared subjectivity between client and therapist, and is very different from conventional verbal therapy as it is non-verbal through the modes of sound and music. The ability to listen is acquired over a lifetime and is a part of our overall perception in order to organize, identify, and interpret sensory stimuli. Listening requires significant effort, mental skills, practice, and attention (Kenny 2006).

When we communicate, we tend to focus our attention on words, but unconsciously we listen even more so to the voice that carries the words. We listen to the timbre, harmonic quality, rhythm, movement, or melody in the speech or song, and the intensity and loudness of the voice. These qualities color our perception and help us interpret the communications of others and understand their emotional states. The sound of the voice can work as a mirror as it is an outward

---

1   The definition of the sounding space follows Kenny's (1989, 2006) definition of a musical space and is a field of existence explored and shared by the client and the therapist through sound.

expression of an internal state. Related to VOIAS and my clinical approach, the listening perspectives can both function as directives for choice of vocal as well as body activities and assessment of these, and through voice work interventions facilitate further personal development in the music therapy treatment processes.

Development of VOIAS

The selection of vocal parameters

In order to identify, extract, and operationally define relevant vocal parameters for VOIAS, a literature review was performed to identify studies on vocal assessment within music therapy, and vocal music therapy approaches (Storm 2013). VOIAS was developed within the field of depression because my clinical experience of vocal change of people recovering from severe depression was very audible. The purpose of the first version of VOIAS was to examine its clinical applicability and relevance, which has formed the basis for the current version of the tool.

Based on VOIAS research, not all measurable parameters and sound qualities found were relevant to study and analyze. It was found that the most reliable VOIAS assessment consists of carrying out three core vocal exercises, and involves observing and evaluating the human voice from different perspectives with an emphasis on clinical application (Storm 2013). The vocal exercises chosen for the current version are free from semantics and linguistics. VOIAS includes a subjective analysis of evaluating vocal sound data collected (VOIAS-1) and an objective analysis (VOIAS-2) using soundwave software.

VOIAS-1 consists of three assessment sheets with one sheet for each vocal exercise. A manual explains how each parameter is assessed, including clear definitions of the different vocal parameters and clear guidelines (Storm 2013). Each vocal parameter is evaluated according to a five-point Likert scale, ensuring a structured and controlled method of scoring. A voice can be more or less rich in overtones. It is the amount of overtones that partly determines how rich or full the voice sounds. The more overtones, the richer the voice and the more the voice resonates. When lacking resonance and overtones, the quality of the voice sounds thin and flat. The sound of the voice can be breathy or tense. If the sound is breathy, there is audible air escaping during giving sound. The voice lacks clarity and is usually reduced in loudness. If the sound is tense, there is a "hard edge" to the sound, or it can even sound creaky or harsh. A modal voice is a voice where air and pressure are balanced and produce a free clear sound (see Figure 16.1).

3 Richness	**4 Tense/Breathy**
☐ Very full/rich	☐ Very tense pressed voice
☐ Full/rich	☐ Modal voice
☐ Very flat/thin	☐ Very breathy voice

Figure 16.1: Likert rating of CoreTone

VOIAS-2 assesses and analyzes the human voice quantitatively by implementing software (PRAAT[2] and MIR toolbox[3]) that carries out a psychoacoustic analysis of the three vocal exercises.

Procedure and data collection

The assessment protocol for VOIAS is structured, fluent, and dynamic, with one activity naturally leading to the next. Each assessment session starts with mandatory grounding exercises, based on elements of psychodynamic voice therapy. The introductory activities aim to nourish a grounding sensation and increase the self-awareness of the client in preparation for the following three vocal exercises. Usually the assessment session lasts around 30 minutes.

---

2   PRAAT is a Dutch word for *talk*, but it is also the name of a free scientific software program for the analysis of speech in phonetics. It has been designed by Paul Boersma and David Weenink from the Institute of Phonetic Sciences, at the University of Amsterdam, The Netherlands.

3   The MIR toolbox was originally composed to analyze music and was devised by Olivier Lartillot, Petri Toiviainen, Pasi Saari, and Tuomas Eerola, who were members of the Finnish Center of Excellence in Interdisciplinary Music Research.

The vocal exercises increase gently in complexity and degree of challenge. The first vocal exercise is an open glissando movement, including an ascending and descending glissando. The second vocal exercise consists of the client finding and giving sound to one note: the CoreTone. This note is not a spontaneously chosen pitch, but a pitch found following the instructions of the music therapist. In the last vocal exercise, the client performs a vocal improvisation following specific instructions of the music therapist in order to improvise freely. The assessment session is audio-recorded in a WAVE file format, in order for the trained music therapist to analyze the vocal sound in detail.

Data analysis and report

As mentioned earlier, VOIAS includes a subjective analysis of evaluating vocal sound data (VOIAS-1) and an objective analysis (VOIAS-2) using software. A five-step procedure is performed for both VOIAS-1 and VOIAS-2. The sixth step involves writing up the conclusion and choosing how to disseminate the analysis in a clear and concise way.

Analysis procedure

First impressions are noted by the therapist, which include subjective spontaneous associations while listening to the recordings of the human voice carrying out the vocal exercises.

1. The therapist writes down the first impressions and spontaneous associations of the voice.

2. Focusing on the specific vocal parameters connected to each vocal exercise, the therapist describes the observation objectively, leaving out subjective interpretations.

3. Studying the individual vocal parameters and their relationship, the therapist takes a comparative look within each vocal exercise and finally across the three vocal exercises. All the

defined individual vocal parameters of the human voice are observed, studied, and described.

4. The therapist uses a theoretical framework based on my approach to voice work to conduct a psychological interpretation of the psychoacoustic analysis, which is related to the client's clinical process.

5. The therapist draws conclusions and a report is written.

Research and psychometrics

As mentioned earlier, the first study on VOIAS focused on clients diagnosed with severe depression. Two men and two women diagnosed with severe depression were recruited as well as two non-clinical participants—one woman and one man. In total, 87 different sound files were collected, including sound samples from the first, seventh, and twelfth sessions in music therapy treatment, and sound files collected from non-clinical participants.

Reliability

Three independent and experienced music therapists and I carried out analyses of the 87 sound files. The inter-rater agreement was examined, as well as the possibility of VOIAS-1 to evaluate change over time. The results of the statistical analysis were promising, as inter-rater reliability was established. Pearson's correlation determined that the value of rho was between .895 and .978 between each of the raters, also demonstrating significant correlation ($p < .01$) and therefore a small variation of differences in the evaluation of the different sound samples.

Furthermore, a Repeated Measures ANOVA was completed using all raters' scores at each of the three time points and between the first and third time points. Bonferoni's post hoc analysis was completed to analyze significant changes over time. From the first to the second assessment there were no significant differences ($p < .17$). However, there was a significant difference from the second to the third assessment (p < .00) and from the first to the third assessment (p < .00). Mauchly's test was violated, so a Greenhouse-Geiser correction was reported as $F (1.43, 21.50) = 15.13$, p < .00. This showed that VOIAS-1 has the potential to document significant changes over time. A more in-depth description of these results is available online (Storm 2013).

Validity

The first study on VOIAS showed that VOIAS-2 (objective data collection through software) has the potential to capture changes as well as to provide in-depth descriptions of the person being assessed (Storm 2013). As an example, the psychoacoustic analysis of the Glissando exercise offers the opportunity to look into a time-based analysis of the exercise as well as accurate differences in starting and ending pitches, and in this way capture small changes over time. In the VOIAS study, the objective VOIAS-2 measurements were related to the clinical description of the client's recovery process. These descriptions have been a very important parameter in providing relevant information and disseminating to the interdisciplinary team as well as to the client (Storm 2013). Furthermore, the software analysis offers the possibility of studying the graphic representations (see Figure 16.2).

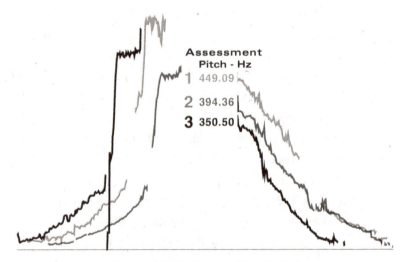

Figure 16.2: Pitch descending glissando

Figure 16.2 shows an analysis of one single vocal parameter in the glissando performed by a male client: the highest Hz (pitch) of the descending glissando in the first (light gray), the second (medium gray), and the third/last assessment (black). Studying the graphic representation, it is clear that the client performed the highest pitch in the descending glissando in the first assessment (light gray) and the lowest pitch in the descending glissando in the third and last assessment (black). It is furthermore very easy to adapt the time differences of the three descending glissandi and the time used for breathing in between the ending pitch of the ascending glissandi and starting pitch of the descending glissandi. The longest descending glissando in time is clearly performed in the second assessment (medium gray), and the difference between the ascending and descending glissando is smallest in time in the second assessment (medium gray).

In the same study, data was collected to analyze the validity aspects of VOIAS, looking at how VOIAS data was connected to other measures of depression (construct validity), as well as how it compared to the experience of the therapist and the client's self-experience (criterion and content validity). A triangulation analysis was carried out, including both qualitative and quantitative data (Storm 2013, 2016). The triangulation consisted of:

- a clinical description of the pattern of the music therapeutic process

- the client's own experience expressed through quotes and drawings from the music therapy process

- VOIAS data from the first, seventh, and twelfth sessions

- scores from the Hamilton Rating Scale for Depression (Hamilton 1967) in the first and twelfth session

- the client's self-assessment on a ten-point Visual Analog Scale (VAS).

The description and illustration of the patterns of the therapeutic process were congruent with VOIAS data, providing various forms of validity evidence for VOIAS including treatment validity. It seems VOIAS can provide clinically relevant information within the field of depression, including the therapeutic process and the client's state of being. However, one case triangulation is insufficient in establishing validity, although the study provides an encouraging starting point for future research.

Furthermore, a master's thesis in music therapy (Buchhave 2016) analyzed the human voice of a client diagnosed with bipolar disorder using one exercise—the CoreTone. The analysis integrated the client's experiences of voice work to contextualize and complement the results of the voice analysis. The client experienced an inability to connect emotionally to himself and found it difficult to know the differences between his symptoms and his *true* self. The VOIAS analysis of the CoreTone also indicated that the client was disconnected from his core self at the beginning of treatment and then further illustrated the therapeutic process from dissociation to a subtle experience of an integrated self. Additionally, VOIAS showed that two of the exercises—the Glissando and the Improvisation—revealed important information about the client's mental state that was not discovered elsewhere. The client was initially perceived as energetic, but the voice analysis underlined the mixed state from which he suffered (Buchhave 2016). This study is also promising for the treatment validity of VOIAS. It is important to note that, to ensure reliability, VOIAS assessment has to include all parts and all exercises.

Training

Training and certification are needed to ensure ethical, reliable, and appropriate use of VOIAS. The music therapist must be trained to conduct the assessment protocol and the exercises in an authentic and supportive way without influencing the performance of the client. Trainees have to acquire knowledge about the purpose of the exercises and what information the different vocal exercises can provide. Preferably, trainees should rate audio samples in a class with others to calibrate their ability to make judgements on those vocal exercises. In order to understand the approach and possible interpretation of assessment data, the analysis of some of the vocal parameters precedes self-experience with VOIAS as a therapist (also see discussion section). Training ensures the strengthening of listening attitude in the therapist and a reliable use of VOIAS.

Future plans

A current research project focuses on strengthening the psychometrics of VOIAS and increasing clinical applicability. This includes developing more structured and systematic procedures for collecting and analyzing data and a refinement of data interpretation. VOIAS-1 has to be adjusted according to recommendations and conclusions from the first study of VOIAS (Storm 2013). In order to validate VOIAS-2 and design a clinically applicable psychoacoustic analysis of data, an interdisciplinary research collaboration is needed. The collaboration should include the field of music psychology and, preferably, a music therapist experienced in using the voice and body as primary instruments in music therapy.

A benchmark and a reference group

The aim is to standardize VOIAS by establishing a complete set of norms. A non-clinical reference group as a benchmark and point of reference seems necessary in this regard. A non-clinical reference group would enable VOIAS to capture data on how vocally untrained persons experiencing subjective emotional well-being would behave during VOIAS administrations, thus enabling a distinction between "healthy" persons and those suffering from depression. A current research project involves collecting VOIAS data from a large group of women suffering from perinatal depression; this provides an opportunity to narrow the variation of depression, gender, and age in comparison to non-clinical data. Furthermore, the perinatal depression study explores test-retest reliability to further strengthen VOIAS's capacity as an outcome measure and measure of change.

Discussion and summary

Initial study of VOIAS provides evidence on the psychometric properties and a capacity to discover changes of the therapeutic process as well as provide a broader description of the person being assessed. VOIAS clarifies psychological interpretation of dynamic features within the human voice through visual empirical evidence that supports the effectiveness of music therapy treatment.

I am often asked if I find it difficult to apply the human voice as a primary instrument in music therapy. The human voice is a very private instrument, and clients using their voice can feel very exposed. Applying VOIAS in clinical practice is challenging because the assessment takes place during the second meeting. One may wonder whether sufficient time has passed to build the trust necessary for this to occur. In my clinical experience, accepting my own voice and allowing the sound of my voice to fill the room is important in the process of building trust. If I am comfortable with my own voice and the vocal exercises, there will be an opening for positive countertransference in meeting the client. Therefore, training in the use of VOIAS is of great importance. It is crucial not only to *know something about* voice work or the vocal exercises, but also to have personal experience with it—to know what the voice work might put into motion, and at the same time not be afraid of how a human voice sounds in such a process. This includes accepting and allowing all sound qualities to be performed without judgement. Still, in order to use VOIAS, the client should be able to understand the instructions and carry out the three different vocal exercises without feeling intimidated.

Clinical application

I believe it is possible to use VOIAS with various populations. It should, however, be taken into consideration that the present version is highly influenced by my own experience with the human voice. I use the voice as a primary instrument in therapy working with personal development or people suffering from psychiatric problems, and not suffering from any physical vocal disorder.

In audio-recording the vocal assessment, it is important to focus on the client's primary needs and what is realistic in practice. The idea of using headsets for recording the assessment data was excluded because I found it too intimidating for the client. Instead, I developed a way to position the client in approximately the same position in the music therapy room. The client needs to be able to carry out the exercises, and it is up to the music therapist to establish a setting enabling the client to succeed in doing all the activities.

I have presented my research outside the music therapy field several times. On these occasions, I presented graphs generated from the software program in order to illustrate the therapeutic process and the connection between the human voice and depression. The visual presentation of the psychoacoustic calculations seems comprehensible and provides easy access to understanding the implications of depression as well as the improving therapeutic process on the human voice.

If the music therapist applies the human voice as a primary instrument and uses core elements from psychodynamic voice therapy, it is possible to study and analyze individual vocal exercises over time (Buchhave 2016). VOIAS shows some promise as an assessment tool in this regard.

References

Bonde, L. O. (2009) *Musik og Menneske: Introduktion til Musikpsykologi* [*Music and Man: An Introduction to Music Psychology*]. Copenhagen, Denmark: Samfunds litteratur.

Buchhave, S. (2016) 'Den Menneskelige Stemme som Indikator på Psykisk Tilstand – et Casestudie med Fokus på Stemmeanalyse og Stemmeassessment' [The Human Voice as a Monitor of the Mental State – A Case Study Focusing on Voice Analysis and Voice Assessment]. Unpublished master's thesis, Aalborg University.

Damasio, A. (1999) *The Feeling of What Happens: Body and Emotion in the Making of Consciousness.* New York, NY: Harcourt Books.

Fuchs, T. (2005) 'Corporealized and disembodied minds: A phenomenological view of the body in melancholia and schizophrenia.' *Philosophy, Psychiatry, & Psychology, 12,* 2, 95–107.

Fuchs, T. (2009) 'Embodied cognitive neuroscience and its consequences for psychiatry.' *Poiesis Praxis, 6,* 3–4, 219–233.

Hamilton, M. (1967) 'A rating scale for depression.' *Journal of Neurology, Neurosurgery, and Psychiatry, 23,* 56–62.

Hart, S. (2012) *Neuroaffektiv Psykoterapi med Voksne* [*Neuroaffective Psychotherapy with Adults*]. Copenhagen, Denmark: Hans Reitzels Forlag.

Howard, D. M. and Angus, J. (2006) *Acoustics and Psychoacoustics* (3rd edition). New York, NY: Focal Press/Elsevier.

Kenny, C. (1989) *The Field of Play: A Guide for the Theory and Practice of Music Therapy.* Atascadero, CA: Ridgeview Publishing Company.

Kenny, C. (2006) *Music & Life in the Field of Play: An Anthology.* Gillum, NH: Barcelona Publishers.

Merleau-Ponty, M. (2002) *Phenomenology of Perception.* London: Routledge Classics.

Panksepp, J. and Trevarthen, C. (2009) 'The Neuroscience of Emotion in Music.' In S. Malloch and C. Trevarthen (eds) *Communicative Musicality: Exploring the Basis of Human Companionship.* London: Oxford University Press.

Stern, D. (2000) *The Interpersonal World of the Infant: A View from Psychoanalysis and Development.* New York, NY: Basic Books.

Stern, D. (2010) *Forms of Vitality: Exploring Dynamic Experience in Psychology, the Arts, Psychotherapy and Development.* London: Oxford University Press.

Storm, S. (2007) 'Den menneskelige stemme—psykologi og psykodynamisk stemmeterapi' [The human voice—psychology and psychodynamic voice therapy]. *Psyke & Logos, 28,* 447–477.

Storm, S. (2013) 'Research into the Development of Voice Assessment in Music Therapy.' Unpublished PhD thesis, Aalborg University.

Storm, S. (2016) 'VOIAS: Et Stemme-Assessmentredskab til Vurdering af Klientens Psykiske Tilstand og Terapeutiske Proces; en Undersøgelse af Dens Kliniske Relevans Fra et Case-Perspektiv.' [VOIAS: A Voice Assessment Profile Evaluating the Client's Psychological State of Being and Therapeutic Process; an Examination of Its Clinical Relevance from a Case Perspective. In N. Hannibal (ed.) *Musikterapi i Psykiatrien Online.* Vol. 11 (1), pp. 57–73. Aalborg, Denmark: Musikterapiklinikken, Aalborg University.

Storm, S. (2017) 'Den Menneskelige Stemmes Stimulering af Krop og Psyke—Psykodynamisk Stemmeterapi mod Prænatal Angst og Depression' [The Human Voice Awakening Body and Mind—Psychodynamic Voice Therapy]. In C. Lindvang and B. D. Beck (eds) *Musik, Krop og Følelser. Neuroaffektive Processer i Musikterapi* [*Music, Body, and Feelings: Neuroaffective Processes in Music Therapy*]. Copenhagen, Denmark: Frydenlund Academic.

Trevarthen, C. and Malloch, S. N. (2000) 'The dance of wellbeing: Defining the musical therapeutic effect.' *Nordic Journal of Music Therapy, 9,* 2, 3–17.

Trevarthen, C. and Malloch, S. (2009) *Communicative Musicality: Exploring the Basis of Human Companionship.* London: Oxford University Press.

CHAPTER 17

The Psychiatric Music Therapy Questionnaire

Michael D. Cassity

Introduction

The assessment of clients has long been considered essential to the practice of music therapy, with the prominence of assessment codified over the years in the standards of practice of the National Association for Music Therapy (NAMT) (National Association for Music Therapy 1993) and later the American Music Therapy Association (AMTA) (American Music Therapy Association 2017). The standards for psychiatric/mental health music therapy since 1993 have specified that assessment, among other requirements, must be appropriate for the chronological age (CA) and developmental level of the client. The standards also have long specified that any interpretation of test results shall be based on norms or criterion-referenced data.

Although the importance of assessment has long been established, in 1994 when Cassity and Cassity (1994a) published assessment data in the *Journal of Music Therapy* laying the foundation for the Psychiatric Music Therapy Questionnaire (PMTQ) and its clinical manual, *Multimodal Psychiatric Music Therapy* (*MPMT*), empirical research examining assessment practices in psychiatric music therapy was scarce, with few published assessment tools (Cassity and Cassity 1994a). Two notable exceptions were a study defining music therapy assessment practices with domestic violence clients according to CA classification and gender (Cassity and Theobold 1990), and a music/activity therapy intake assessment designed to collect data according to CA, diagnosis, and attitude (Braswell *et al.* 1986). Other psychiatric assessment tools published by 1994 were the Music Therapy Assessment for Disturbed Adolescents (Wells 1988), the Hamilton Rating Scale for Depression and Rhythmic Competence (Migliore 1991), the Patient Evaluation of Treatment (Heaney 1992), and the Music Therapy Effects Scale (Thaut 1989). Wheeler (2013) and Crow (2007) provide additional information concerning these assessment tools.

Although the above tests had been published, Cassity and Cassity's (1994a) survey of psychiatric assessment practices revealed that 79 percent of clinical training directors (CTDs) indicated a need for a standardized test that could be used by psychiatric music therapists and 92 percent indicated a need for a treatment manual. Why did such a large percentage of CTDs report they needed a psychiatric music therapy assessment tool when the assessment tools cited above had already been published? I concluded that (1) music therapists needed an assessment tool that could be shared by all music therapists (i.e. one that contains comprehensive, common assessment practices shared by the total population of psychiatric music therapists), and (2) the assessment results must directly lead to the establishment of music therapy goals, objectives, procedures, and evaluation as prescribed in the NAMT Standards of Clinical Practice (1993). The former need was met by producing the PMTQ, and the latter need was met by developing the *MPMT* treatment manual. The second edition of the *MPMT* containing the PMTQ with the tutorial for program planning was published in 1994 (Cassity and Cassity 1994b), and remains in publication today as the third edition (Cassity and Cassity 2006). The empirical construction of the PMTQ may have allowed it to generalize to the target population of psychiatric music therapists.

Even though the PMTQ continues to be used today as evidenced by its continued publication, there remains a need for more psychiatric music therapists to use assessments such as the PMTQ. Eyre (2013a) has expressed concern that the failure to use population-specific assessments may promote the image of music therapy as a profession that lacks identity in the facilities where music therapy is practiced. One way to achieve professional identity may be for music therapists to use specific population assessment tools that are based on the common body of assessment knowledge for the specific population. As such tools are developed, they should be introduced into university music therapy curricula to encourage future music therapists to use assessment tools that promote professional identity. The development section of this chapter provides a description of the common body of knowledge identified in the process of developing the *MPMT* and the PMTQ.

Setting and motivation

At the 1988 annual conference of the NAMT in Atlanta, I noticed there was usually standing room only in sessions related to psychiatric music therapy, and in my session relating to assessments and interventions used by music therapists in domestic violence (Cassity and Theobold 1988). It occurred to me that I could use similar methodology previously used in the domestic violence study for the purpose of determining assessments and interventions used in general psychiatric music therapy, and that this data could be used to construct a treatment manual. Once the domestic violence study was published (Cassity and Theobold 1990), I began developing the initial questionnaire to survey psychiatric music therapy assessment practices.

The setting in which the *MPMT* was developed largely contributed to its evolution across three editions. I was a professor of music therapy at Southwestern Oklahoma State University, and the co-author was a psychiatric music therapist at a nearby community mental health center. This arrangement with the mental health center ensured the availability of all ages of clients to adequately field test the clinical manual at every stage of development, including the effectiveness of the PMTQ as a music therapy assessment tool. In addition, the extensive field testing resulted in a tutorial guide for instructing professionals and students in the appropriate use of the PMTQ and the accompanying clinical manual in planning efficient and effective psychiatric music therapy. The interaction between university research and clinical practice during the development of the *MPMT* resulted in the production of a practical clinical model in psychiatric music therapy as derived through scientific research.

Theoretical background

The multimodal and brief therapy model used in the *MPMT* has been cited as being very eclectic, with emphasis on the total person rather than a psychiatric diagnosis or target behavior (Krout 1996). This theoretical orientation is in agreement with most psychiatric music therapists who describe their primary orientation as eclectic (Silverman 2007). Lazarus (1976, 1989) refers to the type of eclecticism used in multimodal therapy as *technical eclecticism*. Rather than using new techniques in a shotgun manner, therapists "take great pains to determine precisely what relationship and what treatment strategies will work best with each client and under which particular circumstances" (Corey 2005, p. 251).

One should not assume that because the word *psychiatric* is in the *MPMT* name that the manual follows the psychiatric treatment model. At the time as the groundwork was laid for the *MPMT* (Cassity and Cassity 1994a), the term *psychiatric music therapist* was established in the music therapy literature, referring to music therapists employed by, or working in, psychiatric settings. The usage was consistent with literature at that time (Tyson 1982), as indicated by the *Music Therapy Perspectives* special issue on Psychiatric Music Therapy (Goldberg 1994).

Secondary theoretical approaches inherent in the PMTQ are the assessment of initial problem behavior in the absence of music conditions, the use of assessment based on a common body of knowledge (Cassity and Cassity 1994a) to promote generalization and professional identity, the use of the Lazarus (1976) BASIC-ID theoretical model for classifying PMTQ subscales and music therapy assessment practices, the theoretical potential of the PMTQ to obtain unique assessment information, and the use of the PMTQ to obtain global assessment information across diverse areas of the BASIC-ID. What follows here is a description of each theoretical approach.

The PMTQ assesses initial problem behavior in the absence of music conditions

In traditional music therapy assessment, the assessment results of other professionals are commonly examined as part of the assessment (Eyre 2013b). The PMTQ, which is administered under non-music conditions, provides additional information related to client problems most effectively treated *using music*. Furthermore, the traditional, informal checklists music therapists use to assess non-music behavior typically do not indicate music therapy interventions for specific problems (Doak 2013). However, the PMTQ provides clinicians with music therapy interventions most effective for treating each specific problem. The PMTQ, therefore, may contribute to the amount of assessment information available to the music therapist. According to Cruz and Feder (2013a), it is important for the therapist to rely on as many data sources as possible to obtain the most complete picture possible. The PMTQ, like traditional assessment, continues to assess the client in subsequent music therapy activities once base rate behavior is observed.

The initial assessment of non-music behavior in the absence of intervention is closely related to practices in research and related professions. Like the PMTQ, in applied behavior analysis, base rate behavior is commonly observed prior to introducing the music therapy intervention (Jones and Brown 2016), with assessment and treatment, including goals and objectives, a characteristic of behavior therapy (Cruz and Feder 2013b). In addition, base rate scores of standard psychological tests such as the Millon Clinical Multiaxial Inventory (MCMI) are commonly used to interpret results (VandenBos 2007). Some music therapy assessment tools assess behavior under music conditions. Because behavior under music conditions may be "radically different" (Michel and Rohrbacher 1982, p. iii), music therapists should avoid "base-rate fallacy" (VandenBos 2007, p. 103) when attempting to correlate assessment results obtained under music conditions with those of formal tests measuring base rate behavior. The PMTQ, however, like the above psychological tests, establishes base rate scores (prior to introducing music conditions), which in turn may make validation with these tests more achievable.

The PMTQ promotes professional identity

The PMTQ is the first psychiatric music therapy assessment tool promoting awareness among other professionals that a common body of knowledge exists in the profession of music therapy (Cassity and Cassity 1994a), and that a valid test exists to test that knowledge. Most professionals would agree that no profession can exist for very long without a common body of knowledge. The PMTQ is derived from problems or symptoms contained in the *MPMT* manual. Likewise, symptoms in numerous psychological tests, such as the Beck Depression Inventory, are keyed to the *Diagnostic and Statistical Manual of Mental Disorders* (*DSM*) (Cruz and Feder 2013c). Psychological tests can be keyed to the *DSM* because it serves as a "standard reference for clinical practice in the mental health field" (American Psychiatric Association 2013, p. xli).

The existence of the PMTQ may be instrumental in obtaining state licensure for music therapists because of its criterion-referenced orientation based on common music therapy assessment and treatment procedures (Cassity and Cassity 1994a), and its apparent validity with psychometric instruments that assess symptoms and underlying personality constructs (Anderson and Krebaum 1998). Public protection issues related to unqualified persons using the PMTQ to assess and treat clients may strengthen the case for the licensure of music therapists.

The PMTQ uses the Lazarus (1976) BASIC-ID theoretical model for classifying PMTQ subscale items

The Lazarus (1976, 1989) multimodal therapy model was chosen as the theoretical model for classifying the PMTQ subscale items and for organizing the problem-oriented statements and their respective interventions in the *MPMT* manual. The rationale for choosing the Lazarus model was twofold. First, the areas of assessment extracted from the music therapy literature and included in the questionnaire were too numerous to be used in an assessment tool or in the manual. For example, 23 areas had been extracted for adults, 42 areas for adolescents, and 20 areas for children (Cassity and Cassity 1994a). Second, the reliability with which CTDs listed problems in the various areas was low, with a median inter-therapist agreement of 25.72 percent for adult male clients and 35.65 percent for adult female clients. For a detailed description of all percentages of inter-therapist agreements for all assessment areas, the reader is referred to Cassity and Cassity (2006).

The multimodal therapy model served as a brief but comprehensive model for classifying all problems from the survey, as well as serving as a model for comprehensive assessment and intervention across a person's BASIC-ID (or basic identity). This model previously had been recommended for music therapy (Adleman 1985) and also was previously used as a model for music therapy assessment and treatment with domestic violence clients (Cassity and Theobold 1990). According to Lazarus (1976), "Our personalities are the products of our ongoing *Behaviors, Affective Processes, Sensations, Images, Cognitions, Interpersonal Relationships,* and *Biological Functions*" (p. 13). Transferring patient problems from the PMTQ to the BASIC-ID form provides the *big picture* of the client's overall functioning. It is very important to remember that the modalities are dependent on one another so that problems in one modality will likely influence problems in another modality. To illustrate, consider the following case of Laura:

- Laura has trouble asserting herself (behavior).

- She feels frustrated (affect).

- She experiences life as being extremely stressful resulting in feelings of chronic fatigue (sensation).

- She fantasizes about how she could "get even" (imagery).

- She believes others are always taking advantage of her by manipulating her into doing what they would like to do instead of doing what she would like to do (cognitive).

- She sometimes acts in a passive-aggressive manner with her friends (interpersonal).

- She abuses alcohol and prescription medication to decrease feelings of fatigue (drugs).

(Cassity and Cassity 2006, p. 7)

Lazarus (1989) has documented impressive outcomes with multimodal therapy. Perhaps by using this model in music therapy we also will experience greater treatment success. Further discussion of how the multimodal therapy model influenced the development of the PMTQ and the *MPMT* manual is provided later in the section of this chapter relating to the design of the PMTQ.

The PMTQ provides unique assessment information that may not be obtainable from related professionals or by using traditional music therapy assessment procedures

The PMTQ provides unique assessment information, because unlike assessment tools in related professions, it focuses exclusively on problems *music therapists* assess and treat most frequently. Unlike traditional music therapy assessment, it provides a comprehensive picture of client problems most effectively treated using music therapy in addition to the interventions considered most effective for treating each problem. Although the use of this information as well as other assessment information is the option of the clinician, as indicated previously, as much assessment data as possible should be collected.

The PMTQ provides a global assessment of psychiatric music therapy functioning across diverse areas

Standard 2.1 of the American Music Therapy Association's Standards of Clinical Practice specifies a global music therapy assessment (American Music Therapy Association 2017) spanning the areas of music, psychological, cognitive, communicative, social, and psychological functioning appropriate for diagnosis, chronological age, level of functioning, and culture. In addition, Standard 2.9, under Mental Health Assessment, specifies 11 more areas to be addressed during assessment (American Music Therapy Association 2017). In traditional music therapy clinical assessment, music therapists often are involved in making a global assessment when examining the assessment results of related professionals (Kaser 2013). Likewise, the PMTQ covers diverse areas of functioning across the BASIC-ID model, and clinicians are advised to also examine the assessments of related professionals. Music therapists who do not have access to the assessments of related professionals may administer the Multimodal Life History Questionnaire (Lazarus 1989).

Procedure and data collection

Administration

Part I is a brief five-item inventory measuring music preferences. The client rates their preferred style of music using five-point Likert scales, as well as indicating their desire to participate in singing and playing instruments. Part II, Multimodal Problem Analysis of the PMTQ, requires clients to rate themselves on 70 statements using five-point Likert scales. The anchors of the scale are Strongly disagree (1), Disagree (2), Neutral (3), Agree (4), and Strongly agree (5). The statements are problem oriented, with the exception of occasional items that are reversed to reflect positive behavior (i.e. "It is easy for me to talk to people"). An example of a problem-oriented statement is "People cannot tell when I am happy, sad, or excited" (Cassity and Cassity 2006, p. 233). The PMTQ for children is administered to a significant other who is familiar with the child.

The PMTQ takes approximately 30 minutes to administer. Typically, the music therapist gives the client a copy of the Likert scale, reads the PMTQ statements, and records the client's responses in the PMTQ. The PMTQ may be administered to groups of clients. During the field testing phase of developing the *MPMT* the author and clients found group *MPMT* to be satisfactory and effective. The *MPMT* manual provides a tutorial for administering the PMTQ in a group setting and for translating the assessment results into a group music therapy program. Alternate answer sheets included in the manual may be used for clients to record their responses to the PMTQ. Group therapy is one of the most important features of the *MPMT* since most psychiatric music therapists in the USA do group therapy (Silverman 2007).

Scoring

The method used to score the PMTQ depends on the purpose for which it is being used. The PMTQ was designed to make intra-individual comparisons rather than inter-individual comparisons. When scoring the PMTQ to make intra-individual comparisons, the examiner extracts problems that the examinee rated as a 4 or 5 (1 or 2 for positive test items) and places them in the BASIC-ID form. Scoring techniques used by other researchers for purposes other than the purpose for which the PMTQ was designed (criterion-referenced assessment) are discussed in the research and psychometrics section of this chapter.

Development

The content of the PMTQ was obtained by sending questionnaires to music therapy CTDs. For a detailed description of the methodology, the reader is referred to Cassity and Cassity (1994a). Separate questionnaires were designed for adult males, adult females, adolescents, and children. These questionnaires, containing areas of age-appropriate psychiatric music therapy assessment derived from the music therapy literature (Adleman 1985; Cassity and Theobold 1990; National Association for Music Therapy 1989, 1993; Wood et al. 1974), were then sent to all psychiatric music therapy CTDs who had previously indicated the chronological age classification of their clients. CTDs were asked to choose areas they most frequently assess and treat during music therapy sessions. Following each area they chose, they were asked to list two specific client problems they assess and treat most frequently. Finally, next to each problem they were asked to list two music therapy interventions they use most frequently to treat the problem.

CTDs also were given a copy of the GAF (Global Assessment of Functioning) taken from the *Diagnostic and Statistical Manual of Mental Disorders-Revised* (*DSM-III-R*) (American Psychiatric Association 1987) and asked to assign a GAF score to each intervention to indicate the level of functioning of the client for whom the intervention was appropriate. This procedure was implemented because the NAMT Standards of Clinical Practice for adult psychiatry required assessment to be appropriate for the client's level of functioning (National Association for Music Therapy 1993). The reader is referred to Cassity and Cassity (1994a) for a discussion of the reliability and validity of the GAF. For further discussion of the GAF see the "Future plans and discussion" section of this chapter.

CTDs also were given, in the questionnaire, areas of music assessment from the literature (Carroccio and Quattlebaum 1969; Cassity 1976; Ficken 1976; Freed 1987; Noland 1983; Rubin 1976; Wood et al. 1974) and requested to list music behavior assessed and music interventions in the same manner as above for non-music behavior. Finally, CTDs were given 42 areas of activity assessment suggested in the music therapy literature (Braswell et al. 1986; Cohen and Gericke 1972; National Association for Music Therapy 1989) and requested to rank order the ten areas they assess most frequently in their practice.

The results of the above survey, in addition to other assessment data, yielded 200 client problems, 801 music therapy interventions for treating the problems, and 354 music interventions CTDs submitted for assessing music behavior. Once obtained, these problems and interventions posed a need for a brief, comprehensive model for their classification. As indicated earlier, the Lazarus BASIC-ID model was chosen as the classification model.

Once the problems were classified into the BASIC-ID model, questions emerged concerning the extent that the data represented a common body of knowledge in psychiatric music therapy. Stated differently, does little commonality exist in the assessment practices of music therapists, or do music therapists as a group assess certain problems and use certain interventions to treat the problems significantly more often than other problems and interventions? This question was considered an important one pertinent to the generalization of a future assessment tool to the population of psychiatric music therapists.

To investigate the possible existence of a common body of knowledge, Cassity and Cassity (1994a) performed a statistical analysis of the above survey results to determine if certain assessment practices occur significantly more often than others. The results of the analysis indicated the existence of a significant common body of knowledge in music therapy assessment. "The commonality is significant and extensive for all CA levels of patients, and encompasses patient diagnoses, levels of functioning, areas of assessment, specific patient problems assessed and treated, and music therapy interventions" (Cassity and Cassity 1994a, p. 23). As indicated earlier, additional information collected in the survey revealed that although 79 percent of CTDs indicated a need for a standardized test that could be used by psychiatric music therapists, 92 percent indicated a need for a treatment manual. A treatment manual clearly was perceived as the greatest need.

Once the common body of knowledge had been identified for psychiatric music therapy, attention was focused toward constructing a treatment manual based on this knowledge. Because the PMTQ was an outgrowth of the treatment manual, and was designed to serve the treatment manual, the PMTQ needed to produce test results that would directly lead to intervention. Before constructing the PMTQ, I conducted an extensive review of both norm-referenced and criterion-referenced tests and literature. This review influenced the construction of the PMTQ in that the items with their early five-point Likert scales resemble many normative tests, but the results are given a criterion-referenced interpretation. The structured behavioral interview, or cognitive behavioral self-report (Cruz and Feder 2013b; Groth-Marnat 1990), was chosen as the model for the PMTQ items because of the objective nature of the problems that CTDs submitted.

The PMTQ may be considered a criterion-referenced test because the results are a measure of intra-individual differences referenced to a standard or criterion rather than to the performance of others. According to Coleman and Brunk (2003), "*Criterion-referenced* tests describe a student's performance in terms of specific behaviors or skills. The objective of a criterion-referenced test is not to determine a mental age or IQ, but rather to evaluate the student's ability to perform particular skills in a particular setting" (p. 21). "A good criterion-referenced test provides a picture of just what the examinee can or cannot do (Popham 1978), or in the case of the PMTQ, just what problems the examinee does or does not have in terms of the problems music therapists most frequently treat (the criterion)" (Cassity and Cassity 1994b, 2006, p. 42).

Design of the PMTQ

The music preferences assessment in Part I, Music of the PMTQ, consists of five items developed from the 354 music interventions CTDs submitted for assessing music behavior. These interventions were placed in the music section of the *MPMT* manual as supportive information for intervention purposes (pp. 114–156 of the manual).

Part II, Multimodal Problem Analysis of the PMTQ, contains five subscales. Adapted from the Lazarus (1976) multimodal therapy model, these five subscales, followed by the number of items in each subscale of the PMTQ for adults, were Interpersonal (17 items), Affect (21 items), Cognitive (15 items), Behavior (11 items), and Drugs (8 items). The domain of problem-oriented test items in Part II of the PMTQ was selected from the 200 client problems collected from the survey. These 200 problems along with their respective 801 music therapy interventions were classified in the manual under each BASIC-ID modality (i.e. problems that were overt behavior, such as lack of assertiveness, were classified under Behavior, and so on) in order of frequency of usage for purposes of follow-up intervention (pp. 46–113 of the manual). However, the above five subscales in Part II of the PMTQ were not in the same order as the BASIC-ID (Lazarus 1976, 1989) but, rather, were in the order of frequency they were assessed by CTDs.

In accordance with the Lazarus (1976) multimodal therapy model, the Part II PMTQ Interpersonal subscale focuses on problems involving other people. For example, client statements indicating reclusive withdrawn behavior would be interpersonal issues. The subscale Affect is concerned with strong feelings or emotions. For example, music therapists most frequently focus on the inability to identify feelings in self or others. The third subscale, Cognitive, refers to irrational thoughts, ideas, and opinions. The cognitive problem music therapists most frequently target is low self-esteem as evidenced by a low opinion of self and negative self-statements. The Behavior subscale is a measure of overt behavior, or what the client does or does not do. Behaviors music therapists most frequently target are lack of assertiveness, inability to remain on task, and lack of awareness of personal boundaries such as interrupting others during group discussion and inappropriate verbal behavior toward peers. The Drugs subscale includes substance use or abuse and physical and communication problems, such as physical speech problems. According to Lazarus, the word Drugs was used rather than the word Biology so that a sensible acronym could be formed (BASIC-ID as opposed to BASIC-IB). The PMTQ did not include a subscale for Sensation and Imagery because an insufficient number of music therapists submitted assessments and interventions for those areas.

The BASIC-ID model was adequate for classifying in the manual all 200 problem-oriented behaviors assessed and treated by music therapists. This would seem to support the claim by Lazarus that the BASIC-ID can account for every condition a person encounters.

> The BASIC-ID represents the fundamental vectors of human personality just as ABCDEFG represents the notes in music. There are no HIJKLMNOP. Combinations of ABCDEFG (with some sharps or flats) will yield everything from "Chopsticks" to Mozart. (Lazarus 1989, p. 16)

In Part III, Post Interview Observations, items were selected from client problems assessed during activity therapy. As indicated above, these problems had previously been taken from the music therapy literature and ranked by CTDs according to frequency of usage. For example, following conclusion of the client interview, the examiner rates the client on 15 behaviors such as eye contact, posture, and grooming.

Documentation and report

Problem behaviors indicated by PMTQ ratings are transferred to the BASIC-ID form (p. 13 in the manual). The BASIC-ID format allows the examiner to compare PMTQ results with assessment results reported by other professionals as well as to provide the client with an overview of the problems that may need to be addressed. The client problems in the BASIC-ID are subsequently transferred to the *MPMT* (pp. 14–15) where music therapy interventions are chosen, in consultation with the client or clients, for the problems. Items in the PMTQ are referenced to problems in the manual, each followed by their respective music therapy interventions that have been recommended by CTDs.

Data analysis and interpretation

Following completion of the *MPMT*, a series of forms are completed and referred to as the Music Therapy Intervention Plan (pp. 16–17), the Implementation Strategy (pp. 17–18), and the Music Therapy Progress Report Chart (p. 18) (Cassity and Cassity 2006). Goals and objectives are written into the Intervention Plan, and strategies for achieving the goals and objectives are written in the Implementation Strategy. Detailed instructions and examples for completing the forms as well as the tasks of scoring, program planning, and evaluation are described in the clinical manual containing the PMTQ. Blank forms are provided in Appendix IV for the practitioner to copy and use. Also, multiple examples are provided throughout the clinical manual of how the PMTQ results are translated into client goals, objectives, and interventions. Alternate formats (pp. 37–38) also are provided for evaluating the results of music therapy intervention.

A major strength of the PMTQ is its ability to provide information that can lead to program planning. As indicated above, the PMTQ was not designed as a norm-referenced test to compare a client's performance with that of other clients. Instead, the PMTQ was designed to determine the strengths and weaknesses of an individual client in terms of the problems music therapists most frequently treat.

Research and psychometrics

Because the PMTQ was designed as a criterion-referenced test, it was initially evaluated in terms of the type of validity considered in the literature as important for criterion-referenced tests. A review of literature conducted at the time the PMTQ was developed indicated that the type of validity considered important for criterion-referenced tests is content validity (Gronlund 1973; Popham 1978; Popham and Husek 1969; Schoenfeldt *et al.* 1976; Swezey 1981). "The above question concerning the extent that patient problems reflected in the PMTQ represent problems music therapists most frequently treat would therefore be a question of content validity"

(Cassity and Cassity 2006, p. 42). The PMTQ, therefore, initially was evaluated according to three types of content validity referred to by Popham (1978) as *domain-selection validity, descriptive validity,* and *functional validity*. Domain-selection validity refers to how the content of the PMTQ was selected; descriptive validity refers to the extent the PMTQ test items are congruent with the descriptions, or problem-oriented behaviors, in the test manual (*MPMT* manual); and functional validity refers to the extent a criterion-referenced test satisfies the purpose for which it is being used.

Domain-selection validity

The content of the PMTQ was selected from the questionnaire data. Content validity was established for the initial questionnaire *before* it was sent to CTDs. The questionnaire was sent to a panel of five registered psychiatric music therapists employed in NAMT-approved clinical training facilities. They were asked to judge the questionnaire in terms of its clarity, the ease with which responses could be made, and whether they believed the questionnaire adequately surveyed the topic it was designed to survey (i.e. assessment practices). Stated differently, was the questionnaire adequate for the purpose for which it was intended? None of the panel participated in the study other than to judge the questionnaire. Four of the therapists were eclectic and one was of psychodynamic orientation. The four eclectic therapists reported that the questionnaire was adequate for the purpose for which it was to be used. The psychodynamic music therapist telephoned to say the questionnaire did not relate to her practice of music therapy. The response of the psychodynamic music therapist was considered an outlier and was discarded from the content validity results. Caution should therefore be exercised in using the PMTQ in psychodynamic settings.

As indicated earlier, the reader is referred to Cassity and Cassity (1994a) for a detailed description of survey methodology. Following the conclusion of the survey and collection of data, the manual was developed from the resulting data, and client problems most frequently targeted by CTDs were written into the PMTQ. All problems and interventions collected in the survey were placed in the manual.

Descriptive validity

Descriptive validity was obtained following the construction of the PMTQ. Since the patient population for whom the items were targeted had a mean GAF (American Psychiatric Association 1987) of 36.5 with a median of 33, the wording of the PMTQ items had to be simplified and could not contain technical terms. For example, patient problems such as reclusive, withdrawn behavior were assessed by asking questions such as "I would rather be alone than be with people" (Cassity and Cassity 2006, p. 43).

As indicated above, it was important to establish descriptive validity to determine whether the items (simplified problem-oriented questions) in the PMTQ were still congruent (had the same meaning) with the problems in the manual that CTDs had provided in more technical terms. Descriptive validity was determined by giving PMTQs to a master's level music therapist and a psychologist who were employed at a community mental health center serving psychiatric clients with similar GAF scores the PMTQ was designed for. They were asked to judge the PMTQ items to determine whether they were written clearly enough for clients to understand, and to determine whether the meaning of the items was preserved in the process of simplification, as compared to their wording in the clinical manual. Following minor revisions, both judges agreed that the PMTQ was adequate for the purpose for which it was designed.

Functional validity

As indicated earlier, Popham (1978) defines functional validity as the extent a criterion-referenced test satisfies the purpose to which it is being put. The extensive field testing of the *MPMT* manual and the PMTQ at the community mental health center and university clinic where it was developed indicated satisfactory functional validity.

The criterion-referenced assessment information produced by the PMTQ led to a viable music therapy program that was satisfactory to clients, staff, and music therapy clinicians. The fact that the *MPMT* continues to be published today not only may indicate it has become a standard resource in psychiatric music therapy, but that its apparent functional validity may have generalized to the target population of psychiatric music therapists.

Traditional psychometric research

Although the PMTQ was designed to produce criterion-referenced data, and was evaluated in terms of the types of validity recommended for criterion-referenced tests, other researchers sought to evaluate the PMTQ from the perspective of traditional reliability and validity. It was possible to apply traditional psychometrics to the PMTQ because the resulting ratings for each item could be added and totaled for each subscale. A total or composite score is obtained by adding the subscale scores. While the following studies were presented at poster research sessions at either NAMT or AMTA conferences, they have not previously been published.

Reliability

Soon after the publication of the PMTQ, Blodgett and Davis (1994) and Murray (1994) estimated the test-retest reliability of the PMTQ. Although these studies were pilot in nature, they should be reviewed for two reasons. First, even though they are pilot studies with limitations, both studies, in my opinion, have valuable implications for much-needed future research. Second, subsequent research by Anderson and Krebaum (1998) supporting the concurrent and construct validity of the PMTQ with major personality inventories may also support the reliability findings of Blodgett and Davis (1994) and Murray (1994). According to Kerlinger and Lee (2000), "if we have a valid measure then we also have a reliable one" (p. 684).

Blodgett and Davis (1994) administered the PMTQ to 20 university music students and then tested them again following a three-week interval. Each student was tested individually. Using the Spearman rank order correlation, the resulting composite reliabilities were Part I: Music, rs = .79; Part II: Multimodal Problem Analysis, rs = .90; and Part III: Post Interview Observations, rs = .76. Reliability estimates for the Part II: Multimodal Problem Analysis subscales were Behavior, rs = .76; Cognitive, rs = .83; Affect, rs = .82; Interpersonal, rs = .49; and Drugs, rs = .84.

Blodgett and Davis also investigated the Inter-scorer agreement of the PMTQ. Inter-scorer agreement refers to reliability based on agreement, or the extent that two or more examiners will score the test similarly (Waldon 2016). University participants were administered the PMTQ twice in succession. Half of the students were administered the PMTQ by examiner A first and the other half were administered the PMTQ by examiner B first. The inter-scorer composite reliability estimates were Part I: Music, rs = .92; and Part II: Multimodal Problem Analysis, rs = .94. Inter-scorer agreement for Part III: Post Interview Observations was not reported. Inter-scorer agreement estimates for the Part II: Multimodal Problem Analysis subscales were Behavior, rs = .84; Cognitive, rs = .93; Affect, rs = .93; Interpersonal, rs = .50; and Drugs, rs = .76.

Reliability appeared to be somewhat higher when the PMTQ was administered to the client population for which it was designed. Murray (1994) administered the PMTQ to 12 psychiatric clients, including adults, adolescents, and parents in the case of children. Each participant was administered a PMTQ for either adults, adolescents, or children, depending on their chronological age classification. A larger pool of participants was not possible because of institutional research restrictions. With a three-week intervening interval between test and retest, using the Spearman rank order correlation, composite reliabilities followed by levels of significance were Part I: Music, rs = .77, p < .01; Part II: Multimodal Problem Analysis, rs = .90, p < .001; and Part III: Post Interview Observations, rs = .92

(no significance level provided). Part II: Multimodal Problem Analysis subscale reliabilities were Behavior, rs = .90, p < .001; Cognitive, rs = .95, p < .001; Affect, rs = .97, p < .001; Interpersonal, rs = .95, p < .001; and Drugs, rs = .94, p < .001.

Construct validity: Chandra L. Anderson and Steven R. Krebaum

Anderson and Krebaum (1998) compared the PMTQ subscale scores with those of standard psychological tests and found evidence of convergent and discriminate validity. This type of validity is demonstrated when test scores correlate higher with other tests purportedly measuring similar constructs (convergent validity) and lower with tests purportedly measuring dissimilar constructs (discriminate validity) (Waldon 2016).

The standard psychological tests compared to the PMTQ were the Millon Clinical Multiaxial Inventory-III (MCMI-III), the Symptom Checklist-90-R (SCL-90-R), and the Beck Depression Inventory (BDI). The MCMI-III (Millon, Millon, and Davis 1994) contained 175 self-report true or false items and was designed for adults with interpersonal and emotional problems. The SCL-90-R (Derogatis, Lipman, and Covi 1973), designed for use in medical and psychiatric facilities, contained 90 items requiring self-report of symptoms. The BDI (Beck et al. 1961) was designed to measure depression in both psychiatric and non-psychiatric populations. It has 21 self-report items that are rated 0–3, with higher numbers scoring greater severity.

Anderson and Krebaum presented this research in 1998 at the research poster session held at the first annual conference of the American Music Therapy Association in Cleveland, Ohio.

Anderson was a music therapist at an urban Midwestern community mental health center. All clients at the center participated in an interdisciplinary initial assessment, with Anderson using the PMTQ as the music therapy assessment tool. Krebaum was employed as a testing consultant by the mental health center to evaluate all client assessment tools in use at the facility. Anderson and Krebaum (1998) subsequently correlated the subscale scores of the PMTQ with the subscale scores of standard psychological tests in use at the facility.

Participants were 40 general psychiatric clients with a wide array of *DSM-IV* disorders including substance abuse, mood disorders, and personality disorders. The participants were reported by Anderson and Krebaum (1998) to have a mean chronological age of 42 with a range of 22–58, a gender ratio of 47 percent female and 53 percent male, with an ethnicity of 73 percent White, 18 percent Black, 4 percent Hispanic, and 4 percent Asian.

Anderson and Krebaum (1998) used Pearson product moment correlations to compare PMTQ and MCMI-III subscales, as illustrated in Table 17.1.

TABLE 17.1: PMTQ AND MCMI-III PEARSON CORRELATION COEFFICIENTS (R)

MCMI-III scales	PMTQ scales				
	Interpersonal	Affect	Cognitive	Behavior	Drugs
Schizoid	–	–	–	–	–
Avoidant	.33	–	–	.37	–
Depressive	–	.56	.53	–	–
Dependent	–	–	–	–	–
Histrionic	–	–	–	–	–
Narcissistic	–	–	–	–	–
Antisocial	.36	–	–	–	–
Aggressive/ Sadistic	–	.56	–	.74	–
Passive-Aggressive	–	–	–	.56	–
Self-defeating	–	–	.39	.42	–

cont.

MCMI-III scales	PMTQ scales				
	Interpersonal	Affect	Cognitive	Behavior	Drugs
Schizotypal	–	–	–	–	–
Borderline	–	–	–	–	–
Paranoid	–	–	–	–	–
Anxiety D/O	–	.62	–	–	–
Somatoform D/O	–	–	–	–	–
Bipolar: Manic	–	.40	–	.46	–
Dysthymic	–	–	.31	–	–
Alcohol dependent	–	–	–	–	.64
Drug dependent	–	–	–	–	.76
Post-traumatic stress	–	.64	–	–	–
Thought disorder	–	–	.53	–	–
Major depression	–	.49	.42	–	–
Delusional disorder	–	–	–	–	–

Table 17.2 contains the PMTQ and BDI Pearson correlation coefficients (r).

TABLE 17.2: PMTQ AND BDI PEARSON CORRELATION COEFFICIENTS (R)

	PMTQ scales				
	Interpersonal	Affect	Cognitive	Behavior	Drugs
BDI total score	.59	.59	.70	.41	.40

In Table 17.3 the PMTQ and SCL-90-R Pearson correlation coefficients are illustrated.

TABLE 17.3: PMTQ AND SCL-90-R PEARSON CORRELATION COEFFICIENTS (R)

SCL-90-R Scales	PMTQ scales				
	Interpersonal	Affect	Cognitive	Behavior	Drugs
Somatization	–	.65	–	.51	–
Obsessive Compulsive	–	.56	–	.37	–
Interpersonal Sensitivity	–	.53	.52	.38	–
Depression	–	.60	.46	–	.35
Anxiety	–	.60	.38	.40	.30
Phobic Anxiety	–	.51	.42	.49	–
Paranoid Ideation	–	.61	–	.52	–
Hostility	.30	.56	.40	.55	–
Psychoticism	–	.64	–	.50	–
Global Severity Index	–	.63	.45	.43	–
Positive Symptom Distress Index	–	.61	.50	.44	–
Positive Symptom Total	–	.51	–	–	–

Note: Correlation coefficients below .30 were omitted from these tables. The data in these tables is from 'An Analysis of the Psychiatric Music Therapy Questionnaire (PMTQ) and Standard Personality Questionnaires' by C. L. Anderson and S. R. Krebaum, 1998. Paper presented at the first annual conference of the American Music Therapy Association, Inc. (AMTA), Cleveland, OH. Reprinted with permission.

Based on data in the above tables, Anderson and Krebaum (1998) reported the following five conclusions concerning the PMTQ:

- The PMTQ appears to correlate with other psychometric instruments that assess symptoms and underlying personality constructs.

- Correlation coefficients are higher between similar constructs and lower for dissimilar constructs, supporting the concurrent and construct validity of the measure.

- The PMTQ appears to be an effective assessment tool for music therapy if reliability and validity gain further support. Additional research is warranted to fully evaluate its psychometric properties.

- Strengths of the PMTQ include: (1) it provides useful clinical information for treatment planning; (2) it is easily administered and acceptable in clinical practice; and (3) it may withstand the rigorous review of third-party payers who make decisions about funding treatment.

- The PMTQ is recommended as one appropriate option for music therapy assessment in psychiatric settings. It also appears to provide clinically useful data that could be utilized to evaluate progress over the course of treatment.

Training

Ease of administration is an attribute of the PMTQ as cited above by Anderson and Krebaum (1998). In addition, the manual is apparently not difficult to follow from the comments I have received over the years from both students and colleagues. However, training seminars should not be discounted. The early *MPMT* workshops the authors gave at music therapy conferences apparently were valuable considering the excellent ratings given by the participants. Perhaps these workshops should continue in the future considering subsequent research supporting the validity of the PMTQ (Anderson and Krebaum 1998).

As indicated earlier, in order to promote professional identity, universities should provide instruction in assessment tools that have been empirically determined to be representative of assessment practices employed by psychiatric music therapists. These could be music therapists working in general psychiatric populations, as with the PMTQ, or working with specific populations such as domestic violence or substance abuse.

Future plans and discussion

The GAF is not printed in the *DSM-5* (American Psychiatric Association 2013), having been replaced by the World Health Organization Disability Assessment Schedule, Version 2.0 (WHODAS 2.0) (Waldon 2014). The GAF was discontinued after being included in the *DSM-III-R* through the *DSM-IV-TR*. The exclusion of the GAF has not been without controversy. Morrison (2014), following a review of the focus, strengths, and weaknesses of both the GAF and the WHODAS, concluded the latter so heavily emphasizes physical abilities that "it poorly reflects the qualities mental health clinicians are interested in. Some of the most severely ill mental patients received a [*sic*] only a moderate WHODAS 2.0 score" (p. 7). Continuing, Morrison recommends, "Go ahead and use the GAF. Nothing says that we can't, and I find it sometimes useful for tracking a patient's progress through treatment" (p. 8). The GAF may be found in the appendix of Morrison's book. I advise future researchers to read Morrison's review when choosing a tool to establish level of functioning in future surveys of assessment practices.

The above research supporting concurrent and construct validity with major psychological tests may make the PMTQ a viable candidate for adding a normative and standardized component. Once norms were added, the PMTQ could be used either to make inter-individual or intra-individual comparisons. However, from a psychometric point of view, both the criterion-referenced test and the norm-referenced standardized test, because of their orientations, would need to remain independent, requiring different types of validity.

It is recommended that research leading to the production of the PMTQ and its manual be replicated to provide assessments for areas of practice that have no standard assessment tool such as abused women (Curtis 2013), traumatized males (Hatcher 2013), and substance abuse (McFerran 2013; Murphy 2013). The Delphi technique (Cassity 2007) has been used in the production of assessment tools in other professions (Cassity 2016), and therefore may have the potential to shorten the process of constructing the above music therapy assessment tools compared to the survey methodology originally used to produce the PMTQ.

The validity coefficients in the above tables may indicate productive areas for future research and practice in that they may represent areas where music therapy is most effective. Because the PMTQ tests problems most effectively treated using music, it is logical that the areas with the highest validity coefficients may represent areas most effectively treated using music therapy. For example, the .70 validity coefficient between the BDI and the PMTQ may support music's effectiveness with mood disorders. Other examples are drug dependence (.76, MCMI-III), aggressive/sadistic clients (.74, MCMI-III), post-traumatic stress (.64, MCMI-III), psychoticism (.64, SCL-90-R), and anxiety (.62, MCMI-III). It is recommended, therefore, that future researchers investigate areas with higher validity coefficients to determine the potential effectiveness of music therapy in these areas, and to promote future areas of music therapy practice.

While it has been established that music therapists treat certain disorders and certain problems significantly more often than others, and use certain interventions to treat the problems significantly more often than other interventions (Cassity and Cassity 1994a), it remains a task for future researchers to investigate whether these interventions used most frequently are the most effective for treating each problem. For example, Spencer (1988) found that movement activities were more effective than instrumental activities for developing the ability of participants with intellectual disabilities to follow directions. However, an earlier survey by Cassity (1985) had revealed that music therapists, in actual practice, used instrumental activities more often than movement activities to develop the ability to follow directions. Future research to determine the most effective interventions, therefore, is important, especially given the increased emphasis on evidence-based practice. Delphi research has indicated that evidence-based music therapy required by healthcare systems is the third most likely scenario of 28 future scenarios (Cassity 2007).

The PMTQ eventually will need to be revised. Decisions of whether to revise the PMTQ should not be based on recent trends or changes in the mental health field. Likewise, neither should popular or future modes of assessment and treatment in music therapy govern decisions to revise the PMTQ. The single criterion of whether to revise the PMTQ is whether the items in the PMTQ (sample), as well as the content of the manual, are representative of the current common body of knowledge relating to psychiatric music therapy assessment (population) (Cassity and Cassity 1994a). Sampling the assessment practices of psychiatric music therapy internship directors, as opposed to repeating the survey, may provide the requisite information needed for determining whether a revision is necessary.

Limitations should be observed when using the PMTQ internationally. Because the questionnaire survey data used to construct the PMTQ was obtained from psychiatric CTDs in the United States, caution should be exercised when attempting to generalize the PMTQ to other populations, nations, or cultures. The clinician should be aware that all problems and interventions in the *MPMT* may not be appropriate for all cultures outside the United States. The investigation of trans-cultural uses of the PMTQ remains a task for future researchers.

References

Adleman, E. J. (1985) 'Multimodal therapy and music therapy: Assessing and treating the whole person.' *Music Therapy, 5,* 12–21.

American Music Therapy Association (2017) *Standards of Clinical Practice*. Available at: www.musictherapy.org/about/standards.

American Psychiatric Association (1987) *Diagnostic and Statistical Manual of Mental Disorders-Revised (DSM-III-R)*. Washington, DC: American Psychiatric Association.

American Psychiatric Association (2013) *Diagnostic and Statistical Manual of Mental Disorders* (5th edition). Arlington, VA: American Psychiatric Association.

Anderson, C. L. and Krebaum, S. R. (1998, November) *An Analysis of the Psychiatric Music Therapy Questionnaire (PMTQ) and Standard Personality Questionnaires*. Paper presented at the first annual conference of the American Music Therapy Association (AMTA), Cleveland, OH.

Beck, A. T., Ward, C. H., Mendelson, M., Mock, J., and Erbaugh, J. (1961) 'An inventory for measuring depression.' *Archives of General Psychiatry, 4*, 561–571.

Blodgett, G. and Davis, D. (1994) *Reliability of the Psychiatric Music Therapy Questionnaire for Adults: A Pilot Study*. Paper presented at the National Association for Music Therapy Conference, Orlando, FL.

Braswell, C., Brooks, D., Decuir, A., Humphrey, T., Jacobs, K., and Sutton, K. (1986) 'Development and implementation of a music/activity therapy intake assessment for psychiatric patients. Part II: Standardization procedures on data from psychiatric patients.' *Journal of Music Therapy, 23*, 3, 126–141.

Carroccio, D. F. and Quattlebaum, L. F. (1969) 'An elementary technique for manipulation of participation in ward dances at a neuropsychiatric hospital.' *Journal of Music Therapy, 6*, 108–109.

Cassity, M. D. (1976) 'The influence of a music therapy activity upon peer acceptance, group cohesiveness, and interpersonal relationships of adult psychiatric patients.' *Journal of Music Therapy, 13*, 66-76.

Cassity, M. D. (1985) *Techniques and procedures and practices employed in the assessment of adaptive and music behaviors of trainable mentally retarded children*. Ann Arbor, MI: University Microfilms International.

Cassity, M. D. (2007) 'Psychiatric music therapy in 2016: A Delphi poll of the future.' *Music Therapy Perspectives, 25*, 2, 86–93.

Cassity, M. D. (2016) 'The Delphi Technique.' In B. L. Wheeler and K. Murphy (eds) *Music Therapy Research* (3rd edition). Dallas, TX: Barcelona Publishers.

Cassity, M. D. and Cassity, J. E. (1994a) 'Psychiatric music therapy assessment and treatment in clinical training facilities.' *Journal of Music Therapy, 31*, 1, 2–30.

Cassity, M. D. and Cassity, J. E. (1994b) *Multimodal Psychiatric Music Therapy: A Clinical Manual* (2nd edition). Weatherford, OK: C&C Publications.

Cassity, M. D. and Cassity, J. E. (2006) *Multimodal Psychiatric Music Therapy: A Clinical Manual* (3rd edition). London: Jessica Kingsley Publishers.

Cassity, M. D. and Theobold, K. A. (1990) 'Domestic violence: Assessments and treatments employed by music therapists.' *Journal of Music Therapy, 27*, 4, 179–194.

Cassity, M. D. and Theobold, K. A. (1988, November) *Domestic Violence: Assessments Employed by Music Therapists with Battered Women, Battering Men and the Children of Battered Women*. Paper presented at the annual conference of the NAMT, Atlanta, GA.

Cohen, G. and Gericke, O. L. (1972) 'Music therapy assessment: Prime requisite for determining patient objectives.' *Journal of Music Therapy, 9,* 161–189.

Coleman, K. A. and Brunk, B. K. (2003) *SEMTAP: Special Education Music Therapy Assessment Process Handbook* (2nd edition). Grapevine, TX: Prelude Music Therapy.

Corey, G. (2005) *Theory and Practice of Counseling and Psychotherapy* (7th edition). Belmont, CA: Brooks/Cole-Thomson Learning.

Crow, B. (2007) *Music Therapy for Children, Adolescents, and Adults with Mental Disorders.* Silver Spring, MD: American Music Therapy Association.

Cruz, R. F. and Feder, B. (2013a) 'Clinical Assessment.' In R. F. Cruz and B. Feder (eds) *Feders' The Art and Science of Evaluation in the Arts Therapies* (2nd edition). Springfield, IL: Charles C. Thomas.

Cruz, R. F. and Feder, B. (2013b) 'Behavioral Assessment.' In R. F. Cruz and B. Feder (eds) *Feders' The Art and Science of Evaluation in the Arts Therapies* (2nd edition). Springfield, IL: Charles C. Thomas.

Cruz, R. F. and Feder, B. (2013c) 'Objective Tests.' In R. F. Cruz and B. Feder (eds) *Feders' The Art and Science of Evaluation in the Arts Therapies* (2nd edition). Springfield, IL: Charles C. Thomas.

Curtis, S. L. (2013) 'Women Survivors of Abuse and Developmental Trauma.' In L. Eyre (ed.) *Guidelines for Music Therapy Practice in Mental Health.* Gilsum, NH: Barcelona Publishers.

Derogatis, L. R., Lipman, R. S., and Covi, L. (1973) 'The SCL-90: An outpatient psychiatric rating scale.' *Psychopharmacology Bulletin, 9,* 13–28.

Doak, B. (2013) 'Children and Adolescents with Emotional and Behavioral Disorders in an Inpatient Psychiatric Setting.' In L. Eyre (ed.) *Guidelines for Music Therapy Practice in Mental Health.* Gilsum, NH: Barcelona Publishers.

Eyre, L. (2013a) 'Introduction.' In L. Eyre (ed.) *Guidelines for Music Therapy Practice in Mental Health.* Gilsum, NH: Barcelona Publishers.

Eyre, L. (ed.) (2013b) *Guidelines for Music Therapy Practice in Mental Health.* Gilsum, NH: Barcelona Publishers.

Ficken, T. (1976) 'The use of songwriting in a psychiatric setting.' *Journal of Music Therapy, 13,* 43–51.

Freed, B. S. (1987) 'Songwriting with the chemically dependent.' *Music Therapy Perspectives, 4,* 13–18.

Goldberg, F. S. (1994) 'Guest editorial.' *Music Therapy Perspectives (Special Edition on Psychiatric Music Therapy), 12,* 2, 67–69.

Gronlund, N. E. (1973) *Preparing Criterion-Referenced Tests for Classroom Instruction.* New York, NY: The Macmillan Company.

Groth-Marnat, G. (1990) *Handbook of Psychological Assessment.* New York, NY: John Wiley & Sons.

Hatcher, J. H. (2013) 'Adult Male Survivors of Abuse and Developmental Trauma.' In L. Eyre (ed.) *Guidelines for Music Therapy Practice in Mental Health.* Gilsum, NH: Barcelona Publishers.

Heaney, C. J. (1992) 'Evaluation of music therapy and other treatment modalities by adult psychiatric inpatients.' *Journal of Music Therapy, 29,* 70–86.

Jones, J. D. and Brown, L. S. (2016) 'AB, ABA, ABAB, and Other Withdrawal Designs.' In B. L. Wheeler and K. Murphy (eds) *Music Therapy Research* (3rd edition). Dallas, TX: Barcelona Publishers.

Kaser, V. (2013) 'Adult Males in Forensic Settings.' In L. Eyre (ed.) *Guidelines for Music Therapy Practice in Mental Health*. Gilsum, NH: Barcelona Publishers.

Kerlinger, F. N. and Lee, H. B. (2000) *Foundations of Behavioral Research* (4th edition). Fort Worth, TX: Harcourt Inc.

Krout, R. (1996) 'Book reviews.' *Music Therapy Perspectives, 14,* 2, 100.

Lazarus, A. A. (1976) *Multimodal Behavior Therapy*. New York, NY: Springer.

Lazarus, A. A. (1989) *The Practice of Multimodal Therapy*. Baltimore, MD: The Johns Hopkins University Press.

McFerran, K. S. (2013) 'Adolescents with Substance Use Disorders.' In L. Eyre (ed.) *Guidelines for Music Therapy Practice in Mental Health*. Gilsum, NH: Barcelona Publishers.

Michel, D. E. and Rohrbacher, M. (eds) (1982) *The Music Therapy Assessment Profile for Severely/Profoundly Handicapped Persons. Research Draft III (0–27 Months Level)*. Denton, TX: Texas Woman's University.

Migliore, J. J. (1991) 'The Hamilton Rating Scale for Depression and Rhythmic Competency: A correlational study.' *Journal of Music Therapy, 28,* 211–221.

Millon, T., Millon, C., and Davis, R. (1994) *Millon Clinical Multiaxial Inventory-III (MCMI-III)*. Minneapolis, MN: NCS.

Morrison, J. R. (2014) *DSM-5 Made Easy: The Clinician's Guide to Diagnosis*. New York, NY: Guilford Press.

Murphy, K. M. (2013) 'Adults with Substance Use Disorders.' In L. Eyre (ed.) *Guidelines for Music Therapy Practice in Mental Health*. Gilsum, NH: Barcelona Publishers.

Murray, A. (1994, November) *Reliability of the Psychiatric Music Therapy Questionnaire with Psychiatric Patients: A Pilot Study*. Paper presented at the National Association for Music Therapy Conference, Orlando, FL.

National Association for Music Therapy, Inc. (1989) *Sample Job Descriptions*. Silver Spring, MD: National Association for Music Therapy.

National Association for Music Therapy (1993) *Standards of Clinical Practice*. Silver Spring, MD: National Association for Music Therapy.

Noland, P. (1983) 'Insight therapy: Guided imagery and music in a forensic psychiatric setting.' *Music Therapy, 3,* 1, 43–51.

Popham, W. J. (1978) *Criterion-Referenced Measurement*. Englewood Cliffs, NJ: Prentice-Hall, Inc.

Popham, W. J. and Husek, T. R. (1969) 'Implication of criterion-referenced measures.' *Journal of Educational Measurement, 6,* 1–9.

Rubin, B. (1976) 'Handbells in therapy.' *Journal of Music Therapy, 13,* 49–53.

Schoenfeldt, L. F., Schoenfeldt, B. B., Acker, S. R., and Perlson, M. R. (1976) 'Content validity revisited: The development of a content-oriented test of industrial reading.' *Journal of Applied Psychology, 61,* 581–588.

Silverman, M. (2007) 'Evaluating current trends in psychiatric music therapy: A descriptive analysis.' *Journal of Music Therapy, 44,* 4, 388–414.

Spencer, S. L. (1988) 'A comparison of the efficiency of instrumental and movement activities for developing the ability of mentally retarded adolescents to follow directions.' *Journal of Music Therapy, 25*, 44–50.

Swezey, R. W. (1981) *Individual Performance Assessment: An Approach to Criterion-Referenced Test Development.* Reston, VA: Reston Publishing Company, Inc.

Thaut, M. H. (1989) 'The influence of music therapy interventions on self-rated changes in relaxation, affect, and thought in psychiatric prisoner-patients.' *Journal of Music Therapy, 26*, 155–166.

Tyson, F. (1982) 'Individual singing instruction: An evolutionary framework for psychiatric music therapists.' *Music Therapy Perspectives, 1*, 1, 5–15.

VandenBos, G. R. (ed.) (2007) *APA Dictionary of Psychology.* Washington, DC: American Psychological Association.

Waldon, E. G. (2014) '*DSM-5*: Changes and controversies.' *Music Therapy Perspectives, 32*, 1, 78–83.

Waldon, E. G. (2016) 'Overview of Measurement Issues in Objectivist Research.' In B. L. Wheeler and K. Murphy (eds) *Music Therapy Research* (3rd edition). Dallas, TX: Barcelona Publishers.

Wells, N. F. (1988) 'An individual music therapy assessment procedure for emotionally disturbed young adolescents.' *The Arts in Psychotherapy, 15*, 47–54.

Wheeler, B. (2013) 'Music Therapy Assessment.' In R. F. Cruz and B. Feder (eds) *Feders' The Art and Science of Evaluation in the Arts Therapies* (2nd edition). Springfield, IL: Charles C. Thomas.

Wood, M. M., Graham, R. M., Swan, W. W., Purvis, J., *et al.* (1974) *Developmental Music Therapy.* Silver Spring, MD: National Association for Music Therapy.

CHAPTER 18

The Intramusical Relationship Scale

Karina Daniela Ferrari

Setting and motivation

Observation of the music therapy process requires different forms of assessment in the field of special needs, which are mostly focused on the relationships that the client establishes with the music therapist within the "musical play" (Carpente 2016). However, it is important to develop means of analysis to enable professionals to carry out a proper prior assessment based on the intramusical relationships that the client builds with their own musicality, which will be critical for a future intermusical relationship. In my clinical practice working with people with difficulties of social interaction, verbal and non-verbal communication, and isolation, it is interesting to observe how these clients first begin to establish a bond with the music itself (a relationship that will be foundational for future communicative experience with the music therapist). The music therapist can assess this intramusical construct, and this is the main goal of the Intramusical Relationship Scale, which will be described in this chapter.

Theoretical background

Because of a literature review on assessment in music therapy, I have found several studies which discuss different scales to assess the relationships based on the intermusical analysis (Bruscia 1987, 1997; Pavlicevic 1995; Wigram 1999a, 1999b, 2000; Wigram, Bonde, and Nygaard-Pedersen 2002; Wosch and Wigram 2007, among others). These tests observe attitudinal aspects of musical experience, relative to the bond the client creates with others within the musical play.

Tests based on intermusical relationship are functional when the client has the minimum of capacity to engage in the musical play. However, there are cases where clients do not show clear possibilities to interact and can present severe challenges even to recognize the presence of the therapist in the setting, as observed in some cases of autism and multiple disabilities (Ferrari 2013). For children with severe difficulties related to connecting, communicating, and socializing, normally there is a process of adaptation to the music therapy environment in the first sessions where the therapist might have the feeling that nothing has happened. In many cases, the music therapist begins this process trying to build a meaningful bond with the client, taking the establishment of the client's own musical singularity from intramusical aspects.

In this sense, my practice is first to observe how the client creates bounds with their music, then explore and qualify these bounds and create situations and conditions to promote the intermusical relationship. Based on the Dynamic Music Therapy Model, MTD (Ferrari 2013), I propose the idea that, along our lives, all people construct a unique musical identity, which evolves from their own experiences in relation to themselves and in relation to the environment around them. This inherent human characteristic, constitutive of their identity, is called "musical singularity" (Ferrari 2013), and this is in line with the concept of communicative musicality described by Trevarthen and Malloch (2009). In my clinical experience working with people with special needs, I observed that even though many people were born with a communicative capacity, this capacity is often not developed in relation to music (Ferrari 2013). It means that to achieve the clinical goals in music therapy it is necessary to explore the musical singularity, because this dimension might facilitate the use of music to explore non-musical demands. Therefore, the client starts from an "expressive musical singularity" (intramusical) and can reach a "communicative musical singularity" (intermusical), based on the clinical work done by the music therapist.

The Intramusical Relationship Scale (IRS)

Inspired by the Music Interaction Rating Scale (MIR), developed by the music therapist Mercedes Pavlicevic (1995), I have created a nine-level Likert scale to assess the relations that the client establishes with their own musicality. The main objective of the scale is to provide an assessment that enables music therapists to observe and analyze the client's attitudes towards the construction of this "musical singularity" from the intramusical context. This Intramusical Relationship Scale (IRS) is to be used with clients who have intrapersonal challenges. As a form of intervention, the music therapist accompanies the process, offering musical instruments according to the client's needs, thus allowing the client to present the expressive musical singularity that will later turn into communicative singularity.

The IRS consists of nine levels ranging from no awareness of the musical instruments to total awareness, where the instruments are used as an interacting tool with the therapist. Levels 1 through to 4 assess intramusical relationships established by the client in a pre-musical form; levels 5 to 8 evaluate client relationships established in a musical form; and level 9 assesses the client relationships established in a musical form but with an intermusical intentionality.

This scale can be very useful, especially with clients whose changes are subtle and may go unnoticed. It is important to understand that the registration of these changes would enable the therapist to become aware of important aspects of expressive musical singularity. Although this self-awareness of the musical aspects is built during the client's interaction with their environment, the music therapist has an active role in the promoting of musical experiences and situations to facilitate this process.

Description

The dimensions listed in this scale range from a pre-musical level through to a musical level, reaching the musical level with intermusical intentionality, which evolves in this order.

Pre-musical dimension

This dimension accounts for the first contact the person has with the musical instruments, including awareness, examination, and manipulation of the same, with only sensory-perceptive intentionality.

Musical dimension

Once contact has been made from the perceptive level with a musical instrument, the person begins to interact with them with a musical executive intentionality, trying to make music with them. Initially this will occur in a more primary way, trying to connect with the instrument, looking for the emergence of a sound, and then trying and testing different sound forms, which allows the emergence of structured sounds in time. In this sense and for this dimension to be possible, the performer must have the idea of differentiating themselves from the objects already installed, in order to establish a relationship.

Musical dimension with intermusical intentionality

After the object is registered and can be categorized as a musical instrument, there appears a more evolved dimension in which the person tries to interact with another through the sound execution. Note that this dimension will imply "intentional" aspects involving a total awareness not only of oneself but of another as well, with increased tolerance to the shared execution and a search for the other making music.

Score determination given to the item categories

The scores range from 1 to 9 in a progressive order—from a non-registration to a total musical instrument registration with a communicative purpose.

Levels of IRS

Detailed below are the nine levels (indicators) with their respective attitudes to evaluate.

1. No register: the client does not register musical instruments even though the music therapist offers them and invites the client to interact with them.

2. Register: the client records the presence of musical instruments but is not related to them, meaning that they can take them or leave them as anything else, unaware of their characteristics or functionality.

3. Handling: the client interacts with the musical instruments, discovering shapes, colors, and sizes, but yet without any intentionality. It may happen that the client makes some kind of extra-musical play transforming it into a car, a plane, or a train, but still without noticing its particular sound.

4. Exploration: the client begins to have some connection with the musical instruments, discovering their sounds but only with an exploratory intentionality, unable to "own" them. Here the client begins to recognize a certain sonority of that object, smiling at the occurrence of sound or discovering its musical uniqueness, hitting it, shaking it, but only for short periods, without any appropriation. This is the beginning of a future musical relationship with them.

5. Persistence in using one instrument: the client can appropriate one of the instruments, using it on more than one occasion or choosing them steadily in several sessions. Here we can

find cases of clients who resort to the same instruments in a stereotyped way, organizing routines with them and thus being able to establish some sort of relationship with them. At this level, when the music therapist attempts to provide new instruments, the client cannot accept this proposal. Although the music therapist must always be playing music together with the client, this type of intervention will aim to promote the appropriation of the client's own musicality. It is understood that this scale is for the music therapist to observe if the client can move on a little, discovering their musicality—that is to say, that those sound objects make sound and that their own interaction with that sound object is the one that produces that sound.

6. Performance of some activity from them: the client begins to use different instruments with an expressive intentionality; that means, unlike the previous level, that the utilization of the instruments is with a greater variability, alternating the use of more than one. At this level, there is a greater flexibility in the choice of different musical instruments, finding similarities and differences and a better recognition of the instrumental set that has been offered. Another characteristic of this level is the use of musical games; although the client cannot use the instruments with the purposeful pursuit of playing music with them, they use them to do some ludic activity. The client recognizes them as instruments, and can use them at the suggestion of the music therapist. The musical instruments are transformed into objects that give sound to the activity, but out of the activity, they have no meaning. At this stage, the client uses the instruments, making some sounds with them, but just accompanying extra musical games. The expressive intention is prior to the communicative, and resembles the first babbles made by a baby before discovering that this will generate an effect on the listener. Its greatest purpose is expression in itself, and it is a purely spontaneous act (Ferrari 2013).

7. Brief musical use: the client begins to interact with musical instruments for short periods of time, and sometimes with an intentional musical execution. At this level, the client shows their need to be related to the musical instrument, without needing the instrument to be part of an extra musical activity. They can point, name, or appeal to the instrument to play music spontaneously or when the music therapist proposes it. Despite this, the relationship established with the musical instrument is for short periods, and the client is unable to focus attention for long periods of time.

8. Intentional prolonged musical use: the client starts to interact with musical instruments, holding for longer periods of time an intentional musical performance. This highlights the beginning of a search for holding musical forms, repeating and performing them on more than one occasion, realizing their expressive musical singularity. Despite the prolonged use of musical instruments, at this stage they do not tolerate the participation of another person in the musical play, removing the music therapist's hands if they try to play that instrument, or directly taking the instrument away if the therapist attempts a shared experience. It may also be that the client tolerates another instrument performed simultaneously but attention is so focused on their own performance that they cannot perceive the other sounds proposed, thus presenting many difficulties in the attention deferred.

9. Musical use with an intermusical intention: not only does the client use musical instruments but they also interact with others through them. In this sense, the client begins to become aware of joint musicality, sharing instruments, offering and accepting sounds proposed, and being prepared for an intermusical interaction.

Documentation and report

The role of the music therapist

Although this scale assesses the development of clients' attitudes towards the building of expressive musical singularity and its evolution to a communicative form, the music therapist must intervene in various ways to assist in this development—namely:

- knowing the client's musical story

- providing musical instruments in relation to each client's chronological age, socio-cultural characteristics, and capabilities

- tailoring the set of instruments and making interpretations based on the client's motor possibilities (if the client has motor disabilities)

- volunteering as a mirror in relation to the instrument use and its handling

- providing musical sound references for the client to take as theirs

- using voice and songs to provide musical plays that enable client interaction with the musical instruments

- encouraging the client and celebrating progress and findings on their part

- offering musical interactions for installing the intramusical idea—the "sense of self" in music—which will be the foundation for further interaction with others in music.

It is important to understand that all these interventions must be made by focusing the analysis on the relationship that the client is establishing with their own musical play, and monitoring this process.

Application of the scale

The scale may be used to analyze a part of an improvisation, a complete improvisation, or relevant aspects of the session as a whole. In terms of microanalysis (Wosch and Wigram 2007), it can be used to observe moment-by-moment changes, an episode, or a therapeutic event. If the desire is to analyze only one episode, it is advisable to state the most significant level of each session, even though the client may go through more than one level in the same session.

Recording

The recommended recording media for using this scale is video recording, since if only audio recordings are used, many levels can go unnoticed. The video recording must be complemented with the IRS table as a written record. Thus, each professional will be able to create easy-to-use session files containing this type of scale, where, just by marking with a cross, it is possible to get a vertical view of the kind of relationship the client has developed in the session and compare it with other sessions. This can also be used as a record for informing the family or other professionals who care for the client. An example is shown in Table 18.1

TABLE 18.1: EXAMPLE OF THE APPLICATION OF THE IRS IN A CLIENT WITH AUTISM DURING SEVEN SESSIONS

	Session 1	Session 2	Session 3	Session 4	Session 5	Session 6	Session 7
Level 9							
Level 8							
Level 7							
Level 6							x
Level 5					x	x	
Level 4				x			
Level 3			x				
Level 2	x	x					
Level 1							

Research and psychometrics

In collaboration with the music therapist Gustavo Gattino (Ferrari and Gattino 2013), I conducted an investigation to observe the first validity evidences regarding the IRS. This research included a total of 30 clients (aged between 4 and 20 years) organized in two groups. Different Argentine music therapists attended each group. Group 1 consisted of clients with autism and pervasive developmental disorder (PDD); group 2 consisted of clients with pathologies including cognitive problems (mental weakness, Down syndrome, West syndrome).

The main aim of this study was to observe the criteria validity where it was expected that the clients in group 1 would present lower scores compared with clients in group 2.

The scale was applied for six months with populations who had already started music therapy treatment once a week. Each music therapist used musical instruments adapted to each client, performing improvisational music therapy interventions. At the end of each session, the music therapist completed an analysis card based on the nine levels. In addition, the scale was sent to different music therapists with experience in the field of special needs to observe the clarity and relevance of each level of the IRS.

The results confirmed the previous hypothesis: the scores in group 1 were lower in comparison with group 2, with a statistical difference of $p < .001$ (according to the Mann-Whitney test). Moreover, regarding face validity, the results of the analysis carried out by music therapist experts in special needs showed that all items presented a high level of clarity and relevance. For future studies, it is necessary to explore larger samples, as well as to compare the scale with other assessments in order to establish convergent and discriminant validity. Furthermore, it is necessary to translate and adapt the scale to other countries and cultures to detect if the psychometric properties maintain good results.

Conclusion

Using specific tools to perform an assessment in music therapy involves accounting for changes in musical play. For music therapists, it is important to have specific records that help reflect the effect of the music therapy process. Likewise, it is important for the music therapy practice to use assessment tools that can be easily applicable.

The development of the IRS as an assessment instrument attempts to add a strand of analysis to improve the understanding of what happens in a session, to account for the intramusical behavior development of the client. Having records of those often imperceptible changes is essential for use with clients with severe pathologies who need first to develop an "appropriation" process of a music experience, and pass through a pre-musical to musical stage. The analysis of those "small big changes" will allow the design of intervention strategies based on music according to the needs of these clients. At the same time, the development of the scale will help us to understand when the client is ready for an intermusical experience and we can accompany their process. The use of this scale will not only allow visualization of the intramusical path but it can also be used for conducting research, since it has already been validated for the Spanish language, and is in the process of validation for the Portuguese language.

It is expected that the IRS as a specific tool will contribute to the understanding and analysis of music therapy sessions. The contribution of music therapy to the health sciences will be strengthened with the development and application of assessment tools that help to account for the benefits of music therapy.

Acknowledgement

I want to thank all those who have contributed to the writing of this chapter in the English version, especially Dr. Gustavo Gattino.

References

Bruscia, K. E. (1987) *Improvisational Models of Music Therapy*. Springfield, IL: Charles C. Thomas.

Bruscia, K. E. (1997) *Definiendo musicoterapia [Defining Music Therapy]*. España: Editorial AMARU.

Carpente, J. A. (2016) 'Investigating the effectiveness of a developmental, individual difference, relationship-based (DIR) improvisational music therapy program on social communication for children with autism spectrum disorder.' *Music Therapy Perspectives, 35,* 2, 160–174.

Ferrari, K. (2013) *Musicoterapia: Aspectos de la Sistematización y Evaluación de la Práctica Clínica [Music Therapy: Aspects of the Systematization and Assessment of the Clinical Practice]*. Buenos Aires, Argentina: Ediciones MTD.

Ferrari, K. and Gattino, G. (2013) *Proceso de validación de la escala de relaciones intramusicales (ERI) [Validation of the Scale of Intramusical Relationship Scale (ERI)]*. Proceedings of the IV Latin American Music Therapy Conference, Sucre, Bolivia.

Pavlicevic, M. (1995) 'Interpersonal Processes in Clinical Improvisation: Towards a Subjectively Systematic Definition.' In T. Wigram, B. Saperston, and R. West (eds) *The Art and Science of Music Therapy: A Handbook*. London: Harwood Academic Publishers.

Trevarthen, C. and Malloch, S. (2009) *Communicative Musicality: Exploring the Basis of Human Companionship*. Oxford: Oxford University Press.

Wigram, T. (1999a) 'Assessment methods in music therapy: A humanistic or natural science framework?' *Nordic Journal of Music Therapy, 8,* 1, 7–25.

Wigram, T. (1999b) 'Variability and Autonomy in Music Therapy Interaction: Evidence for Diagnosis and Therapeutic Intervention for Children with Autism and Asperger's Syndrome.' In R. Pratt and D. Erdonmez Grocke (eds) *MusicMedicine 3: MusicMedicine and Music Therapy: Expanding Horizons*. Melbourne: Faculty of Music, University of Melbourne.

Wigram, T. (2000) 'A Model of Diagnostic Assessment and Analysis of Musical Data in Music Therapy.' In T. Wigram (ed.) *Assessment and Evaluation in the Arts Therapies: Art Therapy, Music Therapy and Dramatherapy*. Radlett: Harper House Publications.

Wigram, T., Bonde, L. O., and Nygaard-Pedersen, I. (2002) *A Comprehensive Guide to Music Therapy: Theory, Clinical Practice, Research and Training*. London: Jessica Kingsley Publishers.

Wosch, T. and Wigram, T. (2007) *Microanalysis in Music Therapy – Methods, Techniques and Applications for Clinicians, Researchers, Educators and Students*. London: Jessica Kingsley Publishers.

CHAPTER 19

The Music in Dementia Scale

Orii McDermott

Setting and motivation

Dementia affects not only a person's cognitive and physical abilities but also their communication skills and their relationships with the wider social world. Even though dementia is frequently discussed in the public domain, perceived and actual stigma attached to people diagnosed with dementia still exists (Prince, Bryce, and Ferri 2011). People may begin to struggle with communicating using language as their dementia progresses. This can lead people with dementia to feel isolated and begin to be cut off from the world around them. Offering alternative means to building relationships with other people while supporting the uniqueness of individuals is extremely important to maintain the quality of life for people with dementia.

Music therapy is widely acknowledged as beneficial for the well-being of people with dementia. Recent studies have shown that music therapy can help reduce dementia symptoms such as agitation (Ridder *et al.* 2013; Vink *et al.* 2013) and depression (Guétin *et al.* 2009). While reductions in dementia symptoms will certainly improve the quality of life for a person with dementia, the aim of music therapy is not merely the reduction of undesirable or difficult behaviors but the improved well-being of unique individuals. Qualitative studies on music therapy with people with dementia consistently highlight increased "positive" behaviors and improved mood; for example, abilities to regulate emotions (Ridder and Aldridge 2005), increased willingness to communicate with people around them, and changes in body language and facial expression, such as longer eye contact. The majority of quantitative studies in music therapy and dementia use validated outcome measures widely used in psychiatry and psychology, and the primary focus of these studies tends to be the impact of music therapy on neuropsychiatric symptoms: the behavioral and psychological symptoms of dementia (BPSD). Targeting the reduction of BPSD is common not only in music therapy studies but also in other psychosocial ("non-pharmacological") psychological/behavioral/sensory interventions for dementia (Livingston *et al.* 2014). The potential problem of focusing too much on the BPSD reduction in psychosocial research may be that it can enforce the culture of "problem management" among frontline staff instead of developing holistic care to match the individual physical, cognitive, psychological, and social needs of people with dementia. Furthermore, even though reduction of BPSD is often a primary aim of a music-intervention study for dementia, what people with dementia themselves value when they participate in music therapy and other music activities has not been sufficiently investigated.

Theoretical background

The essentiality of engaging directly with the experience of people with dementia and trying to understand the world from their perspective became prominent in the 1990s (Brooker 2007; Brooker and Latham 2015). The importance of understanding the underlying reasons for behavioral and psychological symptoms has been debated widely throughout the literature (Bird and Moniz-Cook 2008; Brooker 2007; Brooker and Latham 2015; Goldsmith 1996; Kitwood 1997a, 1997b). Kitwood discussed extensively how the personal psychology of the person with dementia is affected by the social psychology of the care culture and how the clinical manifestation of a dementia may arise from a complex interaction between personality, biography, physical health, neurological impairment, and social psychology (Kitwood 1993a). The quality and sensitivity of the interpersonal process between a person with dementia and a carer plays a crucial role in supporting the personal psychology of the person and nurturing the social psychology of care culture. Kitwood's debate on the interpersonal process is particularly relevant to music therapy where relationship building through reciprocal musical interactions is the core of the therapeutic intervention. Trevarthen and Malloch (2009) argued that music making was a human activity that communicates motives.

The theory of communicative musicality (Trevarthen and Malloch 2009) resonates with Kitwood's argument on the essentiality of valuing and supporting the communicative attempt made by people with dementia (Kitwood 1993b). In music therapy research with people with dementia, in-depth musical and interpersonal processes are usually investigated qualitatively (e.g. Coomans 2016; Ridder 2003). The validated outcome measures frequently used in quantitative studies—such as the Neuropsychiatric Inventory (Cummings *et al.* 1994) and the Cohen-Mansfield Agitation Inventory (Cohen-Mansfield, Marx, and Rosenthal 1989)—are measures developed for psychiatry and psychology and are not designed to evaluate the music therapy process. There was a need to develop and evaluate an outcome measure that captures components of the interpersonal process, communicative musicality, and the communicative attempt that are relevant to the musical experiences of people with dementia.

Development

The development and evaluation of the Music in Dementia Assessment Scales (MiDAS) was conducted as a doctoral study (McDermott 2014). It aimed to produce a clinically relevant and scientifically rigorous dementia-specific music therapy outcome measure utilizing the mixed methods sequential exploratory design: the instrument development model (Creswell and Clark 2007). This exploratory design consists of three key phases: gathering and analyzing qualitative data (Phase 1), and using the analysis to develop an instrument (Phase 2) that is subsequently administered to a sample population (Phase 3).

Phase 1

Following ethics approval, we conducted focus groups and interviews with people with dementia, family members, care home staff, and music therapists (McDermott 2014; McDermott, Orrell, and Ridder 2014; McDermott, Orrell, and Ridder 2015). We aimed to develop a comprehensive picture of what people with dementia valued when participating in music therapy and music activities. We asked people with dementia (n = 16) if music was important to them, and if so, what aspects of musical experiences were particularly meaningful. We asked family members (15), care home staff (14), and music therapists (8) what they observed when people with dementia found their musical experiences valuable, and how they knew the music was meaningful to the person. Since our aim was to collect observable responses to music, we asked them to focus on describing what they saw rather than providing their views on why music may be important to people with dementia. A total of six focus groups and 19 interviews were conducted (McDermott, Orrell, and Ridder 2014). Audio recordings of focus groups and interviews were transcribed and were analyzed using the general inductive approach (Thomas 2006) to produce transcription cards. The long-table approach (Krueger and Casey 2000) was applied to categorize the 270 transcription cards. Initial grouping of the cards and the analysis were presented to external researchers and their critical feedback was used to refine the themes and develop a theoretical model: the psychosocial model of music in dementia (McDermott, Orrell, and Ridder 2014).

Phase 2

We began to formulate potential scale items after consensus on the key themes was achieved within the research team. An expert consultation with Dr. Chris Gilleard at University College London was held. Visual Analogue Scales (VAS) without anchor points were chosen over other types of scale (e.g. Likert scale) because VAS focuses on subjective experiences (Gift 1989; McCormack, David, and Sheather 1988) and was deemed most suitable to capture the unique musical experiences of individuals. Each VAS comprises a 100mm line without intervals, with the two extremes of the scale labeled as "none at all" and "highest." "Highest" means the optimal level of the unique individual which will be different from another resident. The optimal level may also change as their dementia progresses. The MiDAS consists of: (1) five VAS items: Interest, Response, Initiation, Involvement, and Enjoyment; (2) a supplementary checklist of notable behavior and the mood of the person (agitation/aggression, withdrawn/low in mood, restless/anxious, relaxed mood, attentive/ interested, and cheerful/smiling); and (3) space for raters' comments. Examples of behavior (e.g. "try to communicate") and mood (e.g. "become animated") are provided for each VAS scale. The checklist items are a description of the mood and behavior of residents frequently identified by staff, families, and music therapists during the focus groups and interviews. The checklist is intended to aid the clinical interpretation of MiDAS scores but the checklist items are not added as scores. The total scores of the five VAS items (100mm line = score 100 × five VAS items = 500) are reported as MiDAS scores (McDermott 2014; McDermott et al. 2015).

Procedure and data collection

The MiDAS is an observational outcome measure designed to evaluate the musical engagement of people at mid to advanced stages of dementia who may not be able to provide concrete verbal feedback on their experiences. The MiDAS is designed as a same-day scale to capture the presentation of the person on the day. Therapists and carers are required to rate the person on the day of the session, although some studies have been exploring the use of the MiDAS to aid video analysis of music therapy. A MiDAS rater is expected to reflect on the person's optimal level for each VAS item, compare it to the levels of Interest, Response, Initiation, Involvement, and Enjoyment that the rater observed in the person on the day, and make a vertical mark on the 100mm line. It is crucial the rater knows the person sufficiently well since each person's optimal level is different. Furthermore, engagement of the person's optimal level is likely to differ between raters. Consistency in having the same staff member rating the same person is important to ensure accuracy of MiDAS scores. This will be a challenge in care home settings where staff do shift work or use temporary staff. Some music therapists using the MiDAS in their practice have reported that they identified two or three staff members who worked regular hours and were interested in therapeutic activities in general, and therefore keen to support them as, for example, activity coordinators.

Two MiDAS forms should be completed per participant by the same rater on the day of the intervention to evaluate potential changes. The MiDAS was designed as a same-day scale because focus group participants and interviews highlighted that residents with moderate to advanced dementia often did not seem to remember their musical experiences beyond the day, but here-and-now experiences on the day were important to them (McDermott, Orrell and Riddler 2014). While the MiDAS was developed as a dementia-specific music therapy outcome measure, it is also suitable for evaluating music activities facilitated by non-therapists such as care home staff. The term "therapist" is used broadly for the purpose of the MiDAS form and it implies a "facilitator of a music-based intervention."

In our study (McDermott 2014; McDermott, Orgeta, Ridder, and Orrell 2014; McDermott, Orrell, and Ridder 2014; McDermott et al. 2015), care home staff completed one form before and another after a music therapy session on the same day. Therapist and staff MiDAS forms are identical. The therapists completed two forms immediately after each session: one based on the observation of a client during the first five minutes of the session as a baseline score for that day, and another based on the observation of a client during their "best five minutes" of that session. The "best five minutes" implies the section of the session that the therapist judged as most clinically important for the particular client on the day. Since each client's therapy process and their relationships with therapists are unique, we did not indicate what components they needed to consider as their "best five minutes," but left it to the clinical judgement of each therapist. Staff raters should complete an after-form not immediately after the music session but several hours after the session to evaluate the short-term (same-day) effects of the intervention (McDermott, Orrell, and Ridder 2014; McDermott *et al.* 2015).

Data analysis and interpretation

Although the total of the five VAS scores is ultimately the MiDAS score, it is also important to record and evaluate the changes in individual VAS scores since some VAS items may be more clinically important or relevant depending on the severity of their dementia and their needs. For example, people with advanced dementia may have limited means to initiate their ideas and the length of their engagement with music may fluctuate. In such cases, it would be more realistic to expect potential changes in their Interest and Response scores but not necessarily in their Initiation and Involvement scores. Therefore, evaluating the potential changes in their Interest and Response scores individually might provide a clinically accurate picture, rather than looking at the MiDAS overall scores, when working with the person with advanced dementia. However, each client's clinical presentation and their relationship with the therapist are unique. Therefore, interpretation of the MiDAS scores always needs to be contextualized. Furthermore, clients attending music therapy often use the space to explore their difficult experiences and emotions such as frustration and anger. As their sessions progress, Enjoyment scores can decrease while Interest, Response, Initiation, and Involvement scores may increase. Therefore, interpretation of MiDAS scores requires understanding of the clinical needs of each participant. Evaluating the differences in the VAS scores over the course of an intervention and examining the patterns of score changing are more important than simply aiming for higher MiDAS scores. Comparing the changes between the facilitators' scores (effects during the intervention) and the staff scores (observable effects following the intervention) is important. Pooling the MiDAS scores of research participants to evaluate the impact of a music intervention is appropriate, but score changes need to be interpreted in context (e.g. types of study participants, realistic, observable changes following a time-limited intervention).

Research and psychometrics
Phase 3

The final stage of the "mixed methods sequential exploratory design: the instrument development mode" was a psychometric evaluation of the MiDAS conducted in two care homes in London (McDermott, Orgeta, Ridder, and Orrell 2014). Nineteen care home residents (5 male, 14 female) with moderate to advanced dementia were enrolled for weekly group music therapy for three months. The participants were: White British/White European (17) or Black British (2), with a mean age of 81 years (standard deviation (SD) 8). The mean stay in the care homes was 20 months (SD 14). Two music therapists with over ten years of experience working with this client group ran weekly group sessions independently in the two homes. Each music therapy group consisted of between four and six members. Each session lasted between 45 minutes and one hour. The content of each session was guided by the clinical judgements of the therapists and typically included a mixture of pre-composed songs and instrumental or vocal improvisations. Up to ten sessions were offered to each resident. Two residents declined to attend after initially agreeing to take part. Mean attendance of the 17 residents was seven sessions (range 3–9). The two music therapists distributed the MiDAS forms to staff and collected the completed forms on the day, as well as completing their own therapist MiDAS forms. A total of 31 care home staff (qualified nurses, healthcare assistants, and an activity coordinator) completed staff MiDAS forms. A total of 629 MiDAS forms (staff = 306, therapists = 323) were completed. Statistical analysis was conducted with *Statistical Package for the Social Sciences* software version 21.

PSYCHOMETRIC PROPERTIES OF MiDAS

The mean MiDAS total score was 239 (SD 136). Distribution of the MiDAS scores covered the full range and no floor and ceiling effect was observed.

Reliability

Therapist inter-rater reliability was high (Intraclass Correlation Coefficient (ICC) range .768–.820). Staff inter-rater reliability was low (ICC range .127–.362) but staff test-retest reliability was acceptable (ICC range .498–.609) (McDermott, Orgeta, Ridder, and Orrell 2014). The low staff inter-rater reliability could be explained by the differences in: (1) their experiences of working with people with moderate to severe dementia, which may have affected their observation skills, and (2) their willingness for reflective practice and participation in research, which may have impacted on their attitudes towards completing MiDAS. Internal consistency between the five VAS items was high: α = .967 (McDermott, Orgeta, Ridder, and Orrell 2014).

Validity

Face and content validity were established during the MiDAS development through consensus meetings and expert/peer consultations, and by collating feedback from therapists and staff who participated in the pilot study (McDermott *et al.* 2015). We consistently checked with dementia specialists (music therapists and non-music therapists) if they comprehended what the scale items aimed to measure. QoL-AD (Logsdon *et al.* 1999) was used at three time points (baseline, mid-treatment, end treatment) to evaluate concurrent validity (McDermott, Orgeta, Riddler *et al.* 2014).

The outcome of Spearman's Rank Correlation Coefficient for each time point was acceptable: .524, .469, and .474 respectively. Principal Component Analysis, which reduces multiple variables into fewer components that summarize their variance, was conducted to evaluate construct validity of the five VAS items. Correlations between the items were very high, ranging from .754 (Initiation and Enjoyment) to .947 (Interest and Response). Although high correlations between the items indicates that the MiDAS has "good" construct validity, it can also be argued that some raters might have found it difficult to differentiate the five items, resulting in similar scores. This highlights the importance of making sure new MiDAS raters understand what each VAS item means.

It is possible to conclude the MiDAS is an outcome measure with high therapist inter-rater reliability, low staff inter-rater reliability, adequate staff test-retest reliability, adequate concurrent validity, and good construct validity. An investigation on MiDAS Sensitivity to Change (McDermott 2014) has shown that the MiDAS score-changes over the course of music therapy are closely related to the clinical changes within the music therapy sessions as well as staff observations. This indicates that the MiDAS is an appropriate tool to evaluate clinical practice as well as to use as a validated outcome measure in research.

Documentation and report

A potential drawback of using the MiDAS in resource-limited clinical practice or in a large study is that an evaluator needs to measure the line manually, then enter the data into a separate score sheet. We have started developing an Excel score sheet that allows immediate visual presentations of MiDAS scores. Visual presentations seemed to work well when clinicians tried to demonstrate the changes to care professionals who might not be that familiar with interpreting numerical data. It is important MiDAS raters make sure the VAS items on their forms are exactly 100mm when they prepare MiDAS forms.

Some printing options and photocopying often shorten the VAS lengths slightly (e.g. 96mm). We have been considering developing a MiDAS app so that a rater can mark the VAS scales on tablets, and scores are automatically saved. Development of a MiDAS app will save raters' time and resolve issues of shortened VAS lengths.

We have been asked whether it is possible to complete only therapist and facilitator forms without staff forms and report them as MiDAS outcomes. Our study indicates both staff MiDAS and therapist MiDAS have adequate to good psychometric properties—therefore it should be possible to use them as a therapist-only or staff-only stand-alone tool. Low staff inter-rater reliability identified in the MiDAS psychometric evaluation reinforces the importance of consistency of using the regular staff MiDAS raters. We are aware that involving staff regularly in MiDAS raters is not always possible or practical. Nevertheless, we would encourage both facilitators of a music intervention and care home staff who provide day-to-day care to the person with dementia to complete MiDAS forms to evaluate observable changes over the course of the intervention. Few music-based intervention studies in dementia have measured the changes in "positive" mood and behavior beyond decreased neuropsychiatric symptoms. To have both facilitator and staff MiDAS ratings would increase the validity of observable positive behavior/mood changes following a music intervention.

Training

Using the MiDAS does not require specialist training. Nevertheless, it is essential that a new MiDAS rater understands the concept of VAS and is aware that a rater needs to have sufficient knowledge of the person they are rating. Scoring the MiDAS requires a rater to stop and reflect on the person's presentations in relation to their unique optimal level. Furthermore, each person's optimal level may change as their dementia progresses. Thus completing the MiDAS requires a rater to be able to conceptualize the person's current optimal level fairly quickly. Music therapists seem to have few problems understanding the MiDAS procedure. We have observed some care home staff struggling to grasp the idea of comparing the person's presentation on that day to their presentation when they are at "their best" (most responsive and interactive). Another challenge was that if staff were under pressure to complete many practical tasks, they were less likely to reflect on each resident when completing MiDAS forms. Staff members who said the MiDAS was easy to complete also acknowledged the initial challenge of understating the VAS scales, but as one added, "You get quicker [at completing a form] once you get used to thinking about the person like that." This highlights the importance of training a new MiDAS rater. Although we hope the instruction on the MiDAS form is sufficient for a new staff member to start using the tool, we would certainly encourage a team to set up an introductory practice session for new raters if a more experienced MiDAS rater is available on site.

Discussion and future plans

The MiDAS was designed to evaluate observable presentations of people with moderate to advanced dementia who may not be able to provide concrete verbal feedback on their experiences of music therapy and other music activities. It focuses on observable (visible) presentations—therefore it does not evaluate less visible but important effects of music on emotions and feelings. When we held focus groups and interviews, participants with dementia frequently used the word "happy" to emphasize the importance of music for themselves, for example "music makes me happy," "music and happy memories." Although we recognized happiness as one of the key components of musical experiences, we did not create a VAS item, because happiness is a subjective experience which may or may not be visible and it is highly likely to be influenced by a rater's own interpretation. It should be noted that the MiDAS does not intend to represent all the key musical experiences of people with dementia since emotionally profound musical experiences are not easily or accurately observable. If any significant emotional responses are expressed, a rater should describe this in the box provided.

Since its publication (McDermott, Orgetta, Riddler, and Orrell 2014; McDermott *et al.* 2015), the MiDAS is being used in over 13 countries and is being translated into Danish (Ridder, Lykkegaard, and McDermott 2018), Norwegian, Spanish, and Portuguese. We have produced guidance on translating music therapy outcome measures (Ridder, McDermott, and Orrell 2017) and have encouraged the MiDAS translators to follow the procedure to ensure its rigor and validity. The translation procedure we recommend requires a team of translators and time commitment, which may not be easy to organize for sessional or lone workers. However, this process and psychometric evaluation of the translated MiDAS is essential to use the MiDAS as a validated outcome measure.

We have also set up a MiDAS website (www.musictherapy. aau.dk/midas). A list of translation collaborators is available from the website.

A diverse range of music-based interventions for people with dementia is available but not all interventions have been rigorously developed nor been thoroughly evaluated. The MiDAS was developed aiming to measure the observable impact of music that people with dementia themselves consider important. Measuring Interest, Response, Initiation, Involvement, and Enjoyment does not portray a full range of musical experiences of people with dementia, but the changes in the MiDAS scores are likely to show whether people with dementia find the music intervention meaningful for themselves, or not. In research, the MiDAS may be a useful measure when used in conjunction with other established outcome measures such as the Neuropsychiatric Inventory (NPI) that evaluates changes in symptoms. Further development and evaluation of outcome measures that incorporate the views and perspectives of people with dementia will be important in future dementia research.

Acknowledgements

The doctoral study "Development and Evaluation of Music in Dementia Assessment Scales" was funded by Aalborg University and the Danish Council for Independent Research. The author would like to thank MiDAS co-creators Prof. Martin Orrell and Prof. Hanne Mette Ridder. We are grateful for the support of Central and North West London NHS Foundation Trust and for contributions from music therapists Rosslyn Bender and Maria Radoje during the MiDAS evaluation phase.

References

Bird, M. and Moniz-Cook, E. (2008) 'Challenging Behaviour in Dementia: A Psychosocial Approach to Intervention.' In B. Woods and L. Clare (eds) *Handbook of the Clinical Psychology of Ageing* (2nd edition). Chichester: John Wiley & Sons, doi: 10.1002/9780470773185.ch33.

Brooker, D. (2007) *Person-Centred Dementia Care: Making Services Better.* London: Jessica Kingsley Publishers.

Brooker, D. and Latham, I. (2015) *Person-Centred Dementia Care: Making Services Better with the VIPS Framework.* London: Jessica Kingsley Publishers.

Cohen-Mansfield, J., Marx, M. S., and Rosenthal, A. S. (1989) 'A description of agitation in a nursing home.' *Gerontologist, 44,* 3, 77–84.

Coomans, A. (2016) 'Moments of Resonance in Musical Improvisation with Persons with Severe Dementia: An Interpretative Phenomenological Study.' Unpublished PhD thesis, Aalborg University, Denmark, doi: 10.5278/vbn.phd.hum.00018.

Creswell, J. W. and Clark, V. L. P. (2007) *Designing and Conducting Mixed Methods Research.* Thousand Oaks, CA: Sage Publishers.

Cummings, J. L., Mega, M., Gray, K., Rosenberg-Thompson, S., *et al.* (1994) 'The Neuropsychiatric Inventory: Comprehensive assessment of psychopathology in dementia.' *Neurology, 44,* 2308–2314.

Gift, A. G. (1989) 'Visual analogue scales: Measurement of subjective phenomena.' *Nursing Research, 38,* 5, 286–287.

Goldsmith, M. (1996) *Hearing the Voice of People with Dementia: Opportunities and Obstacles.* London: Jessica Kingsley Publishers.

Guétin, S., Portet, F., Picot, M., Pommié, C., *et al.* (2009) 'Effect of music therapy on anxiety and depression in patients with Alzheimer's type dementia: Randomised, controlled study.' *Dementia and Geriatric Cognitive Disorders, 28,* 1, 36–46.

Kitwood, T. (1993a) 'Person and process in dementia.' *International Journal of Geriatric Psychiatry, 8,* 7, 541–545.

Kitwood, T. (1993b) 'Towards a theory of dementia care: The interpersonal process.' *Ageing and Society, 13,* 1, 51–67.

Kitwood, T. (1997a) *Dementia Reconsidered: The Person Comes First.* Buckingham, PA: Open University Press.

Kitwood, T. (1997b) 'The experience of dementia.' *Aging Mental Health, 1,* 1, 13–22.

Krueger, R. and Casey, M. (2000) *Focus Groups: A Practical Guide for Applied Research.* Thousand Oaks, CA: Sage Publishers.

Livingston, G., Kelly, L., Lewis-Holmes, E., Baio, G., *et al.* (2014) 'Non-pharmacological interventions for agitation in dementia: Systematic review of randomised controlled trials.' *The British Journal of Psychiatry, 205,* 6, 436–442.

Logsdon, R. G., Gibbons, L. E., McCurry, S. M., and Teri, L. (1999) 'Quality of life in Alzheimer's disease: Patient and caregiver reports.' *Journal of Mental Health and Aging,* 5, 21–32.

McCormack, H. M., David, J. d. L., and Sheather, S. (1988) 'Clinical applications of visual analogue scales: A critical review.' *Psychological Medicine, 18,* 4, 1007–1019.

McDermott, O. (2014) 'The Development and Evaluation of Music in Dementia Assessment Scales (MiDAS).' Unpublished PhD thesis, Aalborg University, Denmark.

McDermott, O., Orgeta, V., Ridder, H. M., and Orrell, M. (2014) 'A preliminary psychometric evaluation of Music in Dementia Assessment Scales (MiDAS).' *International Psychogeriatrics, 26,* 6, 1011–1019, doi: 10.1017/S1041610214000180.

McDermott, O., Orrell, M., and Ridder, H. M. (2014) 'The importance of music for people with dementia: The perspectives of people with dementia, family carers, staff and music therapists.' *Aging Mental Health, 18,* 6, 706–716, doi: 10.1080/13607863.2013.875124.

McDermott, O., Orrell, M., and Ridder, H. M. (2015) 'The development of Music in Dementia Assessment Scales (MiDAS).' *Nordic Journal of Music Therapy, 24,* 3, 232–251.

Prince, M., Bryce, R., and Ferri, C. (2011) *World Alzheimer Report 2011: The Benefits of Early Diagnosis and Intervention.* London: Alzheimer's Disease International.

Ridder, H. M. (2003) 'Singing Dialogue: Music Therapy with Persons in Advanced Stages of Dementia: A Case Study Research Design.' Unpublished PhD thesis, Aalborg University, Denmark.

Ridder, H. M. and Aldridge, D. (2005) 'Individual music therapy with persons with frontotemporal dementia: Singing dialogue.' *Nordic Journal of Music Therapy, 14,* 2, 91–106.

Ridder, H. M., Lykkegaard, C., and McDermott, O. (2018) 'Dansk oversættelse af Midas—et redskab til assesment af musikterapi for personer med demens.' *Dansk Musikterapi, 15,* 1, 3–16.

Ridder, H. M., McDermott, O., and Orrell, M. (2017) 'Translation and adaptation procedures for music therapy outcome instruments.' *Nordic Journal of Music Therapy, 26,* 1, 62–78.

Ridder, H. M., Stige, B., Qvale, L. G., and Gold, C. (2013) 'Individual music therapy for agitation in dementia: An exploratory randomized controlled trial.' *Aging Mental Health, 17,* 6, 667–678.

Thomas, D. R. (2006) 'A general inductive approach for analyzing qualitative evaluation data.' *American Journal of Evaluation, 27,* 2, 237–246.

Trevarthen, C. and Malloch, S. (2009) *Communicative Musicality: Exploring the Basis of Human Companionship.* Oxford: Oxford University Press.

Vink, A. C., Zuidersma, M., Boersma, F., Jonge, P., Zuidema, S. U., and Slaets, J. (2013) 'The effect of music therapy compared with general recreational activities in reducing agitation in people with dementia: A randomised controlled trial.' *International Journal of Geriatric Psychiatry, 28,* 10, 1031–1038.

CHAPTER 20

The Music Therapy Assessment Tool for Awareness in Disorders of Consciousness

Wendy L. Magee

Setting and motivation

Imagine this: you are a relatively newly qualified music therapist, and gain a job in a newly established clinical service that offers innovative care to a specialized population. The setting is energetic, with complex patients/clients, and a dynamic multiprofessional team who are excited about what music therapy will bring to the program. Expectations are high from the rest of the team. This is an opportunity for you to develop expertise and to pioneer a music therapy service.

You receive referrals immediately, and other team members want to observe your sessions. The clinical work is highly challenging, and you have never worked with patients/clients quite this complex before as a student or in the short time since qualifying. You try the things you learned to do—singing songs that are reported as meaningful to the patient, interventions using instruments, designing musical experiences that can meet the goals that other team members have set—and you can see that patients' behaviors change during the music therapy session. Your colleagues observe intently during the sessions they attend and participate in, and seem to use the music therapy sessions to formulate their own assessments. You go to team meetings and case reviews where the team members report on patient progress to set and revise goals. You struggle to know how to report the observations you have made in your sessions: there are no formalized assessments in music therapy for this population; you find it difficult to articulate the changes that you saw in the sessions; you do not know how the music therapy experiences fit into the goals that the multiprofessional team are setting. You search for literature on music therapy with this population: there is none (or barely any). You seek supervision. There still seem to be no clear answers that are a good fit for your situation.

I know that what I have described is the situation for many music therapists when they start a job in the early years after graduating. It was certainly the situation for me, and my colleague Rosie Monaghan, when we started work in 1990 at the Royal Hospital for Neuro-disability (RHN), a facility that provided rehabilitation and continuing care to people with complex needs stemming from acquired brain injury and neurological illness. We were employed to work as part of the newly created "coma arousal program" with adults who had acquired profound brain injury, had emerged from coma, but whose brain injuries resulted in highly complex disabilities: multifaceted physical, cognitive, and sensory impairments resulting in communication and behavioral disabilities. The goals of care were to minimize medical incidents, maintain and improve physical health, and optimize cognitive functioning. Overall, the program aimed to determine one of two trajectories: would a person benefit from skilled nursing care alone or was there a potential for them to benefit from further rehabilitation?

My colleague and I were lucky in that we had each other so that we could brainstorm ideas together, and we had the working model of a previous music therapist who had forged the role for music therapy within the team. However, each patient was so very different and neither of us yet had the experience to draw on our own bank of evidence built from many cases that forms the "expert opinion" level of evidence. Between us we found a handful of articles from the previous decade on music therapy with neurological populations, but none of them described patients as complex as the people we were meeting. At that time, in 1990, patients survived brain injuries of a severity that previously would have resulted in death. Additionally, knowledge was lacking of effective care strategies in the acute stages following injury that could minimize longer-term complications. The disabilities that are sustained from profound brain injury are complex. Physical disabilities can include minimal movement or movement disorders; severe contractures in the arms, hands, legs, and feet; and problems with muscle tone resulting in hyperextension, compromising the possibility of establishing a supportive seating system. These physical disabilities can be exacerbated by sensory impairments such as blindness, tactile hypersensitivity, and auditory sensitivity. All of these disabilities can be further compounded by behavioral difficulties, such as, for example, disinhibition, agitation, problems with mood regulation, cognitive difficulties, and impaired insight stemming from frontal lobe damage. When combined with no means for verbal communication, the clinical presentations of people with profound brain injury challenge professionals and are distressing for the person's family and loved ones.

We learned from our multiprofessional colleagues through observation of their clinical sessions and listening to their feedback at patient case reviews. The Sensory Modality Assessment and Rehabilitation Technique (SMART; Gill-Thwaites 1997) had recently been devised on the unit and was being used as a part of standard care. Other assessments for this population (later to be known as "Prolonged Disorders of Consciousness" or "PDOC") were also being devised by other professional groups on this unit. This provided the opportunity to learn what was important in the assessment and ongoing evaluation of PDOC patients: in particular, assessing responses across the visual, auditory, motor, communication, and arousal domains was important. This realization emerged slowly, reflected in the items that were developed in the assessment documentation described in this chapter.

The assessment tool was originally called the Music Therapy Assessment Tool for Low Awareness States (MATLAS) but changed its name to the Music Therapy Assessment Tool for Awareness in Disorders of Consciousness (MATADOC) to complement the change of terminology used in healthcare. The MATADOC protocol and documentation (incorporating the assessment documentation and score record) were developed in several phases over a 16-year period within clinical work and research at the Royal Hospital. Item development occurred first (1990–93), as we tried to formulate a way of documenting behaviors that we observed during music therapy and the changes in these behaviors that happened over time. Between 1993 and 2004, after Rosie's departure, I continued developing the items through revising the number of incremental levels within each item. This process enabled me to incorporate within each item a larger repertoire of behaviors that I encountered in thousands of sessions with hundreds of patients, making the items more sensitive to even tiny changes in a patient's responsiveness. The number of items in the assessment fluctuated over this period, as redundant items were removed, some items were merged, and new items were incorporated. All of this work was based on experience at case reviews and family meetings and feedback from colleagues, reflecting on what appeared to be helpful in informing on patient responsiveness. Additional feedback was gained from music therapy colleagues working on other (non-PDOC) units when they had complex patients, and the MATADOC assessment documentation provided a framework for assessment.

The opportunity emerged to test the MATADOC's reliability and validity between 2004 and 2006. Taking the MATADOC forward with research involved many people with diverse knowledge and skills. During this phase, the items on the assessment documentation were refined to the assessment's final format of 14 items. To progress with research, we needed a defined protocol and guideline (manual)—this ensured that any two therapists followed the same procedures to elicit patient responses in sessions. The manual provided detailed instructions about how to rate responses including, most importantly, definitions (e.g. what is meant by "consistent"). This ensured that any two therapists interpreted responses in the same way and on repeated occasions. The items were divided into three subscales and a scoring system was developed which produced a framework that included a summed score of responses enabling diagnostic outcomes. The final phase of development was the main research study (2007–11) developing the research proposal for ethics review, gaining funding, data collection, and analysis.

Theoretical background

The MATADOC assessment grew out of clinical practice (i.e. expert opinion) rather than theory, although theory influenced the multiprofessional team's practice, which in turn shaped the MATADOC's development. Emerging from practice rather than theory is an important distinction to make about the MATADOC as it could be considered both a weakness and a strength. An important criterion for PDOC assessments is that the full repertoire of behaviors across the spectrum of PDOC should be reflected in items (Seel *et al.* 2010). Through its development from clinical practice, the MATADOC meets this requirement: each item reflects the range of behaviors that are representative of Vegetative State (VS), Minimally Conscious State (MCS), and Emergent from MCS, as was observed and tested in hundreds of sessions.

Although the MATADOC developed over 14 years in response to the demands of a music therapy service on one unit, the importance and relevance of assessment to the care of people with PDOC also emerged during this time (Seel *et al.* 2010). This has coincided with a growing interest in music as a diagnostic treatment and prognostic tool for PDOC (Magee, Tillmann, *et al.* 2016). People with PDOC present possibly the greatest challenges within rehabilitation: "No other diagnosis within the field of neurological rehabilitation carries with it such a vast range of clinical, medico-legal, ethical, philosophical, moral and religious implications" (Wilson, Graham, and Watson 2005, p. 432). The severity and complexity of disabilities typical of PDOC patients have placed accurate assessment central to care, as most standardized rehabilitation measures are not sensitive enough to identify minimal responses that are typical with PDOC, do not measure the behavioral domains that are important and relevant to PDOC, and cannot meet the complex physical, sensory, communication, and cognitive needs of PDOC. Thus, estimates of misdiagnosis have remained unacceptably high over a 20-year period of investigation: Tresch *et al.* (1991) found 18 percent of patients misdiagnosed as VS, and 18 years later Schnakers *et al.* (2009) found that 41 percent of patients diagnosed in VS were actually MCS, 10 percent were misdiagnosed as being in MCS when they had actually emerged from PDOC, and a further 89 percent of patients were assigned an "uncertain diagnosis" when they were actually MCS. Gaining an accurate diagnosis is important as it helps manage family feelings of stigma and determine appropriate care, including informing decisions about withdrawal of tube feeding.

A number of behavioral and imaging studies have found that the auditory modality may be the most sensitive for identifying awareness in VS patients (Gill-Thwaites and Munday 2004; Owen *et al.* 2005, 2006), possibly explained by the high incidence of undiagnosed visual impairment following profound brain injury (Andrews *et al.* 1996). Furthermore, both VS and MCS populations have demonstrated a greater level of behavioral responsiveness and brain activity when the stimuli used have personal meaning (Boly *et al.* 2005; di Stefano *et al.* 2012; Perrin *et al.* 2006; Schnakers *et al.* 2009; Shiel and Wilson 2005). Auditory stimuli with personal meaning positions music as a useful medium, particularly given that language functioning may be assumed to be severely impaired in PDOC patients.

Recent studies have demonstrated that music boosts cognitive responses (Castro *et al.* 2015) and heightens behaviors indicative of awareness (Verger *et al.* 2014) in PDOC. Music therapy interventions have been shown to heighten arousal and stimulate brain activation indicative of attention in PDOC (O'Kelly *et al.* 2013), and one case with a PDOC patient reported improved performance on measures of awareness during music therapy when compared with other non-music interventions (Lichtensztejn, Macchi, and Lischinsky 2014). Perrin *et al.* (2015) propose that the emotional salience contained within music of personal meaning simultaneously stimulates both the external awareness network involving working memory, language processing, mental imagery, and attention, and the internal awareness networks that involve biographical reference and emotional response.

Despite the interest in recent years of music as a potential tool for assessment and intervention with PDOC and the knowledge that the auditory modality may be sensitive for determining awareness, the standardized PDOC measures have not reflected this (Magee, forthcoming). Although assessments of awareness in PDOC examine responsiveness across the domains of visual, auditory, motor, communication, and arousal, all of these measures are grossly insensitive in the assessment of auditory responsiveness, since tasks such as clapping hands near to the patient's ear or calling the patient's name (Magee, forthcoming) predominate. This positions the MATADOC as the most sensitive assessment tool for auditory responsiveness and an attractive contribution to multiprofessional assessment and treatment for PDOC.

Procedure and population

The current version of the MATADOC is validated for adults with PDOC. PDOC are defined as disorders of consciousness persisting for more than four weeks stemming from sudden onset profound acquired brain injury (Royal College of Physicians 2013). The major causes include trauma, vascular event, hypoxic event, inflammation or infection, or toxic or metabolic incident (Royal College of Physicians 2013).

The MATADOC uses a standardized protocol as this assists with treatment fidelity and reliability. However, the protocol also allows for flexibility so as to respond to the patient's "in the moment" responsiveness and needs, and to provide individually tailored patient-preferred music which is a central part of the protocol. A MATADOC assessment is completed in four sessions over a recommended ten-day period where possible (Magee, Lenton-Smith, and Daveson 2015). This allows for repeated measures to help compensate for patient fluctuation in arousal. The protocol and interpretive guidelines are provided in a published manual (Magee, Lenton-Smith, and Daveson 2015).

Interventions with PDOC patients aim to optimize possibilities for the patient to demonstrate that they can respond differently to contrasting stimuli; that is, the patient needs to show differential responses as this is a diagnostic criterion. The MATADOC protocol involves a minimum of five procedures that include one visual task, one verbal command, and several auditory tasks, all presented using music or music-related stimuli. The number of procedures is expanded with more responsive patients, introducing more complex communication tasks. The auditory tasks involve singing the patient's name within an improvised song, playing/singing a pre-composed song that holds emotional meaning to the individual, and playing isolated musical sounds without any visual stimuli. Using live music, the auditory tasks provide the opportunity to manipulate subtly the musical components (e.g. volume, tempo, timbre) to provide more in-depth information about the individual's responsiveness to their auditory environment (Magee 2007).

Data analysis and results

The MATADOC has three subscales with 14 items that rate responsiveness across the auditory, visual, arousal, communication, and motor domains, reflecting domains assessed in standard PDOC measures (Magee 2007). Five items are specific to the auditory modality (Magee, Siegert, et al. 2014) and a further five relate to communication, encompassing pragmatic, musical, and language-based communication (Magee 2007). One further item rates visual responsiveness, one examines arousal, and two other items rate motor responses. The number of items rating auditory responsiveness highlights the MATADOC's sensitivity in assessing responsiveness in this domain.

The therapist rates responses based on behavioral (including musical) observations within the five procedures. All 14 items are rated by reflecting on the patient's overall responsiveness across the session, rating the highest-level responses observed. Responses are rated using a paper copy of the MATADOC assessment form after finishing the session. These ratings are later converted into three numerical or categorical scores, providing a diagnostic outcome, an indication of musical responsiveness to guide music therapy intervention planning, and functional responses to guide interdisciplinary goal setting (Magee, Lenton-Smith, and Daveson 2015). The principal subscale has five items including visual, auditory, communication, and arousal responsiveness. This subscale has diagnostic utility, based on converting ratings into one summed numerical score (Magee, Siegert, et al. 2014). This score indicates whether the patient is in VS, MCS, or Emergent from MCS. The second subscale rates musical responses across two items. This subscale has no diagnostic utility but assists with evidence-based planning of music therapy intervention based on ratings of the patient's responses to musical components (Magee, Siegert, et al. 2016). The third subscale has seven items that further rate responsiveness across the communication, motor, and auditory domains to assist with identifying patient strengths in order to set patient-centered goals as part of interdisciplinary rehabilitation (Magee, Siegert, et al. 2016). Responses are rated first of all, and then ratings are converted into categorical "scores" aligned with VS, MCS, or Emergent from MCS levels of functioning. This subscale is not diagnostic, but provides a "map" of developing areas of functioning and supports the diagnosis provided by the principal subscale. An overall MATADOC score from the three subscales is not produced, as this would not be meaningful.

Interpretation and report

The published manual provides guidelines for rating behaviors, transforming ratings into scores, and then interpreting the numerical and categorical scores. A diagnostic outcome is determined through examining the majority of principal subscale scores over four sessions. For example, if a patient is scored with a diagnosis of "MCS" for three out of four sessions and a diagnosis of "Emergent from MCS" for just one, then a final diagnosis of MCS is given. Categorical scores from the third subscale are used to support or refute the diagnostic outcome of the principal subscale. For example, if the primary subscale has produced a diagnosis of VS, the third subscale should reflect the patient's functioning at this level. Disparities between the principal and third subscale can help with complex cases where the diagnosis is questioned.

All items of the measure can be used to identify patient strengths or musical factors to elicit optimal responsiveness (e.g. using louder music to enhance arousal; using voice to enhance localization to the therapist), which in turn provides information for interdisciplinary intervention planning. Reporting of the results follows local standards that might include feedback to the treatment team, to the family, or to the funding body supporting the patient's care. The relevance and use of the information is influenced by the philosophy of the setting. For example, diagnostic outcomes are of primary interest in rehabilitation settings where such outcomes influence care trajectories or decisions such as withdrawal of tube feeding. Diagnostic outcomes might be of less importance in chronic skilled nursing care settings where the emphasis is on providing interventions to enhance quality of life.

Training

Training in using the MATADOC is required due to the complexity of the population and the advanced skills required in understanding patient responses from a neurobehavioral perspective. Three-day training institutes use lectures and experiential sessions with role play to develop skills in delivering the protocol, rating, and interpreting responses and scoring. Training is offered at international sites each year, usually with two to four training sessions per annum. Training prepares music therapists to deliver the MATADOC immediately; however, competency can also be gained through preparation of a clinical portfolio. At the time of writing this chapter, 171 professionals from 18 countries have been fully trained in 13 training sessions held at international sites.

Research and psychometrics

The research to date on the MATADOC has focused on establishing its psychometric properties for use with adult PDOC, exploring its clinical utility for use with other minimally responsive populations, and establishing its validity with new populations. One prospective study tested the MATADOC with 21 adult PDOC patients to determine its reliability across the three subscales, overall validity, dimensionality, and to test its internal consistency within the principal and second subscales. The principal subscale has good inter-rater reliability (mean intra-class correlations .83, SD = .11), good test-retest reliability (mean intra-class correlations .82, SD = .05), and excellent concurrent validity with 100 percent agreement on diagnostic outcomes when compared to an external reference standard (Magee, Siegert, *et al.* 2014). Rasch analysis determined the principal subscale to be a unidimensional and homogenous scale, meaning that it measures one construct and that the subscale items have a good fit in terms of measuring awareness. This means that it is valid as a diagnostic tool when raters are trained in its use, and may contribute to interdisciplinary assessments of awareness in adult PDOC.

Results for reliability of the second and third subscales that have no diagnostic power, with nine items assessing musical responsiveness and cognitively mediated functions, were mixed although with generally good agreement between and within raters. Mean inter-rater reliability for the two subscales overall was .41, which can be considered adequate reliability for items that examine a non-central domain (Magee, Siegert, *et al.* 2016). These results included two items that were particularly weak, with one musical response item being weak for both inter-rater and test-retest reliability. As this specific item is most useful for planning music therapy intervention, we made the decision not to remove this item. Although the mixed results for the second and third subscales, and in particular the musical response item, were disappointing, we determined that these subscales hold greater clinical utility rather than psychometric strength. In combination with the principal subscale, the overall measure has combined strength as a comprehensive measure that can rate responsiveness to music-based auditory stimuli in PDOC populations (Magee, Siegert, *et al.* 2016).

Further clinical audit on the MATADOC has examined its sensitivity in assessing behavioral domains of interest in comparison with other standardized measures (O'Kelly and Magee 2013). We audited 42 clinical records, comparing the SMART (Gill-Thwaites 1997) diagnostic and item outcomes with those of the MATADOC. Each measure was found to have different sensitivities, with the SMART having heightened sensitivity for the motor domain in relation to diagnosis and the MATADOC showing heightened sensitivity for the auditory and visual domains (O'Kelly and Magee 2013).

These findings were echoed in an exploratory pilot study (n = 4) with children with PDOC (Magee, Ghetti, and Moyer 2015) in which we explored the clinical utility of the MATADOC with children and examined preliminary validity against three external reference standards. In three of the cases, the MATADOC produced similar diagnostic outcomes to the other assessments; however, in the fourth case it produced an outcome of higher awareness state. We also examined outcomes on comparable items across all four measures (e.g. visual, auditory, etc.), finding that the MATADOC produced findings on most items similar to the other measures, with the exception of three instances where the MATADOC outcomes suggested higher levels of functioning within the visual and auditory domains. These tentative findings suggest that the MATADOC protocol and assessment may be more sensitive in eliciting and rating visual and auditory responsiveness but needs to be tested further in a larger study.

Future plans

Given these tentative yet promising findings with pediatric PDOC, further research is taking place to adapt the MATADOC specifically for a pediatric population. Interventions and measures for use with children with PDOC are seriously neglected and under-researched topics. Drawing on the results from the pilot study (Magee, Ghetti, and Moyer 2015) and expert opinion from MATADOC-trained therapists working with pediatric PDOC, the protocol and assessment documentation have been revised and refined to develop a new measure, the Music therapy Sensory Instrument for Cognition, Consciousness, and Awareness (MuSICCA; Pool *et al.*, forthcoming). A multisite international trial is planned to validate the MuSICCA for youth with PDOC and to establish its psychometric properties.

As the MATADOC was developed from clinical practice to work with minimally responsive populations, there are a number of other populations for whom it might provide a useful tool in music therapy practice, such as, for example, end-stage dementia, end-stage terminal illness, delirium, and profound developmental disabilities. In its current form, the MATADOC scoring and items may not be appropriate for these populations—for example, establishing a diagnosis of VS or MCS is not relevant to these populations. The rationale for exploring the MATADOC's use with new populations is to provide a tool for music therapy clinicians that can establish levels of responsiveness and track changes in these responses. Longer-term plans are to trial the MATADOC in small studies to determine its clinical utility with different minimally responsive populations, adapt the protocol and documentation according to the findings, and validate the revised measure if relevant. One such exploratory pilot study is taking place at the current time to explore its use with end-stage dementia (Magee *et al.* 2017). The findings will determine if the protocol and assessment are useful and identify the changes that need to be made to enhance the MATADOC's use for people living with end-stage dementia who are minimally responsive.

Other plans include translating and validating the MATADOC in other languages. It is already translated into Spanish (Magee, Lenton-Smith, and Daveson 2014), and a validation study for the Spanish version is in development at the current time. The MATADOC will also be translated into Mandarin in the coming months with a plan to validate it in the near future. Translating English-language measures into other languages is important as it provides the international community with common tools that help to consolidate music therapy within healthcare. Validating the measures in other languages provides opportunities for larger international research studies that will build the evidence base for music therapy.

Discussion and summary

The MATADOC is just one measure of awareness that is validated for use with PDOC within the interdisciplinary care of adults who are minimally responsive following acquired profound brain damage. It is an assessment tool that can be used repeatedly over time (i.e. assessment on admission and then later as evaluation) to track patient change. It has diagnostic utility with particular sensitivity within the auditory and visual domains; however, it should be used in combination with other PDOC measures. Best practice demands the multiple perspectives that different measures provide due to the complexity of the population of interest. Further exploration is warranted to explore its clinical utility for pediatric PDOC, end-stage dementia, end-stage terminal illness, and delirium. Refining the protocol and assessment as appropriate to each of these populations promises to offer clinicians tools that optimize patient care through collecting data that can inform individualized treatment. Validating such measures also helps to situate music therapy as a viable and credible intervention.

Acknowledgements

As this work has involved many people over several decades and across continents, I would like to acknowledge all the individuals who contributed to the evolution of the MATADOC to its current point. In particular, I acknowledge the input from Professor Keith Andrews and occupational therapy colleagues Karen Elliot and Helen Gill-Thwaites at the earliest stages of its inception. Refinement of the MATADOC documentation for research was led by Barbara Daveson with input from Wendy Magee, and opinion from occupational therapy colleague Ros Munday and speech and language therapy colleagues Sarah Haynes, Sophie McKenzie, and Susan Farrelly. The scoring system was devised by Barbara Daveson. The MATADOC protocol was developed and refined by Wendy Magee and Gemma Lenton-Smith. Wendy Magee led on the manual development with input from Gemma Lenton-Smith and Barbara Daveson. Revisions for the second edition of the manual were done by Wendy Magee and Gemma Lenton-Smith with input from Eirini Alexiou. Barbara Daveson led on research proposal development and funding applications with input from Wendy Magee. Barbara Daveson and Gemma Lenton-Smith led on ethics applications with input from Wendy Magee. The principal investigators (PIs) of the research changed during the project: Barbara Daveson (2007–09); Gemma Lenton-Smith (2009–10); Wendy Magee (2011). Data collection involved all three PIs, with considerable input from Eirini Alexiou, as well as input from other members of the Music Therapy service: Julian O'Kelly and Rebeka Bodak. Richard Siegert and Steve Taylor were responsible for data analysis. The Spanish translation was provided by Marcela Lichtensztejn and Paula Macchi of APEM, Buenos Aires.

References

Andrews, K., Murphy, L., Munday, R., and Littlewood, C. (1996) 'Misdiagnosis of the vegetative state: Retrospective study in a rehabilitation unit.' *British Medical Journal, 313,* 13–16.

Boly, M., Faymonville, M., Peigneux, P., Lambermont, B., *et al.* (2005) 'Cerebral processing of auditory and noxious stimuli in severely brain injured patients: Differences between VS and MCS.' *Neuropsychological Rehabilitation, 15,* 3, 283–289, doi: 10.1080/09602010443000371.

Castro, M., Tillmann, B., Luauté, J., Corneyllie, A., Dailler, F., André-Obadia, N., and Perrin, F. (2015) 'Boosting cognition with music in patients with disorders of consciousness.' *Neurorehabilitation and Neural Repair, 29,* 8, 734–742.

di Stefano, C., Sturiale, C., Trentini, P., Bonora, R., Rossi, D., Cervigni, G., and Piperno, R. (2012) 'Unexpected neuropsychological improvement after cranioplasty: A case series study.' *British Journal of Neurosurgery, 26,* 6, 827–831.

Gill-Thwaites, H. (1997) 'The Sensory Modality Assessment Rehabilitation Technique – A tool for assessment and treatment of patients with severe brain injury in a vegetative state.' *Brain Injury, 11,* 723–734.

Gill-Thwaites, H. and Munday, R. (2004) 'The Sensory Modality Assessment and Rehabilitation Technique (SMART): A valid and reliable assessment for vegetative state and minimally conscious state patients.' *Brain Injury, 18,* 1255–1269.

Lichtensztejn, M., Macchi, P., and Lischinsky, A. (2014) 'Music therapy and disorders of consciousness: Providing clinical data for differential diagnosis between vegetative state and minimally conscious state from music-centered music therapy and neuroscience perspectives.' *Music Therapy Perspectives, 32,* 1, 47–55.

Magee, W. L. (2007) 'Development of a music therapy assessment tool for patients in low awareness states.' *NeuroRehabilitation, 22,* 4, 319–324.

Magee, W. L. (forthcoming) 'Music in the diagnosis, treatment and prognosis of people with prolonged disorders of consciousness.' *Neuropsychological Rehabilitation,* in preparation.

Magee, W. L., Ghetti, C., and Moyer, A. (2015) 'Feasibility of the Music Therapy Assessment Tool for Awareness in Disorders of Consciousness for use with pediatric populations.' *Frontiers of Psychology, 6,* 698, doi: 10.3389/fpsyg.2015.00698.

Magee, W. L., Kleba, W., Roussek, M., and Lipe, A. (2017) *Exploring the Clinical Utility of the Music Therapy Assessment Tool for Awareness in Disorders of Consciousness (MATADOC) with End-Stage Dementia. Temple IRB Protocol Number: 24356.* Temple University, Philadelphia, PA.

Magee, W. L., Lenton-Smith, G., and Daveson, B. (2014) *Herramienta de Musicoterapia para la Evaluación de la Conciencia en Trastornos de la Conciencia* [Music Therapy Assessment Tool for Awareness in Disorders of Consciousness (MATADOC): Assessment Manual and Instructions for Use. London: Royal Hospital for Neuro-disability]. Philadelphia, PA: W. L. Magee.

Magee, W. L., Lenton-Smith, G., and Daveson, B. (2015) *Music Therapy Assessment for Awareness in Disorders of Consciousness (MATADOC): Assessment Manual and Instructions for Use* (2nd edition). Philadelphia, PA: W. L. Magee.

Magee, W. L., Siegert, R. J., Lenton-Smith, G., Daveson, B. A., and Taylor, S. M. (2014) 'Music Therapy Assessment Tool for Awareness in Disorders of Consciousness (MATADOC): Standardisation of the principal subscale to assess awareness in patients with disorders of consciousness.' *Neuropsychological Rehabilitation, 24,* 1, 101–124.

Magee, W. L., Siegert, R. J., Taylor, S. M., Daveson, B. A., and Lenton-Smith, G. (2016) 'Music Therapy Assessment Tool for Awareness in Disorders of Consciousness (MATADOC): Reliability and validity of a measure to assess awareness in patients with disorders of consciousness.' *Journal of Music Therapy, 53,* 1, 1–26, doi: 10.1093/jmt/trv017.

Magee, W. L., Tillmann, B., Perrin, F., and Schnakers, C. (2016) 'Editorial. Music and disorders of consciousness: Emerging research, practice and theory.' *Frontiers in Psychology, 7,* 1273, doi: 10.3389/fpsyg.2016.01273.

O'Kelly, J. and Magee, W. L. (2013) 'The complementary role of music therapy in the detection of awareness in disorders of consciousness: An audit of concurrent SMART and MATADOC assessments.' *Neuropsychological Rehabilitation, 23,* 2, 287–298.

O'Kelly, J., James, L., Palaniappan, R., Taborin, J., Fachner, J., and Magee, W. L. (2013) 'Neurophysiological and behavioural responses to music therapy in vegetative and minimally conscious states.' *Frontiers in Human Neuroscience, 7,* 884, doi: 10.3389/fnhum.2013.00884.

Owen, A. M., Coleman, M. R., Boly, M., Davis, M. H., Laureys, S., and Pickard, J. D. (2006) 'Detecting awareness in the vegetative state.' *Science, 313,* 1402.

Owen, A. M., Coleman, M. R., Menon, D. K., Berry, E. L., *et al.* (2005) 'Using a hierarchical approach to investigate residual auditory cognition in persistent vegetative state.' *Progress in Brain Research, 150,* 457–471.

Perrin, F., Castro, M., Tillmann, B., and Luauté, J. (2015) 'Promoting the use of personally relevant stimuli for investigating patients with disorders of consciousness.' *Frontiers in Psychology, 6,* 1102, doi: 10.3389/fpsyg.2015.01102.

Perrin, F., Schnakers, C., Schabus, M., Degeuldre, C., *et al.* (2006) 'Brain response to one's own name in vegetative state, minimally conscious state and locked-in syndrome.' *Archives of Neurology, 63,* 562–569.

Pool, J., Taylor, S., Siegert, R., and Magee, W. L. (forthcoming) 'Evaluating the validity, reliability and clinical utility of the Music therapy Sensory Instrument for Cognition, Consciousness, and Awareness (MuSICCA).'

Royal College of Physicians (2013) *Prolonged Disorders of Consciousness: National Clinical Guidelines.* London: Royal College of Physicians.

Schnakers, C., Vanhaudenhuyse, A., Giacino, J., Venture, M., *et al.* (2009) 'Diagnostic accuracy of the vegetative and minimally conscious state: Clinical consensus versus standardized neurobehavioral assessment.' *BioMed Central Neurology, 9,* 35. doi: 10.1186/1471-2377-9-35.

Seel, R. T., Sherer, M., Whyte, J., Katz, D. I., *et al.* (2010) 'Assessment scales for disorders of consciousness: Evidence-based recommendations for clinical practice and research.' *Archives of Physical Medicine and Rehabilitation, 91,* 12, 1795–1813.

Shiel, A. and Wilson, B. A. (2005) 'Can behaviours observed in the early stages of recovery after traumatic brain injury predict poor outcome?' *Neuropsychological Rehabilitation, 15,* 3–4, 494–502.

Tresch, D., Sims, F., Duthie, E., Goldstein, M.D., *et al.* (1991) 'Clinical characteristics of patients in the persistent vegetative state.' *Archives of Internal Medicine, 151,* 930–932.

Verger, J., Ruiz, S., Tillmann, B., Ben Romdhane, M., *et al.* (2014) 'Effets bénéfiques de la musique préférée sur les capacités cognitives des patients en état de conscience minimale' [Beneficial effect of preferred music on cognitive functions in minimally conscious state patients]. *Revue Neurologique, 170,* 693–699, doi: 10.1016/j.neurol.2014.06.005.

Wilson, F. C., Graham, L. E., and Watson, T. (2005) 'Vegetative and minimally conscious states: Serial assessment approaches in diagnosis and management.' *Neuropsychological Rehabilitation, 15,* 3–4, 431–441.

About the Contributors

Anne Lipe most recently served as Adjunct Associate Professor of Music Therapy at Shenandoah University in Winchester, Virginia. She has taught in several academic music therapy programs and has worked clinically with older adults and with individuals in hospital and hospice settings. Her assessment tool, the Music-Based Evaluation of Cognitive Functioning (MBECF), has been the subject of several publications and numerous presentations.

Barbara L. Wheeler taught at Montclair State University from 1975 to 2000 and at the University of Louisville from 2000 to 2011. She presents and teaches in the US and internationally. She has been an active clinician throughout her career and has worked with a variety of clientele. She has edited several books, including *Music Therapy Research* (3rd edition; co-edited, 2016) and *Music Therapy Handbook* (2015), and is the author of other articles and chapters. She is a past president of the American Music Therapy Association and received a Lifetime Achievement Award from the World Federation of Music Therapy in 2017.

Claudine Calvet is a developmental-psychopathology psychologist and a child and family psychotherapist. Since 1990 she has worked in research projects for the development of children with disabilities at the Free University Berlin and at Berlin University of the Arts. She is a specialist in video analysis of interaction (TIA—Therapeutic Interaction Analysis) and works with therapists to use this kind of intervention with at-risk families. She is also a docent and a supervisor for development psychology at the University of Arts in Berlin.

Dorothee von Moreau is Professor of Applied Music Therapy and Psychology and Dean of Studies at the School of Therapeutic Sciences at the SRH University in Heidelberg, Germany. She is also head of the Teaching Clinic Center for Music Therapy and Dance Movement Therapy at the SRH University in Heidelberg. She is a member of the Professional Council of the German Music Therapy Association. She has many years of clinical experience, mainly with psychiatric children and adolescents and psychosomatic adults, and teaching experience at various German music therapy training programs and universities.

Elizabeth York is Coordinator of the Music Therapy Program at Converse College, South Carolina. She is past president of the Music Therapy Association of South Carolina, the Southeastern Region of the American Music Therapy Association, and past co-chair of the AMTA Ethics Board. Dr. York has written and co-authored three articles on the development of the Residual Music Skills Test in both the *Journal of Music Therapy* and *Psychology of Music*. Chapters on her work with women survivors of domestic abuse have appeared in *Feminist Perspectives in Music Therapy* (Hadley, ed.) and the *Music Therapy Handbook* (Wheeler, ed.).

Eric G. Waldon is Associate Professor of Music Therapy at the University of the Pacific in Stockton and San Francisco, California. In addition to being a board-certified music therapist, he is a licensed psychologist in California and specializes in the areas of assessment and psychological testing. He has served on the editorial board for the *Journal of Music Therapy* and *Music Therapy Perspectives*, has published works in various journals and books, and is actively involved with the American Music Therapy Association at both regional and national levels.

Gustavo Gattino is Assistant Professor at Aalborg University in Denmark. He is a member of the International Music Therapy Assessment Consortium (IMTAC) and editor of the *Portuguese Journal of Music Therapy* and the *Brazilian Journal of Music Therapy*. He is co-founder and co-coordinator of the Ibero-American Group of Research in Music Therapy (GIIMT) and guest professor in the master's programs in music therapy at the Valencia Catholic University Saint Vincent Martyr (Spain) and Map Institute (Spain).

Jaakko Erkkilä is Professor of Music Therapy at the Department of Music, Art and Culture Studies, University of Jyväskylä, Finland. Currently he runs music therapy master's training (University of Jyväskylä) and two clinical music therapy trainings (Eino Roiha Foundation). His research focuses on improvisational music therapy for depression and anxiety and he runs an Academy of Finland project (2016–20) called "No Pain No Gain—Integrative Improvisational Music Therapy for Depression" on the topic. He has published several chapters and articles on the theory, practice, and research of psychodynamic and integrative music therapy, lately mainly focusing on clinical improvisation.

John Carpente is Associate Professor of Music Therapy at Molloy College in New York, Founder/Executive Director of The Rebecca Center for Music Therapy at Molloy College, and owner of Developmental Music Health Services. He has published several book chapters and articles related to improvisational music therapy and autism spectrum, assessment, music-centered goal writing, developmental relationship-based music therapy, and outcome studies. His latest book is called *Individual Music-Centered Assessment Profile for Neurodevelopmental Disorders (IMCAP-ND): A Clinical Manual.*

Karin Schumacher is Professor at Berlin University of the Arts and has been working since 1974 as a music therapist and child and adolescent psychotherapist with children on the autism spectrum, and since 1984 as professor of music therapy, founding and continuing the development of the training for music therapy. Her research focus is music therapy and infant research, especially the development and assessment of interpersonal relationship skills.

Karina Daniela Ferrari is Professor of Music Therapy at Buenos Aires University in Argentina. Author of the book *Music Therapy: Aspects of Systematization and Evaluation in Clinical Practice* (2013), she is also creator of the Intramusical Relationship Scale and various asessment protocols in mental health and medicine. Since 2007 she has been conducting research in music therapy evaluation and offering courses in various Latin American countries. She is also coordinator of the music therapy area at the General Hospital Dr Teodoro Álvarez and San Jose Sanatorium, and a founder member of the Ibero-American Music Therapy Research Group.

Michael D. Cassity is President and Chief Executive Officer of Music Therapy and Creative Arts, Inc. He retired as Professor and Founder of Music Therapy from both Drury University and Southwestern Oklahoma State University where he is Professor Emeritus. His 42 years of publications include the first published domestic violence and Delphi studies in music therapy, and *Multimodal Psychiatric Music Therapy* (3rd edition), as senior author. He holds the Harmony Award in research from the Southwestern Region of the American Music Therapy Association (AMTA) and is a past president of the SWAMTA.

Orii McDermott is a Senior Research Fellow at the Institute of Mental Health, University of Nottingham, UK, and the Doctoral Programme in Music Therapy, Aalborg University, Denmark. She specializes in dementia psychosocial research, particularly in music therapy and music-based interventions. She is a registered music therapist and continues to work as a clinician in Central and North West London NHS Foundation Trust. She is a member of INTERDEM (early detection and timely intervention in dementia) and serves on the editorial board of the *Journal of Music Therapy*.

Penny Roberts is one of the six authors of the Individualized Music Therapy Assessment Profile (IMTAP). Her work focuses on the biomedical and psychosocial impact of environmental enrichment on pain, pain medication, and the side effects. She has numerous publications on this topic. Dr. Roberts currently teaches music therapy at Loyola University, New Orleans.

Sanne Storm is leader of an interdisciplinary perinatal team at the Psychiatric Center, member of the research committe of The National Hospital, Faroe Islands, and part-time lecturer and guest researcher at the Music Therapy Department, Aalborg University, Denmark. Her research, teaching, and clinical work are focused on therapy-related body and voice work, and her approach and method—Psychodynamic Voice Therapy as well as VOIAS, a voice assessment profile—evolved during her intensive work in this area. She regularly performs workshops internationally.

Silke Reimer has worked in a home for people with severe and multiple disabilities since 1999. From 2006 to 2011, she also worked with children with autism spectrum disorders in a center for the development of children and adolescents. Since 2006 she has been working with Karin

Schumacher and Claudine Calvet in research projects at Berlin University of the Arts. Her research focus is affect regulation in music therapy with people with severe and multiple disabilities.

Søren Hald is a music therapist and holds a PhD. He has published various book chapters and articles in the area of neurological rehabilitation, acquired brain injury, and interpersonal communication competencies. He is currently working as a counselor and music therapist with people in the early stages of dementia.

Stine Lindahl Jacobsen is Associate Professor and Head of Music Therapy at Aalborg University in Denmark. She currently hosts the International Music Therapy Assessment Consortium (IMTAC) and the research center Arts & Health in North Jutland, Denmark. She has published various books, chapters, and articles in the areas of families at risk, standardized music therapy assessment tools, and effect studies. Currently she trains and certifies music therapists from around the world in the use of the tool Assessment of Parent-Child Interaction (APCI).

Thomas Bergmann is Head of the Therapy Department of Berlin Treatment Center for Adults with Intellectual Disability and Mental Disorder. He recently started to offer music therapy to children on the spectrum using a family-based approach. He is on the editorial board of *Musiktherapeutische Umschau* and has published various articles and book chapters in the field of art therapies, autism, social-emotional development, and diagnostic assessment.

Thomas Wosch is Professor of Music Therapy at the University of Applied Sciences Würzburg-Schweinfurt in Germany. He is also the Head of Music Therapy Laboratory and the MA in Developmental Music Therapy and Music Therapy for Dementia Patients at the university. He has published various books, chapters, and articles especially in microanalysis in music therapy and beyond this in the area of music therapy in dementia care, for late-life depression, automatized assessment, and effect studies. He liaises with the University of Jyväskylä in assessment of clinical improvisation (MTTB, IAP-A-M).

Tony Wigram was Professor and Head of PhD Studies in Music Therapy at the University of Aalborg, Denmark, Honorary Research Fellow in the Faculty of Music at the University of Melbourne, Australia, and Reader in Music Therapy at Anglia Ruskin University, Cambridge, UK. He was Associate Editor of the *Nordic Journal of Music Therapy*, and a former President of both the European Music Therapy Confederation and the World Federation of Music Therapy. He was also Head Music Therapist at the Harper Children's Service in Hertfordshire, UK, and Research Advisor to Hertfordshire Partnership NHS Trust.

Wendy L. Magee is Professor in the Music Therapy Program at Temple University in Philadelphia. Having worked as a clinician and researcher in neuro-rehabilitation since 1988, she is widely published on topics related to music therapy assessment, and treatment in neuro-rehabilitation, including a Cochrane review on music interventions for acquired brain injury. Since 1990 she has been involved in the development and standardization of the Music Therapy Assessment Tool for Awareness in Disorders of Consciousness (MATADOC), as well as its translation to and validation in other languages.

Subject Index

Author Index